FROMMER'S

A SHOPPER'S GUIDE

to the

CARIBBEAN

FROMMER'S

A SHOPPER'S GUIDE

to the

CARIBBEAN

by Jeanne and Harry Harman III

1988-89 Edition

Published by Prentice Hall Press
A Division of Simon & Schuster, Inc.
Gulf + Western Building
One Gulf + Western Plaza
New York, NY 10023

ISBN 0-671-60743-X

Design by J. C. Suarès

Manufactured in the United States of America

CONTENTS

MAPS

A DISCLAIMER: Although every effort was made to ensure the accuracy of the prices and travel information appearing in this book, it should be kept in mind that prices do fluctuate in the course of time, and that information does change under the impact of the varied and volatile factors that affect the travel industry.

~~~~~~

INFLATION ALERT: As you know, inflation has hit the Caribbean as it has everywhere else. In researching this book we have made every effort to obtain up-to-the minute prices, but even the most conscientious reporters cannot keep up with the current pace of inflation. As we go to press, we believe we have obtained the most reliable data possible. Nonetheless, in the lifetime of this edition—particularly its second year (1988)—the wise traveler will add 15% to 20% to the prices quoted throughout these pages.

About This Book...

In the course of living in the Caribbean (St. Thomas) as well as covering the other islands during those years for the *New York Times, Time,* and *Business Week,* we had occasion to do more than our share of both window-shopping and buying. All told, we once estimated we visited close to 2,000 island emporiums of one kind or another, in the line of duty and otherwise.

Not all of them struck us as worth a second visit on our part—or a first one on yours. To maximize the use of your limited time, we therefore limit coverage in this volume to the top contenders for your traveling dollar in terms of variety, quality, reliability, imagination, and taste: in other words, those that seem to be *the best,* day in and day out (none is immune from a stumble now and again: nor, for that matter, are we).

As to which shops are best, you and we are bound not to see eye to eye on occasion. Because of space limitations and other compelling restrictions, we may have left out your pet boutique, or even, heaven forbid, your favorite island.

Things change, especially in the West Indies. A new owner, or new manager, new government regulations, and the whole character of an establishment is transformed.

So please use this guide as a broad, general instrument to point you in some right directions and perhaps alert you to possibilities you might otherwise not have had the time to explore.

As to prices listed on these pages, cost of merchandise is determined by what the retailer must pay the wholesaler, and this fluctuates, sometimes wildly, depending on the rate of exchange, increases in rent, wages, and countless other factors. Always allow for the skittish currency, devaluations, and worldwide inflation.

Despite the blood, sweat, and tears that have gone into this effort, errors are bound to occur. We apologize for them in advance. But if you'll consider the size of the area covered and the sheer volume of addresses, prices, and other information, we think you'll be inclined to excuse some of them. To err is, unfortunately, all too human.

In researching this guide we incurred no obligations whatsoever. Not one penny, not one gift—not even a discount—has been accepted from tourist interests concerned. Nor do our recommendations reflect such ploys as solicitation or free trips, accommodations, and the like, for the purpose of gathering information for this book. Goof we may—and perhaps too often—but if so, these will be honest errors, not praise for pay.

This book is part of our continuing love affair with the Caribbean that began long ago and has never ended. We met in Haiti, married in St. Thomas, and made the islands of the West Indies our full-time home for twenty years. We have been in on the creation of modest mom-and-pop emporiums, and have watched them grow into imposing financial institutions.

We have journeyed through the marketplaces up and down the chain countless times, on assignment for *Time, Sports Illustrated, The New York Times*, and other journals in the course of writing books and articles—or just because we wanted to. This firsthand background information has contributed much to our personal enjoyment of the islands, and we feel perhaps it may also enhance your interest to some degree.

Our sincerest wish is that your journey, even if it's a vicarious one at first, provides you with a fraction of the stimulus and pleasure we have experienced in the course of putting this book together. Your own comments, corrections and additions can only make it better. Please pass them on to us c/o Prentice Hall Press, One Gulf + Western Plaza, New York, NY 10023. We'll appreciate hearing from you.

Jeanne & Harry Harman III

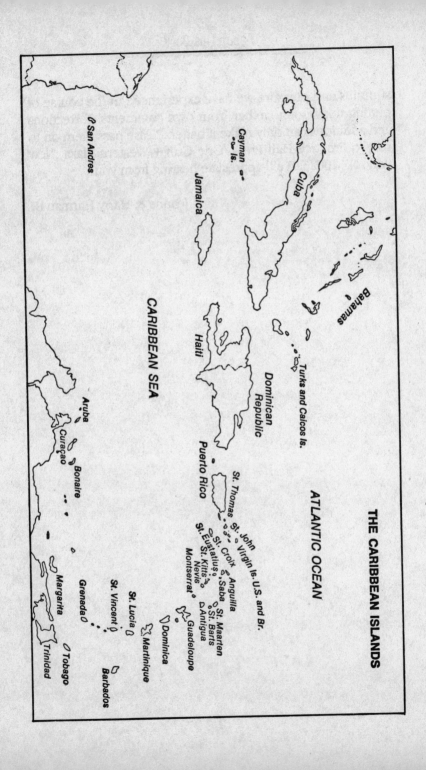

THE CARIBBEAN ISLANDS

ATLANTIC OCEAN

CARIBBEAN SEA

Cuba

Bahamas

Cayman Is.

Jamaica

Haiti

Dominican Republic

Turks and Caicos Is.

Puerto Rico

St. Thomas St. John
Virgin Is. U.S. and Br.
St. Croix Anguilla
Saba St. Maarten
St. Eustatius St. Barts
St. Kitts
Nevis Antigua
Montserrat
Guadeloupe
Dominica
Martinique
St. Lucia
St. Vincent
Barbados
Grenada
Margarita
Tobago
Trinidad

San Andres

Aruba
Curaçao
Bonaire

AN INTRODUCTION TO CARIBBEAN SHOPPING

According to one American Express tour guide, people travel for three reasons: "To buy beads, send postcards, and say they've been there." Exaggeration though this may be, there is no denying that shopping ranks as a favorite traveler's pastime, not only for the thrill of the chase, but also for the pleasant memories various acquisitions evoke back home.

What Makes the Caribbean So Special for Shoppers?

However violently romantics may object to the perception of the West Indies as one big bargain center, a series of floating shopping bags surrounded by some of the world's loveliest sun, sand, and sea—there is a certain amount of truth to the image. In this nearby archipelago you will find assembled the cream of the merchandise crops of Europe, the Middle East, the Pacific—from just about every country in all sorts of categories, from aquavit to zircons.

Special Customs Allowances

In addition to the more liberal customs allowances of today—you may bring up to $400 (retail value) worth of articles acquired abroad back to the U.S. duty free **if**: the articles are for personal use or gifts; you have been out of the country for at least 48 hours; and you have not claimed the exemption within the preceding 30 days. The next $1,000 in items is dutiable at a flat 10% rate—special tariff exemptions and privileges apply on virtually every island, and these make possible anywhere from sizable to sensational savings.

The U.S. Virgin Islands, for example, offer double the tax-free allowance ($800) per person, in which you may include five cartons of duty-free cigarettes, five fifths of duty-free liquors (plus a sixth if it is Virgin Islands-made)—and right to mail (minimal restrictions) an unlimited number of gifts worth $100 or less. There is a flat 5% duty charged on anything over the $800 exemption. In addition, items made in the U.S. Virgin Islands can be brought back in any amounts. Check the U.S. Custom Services pamphlet **Know Before You Go** for all the small details.

In non-U.S. flag islands, Customs inspectors applying duty charges work from something known as the *Tariff Schedules of the United States Annotated*, which contains 5,348 different merchandise classifications. Over half of these (2,766) are eliminated from the dutiable category if they originate in a developing economy. And the **Generalized System of Preferences** (GSP), which makes the judgment call, has accepted every island in the Caribbean/Bahamas—except Guadeloupe and Dependencies (St. Barthélémy, St. Martin, etc.) and Martinique. Because of their Departement status, these are considered part of France. They have their own incentives, of which more later.

This means that Jamaican high fashions, hand-drawn Saban tablecloths and mats, and totes and headscarves silk screened from the world-famous Bagshaw atelier of St. Lucia—these and countless other locally made collector's items—can be brought back to the United States 100% duty-free. Those articles which are grown, manufactured, or produced locally include metals, home furnishings, sporting goods, toys, jewelry, handbags, and spices, among countless others. These provisions allow you to spend your entire Customs allowance on such European or Far Eastern imports which, having been manufactured outside the Caribbean, do not qualify under **GSP**.

6

But bear in mind that not all island merchandise is duty-exempt—watches, certain footwear, those steel and electronic items that could contain imported components, and some apparel are excluded.

World-Class Merchandise

Because of the favorable tariffs, and the cosmopolitan, multinational heritage of the Caribbean, imports represent the cream of production from all over the world: Hermès, Gucci, Yves St. Laurent, Piaget, Baccarat, Patou—these and others you will find all outstandingly well represented and temptingly priced.

Six Additional Reasons for Shopping the Caribbean

Besides the obvious saving of the time and money you would need to acquire these products in their country of origin, Caribbean browsing has still more going for it:

1. On almost every single island you can carry on your negotiations in English, without resorting to an interpreter, dictionary, or phrasebook.

2. Caribbean shops are generally manageable in size, unlike the multi-floored monoliths serving non-vacation-oriented communities.

3. The turnover of merchandise is rapid here, thus the inventory is usually fresh.

4. Wherever possible, island merchants buying abroad specify American sizing instead of European, thereby making much better fits for American physiques.

5. Boutiques usually concentrate in a small area, either on one main street or in clusters in and around resort facilities. The resulting ease in going from one mart to the other means impressive savings in time, temper, and shoe leather.

6. Finally, Caribbean shops benefit from an added ingredient—the special talent and taste of their owner-buyers. Many of them are discerning individualists with a flair for finding attractive off-trail manufacturers and out-of-the-ordinary conversation pieces.

For many dedicated shophounds, these are the raisins in the cake, the bonuses that make the browsing game worth it—not just dollar-and-cent savings, however impressive.

Some Minor Problems You May Encounter

Occasional flies do appear in the ointment. For example, if you arrive after a banner tourist season, you may find stock seriously depleted, the best buys gone, and replacements still on the high seas.

Every now and then a communications gap develops between the leisurely islander and the shoppper in a hurry. Laconic sales personnel may appear sullen. If you have a problem in the Caribbean, do as you would at home, **complain and ask for the manager**.

Remember that some of those "bargains" do not in fact represent real finds. Know your hometown "best price" for a particular watch or camera before you make your island purchase; you may discover that your local discount house can match or even better the Caribbean price. Other categories at risk will be pinpointed in the sections that follow.

On the whole, however, disappointments in the marketplace are the exception, fortunately not the rule. In general, you will find Caribbean shopping an exciting adventure, a rewarding experience encompassing very little bitter with the better.

To achieve maximum satisfaction, however, you too have a responsibility, one which an obscure 19th-century philosopher articulated rather well:

> To acquire money requires valor;
> to keep money requires prudence,
> and to spend money well is an art.

DO'S AND DON'TS OF
SHOPPING THE CARIBBEAN

Golden Rules

To get the maximum value and enjoyment out of your Caribbean shopping, herewith some suggestions:

1.**Before you leave home, study all the catalogs you can**, especially those of houses likely to handle upscale merchandise such as that purveyed in the islands.

Also, collect literature and costs from manufacturers who offer brochures via advertisements in **Town & Country** and other slick magazines. Then you can really decide whether or not you're better off making your purchases at home. Some merchandise comes in at such low tariffs that big chains in the U.S. can easily absorb that, with bulk buying further lowering the wholesale cost.

If you scrutinize and clip the domestic literature, you may well find, as we did, cameras advertised in the United States for less than the cost in a duty-free island shop. Plain cashmere sweaters are not always a buy either, especially if you watch the sales in your local department store. (Beaded or embroidered ones, on the other hand, can represent substantial savings.)

Bear in mind also that you will find considerable made-in-America merchandise in the Caribbean stores, because shoppers from Europe, South America, or other islands appreciate our products. One supposedly experienced traveler reports rejoicing over an exotic piece of West Indian fabric she acquired on her trip, only to note when she got it home that the selvage bore the trademark of a well-known South Carolina mill.

Also be aware that in the past, mainland distributors have howled so bitterly about Caribbean competition that some manufacturers have required, sub rosa or otherwise, that all retailers, regardless of local conditions, stick to the same prices. Watch out, also, for one or a series of middlemen, each taking his percentage off the top, which often results in inflated retail prices.

These conditions do not apply to the majority of items, but they do exist. Therefore, it is important to study your hometown prices—not only for the dollar saved, but as a matter of principle. One of the ways of keeping score in the sport of shopping is by the size of the saving.

2. **Write down the exact name and pattern of any china, crystal, or silver you intend to supplement or replace.**

3. **Bring with you a roughly to-scale floor plan of your house or apartment.** You will find beautiful rosewood chests, khus-khus carpets, handcarved door panels, and other desirables in your Caribbean travels. But will they fit your living space? A color wheel for matching the dominant hues in your existing decor to new acquisitions can also come in very handy.

4. **Avoid, if you possibly can, undertaking to do errands for friends and relatives.** Otherwise, you may very well end up frittering away precious shopping time tramping from one establishment to the next in a futile effort to track down esoteric items either out of stock or long since discontinued.

5. **In making your advance reservations for sight-seeing tours, boat trips, or other activities, be sure to consult the shopping hours and holidays listed in the individual chapters.** Islanders celebrate many holidays. You can easily find everything tight as a drum in honor of West Indies Friendship Day, Hurricane Thanksgiving, or some other local event.

6. **Do NOT change your money at hotels, shops,**

or other non-financial institutions if you can possibly avoid it. Given the volatile state of exchange, nonprofessional moneychangers will, understandably, give themselves the benefit of the doubt on all transactions—to your detriment. So convert your cash in a bank. (There are exceptions to this rule, however—for instance, with converting traveler's checks on certain islands. These will be noted further on.)

7. **Do not rely on credit cards exclusively**. Some merchants will accept specific ones (American Express, Diners Club, MasterCard, Carte Blanche, and Visa being the most common), some will not. In many areas Visa and BarclayCard are interchangeable. Traveler's checks, on the other hand, are not only universally acceptable, but in some cases rate you a 20% discount. (See the chapter on Martinique, for example)

8. **Do not use ocean freight or regular mail for purchases not returning with you**. Specify airmail or air freight whenever possible as long as it's not prohibitively expensive. Not only will the handling be more caring and the expense and hassle of Customs brokers minimized, but you will receive the goods within a reasonable period of time—as, for instance, in your lifetime! Any transport other than by mail can take forever. After all, if it's worth buying—it's worth getting.

9. **Do not hold off buying your favorite camera, watch, or necklace when you see it in one port, on the theory it might be cheaper down the road a bit**. You might find it later for 10% or 15% less—but chances are equally good that the article will be out of stock, discontinued, or just plain not there. Distances are long and time lags affect the process of getting merchandise from manufacturers scattered about the globe to this still somewhat out-of-the-way corner of the world.

Rule One with old Caribbean hands: When you

see it, buy it—or be prepared to do without it entirely. Our comparison shopping, up and down the chain innumerable times, shows absolutely **no one island consistently cheaper than another on everything**. Granted, you might grab the first Omega you see, only to spy it the next day in another port for $20 less. But it could very easily not only be the other way around, but also be absolutely unavailable. By and large, differences are few, far between, and rarely crucial.

10. **Don't turn away from a tempting purchase just because it puts you slightly over your exemption**. You could be passing up a memento to be cherished, and, besides, there are ways to minimize the duty you might pay.

11. **If you are cruising, don't spend all your money until you have checked the shipboard stock. Sometimes you'll do as well here as anywhere, sometimes even better.**

12. **If your purchases exceed your exemption, simply pay duty on the lightly taxed articles and save your credit for those with stiffer assessments.**

"Temporarily" strung pearls, for instance, cost you a mere 3% tariff, while embroidered sweaters or table linen carry substanial charges. In some low-duty categories the price differential between your home store and the island markup is so impressive you can afford to pay full 10% to 12% duty and still save enormously.

As you will find when you compare your U.S. cost with the local tag, this is especially true on perfumes and fine liqueurs. Imported sherry, for example, carries an abkari of around 50 cents per fifth, yet sells in mainland liquor stores for over twice the West Indies cost—which makes it worthwhile to bring in all your state law allows and pay the duty on each: you'll still be saving substantially. Do not hesitate to ask the inspector's help; it is perfectly acceptable for him to advise you regarding which purchases carry the lower charges.

13.**Save all your sales slips until after you've cleared the U.S. border.**

14.**Include in your luggage the official Customs list of what makes of watches and perfume cannot enter the United States at all as well as those restricted in quantity**, due to copyrights, patents, and the like: X ounces of this perfume, only two watches from that manufacturer, etc. No matter how willing you might be to pay for the import privilege, authorities are required to prevent contraband as specified on their listings from coming into the United States.

15.**Do not FAIL to register with your nearest Treasury office any foreign-made cameras, jewelry, timepieces, or non U.S. made articles of value you are taking with you. Or bring with you copies of the original sales slips.** Otherwise, lacking proof of purchase or predeparture ownership, Customs inspectors are fully justified in levying duty on possessions you already had acquired prior to your trip.

The same principle applies, incidentally, should you be sending an imported camera, watch, or other import overseas for repair. Unless you have proof of prior possession, you can be asked to pay full duty on the article when it is shipped back repaired.

16.For those to whom it applies: **Any traveler carrying more than $10,000 in or out of the United States must go directly to a Customs officer before leaving and file a report (Customs Form 4790) or submit one upon their return**. And don't think you might not get caught. As of 1985, a special squad of official dogs are on hand to sniff out American currency; they are trained by weekly doses of shredded money from the mint. However if your cash is in foreign bills, not to worry. The ink is different from that used in the U.S., and as yet the canine squad doesn't recognize it.

Is the Caribbean marketplace worth making all these plans for? Most definitely. One of the most attractive aspects of shopping the islands is their strong sense of place. Each one generates its own ambiance, and that individual character is reflected in the wares it offers. If ever Vive la Difference applied, it is here.

WHAT TO BUY IN THE CARIBBEAN

As you are soon going to discover for yourself, if you have not already, these islands really are a shopper's paradise. In this chapter we'll look at certain categories of merchandise you might want to investigate, along with some sidelights and background information taken from our personal notebook:

ARTS AND CRAFTS

On this subject, consider this episode reported to us by a wealthy and worldly West Indian with less than high regard for the Fourth Estate.

As a public relations gesture, officials on his island had asked him to entertain a delegation of visiting U.S. journalists to impress them with his exquisite home—a treasure trove of museum pieces and artworks he had collected from all over the world.

As the group strolled through one baronial salon after another, one reporter paused at a particularly beautiful 17th-century Gobelin tapestry.

"Tell me," she asked her host brightly, "is this locally made?"

Gobelin does not operate a factory outlet in the Caribbean—as yet. The islanders do, however, produce their own tapestries and wall hangings—along with a rich variety of other original and outstanding creations.

The Caribbean looks back on a long and distinguished

artistic heritage. John James Audubon was a West Indian born and bred. So was Camille Pissarro. Gauguin painted in Martinique. Among contemporary figures, *The New York Times* has named Kapo of Jamaica one of the six top primitive artists in the world. Both Sotheby Parke-Bernet and Christie's are among the prestigious auction houses handling Caribbean works. In 1983, the Smithsonian Institution sponsored an exhibit of Jamaican works that toured major U.S. centers to considerable acclaim.

No question about it. The seminal stimulation of dazzling natural surroundings, combined with the cross-pollination of all the various cultures represented in the area, has produced in the Caribbean a uniquely rich talent—and, to conventional experts, a slightly baffling one. In fact, a critic of *The Times London* once wrote a whole book exploring the whys and wherefores of the West Indian artistic gift—and never did come up with the answer.

Whatever the reason, islanders have been expressing themselves visually for a long time—all the way back to the days when Arawak Indians composed their first petroglyphs using large boulders or cave walls for canvases. Today West Indians still decorate their walls with murals, also brighten up buses and wagons with sprightly paintings in a style which has come to be known as "yard art."

In the absence of easy access to conventional materials, the Arawaks proved astonishingly resourceful. Masterful tapestries acclaimed by connoisseurs as being of museum calibre are made of discarded scraps of cloth. Skillfully assembled, imaginatively conceived, these "thread poems"—as they are sometimes called—are exhibited by better galleries throughout the world. Prized metal sculptures featured in fine metropolitan galleries are fashioned out of discarded fuel drums.

Just as Caribbean shipwrights search the forests for branches that nature has bent in exactly the shape they need to build their boats, so do the woodcarvers select those tropical woods with grains and form best suited for what they have in mind.

As for painters, only comparatively recently have they had access to the usual artists' supplies. (One ingenious inventor drew his pictures on dark cloth with a stick dipped in bleach.) About 40 years ago an American expatriate named DeWitt Peters watched his gardener trying to paint with chicken feathers on shirt boards. He tossed him some brushes and canvas—and thus started a whole new era in West Indian painting. Sisson Blanchard, the gardener, has since exhibited in galleries internationally. As communications improved and the flow of settlers from other parts of the world increased, they added their influence to the mix.

In the area of crafts, the creativity is many-faceted as well. Some islands still utilize the traditional methods of straw-weaving originated by the Arawak Indians centuries ago. Others create carpets of wonderfully delicate design, using the same fragrant grass (khus-khus) from which perfumers obtain the important vetiver extract. To fire their ceramics, potters use the husks of coconuts.

As to where to find the best of local output, it depends on how serious a collector you are. According to Martin Ackerman, a leading Wall Street expert on art as an investment, by and large, unless you're spending at least $5,000, don't buy paintings for economic reasons. Buy what you like, consider the purchase a hobby, not an investment. You could be acquiring a future Blanchard or Kapo or Geoffrey Holder; but if it doesn't turn out that way, you can still enjoy what you choose because you liked it in the first place.

If you're in fact thinking in those $5,000 terms, consult your own expert friends before you leave home regarding what to look for. Once on-island, check with the government tourism authorities. Where there are museums or institutions of higher learning, ask in these places as well.

Whether or not you are that dedicated, keep a sharp eye out

for finds wherever you are. Mahogany sculptures, carved door panels, decorative pieces—the stores are full of them. Wide-eyed urchins will skitter up to you at your hotel or car hawking their wares. Street peddlers are loaded down with pieces—and often, the work is fair to good, the prices incredibly low. Sometimes the creators go on to become highly regarded. The street painter to whom we paid $10 for a 14 x 16 inch oil now commands at least a hundred times that, and is listed among major talents.

As to dickering, how effectively you can bargain depends on how urgent the financial needs of the sellers. In many instances, the casbah philosophy of commerce prevails. If that backroom woodcarver quotes $30 for the bust that catches your eye, he may be happy to sell it for $10. Generally speaking, for amateur hagglers, a final price 35% under the original figure is a pretty good deal. Real pros at arguing do better, sometimes considerably better.

CAMERAS

No two ways about it, photographic equipment does not constitute the best bargain available in the Caribbean marts.

On the other hand, cameras are being bought in considerable quantity, as witness the number of successful stores specializing in this merchandise throughout the islands.

As to why this should be, perhaps it is the impact of all that showy physical beauty and the desire to record it. Or it could be the final gratification of a long-suppressed desire to own really good, first-class equipment.

Uninitiated and/or impatient beginners can acquire cameras that do everything but pose the subject for you: built-in flash, automatic-exposure setting—all the essentials and a good many frills.

Neophytes exposed to the breathtaking drama of their first snorkeling or scuba-diviing experience frequently feel compelled to capture the thrill on film through the magic of underwater photography.

And modern technology makes this marvelously possible. One Nikon camera, as an example, is so waterproof it can function at a depth of 160 feet even without a housing. The die-cast metal body withstands rust, mildew, and fungus. On the ground, it operates just as well in the dust of the desert, in rain, or sometimes even in a blizzard. It comes with an automatic depth-of-field indicator, easy one-operation functioning, and has extra-large controls to facilitate handling it underwater.

For the camera you simply have to have, here and now, cost takes a back seat to availability. In that case, by all means buy from an island dealer who provides informational as well as performance backup.

However, if you are considering making a sizable investment, and have not researched prices in advance, it is worthwhile to pay the price of a long-distance call. The cost is often negligible, to compare. From St. Thomas, for example, you pay as little as 64¢ a minute, prime-time, direct-dial, station-to-station—and during off hours it's as little as 25¢ per minute.

In the unlikely event you don't already have sources of your own, here are just a few phone numbers of U.S. stores selected at random that you might consult for prices.

Executive Photo and Supply Corporation, 120 West 31st St., New York City. Tel. toll free out of New York 800-223-7323; in New York State 212/947-5290.

Focus, 4421 13th Avenue, Brooklyn, New York. Tel. toll free out of New York 800/221-0828; in New York State 718-436-6262.

Forty-Seventh St. Photo, Inc., 67 West 47th St., 116 West 45th St., 115 Nassau St., New York City (all branches). Tel. toll free out of New York 800/221-7774; in New York State 212/260-4410.

Showcase Audio/Video Systems, 2323 Cheshire Bridge Rd., Atlanta, GA. Tel. toll free in Georgia 800/532-2523; out of state toll free 800/241-9738.

Wolf Camera and Video, 150 14th St. NW, Atlanta, GA. Tel. 404/892-1707.

Note: Many of these outlets operate when discounted telephone rates apply, after 5 p.m., for example, and on Sundays. If you plan to check out several items, you might save yourself some charges on **non-toll-free numbers** by calling at low-traffic times.

As we go to press, here are a few sample comparison prices between the islands and the U.S.:

	Caribbean	*U.S. Discount House*
OLYMPUS OM-4	$309	$330
CANON T-50	135	149
CANON AE-1P	170	199
CANON T-70	209	269
NIKON FG	179	169
NIKON F3HP	489	439
MINOLTA X-700	180	209
MINOLTA X-370	115	150

Bear in mind that the discount house prices do not reflect sales tax and/or shipping charges, and that all prices quoted are for the camera only (no extras).

CHINA, CRYSTAL, AND HOME FURNISHINGS

One persuasive inducement to investing in quality china, crystal, and silver is their intrinsic value. Canny connoisseurs are snapping up future heirlooms for not entirely aesthetic reasons: in the face of stock-market volatility and fluctuating dollar values, these articles—concrete, valued objects of established worth—constitute a reassuringly stable financial shelter.

Low overheads, infinitesimal to nonexistent tariffs, and rapid turnover in Caribbean shops make sizable savings possible on many items.

Dine on the same Rosenthal china pattern favored by Elizabeth Taylor—or choose any of a number of other styles. Philip Rosenthal's stable of artists has included such top names as Raymond Loewy, Emilio Pucci, Winblaad—and yet the cost in the islands is little more than you would pay for everyday china at home.

The tiny town of Baccarat on the banks of the Meurthe-et-Moselle River produces crystal so delicately, magnificently elegant that copycats in the U.S. and elsewhere simply cannot come close to imitating it. Decanters, ice buckets, perfume bottles, and exquisite goblets in all sizes and shapes are available in the islands.

The French government chose St. Louis stemware to grace its Palace of Versailles table when entertaining royalty; you can sip from the same shimmering chalice and pay considerably less for it than if you acquired it at home.

In the course of his 85 productive years on this planet, René Lalique exhibited at the Louvre, created stained-glass windows for churches, designed the splashing fountains of the Rond Point on the Champs Élysées, and by inventing his own equipment, blazed new trails in the sculpture of glass and crystal. His son, Mark, carries on the family tradition. You can find exquisite examples for sale in many West Indian emporiums.

Each and every piece of Daum crystal must be signed before the Cristallerie at Nancy, France, will release it. ("In Nancy," 'tis said, "there are no machines, only men and fire.") Each price for export also has to be individually checked.

Waterford needs no introduction to American readers, of course—at least one of our own national monuments features a chandelier hand-cut and blown by this internationally famous Irish firm.

European crystal is an especially good buy in the long run, because Continental regulations require at least 25% lead content in all merchandise that is labeled crystal; this provision does not apply in the U.S.

Other categories offer many more equally appealing buying opportunities: Royal Doulton's Royal Crown Derby bone china and Royal Copenhagen or Bing & Grøndahl figurines. Imported linens and table silver are also good buys. And for practical reasons you may want to purchase Spode stoneware. Fling it to the floor with equanimity—the crushed stone it contains helps make it not only practically unbreakable, but also ovenproof.

Among home furnishings, the items designed and made in the West Indies are equally interesting: hand-sewn lacy rugs made from the same khus-khus grass which grows in the Caribbean, and which constitutes the foundation of many fine French perfumes. Most islands have their own potters and ceramists, firing tableware of original designs that you'll not see anywhere else. The furniture makers of Haiti, the Dominican Republic, Jamaica, Trinidad, and other islands are prized by knowing interior decorators. In many cases the cabinet-maker's skills, learned from experts the planters imported from Europe, have been handed down from one generation to another.

In the process of working with their native woods, islanders have developed some practical and handsome products: stunning mahogany dinner plates, elegant four-poster beds, and tea carts combining six or seven different types and hues of wood. In Jamaica, a whole line of pewter and pottery ware copied from 16th-century implements recovered from the sunken city of Port Royal are conversation as well as museum pieces in themselves.

Another important plus in regard to island furnishings is the fact that workers still craft to order. So if you are outfitting a home, take a little time not only to look around at what's on display, but to inquire about the best local artisans in various disciplines. Your reward may be not only an agreeable reminder of a happy holiday, but a lasting, very special accent to your decor.

FASHIONS

Ever since 2640 B.C., when Empress Si Ling-chi accidentally dropped a worm's cocoon in a container of hot tea, causing the fiber to unwind into a silken thread, fine silk clothing has ranked among the great pleasures of both men and women. To this day, 800 silkworms, each consuming 35 pounds of mulberry leaves, give their lives to produce just one ladies blouse.

Caribbean retailers also make significant sacrifices in their worldwide search for special finery. Bouncing across the African veldt in a zebra-striped bus, sleeping on a straw mat in Japan, cruising up a Bangkok river in a sampan—these and other treks have become routine to island entrepreneurs who each year go straight to their sources, wherever they may be, covering as much as 100,000 miles in four months. First they work with weavers, dyers, tailors, seamstresses, and embroiderers, then they add the personal touch they developed themselves, sometimes when they were first cutting their own patterns on a diningroom table.

Low tariffs and a traditional cultural closeness to European mother countries season the styles with elegant Continental accents. Whether homegrown or imported, fashion is important on the Caribbean shopping scene: inventive, wearable, and interestingly priced.

Of the many designers-in-residence, some are transplanted Americans. By the time these alumnae of New York's top art institutes have lived in the islands a few years, they become expert in the special island look that is so distinctive and appealing and so very Caribbean. At the same time, a new generation of West Indian creators also enjoys the best of both worlds: the understanding and feel for their own land that is hard to duplicate, plus the polish and savoir faire they have acquired by studying abroad.

Typically, Caribbean collections are fresh and fetching, in a colorful kaleidoscope of tropical motifs. Seductive caftans—plunge-backed, high-necked, skinny-shaped, or cinched with a broad obi—come in shells-and-fish, banana, or big bamboo prints for under $100. Or, choose wraparound skirts fashioned from a fabric that depicts jumbo-sized lobsters frolicking on a crimson background. Men's toppers and shorts, zip-up men's boating shirts, featuring silhouetted sleek sailboats and a bottom border of burgees from America's chic yacht clubs—the assortment is interesting and unusual.

The design of the materials often constitutes the main attraction. You'll find silkscreen or batik fabrics framed and hung as works of art in various posh retreats. Batik developed as a decorative art in Indonesia some 700 years ago; it still carries with it a certain mystique. Indonesians wear it as a talisman to ward off illness and attract good fortune, to produce fertility, and to celebrate certain religious rites.

Some patterns indicate the wearer's profession or social status. As for the dyes, these are often a closely held secret. The formula may require combining shredded chicken, fruit, fermented casava, and brown sugar with other undisclosed ingredients to obtain precisely the desired variation in color. Few skilled makers of batik willingly share their formulas.

You will find a considerable amount of handwork in Caribbean fashions: appliqué, embroidery, handmade lace and crochet. And although the shrinking distances of the 20th century have brought mass marketing and mail-order-catalog clothing to every hamlet, you can still locate skilled tailors and seamstresses, especially in the communities with strong links to England and Spain. One West Indian–born designer, for example, spent 11 years working with Balenciaga.

Insofar as world-class couture is concerned, Europe's oldest and most distinguished names are represented in the Caribbean Basin: Gucci, in business for five centuries, supplies several emporiums and has at least one shop all its own; the marchese Emilio Pucci, who traces his lineage to Catherine the Great, furnishes his creations to many islands as well. So do Yves Saint Laurent, Courrèges, Louis Vuitton, Guy LaRoche. Even Ralph Lauren has a "factory outlet" in the Caribbean, where shoppers report saving 30% and more off U.S. prices.

Those luscious Pringle cashmeres, made from the fleece of the Kashmiri goat, transported to Scotland for processing, are available throughout the islands, often at attractive prices. The famous Fair Isle sweaters, each pattern reflecting the choice of the individual knitter, also sell briskly. To make sure you're getting the authentic Fair Isle, look for a telltale seam below the yoke: A hand-assembled Fair Isle has no seam. Check also for the label "Made in Shetland" or "Made in Scotland." Any unscrupulous operator can use the term "Shetland wool" because it has no trademark protection.

As a matter of fact, whenever you are investing in brand-name merchandise, examine it carefully. Counterfeiters have been known to rake off as much as $450 million in illegal profits in just one year. For example, you may find an Izod shirt that looks exactly like the real thing—until you check the emblem. The bona fide garment has that attached with thread of the same color as the alligator on the outside, while on the inside, the thread matches the shirt color. The rip-off version uses colorless thread and a wider border than does the real thing. Inconsistent positioning of the label is another tip: Phonies are placed differently on different garments. Watch, too, for misspellings and packaging discrepancies. And, naturally, be extra-suspicious of the proverbial "million-dollar treasure in a five-and-ten-cent store." Legitimate quality merchandise just doesn't show up in shoddy surroundings.

Watch out also for passed-off goods—items that closely resemble the real thing, with just the tiniest variation: a Guy Laroch, for example, or an Oscar La Renta. By eliminating, replacing, or transposing a single letter, the canny copier can stay within the law. Basically, all well-designed fashions, whether for men or women, follow certain infallible rules. Like works of fine art, they possess a harmonious balance of line, form, texture, proportion, emphasis, and rhythm. Successful designs exhibit all of these qualities, even though they may not be separately distinguishable.

On a more prosaic, practical level, look also at the construction and the fabric: Are the seam allowances adequate? Stitches of proper size? The material free of puckers or stiffness?

Once you invest in a Caribbean fashion, you want it to last a while. You don't expect it to be quite as durable as Charlemagne's 1,200-year-old coronation cloak which still hangs in St. Peter's Church in Rome and still looks great. But that kind of durability is undeniably something to aim for.

FOOD

It has been said that the best way to become acquainted with a people is through their cooking. If this is the case, most visitors will most certainly enjoy getting to know the West Indians.

Islanders are firmly convinced theirs is not only fine food, but, according to Virgin Islanders, it is "the best food existing."

Authentic calypso cuisine is created in the same way as true calypso ballads: the artist improvises as he goes along. To hear islanders tell it, anyone who needs a written-down recipe to cook obviously cannot cook at all.

An islander who married an American was so outraged by

her use of a cookbook that he left her. His farewell note, in calypso form, was addressed to his father-in-law:

> *Mistah, please take back your daughter*
> *She buy a book to learn to cook,*
> *The grub's worse since she got that book.*
> *I'm going back to the Virgin Isles,*
> *Where God's sunshine forever smiles,*
> *Where girls know how to love and cook,*
> *And can do both things without a book.*

Fortunately for visitors who may not share their free-wheeling inventiveness, some of the more expert Caribbean Escoffiers have in fact written down their culinary secrets. Almost every island book- or drugstore carries at least one local cookbook.

In Barbados, the *Bajan Cookbook,* compiled by the Child Care Committee, will tell you how to make "pish pash," "Salmagundy sauce," "Tewahdiddle," and a tropical version of boiled dinner called "Twice laid."

Jamaica's more piquant national dishes include "stamp and go," "rich dumb Johnny cake," and "jerk pork fancy." You will find a wide variety of Jamaican cookbooks on sale, among the best: *Recipe Round-up: Sold for the Jamaica Society for the Blind.*

In Curaçao, Jewell Fenzi has collected the best recipes from all six Dutch islands into one volume entitled *This Is the Way We Cook.* From it you will learn how to prepare cactus and iguana soups, Windward Island pies—not to mention eggplant soufflé, the Caribbean version of Indonesian nasi goreng, the savory and exotic saté sauce, along with a variety of other epicurean finds.

Of those books covering the area as a whole, one of the most outstanding is *Geoffrey Holder's Caribbean Cookbook.* Nationally known in America as a director, costumer *(The Wiz),* painter, and commercial star for such products as 7-Up,

Trinidad-born Holder is also a bon vivant of international repute. "We West Indians entertain at the drop of a hat," he writes, "and entertaining means eating, because you always talk better when food is in your stomach. So I had to learn to cook." And so he did. Curry cascadura, King turtle stew, coconut chicken, coq au rhum, and soursop punch—these are just a few of the delicacies for which his book reveals the formula.

Although several mainland epicures have tried their hand at Caribbean cookbooks, some with commendable results, Caribbean cuisine perplexes many orthodox food writers because of the exuberant, inventive spontaneity with which it is executed. The ingredients themselves are exotic. But now that Puerto Rico, Jamaica, and the Dominican Republic have led the way in canning and packaging some of the more popular ingredients, visitors to these islands, as well as those to many of the others, can easily pick up a tin or two to take home for themselves or a gastronome friend, or to sample on the spot.

Herewith a look at some of the collectors' items you can buy, packaged or canned, in local grocery stores:

Ackee, a beautiful red fruit about the size of an orange, imported to Jamaica by Captain Bligh (of *Mutiny on the Bounty*), comes close to being a national dish in Jamaica. The flesh is roughly akin to scrambled eggs in color and consistency and, to some, also tastes somewhat like them. Ackee has one worthy advantage, in that it contains only 30 calories per 3½ ounces. Combine it with salt fish to be traditional; but most nonislanders prefer it spiced with sharp, grated cheese and a touch of onion. (Add pastry and bacon, and the result is a flavorsome Caribbean quiche.)

Breadfruit, another contribution to the Caribbean vegetable kingdom by Bligh, comes sliced in the can. It is then possible either to fry it in ham or bacon fat, and serve as bite-sized hot appetizers, as a vegetable, or as a side dish, or to puree it as you would mashed potatoes. Creamed with cheese, it becomes a croquette or a soufflé.

Mango marmalade comes in glass jars as well as cans, and so does the mango fruit itself. Caribbean Créole sauce rather resembles a tropical form of A-1 sauce.

Hot-pepper vinegar is a staple in all island households. In addition to the conventional candied papaya, orange, and grapefruit rinds, there's a delicious line of fruit pastes, or "cheeses" as they are sometimes called: translucent concentrates of guava, mango, or orange, akin to gelatin in texture but twice as stiff. Eaten atop a cracker that has been spread with cream cheese, this is a favored dessert among American collegians as well as *becs fins.*

Soupsop, mango, and guava juices and nectars not only make refreshing coolers, alcoholic or otherwise, but also produce tangy, intriguing sherbet and ice cream. Often the labeling is in Spanish (for those processed in the Dominican Republic or Puerto Rico), but you can identify the fruit by the four-color picture on the can.

Guava shells (as the name indicates, the peeled outer core of the fruit) are also savory presented as a finale to a sophisticated meal. Drain the heavy syrup and reserve it for making jelly or other purposes, then marinate the shells in brandy or rum overnight. Serve these also topped with a slice of cream cheese. (Orange shells are available to be used in the same manner.)

West Indian pepper sauce differs from manufacturer to manufacturer in the degree of heat generated, but though versions and color differ, the verve and vitality of the flavor does not. Home-brewed versions of this fiery potion appear in discarded catsup containers, old rum pints—whatever used vessel the confector happens to have handy. In Antigua, look for it in the native market. Grenada grocery stores usually stock a profusion of home-grown mace and nutmeg, the spices for which the island is known. Barbados makes an excellent version of its own sauce.

For a seemingly conventional, but uncommonly succulent, gustatory souvenir, pick up a jar of 100 percent natural, hand-ground, very piquant peanut butter in Haiti (ask for Mamba). Also recommended: the locally made jams prepared at St. Marc by one Madame L. Paultre, sold under the label Pidy.

Where to shop? Puerto Rico and the U.S. Virgin Islands supermarkets stock all the basics; perhaps the easiest source would be the Pueblo chain of markets. The Dominican Republic and Jamaica also have their chains. Sint Maarten/St. Martin offers two small, extraordinarily fine emporiums: on the Dutch side, the Self-Service Supermarket, featuring Dutch/island seasonings, liqueurs, and a wide range of unique staples; on the French side of the island, there are gourmet shops especially worth visiting, although the stock here is mainly European.

For more details and specific addresses, see individual island chapters.

As a parting note to this discussion of Caribbean food, here is the calorie count for approximately 3½ ounces of assorted island food.

Caribbean Calorie Count

ACKEE	30
AVOCADO	94
BANANA	97
BREADFRUIT	61
CASSAVA	60
CHAYOTE	31
COCONUT (MATURE)	296
COCONUT (IMMATURE)	122
COCONUT MILK	296
GUAVA	69
MAMMEE APPLE	47

MANGO (COMMON)	59
PAPAYA (RIPE)	31
SAPODILLA	94
TAMARIND	272
PIGEON PEAS	118
PLANTAIN (YELLOW)	122
PLANTAIN (GREEN)	132
TANNIA	132
YAM	132

Fish, shellfish, chicken, and red meat carry the same caloric values in the Caribbean as elsewhere, as do manmade sweets. Rum, unfortunately, does more damage than scotch, gin, vodka, or other comparable spirits.

JEWELRY

"Equip yourself with weapons of gold, and nothing will be able to resist you. Cover your woman with ornaments of gold and you will have many sons." Those who follow these words of wisdom enunciated by the Delphic oracle to the warrior king of Macedonia will have victory and fertility guaranteed, at least according to legend.

Whether or not the formula works, an awesome number of men and women have had a very good time trying it out over the years. And the Caribbean offers a glittering array of gold finery, both imported and domestic.

You can, for example, acquire in the islands, the exquisite LALAoUNIS renditions of 4,000-year-old Minoan beads, fashioned of 22-karat gold, which Aristotle Onassis chose as a wedding gift for Jacqueline Kennedy. Available in gold also is the arresting, avant-garde line created by Lapponia of Finland. Or, if your tastes are more conventional, choose the patrician, understated elegance of Cartier.

Caribbean designers, and there are many, sometimes prefer to use the area's own bold, tawny-red golds, such as those from nearby Guyana. With it they create their own exuberant designs, inspired by the exotic tropical flora and fauna that surrounds them.

Pieces confected of ancient coins are very prevalent in the area. The Caribbean Sea harbors an infinite number of sunken ships, many of them filled with treasure. (According to *Sports Illustrated*, the Virgin Islands alone contain 100,000 pieces-of-eight still to be retrieved.) Some of the rings, pendants, and pins made from such old gold coins are one-of-a-kind, not sold anywhere else.

All jewelry, of any kind, not only gold, generates a special kind of mystique for both the recipient and the donor. Accordingly, as one of the most popular of all shopping categories, merchants in the Caribbean place special emphasis on all conceivable varieties, both imported and homegrown.

The popularity pearls have been enjoying since Princess Diana wore her heirloom choker (not to mention the yards of imitations sported by Madonna and Cyndi Lauper) has spread to the Caribbean. Their soft glow and inner light flatters every complexion, and as a result you will find every kind and quality of pearl on sale in most islands.

Where once the Roman general Vitellius financed an entire military campaign by selling just one pearl earring, you can now acquire, without paying out a king's ransom, Mikimotos, various grades of *atoya* (the standard round white cultured pearl), black pearls produced by black-lipped oysters, freshwater specimens, and—if you are very lucky indeed—rare pink pearls produced in the Caribbean conch shell.

Other temptations include emeralds from Colombia; the fabulous aquamarines, sapphires, and other precious stones purveyed by H. Stern, listed by *Business Week* as the fourth most important jeweler in the world (after Tiffany, Harry Winston, and Bücherer); elegant creations from Italy's top name designers; diamonds selected by experts; fiery opals from Australia—and some very special gems indigenous to the West Indies.

Caribbean amber—smooth, limpid, glowingly gorgeous—is a top draw with discerning buyers. It is found almost exclusively in the Dominican Republic, around the north coast bay which Christopher Columbus discovered and which his brother named "Puerto Plata." This 20-million-year-old fossilized pine resin comes in various shades, sometimes encasing leaves, bits of wood, pebbles, and prehistoric insects. A drop of dew trapped quivering on a branch has even shown up in some pieces.

Known by the Greeks as *elektron* for its property of generating static electricity (and hence our own word "electricity"), this least heavy of all gems is, along with the diamond, the only one composed of vegetable, not mineral, matter. When presented as a gift, it is said to bring good luck to the recipient. Amber has also been valued for centuries as a weapon to ward off throat ailments, to protect children from evil influences, and it is considered especially lucky for anyone named Anne.

Of interest also from the Dominican Republic is a newer gem, the Larimar. Eleven years ago, Larissa Mendez was strolling along a Dominican beach with her father when a shiny azure pebble caught her eye. The Mendezes investigated further, found several chunks of the material, and traced the source.

They named their find "Larimar" ("Lari" for Larissa and "mar" for ocean). The Mendezes proceeded to mine and market it as a stone duly registered wtih the Gemological Institute of America, which as of this writing classifies it as a "somewhat precious" gem. (Steps are being taken to upgrade the rating.) Very much akin in appearance to the turquoise in American Indian jewelry, Larimar is used in European or Dominican silver or gold settings, and is extremely reasonably priced. Local craftspeople also combine the stone with the ivory of wild-boar tusks.

Jacques Cousteau is credited with making available to Caribbean jewelers another material new to the islands, although it has long been known and used by other civilizations: black coral. A sacred stone for the High Priests of India, valued by the Greeks who named it *Antipathes Grandis,* meaning "against harm and disease." Today's museums in India and Greece contain ancient pieces fashioned from black coral found in the Red Sea.

Two decades ago, while probing the depths of the great Palancar reef off Cozumel, Cousteau discovered this gorgeous Gorgonian in this hemisphere. Since then, divers sufficiently intrepid to brave depths of over 200 feet where black coral lives have harvested specimens in several Caribbean islands. Shaped rather like a bonsai tree, with brown to red veins reflecting various stages of growth, black coral remains expensive, not only because it requires such skill and courage on the part of the divers to gather, but because of its incredibly slow rate of growth: one inch every fifty years!

A Few Precautionary Ground Rules

As with any sizable investment, there are pitfalls to be avoided in buying jewelry: *beware of gold chains on which the gold content is inscribed on the clasp alone*—that 18-karat gold noted might be only in the fastener, and the rest of the piece only gold-filled.

Always weigh, if only in your hand, any prospective purchase. No matter how exquisite the workmanship, in terms of cold dollars and cents, the amount of gold as indicated by the weight takes precedence. It can also tell you in the case of a chain whether you are dealing with solid links or hollow ones. In the latter case, you risk having recurring problems with breakage, and will end up with so much repair soldering, that the chain will become unusable.

Resist also the temptation to invest in a triple herringbone necklace. Constant tangles are impossible to avoid.

Whenever possible, opt for a flexible catch or fastening. Rigid ones undergo more stress and therefore break more easily.

When buying pearls, rub them over the edge of your teeth. If they feel gritty, because of the gradual build-up through which they are created, you have the real article. A fake bead will feel smooth.

To determine value, do as the experts do—check first and foremost on luster. This is the combination of inner and outer glow caused by light striking the pearl's myriad layers of coating. The more luminous the shine, the thicker the topping, and thus the finer the pearl.

According to one professional, you can spot a cheap pearl by rolling a strand across the countertop. If you see winks of light, this means the coating is thin.

Color is not a factor in determining price, so pick the shade most becoming to you. As a rule, creamy pearls go best with brown hair; blondes are more flattered by pinkish tones. When holding them up against your skin, do so in soft, natural light, not in full sun, and never—if at all possible—choose on the basis of what you see by electricity only. Whether or not the pearls are cultured or natural has become virtually an academic question because so few of the natural variety exist. Several thousand oysters will only produce one or two pearls, unless coaxed with an implanted irritant.

To distinguish fake amber from the real thing, rub the piece briskly with wool or felt, then try to pick up a dime-size bit of facial tissue with it. If the tissue clings firmly to the substance as if magnetized, your amber is authentic. You can also test by dropping it on a tile floor; true amber will not shatter.

In selecting already set gems, make sure the stone is anchored in a rim or bezel, and not just glued. Obviously, the latter method is less secure, and the piece less valuable.

Most important of all, make sure of the reliability of the merchant. Obviously no prudent buyer takes his or her patronage to street peddlers. As for the regular shops, scrutinize their literature carefully to see what brand-name watches as well as jewels they feature. While an unscrupulous adventurer might pick up a Piaget, Rolex, or Patek Philippe to establish respectability, he'll not get away with featuring it in his printed brochures unless authorized to do so. Top-flight manufacturers keep a very watchful eye on that sort of thing and act expeditiously to disassociate themselves from fly-by-nights.

In the overall picture, we believe merchants of integrity far outnumber wheeler-dealers, but they do exist, so beware.

LINENS

If you have difficulty believing that there are people in this world who unhesitatingly shell out well over $2,000 for a single bed sheet, send $6 (deductible from your first purchase) to 381 Park Avenue South, New York, NY 10016 to obtain the catalog of Pratesi, supplier to Yves Saint Laurent, Barbara Walters, and Sophia Loren, not to mention the Rockefellers and the Princess of Wales.

Elizabeth Taylor spends $60,000 annually at Pratesi, and according to reporter Susan Harte, Johnny Carson and his most recent spouse even took the question of who would have custody of their joint Pratesis to court.

As to what makes these items so precious, not to mention pricey, the secret, it is said, is in the fabric: fine Oriental silks, African cottons, Irish and Belgian linen with a thread count of 320-per-square inch, twice that found in domestic equivalents. And this close weave, fortunate owners will tell you, produces a marvelous softness, not to mention incomparable sybaritic satisfaction.

Unlikely that shoppers in this price bracket should care, but if they do, they may be able to save up to 30% on Pratesi items in some of the islands.

The Caribbean also offers fruitful foraging in less lofty price brackets. Retailers there have been importing hand-embroidered linens from the Orient for years, during times when high import duties and restrictions on trade with the People's Republic of China precluded American shops from stocking much of this merchandise.

Although barriers have now been lowered, West Indian emporiums still maintain, as you will note in the chapters on the individual islands, a very competitive edge. Hand-appliquéed guest towels, meticulously executed, cost 80¢ apiece; luncheon sets with napkins under $10; crib sheets; embroidered pillowcases; lace table-cloths—the assortment is vast.

You will also find interesting and unusual pieces made in the area. In some cases, skills are handed down from one generation to the next. In others, embroiderers learn from skilled European mentors imported for that purpose. Perhaps a local daughter is sent away for schooling to a convent where the nuns teach her a special style of lacemaking; she passes the art on to her compatriots; they in turn share it with their descendants, and a whole industry is born. Or a family of missionaries undertakes to provide depressed economic areas with a means of livelihood. Handwork is especially desirable because it requires so little capital outlay. Add to that the coterie of gifted American professionals, such as the one-time *Reader's Digest* art director who came to employ almost a hundred islanders in his textile operation, and you have an extraordinarily wide variety of goods from which to choose.

Among those brought in from the Orient, note four different styles of embroidery, each from a different province, with possibly the most highly regarded today being that from the province of Hunan. The top practitioner there, a 32-year-old professor at the Hunan Embroidery Research Institute, recently undertook a two-year tour of the United States, demonstrating an astonishing innovation of her own invention, double-sided embroidery. Ms. Rao B-You, who started embroidering at five and became bored with conventional stitchery while still in her twenties, conceived a system so intricate it took her two years to teach it to her first trainee.

As of now, only four women in the world have mastered her style of double embroidery, whereby, using a single needle so fine it is barely visible, the artist produces one image on one side of the cloth, another on the other. There are portraits showing the subject yawning on one side, frowning on the reverse; or wearing court dress on one side, battle regalia on the other. If you're lucky enough to come across some of this work, you'll be hard put to resist throwing all caution to the winds to acquire it.

Island embroidery, in all honesty, cannot compare with the incredible delicacy of Oriental technique—after all, the Chinese have been practicing for ten centuries. Still, there is a verve and color to the West Indian linens, whether batik, silk-screened, or hand-sewn, that projects a special kind of joy. And much of the workmanship is very good indeed. For example, one set of placemats representing various flowers and birds on a background of Belgian linen, is so handsomely executed that we had twenty-four of them framed and they now decorate one entire wall of our library.

There are a couple of other advantages to buying linens in the Caribbean. For one thing, mail order is no problem, nor are Customs formalities. As products of the islands, they are exempt from tariffs. When you get home and scrutinize some of the price lists, such as those offering hand-embroidered cocktail napkins at 50¢ apiece, or a set of six placemats and matching napkins, also all hand-done, for under $10, you may well reach for your checkbook.

Another plus is the fact that you can order articles made precisely to your specifications. It may take a while, but you will receive exactly the size cloth in exactly the pattern and colors you request. On some islands the government operates institutes specializing in handwork, in others you negotiate with nonprofit cooperatives. Or you can, when you feel confident of reliability, deal directly with the individual.

A word of caution: examine the fabrics extra-carefully, especially on items imported from the Orient. That substantial finish which lends such elegance might be little more than sizing, apt to disappear with the first wash.

PERFUMES AND COSMETICS

Perfume and cosmetics constitute one of the best buys to be had in the Caribbean—they are compact, lightweight, and fairly easy to store.

Since fragrances can represent a sizable investment, you may want to do a little research on the science of scent via your nearest public library or computer hook-up. Meanwhile, herewith a few tips.

All scents, mixtures of oils, gums, and chemicals, must be dissolved in odorless alcohol (that derived from rice is best) in order to last and remain stable. In perfume, the mixture is 80% spiritous; toilet water, or parfum de toilette, on the other hand, reduces the extract to 10% to 14%, while in eau de cologne, only 5% is extract base, the other 95% is alcohol. In some instances, moreover, synthetic ingredients are substituted in the cologne for the more expensive natural substances in the perfume.

Glass stoppers are used in luxury packaging because they are more airtight than grooved corks: each one is individually ground to fit its own flask and cannot be exchanged to seal another.

If you have trouble extracting the stopper, one expert suggests the following: "Hold your bottle firmly with one hand and with the other hit the stopper gently upwards and sidewards with a piece of wood such as a tool handle. If this does not work, hold your bottle sidewise and warm the neck of the bottle (NOT the stopper) over the flame of a lighter or a match. Keep turning the bottle so that the neck is heated evenly all around. After 10 to 20 seconds, the neck starts expanding and the stopper usually pops without further prodding."

Good perfume properly packed keeps for years in a cool place. Every once in a great while, capillary action may draw out the liquid, in which case, you're due a refund. Store perfume in a cool, dark place, never in the sun, and always replace your stopper, preferably after wiping it off.

Aerosols and sprays, however convenient, have these hazards: the freon can change the scent of the perfume; moreover, given the space that gas occupies, spray containers give you less volume than the same size bottle of unpressurized perfume or toilet water. You're better off buying a hand-operated, refillable purse atomizer without the gas.

Watered-down perfume? A myth. Add an eye-dropper of H_2O to the aromatic mixture and the whole bottle will turn milky, i.e., either unsalable or immediately returnable to the manufacturer. As to the manufacture of facsimiles, the individually designed bottles and packaging are far too expensive to duplicate.

One bottle of the same brand better than another? It happens. But you need Cyrano's nose to know it in most instances. Quality of floral crops vary from year to year; some ingredients, such as the musk from Tibetan goats, becomes virtually impossible to obtain. But olfactory scientists are whizzes at chemically reproducing the missing natural substance.

What suits you best? That old saw about the same perfume smelling different on different wearers happens to be true—it has to do with, among other factors, the varying amount of acid in the individual's skin. The most effective way to sample scents is to apply the liquid to the skin, let it dry, and then test it. Apply a drop also to a handkerchief or other piece of cloth. How the fragrance adapts to your clothing, which it will affect even though you may not put it on directly, is equally important. (One giveaway of cheap perfume is its acrid afterbite; the longer you wear it, the worse it gets!)

As to specific brand names, do not be totally snowed by the prestige advertising that accounts for much of a product's success. The Caribbean is the perfect place to experiment— for you, *and* for the manufacturers. New chic varieties have been introduced in smart West Indian shops many months before they hit the American market—and at half the price! Ambergris, Yland, Orris, Myrrh, Musk—all the sensually satisfying ingredients are there, and many of these may be just the perfume signature you've been looking for.

And in the ongoing search for that wondrous, ineffable fragrance that will, if not revolutionize your life, at least give it a new lift, a certain *je ne sais quoi* zing, do not neglect some of the homegrown Caribbean products. Vetiver and patchouli, both key perfume ingredients, are grown on many islands, along with other important elements. In addition, local mixologists, guided by experienced experts, get better every year. Also to be considered is price: as of now, West Indian brands cost way, way below the European variety.

A final note: If you are politically oriented, and/or are considering attending one of the political conventions, the following intelligence, obtained from an absolutely impeccable source—the editor of *Washingtonian* Magazine—provides this important inside intelligence—

Republican Perfumes: Fracas, Giorgio, First, Fidji, Shalimar, Youth Dew, Amazon, White Shoulders, and Tuberose (Nancy Reagan's fragrance of choice). For men: Aramis.

Democratic Fragrances: Oscar, Chloë, Charlie, Estée

Lauder, Joy, Chanel No. 5, Blue Grass, L'Air du Temps, Tatiana, Diorissimo. For men: Paco Rabanne.

Remember, you heard it here.

SPIRITS

> There's nought, no doubt, so much the spirit calms,
> As rum and true religion.
>
> —Lord Byron

Differences of opinion exist as to whether Christopher Columbus introduced the first sugarcane to the New World from the Canary Islands or whether the plant is indigenous to the West Indies. Reports of early explorers do note sugarcane as already growing in Guadeloupe.

Imported or not, it unquestionably played a major role in the evolution of the islands. In an infamous exchange of trade known as the Golden Triangle, molasses made in the Caribbean went to New England to be converted into rum, which in turn was shipped to Africa to buy slaves who were sent to the Caribbean to work the sugar plantation. By 1807, Boston had no less than forty rum distilleries; rum grew to be the Number One, most profitable manufactured article produced in New England.

It also became the principal drink of the American colonies. Congress voted supplies of rum for the American army as a necessity for those facing danger. Considered a medicine, rum was prescribed for the treatment of gallstones, malaria, and was considered a better "restorative" than cod-liver oil. On cold New England evenings, a favorite drink was "flip," a mixture of hot sweetened rum and beer.

In the West Indies, meanwhile, it flowed like the proverbial stream. Author Frank Prial, writing in *The New York Times,* quotes this 18th-century account of one extraordinary rum punch party:

"A marble basin, built in the middle of the garden especially for the occasion, served as the bowl. Into it were poured 1,200 bottles of rum, 1,200 bottles of Malaga wine, and 400 quarts of boiling water. Then 600 pounds of the best cane sugar and 200 powdered nutmegs were added. The juice of 2,600 lemons was squeezed into the liquor. Onto the surface was launched a handsome mahogany boat piloted by a boy of 12, who rowed about a few moments, then coasted to the side and began to serve the assembled company of 600, which gradually drank up the ocean upon which he floated."

At today's prices, even in the Caribbean, you'd have to have J. Paul Getty's bank account to finance such a bash. Indeed, a generation or so ago, rum had plummeted in popularity. Now, thanks to some notable improvement and refinement in the manufacturing process, especially in Puerto Rico, it is regaining favor as a sophisticated and versatile libation, with the United States importing $100 million worth each year.

The product has come a long way since the primitive frontier distillers judged their mixture by combining spirit and gunpowder in equal parts. If the powder failed to burn, the liquor was too weak. If it burned brightly, it was too strong. If it burned evenly, it was "just right." As the mixologists became more sophisticated, so did their output. Indeed, some of the better brands have all the texture and bouquet of a fine armagnac.

In addition, using rum as a base, distillers throughout the Caribbean have confected some suave and popular innovations, especially in the field of liqueurs. Some combine the rum with fine local coffees, others flavor it with coconut, citrus, assorted herbs and spices, or even, in one case, with cactus.

Curaçao's cordial of that name is world-renowned, but other islands also have their specialties, many flavored with tropcial fruits, as for example, the banana of banana daiquiri fame, or Jamaica's Orangique. The secret ingredient in Cointreau is a sweet and seductive peel as tantalizing as white chocolate. Edward Cointreau, Jr., discovered it in Haiti in 1849.

The West Indies are also an excellent place to stock up on conventional liquors—bourbon, scotch, vodka, whatever your pleasure. In that connection consider U.S. cost breakdown on an average bottle of liquor selling for, say, $6.79, as supplied by the Distilled Spirits Council of the United States—federal taxes: $1.99; state and local taxes vary, but for the sake of argument, assume $1.34; for retail distribution, add another $2.02; and for the distiller, $1.75. No wonder, then, that Beefeater Gin priced $11.79 in Manhattan sells for $5.50 in St. Thomas; Seagram's V.O. for $5.75, as opposed to $10.50; or Jack Daniels for $7.50.

Savings on wines tend to be smaller, because the tax is lower. You may still find good buys in the French islands, though, and in the U.S. Virgins Harvey's Bristol Cream sells for $4.95, as opposed to $7.69 in New York.

WATCHES

The traditional shifty-eyed street merchant peddling hot watches on the corner, cliché of cons though it may be, does say something about the care with which you should select your timepiece.

Few objects present greater possibilities for flimflammery: cut-rate workings concealed in an impressive container, bargain-basement imitations of respected brands (these are not difficult to fabricate)—the ways in which the trusting client who values quality but at the same time can't turn down a "good buy" can be euchred are endless. To invest a sizable amount of cash with any but the most responsible merchants, therefore, constitutes the height of folly.

Fortunately, the Caribbean abounds in trustworthy emporiums: houses that stand behind their sales and don't hesitate to issue guarantees and honor them willingly, either at point of purchase or via mainland branch offices.

Every island with any kind of tariff break offers some kind of savings. On one of our early European junkets we followed the standard tourist procedure and paid $200 for a chronograph in Geneva, Switzerland: the same article, we were told, would run 40% more, at the very least, in the United States. True enough. But we found the identical timepiece on sale in the islands at $15 LESS than its country-of-origin tag!

No wonder watches rank among the very choicest buys in the Caribbean—with selection probably unequaled anywhere in the world, INCLUDING Switzerland!

In 1985, the "Today Show" aired an in-depth takeout on a modest innovation that revolutionized the industry and is widely credited with saving it for Switzerland. The new wrinkle is an eye-catching low-cost model known as the Swatch, sold for around $30 in the States. It can be had in the country of origin—and in some places in the West Indies—for perhaps 20% less.

However, a Swiss expert of highest integrity and experience calls our attention to an alternative: a sporty, trendy, even lower-cost version known as the Swiss Swatch. According to our friend, the movement is the same as that of the Swatch, but the price—in St. Thomas, at any rate, where we last spotted it—is a mere $16.50. At that price, you might pick up several.

On top-quality, prestige watches, Switzerland remains unequaled. Vacheron at Constantin, the oldest watch factory in the world, will turn out only nineteen timepieces each day, so painstaking is the hand-finishing that goes into making each and every watch. Napoleon bought one of the early Vacheron et Constantins; so did England's Queen Elizabeth II.

What are the best brands? We have our pets, as undoubtedly do you; and chances are a million to one you'll find them in plentiful supply in the Caribbean in all price ranges.

If you fancy feasting your eyes on beautiful art forms (and who doesn't), have a look at those stunning Piagets featured in slick magazines: 100% hand engraved, cases made in 18-karat gold or platinum only. To complete just one Piaget requires 150 man-hours of labor. Be it the gem-faced model, or one featuring a gold coin, you can save a bundle, by pre-shopping at home and knowing your local market. Piagets are not found on bargain tables, however, either in the U.S. or in the West Indies. The company makes over 500 models. The dials and hands are also gold.

Omega, the watch that has timed so many Olympic games, undergoes no less than 1,497 quality-control checks before being approved for sale. The oil used to lubricate Omega's intricate precision works costs a minimum of $2,000 a gallon.

From the tiny village of Brassus, in the Joux Valley, comes the frankly expensive, painstakingly handcrafted Audemars Piguet creations: slim, flat, completely distinguished. Whatever model you select, know that you are making a sizable saving.

Rolex, good-life connoisseur James Bond's favorite, and possibly the hottest status symbol of all, produces half of all the chronometers manufactured in Switzerland. Rolexes were used on Sir Edmund Hillary's Mount Everest climb. On display at the Smithsonian Institution is the Rolex, which, fitted to the outside of the Trieste bathyscape, withstood a dive of seven miles.

There is indeed something special about owning a Swiss watch: more than a convenience, it's a lasting piece of jewelry, an heirloom in the making—and in these islands, a whale of a buy.

ANGUILLA

ANGUILLA
AT A GLANCE

GOVERNMENT TOURIST OFFICE: Anguilla Tourist Office, The Valley, Anguilla, W.I. (tel. 2759).

CURRENCY: The Eastern Caribbean dollar is the official currency, although U.S. dollars are widely circulated. US$1 equals about EC$2.65.

OFFICIAL HOLIDAYS: New Year's Day, Constitution Day (February 10), Good Friday, Easter Monday, Whit Monday, the Queen's Birthday (mid-June), Carnival (August 1, 4, and 5 are official holidays), Separation Day (December 19, marking Anguilla's secession from the Associated State of St. Kitts and Nevis in 1967), Christmas Day, Boxing Day (December 26).

STORE HOURS: 8 a.m. to noon and 3 to 5 p.m., Monday through Friday—for the most part. Some shops open on Saturdays, and many will on request.

LOCATIONS: For the addresses and telephone numbers of shops, consult the alphabetical list at the end of this chapter.

Shaped like the eel for which it is named, this long, flat (maximum elevation 2,556 inches) beachy island half again as big as Manhattan gained instant notoriety nineteen years ago as the Mouse That Roared, and as the setting of the Bay of Piglets invasion. These references concern the fuss raised by six thousand residents determined to go it alone, free of association with St. Kitts and Nevis.

Britain dispatched 120 paratroopers and 40 policemen to its sandy shores, 69 miles north-northwest of St. Kitts. The self-proclaimed Republic of Anguilla was dissolved. Trouble flared up again briefly in 1977, when the Royal Marines were sent to break up another disturbance.

Anguilla is now a British dependency and the situation seems calm. A favorite refuge of French and Irish freebooters in the halcyon days of piracy, Anguilla lays claim to having introduced the original Sea Island cotton seed into Georgia and South Carolina a century ago. Its current exports consist of varying quantities of spiny lobster, and several thousand barrels of salt a year.

Imports, however, are another story. As more and more jetsetters search for a new winter refuge, talented newcomers have been moving in to cater to them, without as yet despoiling Anguilla's quiet serenity and its friendly, hospitable inhabitants—nor its thirty beautiful beaches.

New resorts are elegant and luxurious. To serve this top-drawer clientele, a number of sophisticated boutiques have sprung up. Although you can pay $300 or more for a dress, you will also find other, much more affordable options.

ARTS AND CRAFTS

For sprightly watercolors of Anguillan scenes, visit artist Judy Henderson at her **Sunshine Boutique**, in South Hill (tel. 2149).

West Indian houses, as woodcarvings and/or painted on wall hangings, have a special charm. You can buy them either at **The Mariners Hotel Boutique** (tel. 2671) or **Riviera Restaurant Boutique** (tel. 2833), both in Sandy Ground.

FASHIONS

Fashion is big on Anguilla: from the Laura Ashley dress you can pick up for $99 at **Janvell's Boutique** on Main Road (no phone) to elegant Italian creations in the several-hundred-dollar range featured at the **Malliouhana Hotel Boutique**, La Semana, Maids Bay (tel. 2741). Assorted slacks, sports clothes, and leather goods can be found at the Malliouhana Hotel Boutique also. Note that the small, shoulder-strapped clutch pocketbook is a good buy, we are told, at $130.

Olive Branch Fashions in The Quarter (tel. 2522) includes local custom-made clothes along with its imports; plan on paying about $30 for a made-to-order summer skirt.

For just $14 you could consider a pair of vinyl slacks (lightweight), if only for fun. Find them at **The Galaxy Supermarket** in The Valley (tel. 2232 or 2332).

And while we're on the subject of supermarkets, you might do some inquiring at **Bennie & Sons Supermarket** in Blowing Point (tel. 2221). We're told that the ready-to-wear department includes a handsome pure linen dress for $35.

Other possibilities:

Locally made pareos, silk-screened or tie-dyed, at **The Mariners Hotel Boutique** in Sandy Ground (tel. 2671).

In the **Cul de Sac Boutique** at Blowing Point (tel. 2741) wrap skirts, bikinis, and $40 Italian imported coverups.

JEWELRY

Make your way through the souvenirs and cosmetics at **The Anguilla Drug Store** in The Valley Settlement (tel. 2738), and you'll spot jewelry imported from here and there—for example, a jade charm for $13.

Riviera Restaurant Boutique, Sandy Ground (tel. 2833), handles costume pieces, some of the more inventive ones retailing for $20.

USEFUL ADDRESSES

The Anguilla Drug Store: The Valley (tel. 2738).

Bennie & Sons Supermarket: Blowing Point (tel. 2221).

Cul de Sac Boutique: Blowing Point (tel. 2741).

The Galaxy Supermarket: The Valley (tel. 2232 or 2332).

Janvell's Boutique: Main Road (no phone).

Malliouhana Hotel Boutique: La Semana, Maids Bay (tel. 2741).

The Mariners Hotel Boutique: Sandy Ground (tel. 2671).

Olive Branch Fashions: The Valley (tel. 2522).

Riviera Restaurant Boutique: Sandy Ground (tel. 2833).

Sunshine Boutique: Main Road, South Hill (tel. 2149).

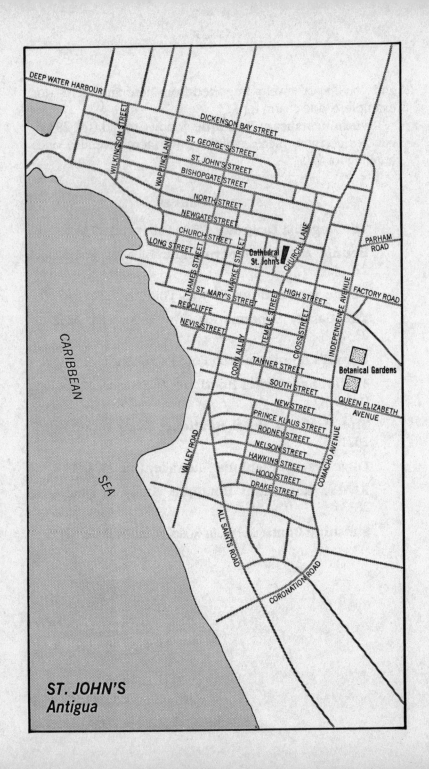

ST. JOHN'S
Antigua

ANTIGUA

ANTIGUA
AT A GLANCE

GOVERNMENT TOURIST OFFICE: Antigua Department of Tourism, Thames and Long Streets, St. John's, Antigua, W.I. (tel. 2-0480).

CURRENCY: The Eastern Caribbean dollar (EC$) is the official currency, available in denominations of $1, $5, $20, $100. Tied to the U.S. dollar at a rate of EC$2.65 equals US$1. Most prices are quoted in both currencies, and U.S. dollars are accepted almost everywhere.

OFFICIAL HOLIDAYS: New Year's Day, Good Friday, Easter Monday, Labour Day (May 1), Whitsun Monday, Queen's Birthday (June 2), State Day (November 1), Christmas Day, Boxing Day (December 26).

STORE HOURS: Shops are most often open from 8:30 a.m. to noon and 1 to 4 p.m. every day except Sunday. Thursday is a half day, generally speaking (although some shops do remain open throughout the afternoon on cruise ship arrival and other busy days).

LOCATIONS: For the addresses and telephone numbers of the shops, consult the alphabetical list at the end of this chapter.

Of all the literally thousands of Caribbean islands to choose from, the exclusive coterie of American socialites who established the Mill Reef Club found Antigua the most desirable. They bought 2,000 acres on the southeastern tip of this lopsided, leaf-shaped island 40 years ago, built their plush clubhouse and started the whole trend toward millionaire enclaves in the Caribbean.

Today the main building of the fabled Mill Reef Club is rimmed with handsome houses; members have included such personages as the Mellons, the Cowles, and other established movers and shakers. Jackie Onassis bought a lot at Half-Moon Bay.

The island continues to attract upper-crust escapists. Peter de Savary, who led Britain's challenge in the 1983 America's Cup Races in Newport a couple of years ago, opened a branch of his elegant London St. James Club on Marmora Bay, close to where Admiral Nelson once based his fleet. (Daily rates begin at around $400 for two, and guests include the likes of Joan Collins, Ann-Margret, and other show-business luminaries.)

What do the well-heeled sun worshippers find so special about this 12-by-14-mile, one-time British colony?

First of all, it is eminently accessible. Thanks to U.S. World War II military installations, the airfield has long been able to accommodate direct international flights. The next greatest lure is the beaches: 365 of them. Some are mediocre, but others are superb—expansive, sparkling, sloping softly into crystal-clear water.

But, especially, there's the atmosphere: Antigua is old-fashioned, off-beat, authentically West Indian. An up-to-date island—up to the date of Queen Anne, it has been said. Nowhere in the Empire has the Crown been more revered than by Antiguan oldtimers. On the night of King George VI's death, one Antiguan hostess received her dinner guests dressed entirely in black—in mourning for the King. On a previous occasion, when a minor member of the royal family visiting the island conveyed the King's apologies for not coming himself although he very much wanted to, a native matriarch clucked sympathetically, "Fancy being King and not being able to do what you like."

One of the country's treasured possessions is the cupboard door on which an early Prince of Wales, while on Navy assignment in Antigua, had scrawled, "Merry Christmas 2 you." Some senior islanders were so upset at Edward VII's giving up his throne for Wallis Simpson that they refused to use a stamp bearing his picture.

Antigua is no longer so tied to the United Kingdom politically. An independent state, it still combines much of the original West Indian flavor with the British ambience that attracted discerning escapists a generation ago and continues to draw them today.

Unlike some other shopping areas in the world, Antigua has not lost its individuality in achieving its independence. As a result, you will find no chrome-and-plate-glass department stores with miles of display counters offering huge stock for sale. No tricked-up boutiques, no mass merchandising. You will, on the other hand, be able to choose from a variety of tasteful items, carefully collected by discerning individual shop owners.

Capital and chief port of the island, St. John's shelters over half the 80,000 population. It is the focal point of government, commerce, and industry. Founding fathers built the streets extra wide to provide maximum cooling by the trade winds. Thus traffic flows rather smoothly and without the sort of congestion you might see in Bridgetown, Barbados, or Charlotte Amalie, St. Thomas, or other shopping centers.

Dominating the town and considered its most imposing monument is St. John's Cathedral (Anglican) built in 1683, rebuilt in 1745, steepled in 1789, razed by an 1843 earthquake.

Today's structure was completed over a century ago, the steeples and interior damaged in the 1974 quake. Other St John's landmarks Antiguans are proud of include the two-in-one Government House Buildings: the original half is 250 years old, the newer section dates back to 1802.

Hamlets of varying sizes dot the rest of the countryside, none of outstanding mercantile interest. You will find clusters of marts here and there, especially around Nelson's Dockyard on the south shore of the island, and some worthy boutiques tucked into the larger resort hotels.

ARTS AND CRAFTS

If you have been looking forward to commissioning a family portrait as soon as you could afford the extravagance, here is your chance. Native son Cadman Mathias is a top favorite with the international trend-setters at such resorts as the Mill Reef Club and the St. James Club, which take turns in hosting a weekly one-man show for this gifted Antiguan, and, considering his talent, his prices are quite attractive. Watercolors begin at $55; for $400 Mr. Mathias will paint your likeness.

Mathias maintains no regular gallery. To get in touch with him, either make arrangements to attend one of the hotel showings or, failing that, ask the **Antigua Tourist Board** on Thames Street in St. John's (tel. 2-0480) to put you in touch with him through the Antigua Arts Society.

Some in-town stores also carry oils and watercolors by Antiguan artists; a few are priced under $20. You might also spot something you like amidst the miscellany in the **Shipwreck Shop** on St. Mary's Street (tel. 2-1322). All stock here is by no means Antiguan, and if you're in the market for souvenirs that just about come right out and say so, here's where you will find them. Within this mind-boggling melimelo of good and bad paintings, conch shells, and island books, you can, if you know what you're about, pick up piquant bits of West Indiana not always found elsewhere. Among our favorite acquisitions from this shop are the coconut birdfeeders made in various islands under the supervision of United Nations experts (they look considerably better than this sounds!!). You will find here Caribbean handcrafts at their worst—and sometimes at their best. As to which is which? That's what makes horse races.

Antigua's number one take-home memento is a brain-twisting parlor game called *warri*, played on a homemade board fashioned with varying degrees of artistry, in mahogany, maho, or other local woods. You'll see islanders hunched thoughtfully over their warri boards at taxi stands, bar counters, or on street corners, concentrating as intently as players in an international chess competition.

Gold Coast slaves brought the game with them from Africa, and for some reason it has persisted in popularity in Antigua more than on any other island. Each contestant starts off with 24 little nicker nuts from the Guilandina plant (younger players have been known to substitute marbles), 4 in each of the 6 cups on his side of the warri board. He removes 4 nuts from one hollow and sows them into the other holes counterclockwise, on both sides of the board. Through a series of maneuvers too complicated to outline here, whoever captures the first 25 nuts wins.

Obviously, there's a great deal more to the game. Once you get the hang of it, warri is almost as fascinating as jousting with knights and pawns. The **Pink Mongoose**, the **Shipwreck Shop**, and **The Coco Shop**, all on St. Mary's Street, have carried a selection of warri boards at one time or another, including one that folds up for traveling. When we bought ours (at the Pink Mongoose), the saleswoman threw in printed instructions, extra nuts, and an on-the-spot lesson as well. Prices begin around $10 or so. Loads of fun, and a real challenge. Known in Africa as "Mankala," the "stone game"—

as it is sometimes called—is beginning to attract attention in the United States also. The Smithsonian Institution is now offering its members folding Mankala boards, with stones and carrying case.

Should the fine points of the game escape you, some Antigua hostesses suggest alternative uses for the warri. A frequent suggestion—use it as a condiment tray for curries or other dishes served with chopped pepper, hard-cooked eggs, and the like.

The **Industrial School for the Blind**, on Market Street near the open market, presents a wide assortment of custom-made baskets, straw placemats for $2 or so, two-foot-long dog beds for under $15, and huge hampers for about the same. Some of the weavers are very skillful, and the hammocks, rugs, and Chinese grass products we have seen there would be a credit to a sighted professional much less to a sightless one.

Closely woven wastebaskets sell for about $10, unisex hats for the same and less, cunning baby chairs with woven sea-grass seats, raffia mesh bags—the stock varies. The dozen or so sightless workers may not earn much (the total weekly payroll can run less than the combined take-home pay of two blue-collar workers in our country), but they have a fine time gossiping, joking, and fellowshipping.

We have not had much luck with the **Handicraft Shop** on Thames Street (same building as the Tourist Office), but perhaps we haven't managed to get there at the right time.

Pottery and ceramics are a favored Antiguan craft. **Seaview Farm** is the home of the rustic potters who make coal pots, flower pots, and the large yabba pots which are traditional cooking utensils. You're welcome to visit and make your purchases directly.

If your stay in Antigua is brief, and you have time for only one stop, make it the aforementioned **Coco Shop** (tel. 2-1128). Pat and Ogden Starr, who own this upscale establishment, are among the original Mill Reef pioneer residents.

They have been running this emporium for the past 35 years. The Starrs have a way of skimming off the cream of the local output, as well, for that matter, as choosing some of the choicest imports. Whatever is worthwhile in the way of Antiguan products, you're likely to find they stock at least one or two examples.

CAMERAS

Compare your hometown prices with those at **Y. de Lima** on High Street, a branch of the Trinidad emporium. (Look for optics here also.)

CHINA, CRYSTAL, AND HOME FURNISHINGS

Waterford, Wedgwood, and Royal Worcester, among other name luxuries, can be found at **The Specialty Shoppe Ltd.** on St. Mary's Street (tel. 2-1198). If you had the foresight to check U.S. costs ahead of time, you may find gratifying savings.

The Scent Shop on High Street (tel. 2-0303) carries Lalique and Baccarat crystal and other treasures as well as its regular line of fine fragrances. **Norma's Duty-Free Shop** on High Street and at the Halcyon Cove Resort, features Rosenthal china and Lladró figurines.

On the island, ceramists Sarah Fuller and Kim Warren design and fire their own dishes, cups, plates, and vases shaped like ginger jars. Items are frequently glazed both inside and out, colors soft and muted in greens and blues, prices run from $10 to $45, at **Nubia** (St. Mary's Street), **The Coco Shop** (St. Mary's Street—tel. 2-1128) or at the artists' ateliers outside of town.

FASHION

We first discovered Heiki Petersen in her **Bay Boutique** on St. Mary's Street (tel. 2-2183) 15 years ago, and we're as impressed now as we were then: clever styling, original touches, and fabulous fabrics. French and Swiss cottons, psychedelic colors where appropriate. You will discover here a rare and special talent. Happily, Frau Petersen has not been lured to more urban pastures. If you don't find what you like in the Boutique, you might be able to track this gifted lady down in another location, **The Studio**, on Cross Street (tel. 2-1034), and talk to her about having just the right thing made to your order.

One of **The Coco Shop** founders trained at the Cranbrook School of Fine Arts in Michigan, and the resulting professional touch is readily evident. The Coco Shop (St. Mary's Street—tel. 2-1128) puts together a series of collections—bathing suits, sundresses, men's windbreakers—in sea island cotton and other fine fabrics. Prices vary between $30 and $100, designs are replaced every two years. Here, too, you will see Liberty lawns, made up or by the yard; English-tailored Daks slacks; along with finds not obtainable anywhere else on the island. This commissary features imports of top quality, and uses local motifs and materials whenever possible. Sprightly sportswear, well-crafted bikinis, islandy skirts, and plenty of pickup items. Be prepared, however, for fairly hefty price tags. Quality seldom comes cheap.

Under the imprint of **Kel-Print**, George Kelsick has been specializing in locally silk-screened products ever since our first shopping foray in St. John's many years ago. His shops on St. Mary's and Temple Street, and at the Coolidge Airport (tel. 2-2189) feature pineapples (the island emblem), steel drummers, flamboyants, or fighting cocks running rampant on cool backgrounds. Have the fabrics made up into skirts or shirts, or, if you're a home stitcher, buy by the yard.

The West Indian Sea Island Cotton Shop carries a line of hand-painted and/or batik fabrics, in bolts or made up. In the $30 to $70 range, they are attracting increasing notice from fashion professionals.

A Thousand Flowers on Redcliffe Quay (tel. 2-4264) features the Indonesian/Java style wraps along with instructions on how to sarong yourself. Well worth a look here also is the sportswear confected locally by Dominic. Find swimsuits, sarongs, and shirts in this boutique and at the sister shop at Buccaneer Cove, or in **Dominic's** own **Boutique** on Marble Hill in Dickenson Bay.

Look for the Ruth Clarage label (see entry in Jamaica chapter under "Fashions") at the **Sugar Mill Boutique** on St. Mary's Street (tel. 2-4523).

If you read *Harper's Bazaar* you know about **The Galley Boutique**, 7 Redcliffe Quay, and at Nelson's Dockyard. The magazine recommends it. The two dynamos who run this operation stock a full line of batiks, silkscreens, floats, patio skirts, and a few things for men. Here is where you will also find the work of St. Barth's internationally recognized Jean-Yves Froment.

FOOD AND DRINK

We had our first taste of two West Indian culinary classics, "wet sugar" and island hot sauce, in Antigua. To this day, Antigua rates high marks for both. The moist, fresh sugar crystals extracted from local cane still come packaged in plain brown paper bags, and sell for pennies in any grocery. Incredibly inexpensive, uniquely flavorsome, the caramelly taste lingers sweetly on the tongue—for discerning *becs fins* at home, an appreciated gift.

West Indian hot sauce is as distinctive as a fingerprint, and can contain as many as 17 ingredients, depending on the whim of the preparer. Local Antiguan ladies put theirs up in discarded ketchup bottles, mayonnaise jars—whatever comes to hand. To aficionados, it is invariably delicious, however packaged.

The sauce's special heat provides natural air conditioning,

islanders will tell you, because it cools by dilating the tiny blood vessels at the skin's surface, thereby releasing a wave of warmth through the body. When the rush of heat subsides and perspiration beads, you will feel cool, they assure you, despite the temperature.

Antiguan honey, with or without the comb, is outstanding as well. Some say it's the pollen from those bright tropical flowers that makes it so good. Mark of preference: Christian Brothers brand.

Insofar as native dishes are concerned, Antiguans favor the traditional West Indian conch curries, roast breadfruit, yams and sweet potatoes.

Groceries in the several island supermarkets seem to be about 80% U.S.-made, 20% imported from England. Local housewives transplanted to America miss the Devonshire cream readily available at **Joseph Dew's** on Long Street in St. John's, or at **Bryson's**, nearby.

The Antiguan black pineapple is so prized for its extraordinary sweetness that the island adopted it as its national emblem. Local mixologists use the juice to whip up memorable fruit coolers, delicious with or without alcohol. You might also sample the nectars of soursop, guava, mango, and papaya.

JEWELRY

If you've logged any time in the chic watering holes of New England, you know Hans and Nancy Smit from their shop in Marblehead, Massachussetts, where they spend the summer. When the frost comes on the pumpkin, they repair to their emporium, **The Goldsmitty**, at 8A Redcliffe Quay (tel. 2-4601). Custom-designed pieces feature handsome stones, first-quality gold, and especially the indefinable cachet that comes from talent combined with care. If, as has been said, genius is basically the capacity for taking infinite pains, the Smits are on the right track.

Other jewelers include a branch of **Y. de Lima** of Trinidad (High Street—tel. 2-0814), billed as the largest manufacturer of gold and silver jewelry in the Caribbean (for specifics see entry in the Trinidad chapter.)

And if you collect pieces strongly reflective of the area where you acquired them, look up the confections of Mrs. Neville Iken, who works with coral, shells, and macramé. If the **Coco Shop** (tel. 2-1128) doesn't have some on sale, phone Mrs. Iken at home. Our notes containing her number seem to have disappeared, but you should find her in the phone book.

PERFUME

Antigua has its own fragrance, an agreeable floral called Frangipani. Affordably priced under $20 the ounce, attractively presented (definitely not in the usual ketchup bottle), you'll find it on sale 'most everywhere.

For imported perfumes, try **The Scent Shop** (High Street—tel. 2-0303) and **The Coco Shop** (St. Mary's Street or branches—tel. 2-1128).

SPIRITS

Cavalier Rum is the local brand. Agreeable, versatile, but not a collector's item among West Indian rums. Nor, on the other hand, will the price break you: on-island you will pay around $2 a bottle; up North it can run three times that.

WATCHES

Shop the **Y. de Lima** branch store first, High Street (tel. 2-0814). This is the place also for cameras and optics.

One of the compelling features that lured the original pioneering winter escapists was the slow pace and low key of Antigua. You could barely hear the muted voices of soft-spoken islanders as they strolled through the luminous tropical nights from a game of cricket or a quick dip before dinner. Now and then the rhythmic beat of an itinerant steel band echoed in the hills (none rise higher than 1,400 feet). Consideration for others was built into the Antiguan character. If anyone was so rude as to talk during a movie, the projectionist stopped the show and turned on all the lights until the unseemly chatter stopped. In case of illness, one of the folk remedies was to change the patient's name—on the theory this would also change his luck and make him well. Among the most popular adopted names in those days were "Penicillin" and "Sulfa."

Times are different now, and so is Antigua. Television has introduced a whole new culture to the formerly insulated island; all "progress" has not been for the better. Nevertheless, once you get home and unpack that Mathias watercolor, the Liberty shirt, those ceramic figurines, and the other treasures you have acquired, chances are you will find wrapped in with them some pretty fond memories of Alec Waugh's own original *Island in the Sun.*

USEFUL ADDRESSES

Antigua Tourist Board: Thames and Long Streets, St. John's (tel. 2-0480 or 2-0029).

Bryson's: St. John's.

Bay Boutique: St. Mary's Street, St. John's (tel. 2-2183).

The Coco Shop: Kensington Court at St. Mary's Street, St. John's (tel. 2-1128).

Dominic's Boutique: Marble Hill, Dickenson Bay.

The Galley Boutique: 7 Redcliffe Quay, St. John's, and Nelson's Dockyard.

The Goldsmitty: 8A Redcliffe Quay, St. John's (tel. 2-4601).

Handicraft Shop: Thames Street, St. John's.

Industrial School for the Blind: Market Street, St. John's.

Joseph Dew's: Long Street, St. John's.

Kel-Print: St. Mary's Street, Temple Street, and at the Coolidge Airport (tel. 2-2189).

Mill Reef Club: Antigua, W.I. (tel. 3-2018).

Norma's Duty-Free Shop: High Street, St. John's, and at the Halcyon Cove Resort.

Nubia: St. Mary's Street, St. John's.

Pink Mongoose: St. Mary's Street, St. John's.

The Scent Shop: High Street, St. John's (tel. 2-0303).

Shipwreck Shop: St. Mary's Street, St. John's (tel. 2-1322).

The Specialty Shoppe Ltd.: St. Mary's Street, St. John's (tel. 2-1198).

St. James Club: P.O. Box 63, St. John's, Antigua, W.I. (tel. 3-1430).

The Studio: Cross Street, St. John's (tel. 2-1034).

Sugar Mill Boutique: St. Mary's Street, St. John's (tel. 2-4523).

A Thousand Flowers: Redcliffe Quay, St. John's (tel. 2-4264).

The West Indian Sea Island Cotton Shop: St. Mary's Street, St. John's.

Y. de Lima: High Street, St. John's (tel. 2-0814).

ARUBA

ARUBA
AT A GLANCE

GOVERNMENT TOURIST OFFICE: Aruba Tourist Office, 2-A Schuttestraat, Oranjestad, Aruba (tel. 23777).

CURRENCY: The Aruban florin, 1.77 equals US$1, tied to the U.S. dollar, not the Netherlands guilder. Silver coins come in 5-, 10-, and 25-cent pieces, plus square 50-cent and 100-cent (1-florin) pieces.

OFFICIAL HOLIDAYS: New Year's Day, Carnival Monday (preceding "Fat Tuesday," or Mardi Gras), Flag Day (March 18), Good Friday, Easter Monday, Queen's Day (April 30), Labor Day (May 1), Ascension Day, Christmas, Boxing Day (December 26).

STORE HOURS: From 8 a.m. until noon and from 2 to 6 p.m., Monday through Saturday. Hotel shops maintain longer hours, including staying open during lunch and on Sunday and holidays when cruise ships are in port (as do some in-town establishments).

LOCATIONS: For the addresses and telephone numbers of the shops, consult the alphabetical list at the end of this chapter.

As was Gaul, so is the royal realm of The Netherlands divided into three parts: Holland, the
Netherlands Antilles (Curaçao, Saba, St. Eustatius,
Bonaire, Sint Maarten) and the six-by-twenty-
mile territory of Aruba. As of January 1986, Aruba amicably
separated from her sister islands. Relations with the mother
country in Europe will be henceforth direct. Aruba will also
manage internal affairs, including setting tariffs, if any, to be
levied on imported merchandise.

Snuggled fifteen miles off the Venezuelan coast, roughly
1,200 miles from Miami and over 1,700 from Manhattan, this
desert-like enclave lies at the epicenter of trade routes. Its very
name comes from the original Indian word *oruba*, meaning
"well placed." As a result of good location and a continuity of
political stability, Aruba has maintained commercial links to
Europe, North and South America, and even the Middle and
Far East for centuries.

In recent years tourists in growing number have begun to
discover the island. Some are attracted by the healthy, Arizona-
by-the-sea climate: with an annual precipitation rate of 24
inches, Aruba offers better odds on a rain-free vacation than
any other Caribbean resort. Others find the unusual scenery
captivating: landscapes with the dry, cactusy look of a healthy
desert rimmed with snowy sands and a turquoise sea.
Thousand-ton dioritic boulders haphazardly scattered one on
top of the other add a fascinating surrealistic moonscape
quality to some sections. Brisk 15-knot northeast trade winds,
much stronger than on most tropical land dots, ruffle the
ubiquitous divi-divi trees as they right angle to the southwest
in their effort to skirt the breeze.

Last, but far from least, on the list of lures attracting growing
numbers of vacationers are the conventional amenities:
modern hotels and restaurants, casinos, and first-rate shopping.

While political ties with the other Dutch islands may have

weakened, commercial links remain as strong as ever. In fact, some of the biggest and best-known emporiums in Oranjestad, the capital city, have their headquarters in Curaçao, with substantial installations in Sint Maarten as well. For more complete descriptions of their wares, consult the chapters on those particular islands. There are also, however, a number of homegrown operations eminently worth your attention.

ARTS AND CRAFTS

Every Tuesday evening from 7 to 10, April 19 through December 20, Arubans meet in the courtyard of Fort Zoutnan in the capital city of Oranjestad, for what is known as the Bonbini ("Welcome" in Papiamento) Festival. There are folkloric presentations, and temporary stalls purvey exotic libations and regional titbits confected by local gourmets. Volunteer members of civic organizations man the booths and profits are earmarked for local worthy causes.

Here is where you will find assembled for sale a representative selection of local handcrafts, woodcarvings, handcrocheted work, paintings, leatherworks, and ceramics.

Other than what's displayed at the Bonbini festival, Aruba does not maintain a high-profile, formally structured arts and crafts program. You will spot, however, individual creative efforts here and there.

One of the most admired Christmas primitives in our collection, for instance, we just happened on down one of Oranjestad's back streets. In a modest shop we found a fourinch-high Aruban cottage made of wood, colorfully decorated with the distinctive hex-like signs found on island houses; its double doors open to reveal a complete hand-carved, handpainted Nativity scene consisting of sixteen three-dimensional figures. The price: US$5. The address? With a cosmic lack of foresight, we neglected to write it down. Fortunately, several alternative browsing grounds exist.

Alex Cox purveys hand-carved wooden figurines in the Boulevard Shopping Center. There too are **Luly's**, for Aruban ceramics, and **Mi Kadushi** (Aruban for "Our Cactus") for handcrafts produced locally and elsewhere in the area.

Artesania Arubiano, at 178 L. G. Smith Boulevard, features an assortment of home-crafted pottery and other objects. (There are branches also at the Ports Cruise Terminal and the Boulevard Shopping Center.)

Attractive artisanry at **Casa del Mimbre**, 76 Nassaustraat (tel. 27268), made of leather, handwoven fabrics, and wools, comes mostly from South America.

For other imports, look in on the **Artistic Boutique**, 25 Nassaustraat (tel. 23142). It carries some interesting batiks on occasion, sometimes made up into men's shirts as well as sold by the yard. You'll also spot Siamese rings, Indian scarves, and other, changing miscellany.

If you're in the market for Dutch wooden shoes, try **Harms Brothers Limited**, 17 L. G. Smith Boulevard (tel. 21597). They also carry dolls, as does the **New Amsterdam Store**, 10 Nassaustraat (tel. 21152)—folkloric ones made in Curaçao, and Dutch dolls imported from Holland.

As for fine arts, we're told **Fantastica**, 82 L. G. Smith Boulevard, in the Shopping Center, exhibits the work of local talents from noon until 7 p.m., but we have not investigated ourselves. To find out more, call 23199.

CAMERAS

A goodly assemblage of choices exists in this category, as, for example, at **Boolchand's**, 51 Nassaustraat (tel. 24092), one of the undertakings you find represented on several islands, or at **El Globo Aruba** at 70 Nassaustraat (tel. 22900), also represented on Curaçao.

The fact that Canon, Elmo, Mamiya, Minolta, Nikon, Vivitar,

and other established manufacturers allow their names to be featured in advertisements from such merchants will, justifiably, instill confidence in prospective buyers.

It is essential to point out, however, when discussing photographic equipment, that worldwide competition is especially keen. If you have not already shopped your home discount sources, you might want to invest in a long-distance phone call before committing to any large investment.

CHINA, CRYSTAL, AND FINE TABLEWARE

Spritzer & Fuhrmann, the Curaçao-based giant in this field, maintains four main stores (two on Nassaustraat—tel. 24360) and several hotel branches in Aruba, with stocks of Wedgwood, Lladrò, Bing & Grøndahl, Baccarat, St. Louis, Lalique, Waterford, and the multifaceted Swarovski. If you don't see what you want, ask about having it flown over from Curaçao. (For a discussion of Spritzer & Fuhrmann, consult both the Sint Maarten and Curaçao chapters.)

A longtime, reliable, and home-grown standby, the **Aruba Trading Company** (known as ATC), operates a kind of mini department store, from beachheads at 14 Nassaustraat (tel. 22600), at the airport (tel. 26759), and at 17 Weststraat in the Palm Beach Hotel (tel. 23950). Here is where you will spot your Hummel and Limoges.

Kan Jewelers fills out its multi-island empire with several Aruba emporiums (main store, 47 Nassaustraat—tel. 21192). Nowhere else on the island will you find the Rosenthal line of crystal, china, and silver offered here, temptingly priced.

Artistic Boutique, 25 Nassaustraat (tel. 23142), displays porcelain and pottery from Spain and Italy, along with rugs, figurines, carved screens, and some antiques.

Raghunath Jewelers, 64 Nassaustraat (tel. 24109), also carry figurines imported from Spain. The **New Amsterdam Store**, 10 Nassaustraat (tel. 21152), features Lladrò, as does

Palais Oriental, corner of Nassaustraat and Emmastraat (tel. 21510), along with Cristofle silver and assorted crystal and glass. **Fanny's**, 7 Nassaustraat (tel. 22621), also carries this kind of merchandise.

You'll find the Dutch Delft featured most everywhere.

FASHIONS

J. L. Penha & Sons, one of the most venerable and highly regarded Curaçao mercantile pioneers, handles some of the best-known names in fashion in its 11 Nassaustraat location (tel. 24161). For feminine shoppers they feature Pringle, Lanvin, Dior, and Castoni. Designs for men include Givenchy, Eminence, D'Gala, Pierre Cardin, and Papillon, among others. Our Liberty jacket acquired at Penha ten years ago is still in use. It was here also that we first discovered those bargain-priced, indestructible Bonaire-made sports shirts. There are souvenirs and perfumes as well. This is a conservative, eminently value-oriented house. It was one of our very early favorites, one we continue to like.

When we first visited Aruba over two decades ago, knowing locals recommended to us their favorite off-the-tourist-track emporium, **Eva's Boutique**, located in the Boulevard Shopping Center (tel. 23199). Eva's Boutique still functions, still largely undiscovered by the guidebooks.

On our first trip Eva's was a modest second-floor walkup in a rickety old native house. It moved uptown to its own headquarters, and the Boulevard Shopping Center premises are filled with temptations. Some things struck us as a bit elevated in cost, but the Gottex beachwear, imported bikinis (these have been known to run up to size double-D cup!), sweaters, and handbags can also be worthwhile. Begun as an egg-money pastime by the wife of the Aruba Spritzer & Fuhrmann director, in partnership with a professional Dutch designer, this house provides no thrills, no steals, but it is a workman-like, knowledgeable operation.

Today's home-grown designer favorite, Etlien Abspoel Oduaber, specializes in bright tropical designs and super-casual lines. See them in her own **Tropical Wave**, at 82 L. G. Smith Boulevard in the Boulevard Shopping Center (tel. 21905).

For avant-garde, with-it, dernier-cri décor and apparel, **Aquarius** (of the Curaçao Aquarius family), at 9 Nassaustraat (tel. 24871), features Maud Frizon, Valentino, Gianfranco Ferre, and other trendy European names.

Entre Nous, in the Boulevard Shopping Center (tel. 32973), also handles elegant and expensive European clothes for men and women.

Gandelman Jewelers, 5-A Nassaustraat (tel. 29143), also a Curaçao offshoot, features Gucci scarves, belts, handbags, and ties.

Certified Jewelry, 75 Nassaustraat (tel. 26845), carries Pierre Cardin accessories and Spalding sunglasses as well as their own regular line of chains, bracelets, rings, and charms.

At the **New Amsterdam Store**, 10 Nassaustraat (tel. 21152), the jammed-to-the-rafters assortment includes Yves Saint Laurent, Rossetti, and Lacoste (of Paris) shirts, beachwear by Israel's Oberson, embroidered blouses, and Italian shoes. Shoes can be found also at **Capri**, branch in the Boulevard Shopping Center (tel. 28070), and at **Ecco** department store (Ferragamo and Magli brands), 22 Nassaustraat (tel. 24726). Find men's wear there as well.

FOOD

While everywhere else in the Caribbean the native Indian population was either being slaughtered or carried off to Europe enslaved, twin quirks of fate spared those living in

Aruba. In the days of Spanish occupation, King Charles V, for reasons not entirely clear, forbade any permanent settlement on Aruba. As a result, the local residents were able to continue their way of life unmolested.

Next, when the Dutch took over, they found it easier to draft the resident aborigines for agriculture and animal husbandry than to import slaves from Africa. As a result, today's Aruban population has as heavy an infusion of original Indian blood as probably any other island in the Caribbean, and fewer natives of African descent. This heritage is distinctly reflected in the island's cuisine. While admittedly mainly Indonesian-Dutch in character, there are special grace notes exclusive to Aruba. *Pastechis,* a plump little pastry filled with spicy meat, shrimp, or fish, substitutes American seasonings for hard-to-find originals, but you will still note the unusual combination of dark-brown sugar and cumin. Another Aruban favorite is *Kari Kari,* accented with achiote seeds and cod and served with plantain.

Dehydrated shrimp toast (*kroepoek oedang*), saté sauce, crushed red-pepper paste in medium, hot, and very hot strengths (*sambals*); these and loads of other condiments, seasonings, and exotica are on sale at any one of several supermarkets. **Nic Habibe** at 108 Nassaustraat (tel. 24920) is one.

Le Gourmet in the Aruba Trading Company at 14 Nassaustraat (tel. 22929) handles all the classic upscale items—including caviar, foie gras, brandied fruits, Dutch chocolates, Fortnum & Mason products, and other comestibles.

Check also **La Bonbonnière** at 75-B Nassaustraat (tel. 22375) and **Harms Brothers Limited** at 17 L. G. Smith Boulevard (tel. 21597).

All food stores and delicatessens carry those fine Dutch cheeses (Edam and Gouda)—U.S. Customs allow you to bring home ten pounds or $25 worth. Or you can purchase these items at the airport cheese counter.

JEWELRY

Spritzer & Fuhrmann, Kan Jewelers, Gandelman Jewelers—these well-known island megamerchants are discussed in detail in the Curaçao and Sint Maarten chapters. For local branches and telephone numbers, check the list at the end of this chapter. There are other special emporia on Aruba, however.

Look at the **Artistic Boutique**'s (25 Nassaustraat—tel. 23142) pieces made of jade, gold jewelry here as well, and those at **Casa del Mimbre** (76 Nassaustraat—tel. 27268) too. **Lucor Jewelers**, 5 Hendrikstraat (tel. 26765), have experts on the premises to create gold or silver settings for the loose diamonds and other gems that are stocked. **Kenro Jewelers** in the Boulevard Shopping Center specializes in diamonds.

LINENS

Linens are an extremely good buy on Aruba. The **New Amsterdam Store**, at 10 Nassaustraat (tel. 21152), offers an extraordinary range of values, from finger towels and muffin servers priced at a dollar or so up to the most elaborate of banquet cloths. **Boolchand's**, with branches at 51 Nassaustraat (tel. 24092) and in the Boulevard Shopping Center (tel. 25989), offers a varied selection as well, as does the **Strada** department store, 4 Havenstraat (tel. 24190).

Other establishments are most definitely worth a second look. **Artistic Boutique**'s (25 Nassaustraat—tel. 23142) collection includes Irish linens, organdies, and items hand-embroidered in Madeira. Shop **Palais Oriental** (branches at 8 and 72 Nassaustraat—tel. 21510 and 21422, respectively), for Chinese embroidered cloths. **Aruba Trading Company** at 14 Nassaustraat (tel. 22600) carries linens, as does **Bon Bini Bazar**, 65 Nassaustraat (tel. 24081). You may find some colorful Central American pieces at **Casa del Mimbre**, 76 Nassaustraat (tel. 27268).

PERFUMES AND COSMETICS

There are worthwhile savings to be made in this category and thus many shops handle fine fragrances and cosmetics. Among them:

Aruba Trading Company, 17 Weststraat (tel. 23950); 14 Nassaustraat (tel. 22600); Airport (tel. 26759)

Botica Del Pueblo, 48 Nassaustraat (tel. 21502)

Ecco, 22 Nassaustraat (tel. 24726)

Fanny's, 7 Nassaustraat (tel. 22621)

Maggy's Tree, Boulevard Shopping Center, Alhambra Center

New Amsterdam Store, 10 Nassaustraat (tel. 21152)

Strada, 4 Havenstraat, across from the Boulevard Shopping Center (tel. 24190)

Brand-name perfumes carried include Guerlain, Lanvin, Dior, Giorgio, Oscar de la Renta, Nina Ricci, Hermès, Van Cleef & Arpels, Chanel, Patou, Lagerfeld, Paco Rabanne—in other words, you name it.

Imported cosmetics are equally well represented. Clinique, for example, is at **Maggy's Tree.** Find Vitabath under its German name of Badedas at the **New Amsterdam Store**.

Do try, however, some of the local products made from the aloe found in the cactus that thrives on Aruba. Once on a trip to another desert resort, Palm Springs, we were taken to an aloe farm where the proprietress, who looked a scant thirty years of age, assured us she was all of sixty-two. The family skeptic contends that the reason she looked thirty was because she WAS in fact thirty. Be that as it may, the beneficial properties of aloe are an established reality. And the Aruba offerings contain plenty of it: Aloe Suntan Lotion in three strengths; Aloe Vera Skin Care Gel; Aloe Multi-Purpose Skin Cream, Aloe Burn Balm, and Aloe Lift Mask. In the unlikely event you have any problems finding these products in the nearest drugstore, query **Aruba Aloe Balm**, 140 L. G. Smith

Boulevard (tel. 24277). Of the various Aruba aloe products, we especially like the Fleur d'Aloe Skin Cream.

SPIRITS

Low-priced liquors are available at **Aruba Trading Company's Le Gourmet**, 14 Nassaustraat (tel. 22929); **Harms Brothers Limited**, 17 L. G. Smith Boulevard (tel. 21597); and the **Bacchus Liquortique** in the Boulevard Shopping Center (tel. 31381). Inasmuch as you can only carry one duty-free bottle home, however, you might consider tasting some of the local elixir, Cucui by name. Originally homemade, reserved for special occasions, most liquor stores now carry it. The flavor of this anise-based creation is vaguely reminiscent of absinthe. (Bacchus is one place you can sample it.)

If Cucui doesn't fascinate you, you might pick up a bottle of Curacao's famous, *Curaçao Liqueur*.

A canny government tourism representative suggests—not for attribution—that we share with you the tip experienced travelers know, namely, find out if the price tag reflects a discount before handing over your payment. Although by no means do all stores structure their tariffs in this fashion, it does happen—sometimes involving a saving of as much as 25%.

WATCHES

Whatever your preference, you can find it in Aruba:

Aquarius, 9 Nassaustraat (tel. 24871): Porsche Design
Gandelman Jewelers, 5-A Nassaustraat (tel. 29143): Baume & Mercier, Citizen, Dior, Gucci, Heuer, Longines, and Raymond Weil
Kan Jewelers, 18 and 47 Nassaustraat, plus branches (tel. 21192): Concord, Eterna, Girard Perregaux, Les must de Cartier, Longines, and Rolex

New Amsterdam Store, 10 Nassaustraat (tel. 21152):
Orbit

Spritzer & Fuhrmann, 27, 29, 32, 34-A Nassaustraat;
plus branches (tel. 24360): Audemars Piguet, Chopard,
Corum, Mido, Nivada, Omega, Patek Philippe, Piaget,
Seiko, Vacheron & Constantin

A general suggestion to help you get the most out of your
shopping time: first, ask the Tourist Bureau or your hotel for a
free copy of **Aruba Holiday!**—or the Green Sheet as it is
called. Now going into its third decade of continuous
publication, this twenty-four page tabloid is packed full of
useful tips on where to dine, what to see, sports facilities—
everything you might want to know to make your Aruba trip
an enjoyable one—INCLUDING shopping!

USEFUL ADDRESSES

Alex Cox: Boulevard Shopping Center.

Aquarius: 9 Nassaustraat (tel. 23142).

Artesania Arubiano: 178 L. G. Smith Boulevard; Ports
Cruise Terminal; Boulevard Shopping Center.

Artistic Boutique: 25 Nassaustraat (tel. 23142); 82 L. G.
Smith Boulevard (tel. 32567); Concorde Hotel.

Aruba Aloe Balm: 140 L. G. Smith Boulevard (tel.
24277).

Aruba Trading Company: 17 Weststraat (tel. 23950);
14 Nassaustraat (tel. 22600); Airport (tel. 26759).

Bacchus Liquortique: 82 L. G. Smith Boulevard (tel.
31381.

Boolchand's: 51 Nassaustraat (tel. 24092); 82 L. G.
Smith Boulevard (tel. 25989).

Bon Bini Bazar: 65 Nassaustraat (tel. 24081).

Botica del Pueblo: 48 Nassaustraat (tel. 21502).

Boulevard Shopping Center: 82 L. G. Smith Boulevard (tel. 26360).

Casa del Mimbre: 76 Nassaustraat (tel. 27268).

Capri: Boulevard Shopping Center (tel. 28070).

Certified Jewelry: 75 Nassaustraat (tel. 26845).

Ecco: 22 Nassaustraat (tel. 24726).

El Globo Aruba: 70 Nassaustraat (tel. 22900).

Entre Nous: Boulevard Shopping Center (tel. 32973).

Eva's Boutique: 82 L. G. Smith Boulevard (tel. 23199).

Fanny's: 7 Nassaustraat (tel. 22621).

Fantastica: 82 L. G. Smith Boulevard (tel. 23199).

Gandelman Jewelers: 5-A Nassaustraat (tel. 29143).

Harms Brothers Limited: 17 L. G. Smith Boulevard (tel. 21597).

J. L. Penha & Sons: 11 Nassaustraat (tel. 24161).

Kan Jewelers: 18 and 47 Nassaustraat; 9 Kruisweg; Aruba Sheraton; Holiday Inn; Americana Hotel; Aruba Concorde; Tamarind Beach Hotel; Airport (tel. 21192).

Kenro Jewelers: Boulevard Shopping Center.

La Bonbonnière: 75-B Nassaustraat (tel. 22375).

Le Gourmet: 14 Nassaustraat (tel. 22929).

Lucor Jewelers: 5 Hendrikstraat (tel. 26765).

Luly's: Boulevard Shopping Center.

Maggy's Tree: Boulevard Shopping Center; Alhambra Center.

Mi Kadushi: Boulevard Shopping Center.

New Amsterdam Store: 10 Nassaustraat (tel. 21152).

Nic Habibe Supermarket: 108 Nassaustraat (tel. 24920).

Palais Oriental: 8 and 72 Nassaustraat (tel. 21510 and tel. 21422).

Raghunath Jewelers: 64 Nassaustraat (tel. 24109).

Spritzer & Fuhrmann: 27-29, 32-34-A Nassaustraat; 63 Zeppenfeldstaat; 5 Waterweg; Divi-Divi Boutique, 93 L. G. Smith Boulevard; Aruba Concorde Boutique, 77 L. G. Smith Boulevard; Holiday Inn, L. G. Smith Boulevard (tel. 24360).

Strada: 4 Havenstraat (tel. 24190).

Tropical Wave: 82 L. G. Smith Boulevard (tel. 21905).

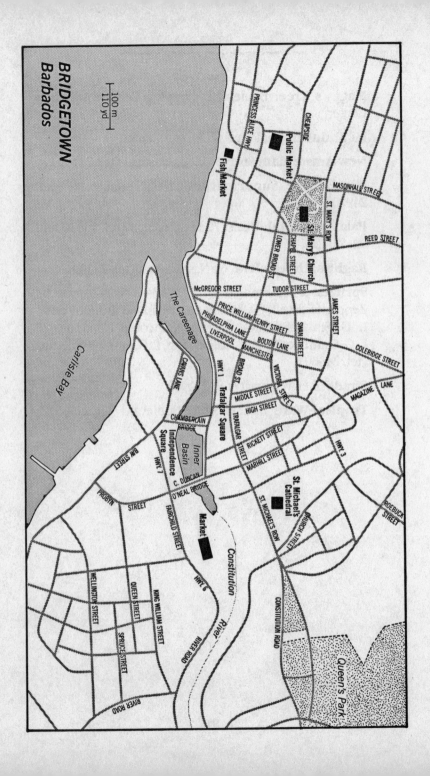

BRIDGETOWN
Barbados

100 m
110 yd

Carlisle Bay

The Careenage

Fish Market

Public Market

CHEAPSIDE

MASONHALL STREET

ST. MARY'S ROW

St. Mary's Church

REED STREET

PRINCESS ALICE HWY.

LOWER BROAD ST.

CHAPEL STREET

McGREGOR STREET

TUDOR STREET

JAMES STREET

PRICE WILLIAM HENRY STREET

PHILADELPHIA LANE

SWAN STREET

COLERIDGE STREET

LIVERPOOL

BOLTON LANE

MANCHESTER

BROAD ST.

VICTORIA STREET

MAGAZINE LANE

MIDDLE STREET

HIGH STREET

HWY. 1

Trafalgar Square

TRAFALGAR STREET

RICKETT STREET

HWY. 3

CAINS LANE

CHAMBERLAIN BRIDGE

MARHILL STREET

Independence Square

Inner Basin

St. Michael's Cathedral

CHURCH STREET

ROEBUCK STREET

BAY STREET

HWY. 7

C. DUNCAN

O'NEAL BRIDGE

ST. MICHAEL'S ROW

PROBYN STREET

Market

Constitution River

CONSTITUTION ROAD

FAIRCHILD STREET

HWY. 6

WELLINGTON STREET

QUEEN STREET

KING WILLIAM STREET

Queen's Park

SPRUCE STREET

RIVER ROAD

RIVER ROAD

BARBADOS

BARBADOS
AT A GLANCE

GOVERNMENT TOURIST OFFICE: Barbados Board of Tourism, Bridgetown, Barbados, W.I. (tel. 427-2623).

CURRENCY: US$1 equals $1.98 BDS (Barbados dollar) at the official rate. The Bajan dollar is divided into 100 cents, available in $20, $10, $5, $2, and $1 notes, as well as $1, 25¢, and 10¢ silver coins plus 5¢ and 1¢ copper coins.

OFFICIAL HOLIDAYS: New Year's Day, May Day (first Monday in May), Whit Monday, Kadooment Day (*Kadomant,* an African word for celebration, signals the climactic end of the Crop Over Festival marking the conclusion of the sugarcane harvest) and Caricom Day (first Monday in August), United Nations Day (first Monday in October), Independence Day (November 30), Christmas Day, Boxing Day (December 26).

STORE HOURS: Officially 8 a.m. to 4 p.m. on weekdays, but more and more shops are beginning to open later. Supermarkets close at noon or 1 p.m. on Saturdays. Hardware stores shutter at noon on Saturday and an increasing number operate Sunday mornings as well. *Tip:* Shops are more crowded in the morning than in the afternoon.

LOCATIONS: For the addresses and telephone numbers of shops, consult the alphabetical list at the end of this chapter.

One thing is certain: Bajans (as the native-born of Barbados are called) don't suffer from a lack of self-esteem. In fact, to them the mere thought that anything closer to paradise on earth exists than their lopsided, mango-shaped little 14 x 21 mile island is quite inconceivable.

Says one islander to a sleeping fellow passenger as their plane swoops in for a landing at the country's handsome Grantley Adams International Airport, "Wake up, man, yonder de WORLD."

Nor should anyone dismiss Barbados as inconsequential in the international scheme of things. The Bajans will soon convince you otherwise. When the hostilities broke out in World War II, the colony gravely cabled the British home government: "Barbados is behind you." Fear not, in other words. And that settled that. Presumably the king slept better that night.

Throughout the various Caribbean upheavals, Barbados sat on the sidelines, always an interested observer, never a participant. True enough, a rare hurricane or two has come its way, and on one or two occasions minor civil disorders have erupted, but basically this land traditionally remained an island-in-the-sun, always steeped in British traditions, peaceful, and quiet. The people have no background of hostility. Their heritage is one of amity, concord, and harmony.

While war, insurrection, strife, and turmoil might be the accepted way of life elsewhere in the West Indies, for 300 years Barbados hummed along distilling rum, growing cane, and minding its own business. Caribbean pirates and freebooters defied kings and their navies—except in Barbados. The seas surrounding other islands turned from turquoise to muddy brown with the spilled blood of fierce fighting—but not here. Tidal waves decimated populations, volcanoes spewed death and devastation—but not on this "singular," special island.

As a result, tourist amenities developed very early in Barbados, and in an orderly, civilized fashion. Claudette Colbert, Ingrid Bergman, Lord Beaverbrook's daughter, Marietta Tree, Lord Thompson of Fleet, Oliver Messel, Noël Coward, David Niven, Raymond Massey, Joan Crawford, Caroline and John Kennedy, Lee Radziwill, Pierre Trudeau, Ronald and Nancy Reagan—these and other celebrities in the past have chosen to spend their time, and money, here rather than elsewhere in the West Indies. Consequently, a well-rounded and civilized shopping complex was growing in Barbados while other islands were still clearing the brush to build their first hotel.

When the Earl of Carlisle took Barbados from Sir William Courteen three centuries ago, he divided his fief into eleven parishes, which he named after saints. You'll be given directions and addresses in terms of saints, according to the parish structure. Now Bridgetown—this bustling, crowded metropolitan capital city in St. Michael's parish—accounts for about a third of the total population (about 100,000) and most of the shopping.

There are satellite retail complexes at The Skyway, Hastings, at Holetown and Sunset Crest, and Speightstown in St. Peter Parish. Shop also in the north of the island and in the specialty shops in many of the hotels.

In order to appeal to the tourist and still collect luxury taxes, Barbados shopping works on two levels: residents contribute their taxes to their government by not shopping duty free, but visitors may shop duty free.

When you buy in one of the duty-free stores (see the list below) you show the salesperson your air or sea ticket and pay for your purchase (at duty-free price). The merchandise is delivered to your point of departure—special counters at the airport or harbor—for you to pick up before you leave. Allow as much time as possible between purchase time and departure for obvious reasons. There is no insurance, but if anything is damaged the shop will replace it if you send a copy of the invoice and a photograph of the damaged goods. There are also fairly well-stocked emporiums at the airport and near the dock, where what you see is what you get instantly.

The system sounds a little frustrating, and it would be preferable to walk out with your acquisitions in hand. But the powers that be have decreed that this is the way it is to be, and in our experience problems are minimal, if any. Overall, the procedure works remarkably well.

Duty-free items include:

Liquor
Bone china
Crystal
Silver flatware
Hollow ware
Electronic equipment
Cameras
Binoculars
Watches
Jewelry
Clothing & accessories
Perfumes

The following are duty-free shops:

J. Baldini Ltd., Broad Street, Bridgetown (tel. 426-5845)

Louis L. Bayley & Son Ltd., 33 Broad St., Bridgetown (tel. 426-3647); branch also at Olive Blossom Shop, Sunset Crest Shopping Centre, in St. James Parish

Bijoux, 3 Swan St., Bridgetown (tel. 429-7266)

Cave Shepherd & Co. Ltd., Broad Street, Bridgetown (tel. 426-2121); branches throughout the island

Correia's Jewellry Store, Ltd., Prince William Henry

Street and on Broad Street in Bridgetown; branches also at Sunset Crest Shopping Centre in St. James Parish, and Grantley Adams International Airport

Da Costa Ltd., Broad Street, Bridgetown (tel. 426-3451); branch also at Sunset Crest Shopping Centre, St. James Parish

De Lima (Barbados) Ltd., 32 Broad St., Bridgetown (tel. 426-5751)

El Matador Ltd., Hilton Arcade, Hilton Hotel, St. Michael's Parish

Harrison's, 1 Broad St., Bridgetown (tel. 426-0720); branches also at the Hilton Arcade in St. Michael's Parish, Paradise Beach Shop at the Paradise Beach Hotel in St. Michael's Parish, Southern Palms Shop in the Southern Palms Hotel in St. Lawrence Parish, and at the Grantley Adams International Airport

India House Ltd., Mall 34, Broad Street, Bridgetown (tel. 429-7237).

Knights, Ltd., 24 Broad St., Bridgetown (tel. 426-5191), and at Sunset Crest Shopping Centre, No. 1, St. James Parish

Lerner Shops, 27 Broad St., Bridgetown (tel. 429-7278)

Nari's, 52 Swan St., Bridgetown (tel. 429-7284); branch also at Hilton Arcade, Hilton Hotel, St. Michael's Parish

The Royal Shop, Nicholas House, Broad Street, Bridgetown (tel. 429-7072); branch also at Mall 34, Bridgetown

Maraj & Sons, 9 Norman Centre, Broad Street, Bridgetown (tel. 429-5631)

In earlier times, being able to acquire Scottish cashmeres, French fragrances, Irish linens, Scandinavian silver, English bone china, Japanese optics, and so on at a fraction of their U.S. price was Barbados's top lure. In recent years, however, a number of other areas of interest have evolved, in some cases even outstripping in popularity the more conventional shopping lures.

ANTIQUES

For those of you interested in antiques, experts in the field inform us you can do very well in Barbados. In fact, dealers from other islands have been swooping down and making off with so much of the national patrimony that strenuous efforts are afoot to curb the wholesale exporting of antiques. If you are contemplating major purchases, you should inquire about export license requirements. Just a few heirlooms that belonged to original colonists may still be located, but note that the reproductions early Bajan craftsmen made, all of mahogany, are collectors' items in themselves: four-poster beds, lovely hand-carved couches, handsome tables.

Even if you don't buy anything, you'll enjoy meeting the Barbadian antiquarians. Owen T. Alder, for example, of **Claradon Galleries** on Pine Road just outside of Bridgetown (tel. 429-4713), has spent a lifetime going to auctions. In addition, Mr. Alder is a man of many talents and interests: longtime politician, connoisseur—one sophisticated Bajan describes him as "a kind of self-taught everything. A most interesting man."

Well worth a look also is **Antiquaria** in the Bradshaw Building on St. Michael's Row, Bridgetown (tel. 426-0635). Every now and then **Women's Self-Help Handicraft and Flowers** (on Broad Street in Bridgetown—tel. 426-2570) comes up with some vintage bits and pieces as well. Of what value—if any—we are not knowledgeable enough to say.

If you'd like to have some things made to your specifications, ask around. There are quite a few Bajans making furniture these days and some of it is excellent.

ART

As in many other islands, native-born Bajans were somewhat

late in finding their own voice. There was an era when the English-garden, pastel style of painting more or less dominated the local art scene.

No more. With the encouragement and guidance of the government's National Cultural Foundation, vibrant and flourishing talents have emerged in the past decade, giving Barbadian art its own distinctive character: very colorful, very Caribbean, very bold—and often very sophisticated as well.

The **National Cultural Foundation** operates its own gallery in headquarters at Queen's Park House, Bridgetown. It's open Monday through Friday from 10 a.m. to 1:30 p.m. and from 2:30 until 6 p.m.; on Saturday the hours are 2 to 6 p.m.

You may also wish to visit:

Bay Gallery on Lower Bay Street, St. Michael's Parish (tel. 426-1604), open Monday to Friday from 9 a.m. to 4 p.m.

Dayrells Gallery at Dayrells Plantation, St. George Parish; by appointment only, with proprietor Denyse Menard-Greenidge (tel. 437-9400).

The **Studio Art Gallery**, Speedbird House, Fairchild Street, Bridgetown (tel. 427-5463). It is open Monday through Saturday.

If you have time for one stop, we suggest you make it Norma Talma's **Talma Mill Art Gallery**. Housed in an old mill, as the name indicates, on Enterprise Road in Christ Church, the gallery receives visitors by appointment only. Call Norma Talma at 428-9383. She herself is an accomplished and highly regarded artist. In addition, she features a discerning selection of other painters' work as well as her own and keeps in touch with the best. If you have a specific artist in mind, Ms. Talma can probably point you in the right direction.

You will find limited-edition prints, watercolors, and collages, including some very beautiful ones done by the owner. She makes her own paper for these out of sugarcane and wild-cotton bark and the results are so striking that collectors do not hesitate to pay $1000 or more for one of mural size. If you would like to see the paper being made, or acquire some, speak to Norma Talma ahead of time.

If you're interested in sculpture, have a look at the **Bertalan Gallery** in Marine Gardens, Hastings, Christ Church (tel. 427-0714). Although prices can range from as high as $1000 or more, you should be able to find pieces in the $40 range as well.

Barbados has at least one major sculptor—Karl Broodhagen. You will see one of his magnificent larger-than-life statues of Bosso, the freed slave, on the roundabout at the St. Barnabas Highway. Broodhagen also did the bust of Barbados's outstanding leader, the late Prime Minister Grantley Adams. You'll notice it outside the Government Headquarters Building in Bridgetown. Mr. Broodhagen has reached the age and eminence to be able to create only what he likes. He is, however, occasionally available for commissions. Again, ask Norma Talma's help if you want to get in touch with him or obtain a look at his catalog.

CRAFTS

With the twin objectives of preserving their heritage and at the same time stimulating employment, the Barbados government established the Barbados Industrial Development Corporation (IDC) to coordinate and market the output of individual traditional craftsmen.

A catalog is available through the **Barbados Industrial Development Corporation**, Handicraft Department, Pelican Industrial Park, Bridgetown, Barbados, W.I. (tel. 426-4391). It includes car seat cushions, bread baskets, and pocketbooks made of lace-stitched dried pandanus leaves; placemats of woven "coconut bones"; handbags made of handwoven cabbage bark or clusia; plant holders of black sage; polished mahogany boxes and nests of trays; rugs and mats of plaited khus-khus grass made to order; black-coral earrings and pins with silver or gold fittings. One set of straw placemats we saw here for $3 apiece are being advertised, as we go to press, at 4 for $45 in one of the fancy Stateside catalogs.

Bajans trace their involvement in handcrafts back to the days of the original Arawak inhabitants. The skills have been passed on through succeeding generations, with generous infusions of European and African influences.

One Arawak specialty was firing unique pieces of pottery out of the first-quality clay available on the island. Not only do today's artisans utilize many of the same Arawak designs but they employ their methods as well, relying on primitive earthen kilns and the old-fashioned potter's wheels.

Africans brought to Barbados their talents in confecting adornments from seashells, coconuts, trical seeds, corals and various *matériaux trouvés*. From the various grasses—wild cane, clusia root, the leaves of the pandanus plant—they wove a wide assortment of straw goods. The European, more contemporary contribution shows in the perfecting of production methods, in fabric prints, and other modern grace notes that adorn today's Barbados shopping scene.

The emergence of the Rastafarians as a cohesive sect is also a comparatively recent addition to the Bajan sociological mix. These admirers of the late Haile Selassie (you'll know them by their long braids—dreadlocks) specialize in leather work, and the real ones are known as upright, peaceable citizens. Unfortunately, some bad actors tend to adopt their outward appearance as camouflage.

Where to view the various crafts? **The Potteries**, a village atop Chalky Mount, District of St. Andrew, shelters local potters in small wooden houses, using old wheels operated by foot treadles.

Pelican Village, along the Princess Alice Highway between Bridgetown and Deep Water Harbour, consists of a three-acre cluster of African kraal-style pyramid-roofed buildings created by the Industrial Development Corporation to serve as headquarters for island handcrafts and artisans. It features individual boutiques devoted to assorted categories of merchandise. One specializes in locally made soft-sculpture-type dolls, another displays the fetching clay miniatures of the local constabulary. **Courtney Devonish's** pottery studio (tel. 436-6126) is particularly worth a look. If you don't find what you like amidst Devonish's "monkeys" (the local name for water pots), platters, and other glazed and unglazed articles, you might have your order custom-made. Some wooden sculptures and macramé are here as well.

For the best examples of local weaving, visit **The Loom House** in the Skyway Shopping Plaza, Hastings, Christ Church (tel. 426-0442). Other crafts are on display as well; Roslyn Watson is in charge.

The Rastafarians operate their own market at **Temple Yard** along the Princess Alice Highway, near Bridgetown. But you might find it worthwhile to stop and look at the wares of some of the street merchants. Many of them do very interesting work.

The Women's Self-Help Handicraft and Flowers showroom on Broad Street near Nelson's statue (tel. 426-2570) offers a collection of local items, among the more fetching of which are the khus-khus root sachets for $3 or $4 (U.S.). Khus-khus, the bushy grass that lines the country roads, is also known to professionals in the perfume industry as vetiver, a key ingredient in many a top-priced scent. Packaged and ribbon-bound for hanging in your closet or use in your dresser drawers, these make pretty and fragrant pick-up gifts.

Scrutinize also, what's on display at the **Best of Barbados** shops at The Skyway Shopping Plaza, the Hilton Arcade, Sam Lord's Castle, and the Sandpiper Inn in St. James Parish. You might look in on **West Indies Handicraft** as well, located at Norman House on Broad Street in Bridgetown. A specialty here is the "tingwing" straw (straw clogs).

If you choose to visit Barbados in the fall, note that the **National Independence Festival of Creative Arts**, better known as NIFCA, takes place during October and November, climaxing on November 30, Independence Day. Spotlighted are music, dancing, singing, painting, drawing, crafts, drama, creative writing, and poetry. For specifics, query the National Cultural Foundation (tel. 426-0914) or the Barbados Board of Tourism (tel. 427-2623).

CAMERAS

The merchants of Barbados have been in the business of handling top-quality imports in the Caribbean for about as long as anyone in the West Indies. Whether you can equal, or even beat, their camera prices at your local discount house is for you to determine. Do your research at home and to make the comparison, check the merchandise at **Louis L. Bayley & Son Ltd.**, 33 Broad St. (tel. 426-3647); **Cave Shepherd & Co. Ltd.**, Broad Street (tel. 426-2121); **Knights, Ltd.**, 24 Broad St. (tel. 426-5191), and other duty-free emporiums in Bridgetown—see the list at the end of this chapter for addresses of branches.

CHINA, CRYSTAL, AND HOME FURNISHINGS

Barbados is big in all these categories. At **Da Costa's** on Broad Street (tel. 426-3451), for example, find Waterford crystal, Capodimonte and Lladrò figurines, Royal Doulton, Coalport, Aynsley, Minton, Belleek, Sèvres china, among others. **Cave Shepherd & Co. Ltd.**, at Broad Street and satellite branches (tel. 426-2121), features the fine figurines and dinnerware of Bing & Grøndahl. **Harrison's**, 1 Broad St. (tel. 426-0720)—see the list at the end of this chapter for addresses of branches—carries an extensive collection of full lead crystal, bone china, and figurines. If none of these shops can satisfy your needs, you'll have no difficulty locating several other purveyors of quality imports.

FASHION

Although perhaps you might not expect such a laid-back, low-keyed little island to be ultra style-conscious, Barbados has been at the forefront of Caribbean fashions for almost two decades. The Yellow Pages of the Caribbean telephone directory lists no less than 71 Barbados boutiques. Their names alone are intriguing in themselves: **Distinctly Different** (Norman House, Broad Street, Bridgetown—tel. 429-7552), **The Impulse Shop** (Bolton Lane, Bridgetown—tel. 427-5534), **Look 'N Good** (McGregor Street, Bridgetown—tel. 429-7491), **Slick Chic** (Balmoral Gap, Hastings, Christ Church—tel. 426-2239), **Sneaky Peep** (3 McGregor St., Bridgetown—tel. 426-2991), and **Word of Mouth** (Broad Street, Bridgetown—tel. 429-7066). Be forewarned, however, that quite a few of them are pretty pricey.

Petticoat Lane in the Bridge House Complex on the waterfront in Bridgetown (tel. 429-7037) is the brainchild of Carol Cadogen, a Barbadian who makes and designs a lot of her merchandise. Her things are islandy—lots of cotton fabric, and cotton lace, some patchwork—but sophisticated enough to wear anywhere, including the most festive occasions.

Simon Foster creates clever originals in a little wooden cottage in Payne's Bay in St. James Parish. They are stitched up right there in his own workshop, and the results are smashing. See them for sale at **Giggles,** a shop just up the road from Simon's atelier at Gibbes Beach (tel. 422-5643). If you catch Simon at his drawingboard and sweet-talk him, it's possible he might whip you up the dress-of-a-lifetime—and overnight at that. According to one elegant Barbadian socialite who commutes between New York and Bridgetown, you don't have to be "special" to get this kind of tender loving care.

"Anyone is special to Simon if they are nice to him. Charm him, he'll go all out to please you." Although we've long heard the praises of Simon Foster sung, we've never actually had the benefit of his personalized expertise. Next time we're in Barbados, we mean to remedy that. *Tip:* If Simon is not there, or, as could happen, not in the mood, ask for his sister, Paula.

Jill Walker has been described as being to Barbados what Ruth Clarage is to Jamaica: a gifted expert at translating into graphics the look and feel of the island. For the most extensive Jill Walker selection, visit the **Best of Barbados** at The Sandpiper Inn in St. James Parish. But you'll spot her work elsewhere also. As for the **Gaye Boutique** (Holetown; St. James—tel. 424-1704), **Quest** (Hilton Arcade, Hilton Hotel, St. Michael's Parish—tel. 436-0596), and the remaining 60-odd fashion shops, it's the luck of the draw as to what's there at the time of your visit. And a matter of your own taste as to what pleases you.

For Liberty fabrics, cashmere sweaters, doeskin gloves, and a variety of other alternative imports, shop the department stores. While in **Cave Shepherd & Co. Ltd.** on Broad Street, Bridgetown (tel. 476-2121), glance at the selection of interesting creations from the island of St. Lucia.

Harrison's (1 Broad St., Bridgetown—tel. 426-0720), **Da Costa Ltd.** (Broad Street, Bridgetown—tel. 426-3451)—many shops, in fact, offer good buys in blazers, slacks, and the like for men. In addition, you might research having something custom-made from the top-quality English woolens available on the island. (If you're a home stitcher, you'll find lots of tempting fabrics all along Swan Street as well as on Broad, as a matter of fact.)

Of the several capable tailors plying their trade in Barbados, Mr. Blackman (no first name, please, the gentleman is customarily known as Mister Blackman) is one of the most highly regarded. His establishment, **Blackman & Tailors**, is on James Street in Bridgetown. For those who prefer trendier styling, consult George Martin at **The Posh Shop**, also on James Street. Another good possibility: **Reward's Bespoke Tailors**, on Prince Alfred Street in Bridgetown (tel. 427-5142) operated by Robert Ward.

FOOD

Cou Cou, Jug Jug, Fish Fash, Twice Laid, sea egg pie, grapefruit meringue, guava fool, yam balls, pickled bread-fruit—local specialties taste as fascinatingly titillating as their names—WHEN you can find them on the menu. Day in and day out, these curiosities do not appear on resort bills of fare, in deference to the rigidly conservative tastes of most of our fellow travelers, we're told. One hotelier reports that the three nights he listed Barbadian turtle pie, only two adventurers among his 60 guests were bold enough to order it.

You can buy tamarind balls, coconut sugar cakes, shaddock rind, peppermint twists, and the like from the **Women's Self-Help** shop on Broad Street or from the street peddler who shows up on lower Broad Street near Trident House once a week, usually on Friday.

As do most other West Indians, Bajans make their own hot sauce, and this one, in our view, is one of the very best. Here, too, the wondrously flavorsome, incredibly inexpensive, locally processed sugar that American epicures treasure, known in Jamaica and some of the other islands as "wet sugar." In Barbados it is called yellow sugar. Not having been refined as much as is the custom with our own white sugar, it has ever so much more flavor and texture.

Under the label Windmill, the Miller Brothers have been packing local delicacies and necessities for a good many years, in the course of which they have established a solid reputation for reliability. Look for their products at most any of the truly huge number of groceries and supermarkets that dot the island.

The **JB's Master Mart**, at Sargeants Village, Christ Church (tel. 426-9830), operated by John Simpson, is one of the biggest and the best. **Goddard's Foodfairs**, in Kensington and Rendezvous, claim to stock over 7,000 food and household items. In both these stores, as well as others, you will find a wide assortment of English teas, jams and jellies, Branston's pickles, and other European items. One of the most popular guides to preparing Bajan food, incidentally, is the Rita Springer cookbook.

Far and away the most famous Bajan delicacy is flying fish: a small creature that soars out of the waves, skipping briskly along the sea surface. Its fine texture and delicate flavor make it an extremely versatile ingredient. You can bake it, broil it, fry it, or stuff it. One remarkable aspect is that it has no salty taste. On the contrary, were you not forewarned, we believe you'd swear you were eating the freshest of mountain trout.

Until recently, flying fish were a treat to be savored on-island and nowhere else. Now **Atlantic Fishmongers**, a modern processing plant, has been established at the Caree-nage in Bridgetown where the flesh is fast, flash-frozen, the water extracted, and the fish vacuum-packed, five fish per pack. They are sold in supermarkets very reasonably ($3 or so the package), and the recipe for preparing them correctly is on the back of the package. Bold souls report that wrapping them in a few layers of newspaper makes it possible to bring them home on a direct flight back to the mainland.

As to how U.S. Department of Agriculture bureaucrats feel about their entry into the United States—we haven't asked! It is worth noting, however, that in their lengthy list of No-Nos, which most definitely includes meat, there is no mention of fish being prohibited that we could find.

JEWELRY

The Guyanese gold pieces are said to be very good buys: heavy, rich in color, high in gold content. There is a drawback in that they are not stamped, thus should you have to resell or in any other way establish and prove the precise value, this could pose a problem. Most Barbados jewelers carry this type of adornment, but you might find it rewarding also to poke through the small Syrian and Lebanese souks on Bond Street as well. If you plan any serious investment, however, either be sure you know what you are about, or take along with you someone who does.

Harrison's on Broad Street in Bridgetown (tel. 426-0720) carry an assortment of imported good jewelry, so do **Maraj & Sons**, 9 Norman Centre, Broad Street (tel. 429-3631).

LINENS

Your best source of quality European and Oriental table linens, once again, is the duty-free department stores. You might, however, glance at what some of the individual Barbados ladies have made themselves and brought in to the **Women's Self-Help** in Bridgetown for sale there: handdone lace tablecloths, assorted embroidered items, and the like. If you don't find what you are looking for, conceivably you might arrange to have it made to order—provided time is not of the essence—and have it shipped on to you.

PERFUME

Da Costas features Fidji, Oscar de la Renta, Lanvin, Yves St. Laurent, and countless other fragrances, all at prices anywhere from 30 to 50% under U.S. list. You will find perfume also at **Harrison's, Cave Shepherd, Melwani's** department store on Broad Street in Bridgetown, a **Touch of Class**, and a number of other shops and boutiques.

Barbados has a **Flower Forest** at Richmond in St. Joseph Parish where visitors can view local blooms, and there are half a dozen florists scattered throughout the island—**Flowers by Gill Wilson** in Holetown, St. James; **Golden Florist** in Hastings, and **Flower Lover** on Broad Street. All of them will dispatch bouquets most anywhere in the world. But despite the availability of blooms, we know of no local perfume presently being manufactured on the island.

SPIRITS

According to one local saying, all Bajans are born with a Bible in one hand and a bottle of rum in the other.

Whether or not you fancy this potion as a rule, do not leave without having tried at least one, small taste of the *vin du pays*. The **Mount Gay Distilleries** mix up several different varieties, each designed for a specific purpose. Special Reserve has the daintiest bouquet; it's tailored especially for Americans, we're told. We like it least. The Liqueur steers a middle course between light and dark; if you're on the fence about this drink, this type might suit you best. It probably has the rummiest of rum flavors; use it in cocktails and punches. But it is Sugar Cane Brandy, mellow, eight years old, which holds the permanent place of honor on our bar. Smooth as aged cognac, of superb quality, this one is impossible to spoil, no matter how many irreverent mixes assault it.

There are several other distilleries on the island; most tourist guidebooks recommend **Cockspur** only. While **Hanschell Innis** unquestionably does make an outstanding rum, we prefer the Mount Gay products. Which one to choose is, of course, purely a matter of your taste.

Actually, it's difficult to get an inferior rum of any label in

Barbados, because when it comes to this libation, the island has a secret weapon: its water. According to islanders one of the purest supplies in the world, it passes twice through the 60,000-year-old, up-to-300-foot-thick layer of coral which underlays six-sevenths of the island: as rain from the sky seeps downward to blend with a system of huge subterranean lakes and rivers, then back through again as it is pumped up, it is not only purified in the process, but also enriched with the minerals leaching into the water as it is drawn back through the coral to the surface.

Bajans have been cultivating sugar ever since Hollander Pieter Blowet brought the first stocks of cane from Brazil to Drax Hall in 1637 (it is still cultivated there). In fact, Barbados claims to have been the first country to export rum, and to have been the first one to call it that. The original word, Rumbullion, was used in Devon, England, to indicate pandemonium. Because donnybrooks so frequently followed the ingestion of this potent brew, hence the name. *The Ins And Outs of Barbados,* one of the best island guides being published in the Caribbean today, tells us further that "punch," as in "rum punch," comes from a Hindustani word, *panch,* meaning five, and was adopted because of the five traditional ingredients in an authentic West Indian rum punch:

> One of Sour
> Two of Sweet
> Three of Strong
> Four of Weak
> Five drops of bitters

We learn further that the first institution French and Spanish pioneers built when they colonized was a church. The Dutch usually constructed a fort. The British began by putting up a tavern. Indeed, 20 years after the first English settlers arrived, there were 120 drinking houses in Bridgetown, making it a "holiday spot of Rumbunctious Rum Revelry for resting Army and Navy Personnel."

Since one acre of land produced three times as much cane as it did cotton (10 tons, which in turn yielded 1 ton of sugar, which in turn was converted into 30 gallons of rum), cane soon became the crop of choice. And the formula for the original rumbullion was mellowed and perfected, until by the 18th century rum had attained such popularity internationally that Barbados was exporting it to North America, West Africa, Ireland, and England in large quantities. In fact, it was only in 1970 that the Royal Navy discontinued its daily rum ration containing Barbadian rum.

Whether or not Barbados rum was the very first in all the categories it lays claim to, one product does seem unique to this special island: a sweet, syrupy rum-based concoction called Falernum, which tastes faintly like Cinzano. Served over shaved ice with a twist of lemon, it may please the light drinker weary of specifying soda, tomato juice, or branch water. Mix it with one or two parts rum or brandy and you have a Barbadian version of a Manhattan. If nothing else, it's a good way to upstage your beverage-name-dropping acquaintances. As, for instance, sauntering into one of those fancy Manhattan East Side saloons and ordering a *fine* and Falernum please—light on the Falernum.

One of the more popular local drinks is Corn Oil: equal parts rum and Falernum, a squeeze of lime, and lots of ice. Other more or less Bajan inventions: a Goat Hair (cane juice, lime, rum, and nutmeg) or a Tewahdiddle (one pint of beer, a tablespoon of brandy, and a teaspoon of sugar with ginger and lemon peel—otherwise known as a Bajan boilermaker). *Note:* Rum and Coke in Barbados means dark rum. If you prefer yours made with white rum (for reasons beyond our comprehension), better so state when you place your order. Ask for "see-through" rum and they'll know you mean white.

Finally. Don't overlook the Barbados beer: Banks by name,

tangy in taste, and an International Gold Award Winner. Again, it's that water.

If rum is not your thing and you choose to use your liquor allowance for choice imports, **Da Costa Ltd.** on Broad Street in Bridgetown (tel. 426-3451), among several freeport shops, offers a wide selection of French brandies, English gins, Russian vodkas, and assorted miscellany.

WATCHES

You name it and you'll find it in Barbados—and like as not save a bundle. An added bonus is the fact that these are no johnny-come-lately street peddlers you're dealing with. **Harrison's** (1 Broad St.—tel. 426-0720) handles Cartier and Patek Philippe, among others. **Maraj & Sons** (9 Norman Centre, Broad Street—tel. 429-5631) feature Baume & Mercier as well as Rado, Seiko, and Casio. **J. Baldini Ltd.** (Cave Shepherd, Broad Street—tel. 426-5845), **Cave Shepherd** itself (Broad Street —tel. 426-2121), **Correia's Jewellry Store Ltd.** (Prince William Henry Street), and **The Royal Shop** (Nicholas Howe, Broad Street—tel. 429-7072) all carry upscale timepieces also.

Some years ago a modest little café in the middle of Bridgetown headed its menu with a little poem we've always remembered:

> When a man loves a woman
> That is his business,
> When a woman loves a man
> That is her business.
> When they love each other
> That is their business.
>
> But when they desire delicious
> Food in comfortable air-
> Conditioned surroundings—
> That is our business.

Overall, this same sentiment can be applied to most of Barbados's merchants: When you desire good shopping in comfortable, air-conditioned surroundings, the Bajans make it their business to try to see that you get it.

USEFUL ADDRESSES

Antiquaria: St. Michael's Row, Bridgetown (tel. 426-0635).

A Touch of Class: Bridgetown.

Barbados Industrial Development Corporation: Handicraft Department, Pelican Industrial Park, Bridgetown (tel. 426-4391).

Bay Gallery: Lower Bay Street, St. Michael (tel. 426-1604).

Bertalan Gallery: Marine Gardens, Hastings, Christ Church (tel. 427-0714).

Best of Barbados: Branches at The Skyway Shopping Plaza, the Hilton Arcade, Sam Lord's Castle, and the Sandpiper Inn in St. James.

Bijoux: 3 Swan St., Bridgetown (tel. 429-7266).

Blackman & Tailors: James Street, Bridgetown.

Cave Shepherd & Co. Ltd.: Broad Street, Bridgetown (tel. 426-2121).

Claradon Galleries: Pine Road, Belleville, St.. Michael (tel. 429-4713).

Cockspur: Hanschell Innis Ltd., Kensington, St. Michael (tel. 426-3544).

Correia's Jewellry Store, Ltd.: Prince William Henry Street, and at Broad Street, Bridgetown; branches also at

Sunset Crest Shopping Centre in St. James Parish, and Grantley Adams International Airport.

Courtney Devonish Gallery: Pelican Village, Harbour Road, Bridgetown (tel. 436-6126).

Da Costa Ltd.: Broad Street, Bridgetown (tel. 426-3451); branch also at Sunset Crest Shopping Centre, St. James.

De Lima (Barbados) Ltd.: 32 Broad St., Bridgetown (tel. 426-5751).

Distinctly Different: Norman House, Broad Street, Bridgetown (tel. 429-7552).

Flower Forest: Richmond Plantation, St. Joseph (tel. 433-8152).

Flower Lover: No. 12, Mall 34, Broad Street, Bridgetown (tel. 427-3755).

Flowers by Gill Wilson: Holetown, St. James (tel. 432-0332).

Gaye Boutique: Holetown, St. James (tel. 424-1704).

Giggles: Gibbes Beach, St. Peter (tel. 422-5643).

Golden Florist & Green House: Balmoral Road, Hastings, Christ Church (tel. 427-0722).

Goddard's Foodfair: one at Kensington and one at Rendezvous.

Harrison's: 1 Broad St., Bridgetown (tel. 426-0720); branches also in the Hilton Arcade in St. Michael, and at the Paradise Beach Shop, Paradise Beach Hotel in St. Michael, plus in the Southern Palms Hotel in St. Lawrence, and at the Grantley Adams International Airport.

The Impulse Shop: Bolton Lane, Bridgetown (tel. 427-5534); St. Lawrence Main Road, Christ Church (tel. 428-7443).

India House Ltd.: Mall 34, Broad Street, Bridgetown (tel. 429-7237); branches also at the Hilton Hotel in St. Michael, and Sunset Crest Shopping Centre, St. James.

J. Baldini Ltd.: Ground Floor, Cave Shepherd, Broad Street, Bridgetown (tel. 426-5845).

JB's Master Mart: Sargeants Village, Christ Church (tel. 426-9830).

Knights, Ltd.: 24 Broad St., Bridgetown (tel. 426-5191); branch also at Sunset Crest Shopping Centre, St. James.

Lerner Shops: 27 Broad St., Bridgetown (tel. 429-7278).

Look 'N Good: McGregor Street, Bridgetown (tel. 429-7491).

The Loom House: Skyway Shopping Plaza, Hastings, Christ Church (tel. 426-0442).

Louis L. Bayley & Son Ltd.: 33 Broad St., Bridgetown (tel. 426-3647); branch also at Sunset Crest Shopping Centre, St. James.

Maraj & Sons: 9 Norman Centre, Broad Street, Bridgetown (tel. 429-5631).

Melwani's: Broad Street, Bridgetown (tel. 436-6128).

Mount Gay Rum Distillery: near Bridgetown.

Nari's: 52 Swan St., Bridgetown (tel. 429-7284); branch Hilton Arcade, Hilton Hotel in St. Michael.

National Cultural Foundation: Culloden Farm, Culloden Road, St. Michael (tel. 426-0914); **Gallery** at Queen's Park House, Bridgetown.

Oliver Blossom Shop: Louis Bayley & Son Ltd., Sunset Crest, St. James (tel. 432-1424).

Pelican Village: Harbour Road, St. Michael.

Petticoat Lane: Bridge House Complex, Wharf, Bridgetown (tel. 429-7037).

The Posh Shop: James Street, Bridgetown. Phone unlisted.

The Potteries: Chalky Mount, St. Andrew.

Quest: Hilton Arcade, Hilton Hotel, St. Michael (tel. 436-0596).

Reward's Bespoke Tailors: Prince Alfred Street, Bridgetown (tel. 427-5142).

The Royal Shop: Nicholas House, Broad Street, Bridgetown (tel. 429-7072); branch also at Mall 34, Bridgetown.

Slick Chic: Balmoral Gap, Hastings, Christ Church (tel. 426-2239).

Sneaky Peep: 3 McGregor St., Bridgetown (tel. 426-2991).

Studio Art Gallery: Speedbird House, Fairchild Street, Bridgetown (tel. 427-5463).

Sunset Crest Shopping Centre: St. James.

Talma Mill Art Gallery: Enterprise Road, Christ Church (tel. 428-9383).

Women's Self-Help Handicraft and Flowers: Broad Street, Bridgetown (tel. 426-2570).

Word of Mouth: Broad Street, Bridgetown (tel. 429-7066).

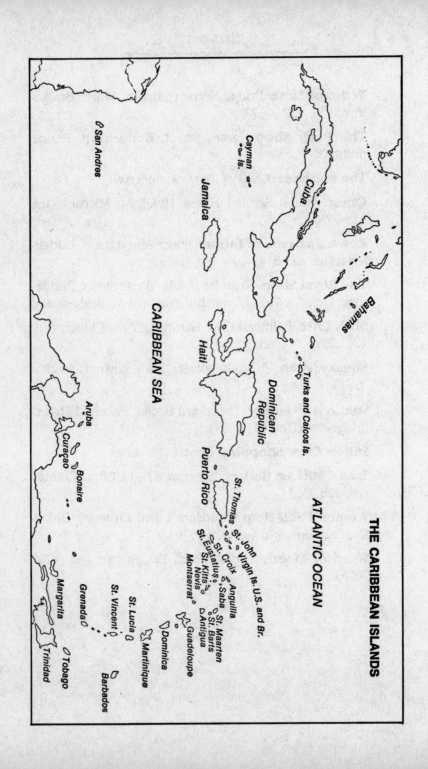

THE CARIBBEAN ISLANDS

San Andres

Cayman
Is.

Jamaica

Cuba

Bahamas

Turks and Caicos Is.

Haiti

Dominican
Republic

Puerto Rico

St. Thomas
St. John
Virgin Is.-U.S. and Br.

St. Croix

Anguilla
St. Maarten
Saba
St. Barts
St. Eustatius
St. Kitts
Nevis
Montserrat
Antigua

Guadeloupe

Dominica

Martinique

St. Lucia

St. Vincent

Barbados

Grenada

Tobago

Trinidad

Margarita

Aruba

Curaçao

Bonaire

CARIBBEAN SEA

ATLANTIC OCEAN

BONAIRE

BONAIRE
AT A GLANCE

GOVERNMENT TOURIST OFFICE: Bonaire Tourist Board, Kralendijk, Bonaire (tel. 8322 or 8649).

CURRENCY: The Netherlands Antilles guilder or florin (NAf), backed by gold and foreign exchange. US$1 equals 1.77 NAf.

OFFICIAL HOLIDAYS: New Year's Day, February Carnival (dates vary), Good Friday, Easter Monday, Coronation Day (April 30), Labor Day (May 1), Ascension Day, celebration of St. John's Day (June 24), St. Peter's Day (June 28), Bonaire Day (September 6), Christmas Day, Boxing Day (December 26).

STORE HOURS: Monday through Saturday from 8 a.m. until noon and from 2 to 6 p.m. Some merchants open on Sunday, holidays, and special occasions. For information call 8322 or 8649.

LOCATIONS: For the addresses and telephone numbers of the shops, consult the alphabetical list at the end of this chapter.

hen you choose Bonaire as your destination, one or more of three primary considerations probably influenced your decision. And none of them was shopping.

If you're an underwater addict, this boomerang-shaped, 112-square-mile-island 50 miles north of Venezuela is an internationally recognized attraction. The prehistoric convulsion which raised Bonaire's underwater caverns, grottos, and reefs above the sea still left plenty of fascinating scenery under the ocean. Visibility ranges from good to unbelievable.

Scientists rate this underwater area among the top three in the Caribbean, and the top ten in the world. Indeed, according to experts quoted by the *New York Times*, here is where you will find the most abundant, untouched, and accessible reefs in the world.

If you're into birds, you may already know that Bonaire has the largest accessible flamingo nesting and breeding grounds in the Western Hemisphere—not to mention the 126 other varieties of feathered friends. There is even a bird mass at Rincon, read before daylight, so the 93% Catholic community can get to the fields to run off airborne predators attacking ripening crops.

But especially for those in search of an untrammeled, uncrowded, and quiet retreat, Bonaire most definitely qualifies. Where some islands think nothing of hosting a million or more tourists annually, Bonaire receives a grand total of 30,000 visitors a year, or an average of 577 a week, at the most. And there are less than five hundred tourist-caliber hotel rooms all told. As to local population, it has been said that sometimes the birds outnumber the humans. A haven, in short, away from the crowds.

Which is not to say you will not find agreeable shopping here. A few of the sophisticated souks of Curaçao and Aruba maintain Bonaire branches, and the local browsing, though small-scale, can be quite diverting.

At the height of the Americans' stampede overseas to take advantage of the strong dollar, an advertising campaign for a film concerning visitors from outer space proclaimed on London billboards, "They came, they saw, they did a little shopping."

So come to Bonaire, feast your eyes on its unexploited expanses, above and below the water—and do a little shopping.

ARTS AND CRAFTS

Each Thursday evening, as the sun sinks below the yard arm, beachcombers, divers, and gregarious residents of artistic inclination congregate at the Flamingo Nest of the Flamingo Beach Hotel & Casino. There they hoist a few libations, pop some corn, exchange news, view each other's handwork—and dicker on the price for which they will part with the watercolors, acrylics, or oils they have produced.

Some are representative scenes of the island. Other works are less traditional. Some, let's face it, do not precisely rank up there with Gauguin or Pissarro insofar as talent is concerned. A few show promise, or even fulfill it. In any case, you'll not be asked to pay a fortune for your souvenir.

The gathering is cheerful, and there's usually no shortage of canvases for sale around $20. You will even find someone in town who can frame your purchase properly. Separating out the touristy items, the painted ashtrays, uninspired shell jewelry, and tortoise shells that show up now and again, your chances of finding something to your liking are fair to good.

Those whose works you might look for are Cheri S. Sweetnam (watercolors); Sonk Frans, pen-and-ink birds; Adi Figeroa, who paints his acrylics on paper and driftwood; or Papa Melaan, who uses acrylics as well as oils.

Twenty years or so ago the United Nations, in one of its more worthwhile endeavors, dispatched a team of professional designers to the Caribbean to help craftsmen in the islands perfect and style their output. In some communities their efforts were not appreciated and their influence has now faded away.

In Bonaire, however, the results remain. At **Fundashon Arte Industria Bonairiano** on J. A. Abraham Boulevard in Kralendijk (tel. 8123) a dozen or two youngsters learn to make all sorts of items for sale—tea carts of local wood; necklaces of black, brown, and green coral; hand-painted shirts and dresses: the assortment varies with the availability of materials and the preferences of the workers. Ask Lydia Alberto, the director there, what's new and interesting.

And while you're about it, you might inquire about having things made-to-order during your stay: trays, boxes, or whatever. *Caution:* Do not attempt to take home anything made of goatskin or tortoise shell. Although other nationals can and do import such objects in bulk, they're contraband in our country.

There are other options. Be forewarned, however, that much of the merchandise in some of these marts comes from, as the islanders put it, "away."

CAMERAS

Boolchand's, on Kaya Grandi (tel. 8497), handles photographic equipment. As is the case in all of the Caribbean, you need to have done your price comparisons ahead of time. If you are considering a sizeable investment, you might well telephone home to check what, if any, savings are involved.

Whether or not you find the difference worthwhile, you do have the reassurance of dealing with an established name here; Boolchand's also maintains beachheads in Curaçao, Aruba, St. Maarten, and St. Thomas.

Heit Souvenirs, on Kaya Bonaire (tel. 8215), carries film, Polaroid cameras, and Dee Scarr's underwater slides—along with diving/snorkeling equipment, dive watches, and assorted coral jewelry.

CHINA, CRYSTAL, AND HOME FURNISHINGS

Spritzer & Fuhrmann, on Kaya Grandi in Kralendijk (tel. 8466), is the biggest game in town insofar as Baccarat, Lalique, Orreförs, Minton, Rosenthal, Royal Copenhagen, Hummel, Royal Doulton, silver souvenir spoons, and the like are concerned. Over half a century in business; jewelers by Appointment to Her Majesty the Queen of the Netherlands; members of the Diamonds International Academy; awarded the Golden Key of the Italian Goldsmiths Association, this partnership of Austrian watch repairmen has amassed some imposing credits which the firm usually, if not invariably, convinces its customers it lives up to. Every now and again, we hear grumbles. On the other hand, with about three dozen stores and hundreds of employees, and given the huge volume of business, perhaps a certain margin of discontent is inevitable. Although *Caveat emptor* is always a sound idea overall, to continue to serve as many customers as they do, in New York as well as in the Caribbean, this house must be doing something right.

Crystal, glassware, and some china turn up in other emporiums from time to time; wooden tableware at **Nastasja and Alexander's** on Kaya Grandi in beautiful downtown Kralendijk, possibly at the **Fundashon** (J. A. Abraham Boulevard) as well. If what you want is not on hand, they just might be willing to order it for you.

Littman Jewelers at 33 Kaya Grandi (tel. 8160) will provide a certificate of authenticity with the Dutch Delft china it sells you.

Also find Delft, and silverplate collector's spoons at $6, in

Things Bonaire, Kaya Grandi (tel. 8423). If you don't spot what you want, ask Jean Weiss, the affable manager there, to help you.

Fashions

Insofar as we have been able to determine, no budding Balenciaga lurks here undiscovered. You will, however, find European and American brand names, along with cool and casual West Indian sportswear, in the **boutiques** at the Bonaire and the Flamingo Beach Hotels. Some wrap skirts, swimsuits, shirts for men and women are at the **Fundashon** and at **Nastasja and Alexander's**, mentioned previously.

Things Bonaire, Kaya Grandi (tel. 8423), features the traditional South American men's guayabera shirts for $11, along with $8 shorts, tote bags, terrycloth dresses ($21), caps, beach towels, and 45 different T-shirt designs ($6).

Aries Boutique at 33 Kaya Grandi (tel. 8901), operated by Esther Littman of Littman Jewelers, has men's and women's casual fashions and jewelry you might want to look over; as an artist herself, Ms. Littman is capable of separating much of the flotsam from the jetsam.

Ki Bo Ke Pakus (which means something like "whatever you desire" in Papiamento) purveys batik fabrics imported from Indonesia, Ecuadorian wall hangings, chunky shell jewelry, and beachwear from its roost in the Flamingo Beach Hotel on J. A. Abraham Boulevard (tel. 8285).

Boolchand's on Kaya Grandi (mentioned earlier) features Adidas sandals, swimwear, and the St. Michael line of fashions and footwear.

If you're into no-nonsense, good quality at a more than fair price, you might investigate what's on sale at **Cambes** on Kaya Grandi or at the Texport "factory outlet" on Kaya Amsterdam (tel. 8325). Acronymically named after the six

Dutch Antilles—Curaçao, Aruba, St. Maarten, Bonaire, St. Eustatius, Saba—the firm manufactures all manner of uniforms for restaurants, ships, hotels, policemen—you name it, they make it, and usually very well indeed. With the remnants of their main endeavor, the thrifty Dutch turn out some extremely comfortable workday toppers: cool as can be, compact (six fit in the same suitcase space occupied by one dress shirt), drip-dry—we pick them up by the half dozen, along with walking shirts, PROVIDED we can find them. Supply is far from constant (when clever cutters make maximum use of the yardage, with no leftovers, you're out of luck), but worth a big try. Should you perchance be in the market for the Bonaire flag, you may buy one here.

FOOD

If you enjoy broadening your culinary horizons, your first purchase might well be a copy of *This Is The Way We Cook*, on sale for about $5 at **Bonaire Boekhandel**, the DeWit Book Store, on Kaya Grandi (tel. 8499). In it you will not only discover recipes for such succulent regional specialties as *giumbo* (gumbo), *sopa di binbja* (wine soup), *keshi yena* (stuffed cheese), pumpkin pancakes, or chocolate trifle, you will also learn a good deal about the Dutch West Indian culture as manifested in its cuisine. If you can't locate the book locally, order one from **Holiday Publications!**, Box 416, Curaçao, Netherlands Antilles.

As in all the West Indies, the Dutch Antillean epicurean heritage is mixed. Spanish, Portuguese, and Latin American Sephardic cuisine contributed the assertive vigor and zing; from the Netherlands came the stick-to-the-ribs substantial style of cuisine; and the Indonesians and West Africans seasoned the whole with their own spicy accent. The result is distinctive, special to these islands, and an attractive addition to anyone's gastronomic lexicon.

To stock up on *sambal manis, kroepoek oedang,* or any of a number of Dutch delicacies (not to mention the cheeses and chocolates), choose from **Cash and Carry** (Kaya Grandi—tel. 8435), **Cultimara Supermarket** (6 Kaya Kerk—tel. 8104), or **Mas Por Menos** (Eutrejol—tel. 8990).

In addition to these and other retailers, thrifty Bonaire householders also have at their disposal **Consales** (near the Flamingo Beach Hotel—tel. 8754), the bargain-priced volume importer. One enterprising transplanted American reports loading up on European canned goods by the case. If you have a school class, bridge club, or other group/troup you need to bring something home to, this might be an answer.

For those of you who rent housekeeping lodgings, note that **Fifoco**, across the street from Consales (tel. 8200), specializes in fresh produce and meat; the owner is a restaurateur.

For Dutch chocolate (and Swiss as well), drop into the **Bonaire Beach Hotel Boutique** (tel. 8448). You'll find it here—along with Spanish pareos, Danskin fashions, jewelry, hats, caps, film, and needlework.

The recent relocation of the **Aries Boutique** to more spacious quarters in the historic Bonairean landmark building at 33 Kaya Grandi has allowed the store to add a new deli section, featuring Dutch specialty foods such as chocolates and cheeses.

JEWELRY

One of the reasons Bonaire is such a superb underwater preserve is because of the ecological consideration with which its residents treat its marine resources. The legendary Don Steward (Cap'n Don, as he is known throughout the Caribbean) conceived the plan to locate the dive sites and then sink buoys around Bonaire, enabling scuba boats to secure themselves to these rather than hooking their anchors into the coral and tearing it up. The law now forbids any spearfishing unless genuinely for nutrition, and allows no removal of coral except under the most carefully controlled conditions.

As a result, the supply of the rare and highly prized black coral is unusually plentiful in Bonaire. Dutch environmentalists carefully and selectively harvest the few pieces used in the manufacture of jewelry by local artisans.

The craftsmen at **Fundashon Arte Industria Bonairiano**, J. A. Abraham Boulevard (tel. 8123), combine the coral with silver. If you would like something a little fancier, talk to Esther Littman at **Littman Jewelers**, 33 Kaya Grandi (tel. 8160), about the possibility of having something special made up. The Indonesian bride of a second-generation American gemologist (Littman's father, Marshall, is an established Philadelphia professional), Ms. Littman has earned considerable kudos in Bonaire for her designs in combining gold with precious and semiprecious stones and other materials. Eighteen-karat gold chains are also on sale here, from $50 for the 16-inch chain up to $500 for one 24 inches long.

Lots of shell pieces of varying degrees of worthiness show up here and there. In the **Krisly Beauty Salon**, Kaya Grandi (tel. 8774), owner-operator Lida Morkos makes her own necklaces, earrings, etc., out of coral of various hues. Have a look while you're having your hair done. And if you're in the mood for a fishing trip, her husband, Chris, is a professional guide.

Kibra Hacha on Kaya Corsow, featuring wall hangings, dresses, and straw hats, mixes in some driftwood and shell artwork and jewelry as well.

For imported baubles and beads, look over the wares of **Spritzer & Fuhrmann**, Kaya Grandi (tel. 8466), as well as those of Littman. If they don't have what you are looking for in here, their larger shops in Curaçao and Aruba are but a plane hop away. Time permitting, they can send for additional stock.

PERFUMES AND COSMETICS

Spritzer & Fuhrmann as well as **Boolchand's** (both mentioned above) carry imported perfumes and cosmetics. If your favorite brand is not on sale there, try **Centro** on Kaya Grandi (tel. 8237): they have one of the island's largest selections of fragrances—along with American lingerie, beach towels, and luggage. Boolchand's carries some perfume.

One thing we try never to leave the Dutch Islands without is a good supply of a Curaçao product known either as Aquamint (turquoise in color) or Alcoholado Glacial (green) both available in most any drug or grocery store. Developed by the same people who manufacture the Curaçao liqueur, this delightfully cooling, unisex liquid functions as an aftershave, a splash cologne, and a poultice for insect bites—among other uses. The label promises to be "Refreshing, Invigorating, and Wholesome." That it is. And inexpensive, too. If our notes are right, we paid about US$3 for the big 16-ounce bottle the last time. Smaller ones are on sale for even less. At **Things Bonaire** on Kaya Grandi (tel. 8423) find Banana Boat aloe sun and skin products.

SPIRITS

The closest thing to a local product would be a pair of favorites from the sister island of Curaçao: Amstel Beer and the internationally acclaimed Curaçao liqueur (see the entry in the Curaçao chapter).

Otherwise, this is your opportunity to pick up a rare European brandy or liqueur minus all those hefty U.S. Bureau of Alcohol, Tobacco, and Firearms taxes. Bonaire has no full-fledged wine and spirits shop dispensing such merchandise only. You will find, however, representative selections in the supermarkets indicated earlier.

WATCHES

Antillean merchants claim to purvey top-name brands at savings of 40%, sometimes even more. To confirm this when you are contemplating investing in a specific timepiece, all you have to do is phone your Stateside dealer of preference. You will find watches in Bonaire at **Boolchand's, Littman Jewelers,** and **Spritzer & Fuhrmann** (all referred to above).

If you are looking for a specific brand, the widest assortment is probably at Spritzer & Fuhrmann: Patek Philippe, Piaget, Omega, Tissot, Seiko, Pulsar, Borel—at least twelve different makes. If you're looking for Rolex and Seiko, you'll find them at Littman. Boolchand's carriers Citizen and Casio, as well as divers' watches from $42.

As indicated earlier, Bonaire does not exactly qualify as the mercantile crossroads of the Caribbean. And to some, therein lies some of its charm: less hustle, less bustle, a more relaxed ambience. On the other hand, if you should suddenly find yourself needing a shopping fix, you'll still be able to take care of it nicely here.

Obviously you will not leave Bonaire without taking at least one glimpse of the fabulous underwater. And if you have any feeling for birds, do include on your agenda a trip to 13,500-acre Washington/Slagbaai National Park. Islanders claim it is not only the first, but the largest such preserve in the Dutch Antilles, if not in the Caribbean. (Take a picnic lunch, maybe.) Some species are original to Bonaire and the flamingos appear most any time. A note of warning, however: bring along plenty of thirst-quenchers. It can get warm. You might also pick up a copy of *Birds of Bonaire* ($6) at **Things Bonaire** on Kaya Grandi to help identify what you spot.

Less well-known, but of considerable interest also, is the fact that little Bonaire has the loudest voice in all Christendom: its 800,000-watt, evangelistic Trans World Radio bleeps out interdenominational Gospel messages in 14 languages from a

30-tower antenna field. As if this isn't enough to qualify the island for the Airwaves' Hall of Fame, Radio Nederland Wereldomroep broadcasts from a 13-tower, 500,000-watter—said to be the globe's most powerful transmitter.

But perhaps the nicest message of all is the one islanders send to the visitors who do make it this far south. And that is their very warm, sincere "Bonbini." *Bonbini* means "Welcome" in Papiamento, the local dialect of the Netherlands Antilles. And Bonbini is one commodity Bonaire dishes out in king-size portions these days.

USEFUL ADDRESSES

Aries Boutique: 33 Kaya Grandi at Gouvernor Debrotweg (tel. 8091).

Bonaire Beach Hotel Boutique: Gouvernor Debrotweg (tel. 8448).

Bonaire Boekhandel: Kaya Grandi (tel. 8499).

Boolchand's: Kaya Grandi (tel. 8497).

Cambes: Kaya Grandi and Kaya Amsterdam (tel. 8325).

Cash and Carry: Kaya Grandi (tel. 8435).

Centro: Kaya Grandi (tel. 8237).

Consales: Wegnaar Terra Corra (tel. 8754).

Cultimara Supermarket: 6 Kaya Kerk (tel. 8104).

Fifoco: Wegnaar Terra Corra (tel. 8200).

Fundashon Arte Industria Bonairiano: J. A. Abraham Boulevard (tel. 8123).

Heit Souvenirs: Kaya Bonaire (tel. 8215).

Ki Bo Ke Pakus: Flamingo Beach Hotel, J. A. Abraham Boulevard (tel. 8285).

Kibra Hacha: 33 Kaya Corsow (Curaçaostraat).

Krisly Beauty Salon: Kaya Grandi (tel. 8774).

Littman Jewelers: 10 Kaya Grandi (tel. 8160).

Mas Por Menos: Eutrejol (tel. 8990).

Nastasja and Alexander's: Kaya Grandi.

Spritzer & Fuhrmann: Kaya Grandi (tel. 8466).

Things Bonaire: Kaya Grandi (tel. 8423).

BRITISH VIRGIN ISLANDS

BRITISH
VIRGIN ISLANDS
AT A GLANCE

GOVERNMENT TOURIST OFFICE: British Virgin Islands Tourist Board, Box 134, Wickham's Cay Road, Tortola, British Virgin Islands (tel. 43134).

CURRENCY: Since 1959, the official unit of exchange has been the United States dollar.

OFFICIAL HOLIDAYS: New Year's Day, Good Friday, Easter Monday, Commonwealth Day (May 24), Sovereign's Birthday (June), Colony Day (July 1), St. Ursula's Day (October 21), Prince of Wales's Birthday (November 14), Christmas Day, Boxing Day (December 26).

STORE HOURS: From 9 a.m. to 4 p.m. Monday through Friday; Saturday from 9 a.m. to 1 p.m.

LOCATIONS: For the addresses and telephone numbers of the shops, consult the alphabetical list at the end of this chapter.

Throughout their 391-year-membership in the British Empire, the British Virgin Islands have specialized in obscurity. At one time the Home Office records in London listed Tortola, the capital, as "the least important place in the realm." On an occasion when Parliament was considering an appropriation for this tiny archipelago, a member inquired as to where exactly they were located. Winston Churchill reportedly replied that he really didn't know either; but presumably they must lie as far as possible from the Isle of Man.

As a point of fact, the British Virgin Islands group consists of more than 50 islands and islets, only 16 of which are inhabited. (Total population in all the islands: 12,000.) The principal centers are Tortola (capital, Road Town), Virgin Gorda, Anegada, and Jost van Dyke.

For Maureen O'Hara and Boy George who built homes in the islands, for Laurance Rockefeller who supplied the British Virgins with their first world-class resort, for Paul McCartney and Benjamin Spock who both cruise their waters, and for a growing number of knowing escapists who make these islets their refuge, this low profile is one of the important lures. Along, of course, with a physical beauty so staggering as to cause one overly lyrical 18th-century poet to describe this as "the place where tired angels pause to rest."

For shoppers, the British Virgin Islands are not a top-priority destination. Even the local Tourist Board concedes that. Indeed, in one of its own fact sheets distributed to the press, the Board states: "The BVI does not offer an abundance of shopping for the visiting tourist."

Having said that, however, the Board goes on to point out, in its own words, some pretty potent plusses:

"But what the British Virgins lack in store-browsing, they make up for in water-oriented activities. The BVI now has the largest bareboat fleet in the world. In addition to bareboating, there is water skiing, windsurfing, power boating, scuba diving, snorkeling, fishing, the works. For those who want to find a quiet beach lined with gently swaying coconut palms on which to collapse and simply soak in the sun, the BVI is the ideal destination. There are mountains that offer the hiker treats unimaginable. Mt. Sage, the highest peak in the BVI, not only offers the opportunity for a trek through a tropical rain forest with its verdant growth, but also views that leave one breathless."

You will not have to go cold turkey as far as shopping is concerned, however. Only one mile separates the British from the American Virgins at their nearest point. You can reach St. Thomas, unquestionably one of the top shopping meccas in the West Indies, on any one of seven short air hops a day. Or take a more leisurely and exquisitely scenic, 45-minute ferry ride.

What to buy in the British Virgins? The traditional top take-home item has been of interest mainly to philatelists; in fact, stamp sales at one time constituted the government's chief source of revenue. Stamps are still a popular buy. One islander who has been commemorated on a stamp is Quaker founding father William Penn. The Penn brothers reportedly tossed for possession of Tortola, the loser having to settle for Philadelphia.

Also honored is William Thornton, the native son whose *Cadmus, a Treatise on the Elements of Written Language* won him the Gold Medal of the American Philological Society at age 29. A little while later his entry in Thomas Jefferson's contest for a Capitol Building design so impressed George Washington that even though the contest had closed by the time the drawings arrived from Tortola, the Father of Our Country had the contest reopened. Thornton not only captured the $500 prize and a city lot in Washington, D.C., but in the process became one of three commissioners delegated to build the capital city, and in 1802 was named the first U.S. Commissioner of Patents.

Another stamp immortalizes John Lettsom, the British Virgin Island-born cofounder of the Medical Society of London, known as "the most distinguished physician of his day." Dr. Lettsom is also credited with composing one of the earliest and most durable of Caribbean calypsos. We most recently heard it quoted, in full, at a formal meeting of Mayo Clinic physicians and patrons. It goes as follows:

> I, John Lettsom,
> Blisters, bleeds and sweats 'em,
> If after that they please to die,
> I, John, Lettsom.

In 1985 the islands caused more than a slight stir when they proposed a new eight-stamp issue featuring, of all things, Michael Jackson's autographed picture. In view of the fact that Michael Jackson is American and not British and has no known ties with the islands, and, further, is the first man to be so honored while still living, the proposal raised quite a few eyebrows—including, apparently, royal ones—because this time the portrait of the reigning British monarch was not authorized to appear jointly on the stamp, as is the custom. The reason given: that Her Majesty's likeness is not to be used in association with another living person. Whatever the facts, the Michael Jackson issue was put on indefinite hold. Less controversial recent British Virgin Islands motifs are of local birds.

If philately doesn't quicken your pulse, be assured that you won't have to do all your shopping at the local post office.

Rodeo Drive Road Town's main street most definitely is not, nor are any of the British Virgins duty-free. Furthermore, given import taxes, the small volume of sales, and the comparatively slow turnover of merchandise, you're not likely to find many huge bargains. Buy what appeals to you and save your big-ticket shopping for other islands. With these circumstances in mind, you can enjoy some pleasant prowling in small shops tucked into the various inns, in shopping complexes such as the one in Virgin Gorda near Little Dix Bay Resort and more particularly, in the "metropolis" of Road Town, capital of Tortola. All of the shops discussed below are on Tortola.

ARTS AND CRAFTS

Roger Burnett's watercolors are subtly drawn, islandy in tones, and as renditions of characteristic local scenes will provide a continuing pleasant reminder of your holiday. You can phone Mr. Burnett at 5-2352 for an appointment. You'll probably also spot some of his aquarelles here and there in various emporiums.

Very definitely worth while also is a visit to Melvin Bellamy's **Coral Creations** on Main Street in Road Town. Here you will see remarkable representations of regional birds, fish, and flora that at first glance appear to have been fashioned from a single piece of coral. The results are handsome and most unusual. Also on display are works of other island talents.

For assorted items crafted in the British Virgin Islands (drift-wood and local stones are among materials used), scout the **Ooh La La Gift Shop** on the Town Square (tel. 4-2433), operated by a trained designer, Sophie. You might find some crafts also at **The Cockle Shop** on Main Street in Road Town (tel. 4-2555).

On Main Street in Road Town as well, the Tortola branch of the **Shipwreck Shop** chain (tel. 4-2587) assembles straw and reeds, shell, woodenware—West Indian miscellany in general, of varying degrees of desirability.

CHINA, CRYSTAL, AND HOME FURNISHINGS

Little Denmark on Main Street in Road Town (tel. 4-2458) carries Georg Jensen, Minton, Spode, Royal Copenhagen, and other imports for the home, as do **Carousel** in the Tropic Aisle Shopping Center in Wickham's Cay (tel. 4-2442), and **The Cockle Shop**. **Past And Presents**, across Main Street from The Cockle Shop (tel. 4-2747), features antique pieces. The stock is somewhat limited, but you might find just what you need if you happen in at the right time. Bibliophiles take note: Past And Presents is known for its collection of books, including some hard-to-find volumes usually available only in Europe.

FASHIONS

Sara Montague-Gray presides over **Bonkers Gallery** on Road Town's Main Street (tel. 4-2535), stocking a wide assortment of slacks, wrap skirts, Gallic sarongs, East Indian batik, and the Java wraps seen throughout the Caribbean. Although we cannot speak from first-hand experience, we have met sharp-eyed visitors who were delighted to report finding some of Sara Montague-Gray's prices on designer items lower than in the country of origin.

Viviana Helm doubles in brass as a trained architect in partnership with her husband and as co-owner of a shop known as **Zenaida** (the Town Square, Road Town—tel. 4-2134), which specializes in sarongs. Some of the fabrics are designed specifically for Zenaida by the onetime director of the British Virgin Islands government's batik-training project. Other variations include arresting African khangas.

The Cockle Shop on Main Street (tel. 4-2555) also features fabrics. Rosemarie Flax runs an interesting fashion operation of her own in conjunction with her husband Keith's extraordinary jewelry atelier (see "Flaxcraft Jewelers" below.)

FOOD

The number one culinary take-home items, **Sunny**

Caribee Herb & Spice Company products, are the creation of New Englander Bob Gunter and his family, headquartered on Wickham's Cay near the Roundabout of Road Town (tel. 4-2178). Included in the stock are all sorts of seasonings, vinegars, condiments, hot sauces, herbal and flowered teas and coffees, and potpourri such as a highly touted secret recipe for a Hangover Cure. The company exports to a number of other islands and by the same token culls the cream of what the neighbors have to offer. Reputedly soon to come, if not already in place, a complete line of fragrances.

British Virgin Islands Caribbean Seasonings, made with sea salt presumably harvested from nearby Salt Island, augmented with herbs and spices, has been featured in a number of U.S. newspapers and magazines.

Honey from the island of Virgin Gorda is prized by connoisseurs. Nothing else tastes quite like it, they say. Shop for these and other delicacies, including such English imports as Fortnum & Mason items, at **The Ample Hamper** in the Village Cay Marina (tel. 4-2494 or 4-2784), or at a **Rite Way Food Market**, the leading supermarket chain; there are branches at Pasea, Main Street, Lower Estate, and Macnamara.

JEWELRY

Top practitioner of the art of jewelry making is Keith Flax, of **Flaxcraft**, off Main Street, Road Town (tel. 4-2892). In addition to his own designs, Mr. Flax can and will custom create one-of-a-kind pieces to your specifications, repair existing items, set gems—you can even have your ears pierced here.

The Jesner jewelry dynasty (the founding father was a successful New York professional) is represented in Tortola by **Crown Jewelers** at Wickham's Cay (tel. 4-3399). This generation has prospered in the Caribbean, offering an array of finery that includes colored stones, diamonds, and gold in a multitude of forms.

Little Denmark on Main Street (tel. 4-2458) features the fine designs of Scandinavia.

Zenaida on the Town Square (tel. 4-2134) carries exotic and primitive pieces from Africa and the Orient.

Collectors Corner at the Village Cay Marina (tel. 4-3550) is known for gold coin jewelry and scrimshaw.

You'll see lots of costume jewelry around and about in the various boutiques. We've heard compliments about, but have not seen, the "Carinia Collection" of coral designs in the **Courtyard Gallery** in the center of Road Town (tel. 4-2455).

LINENS

By and large we believe you can do much better in St. Thomas. However, you might have a look at the merchandise at **Carousel** (mentioned above) or **Pretty Things** on Road Town's Main Street.

PERFUMES

From what we hear at press time, Tortola's own perfume operation is not yet in full swing. On imported perfumes the British Virgin Islands do not make any claim to Freeport status; yet the prices of some French brands can be attractive. You might, as a case in point, take a look at **Turtle Dove** on Flemming Street in Road Town (tel. 4-2211).

SPIRITS

At one time Tortola resembled the West Indian equivalent of moonshine country, with each individual landholder operating his own small still, because the prim Quakers frowned on hard liquor, as on many other frivolities. In fact, two Tortolians were even once reported disowned for dancing. Thus if you chose to imbibe alcoholic beverages in those days, you made your own. And hell's fire brews these often were.

About a decade ago Tortola acquired what might be called its own brand-name rum for the first time. And according to our conversation with Charles Tobias, the integrated-circuits physicist who introduced the product to the islands, there's quite a story as to how it came about. It goes something like this.

On August 1, 1970, Mr. Tobias tells us, after some 300 years, the British Navy ceased producing its specially blended naval rum. Charles Tobias and his associates took over the operation, and moved the blending and bottling process of the five rums involved from Demerara and Trinidad—where they are still made—to Tortola in the British Virgin Islands, which was one of the few islands in the Caribbean not already producing its own rum. The name "Pusser's" is taken from the seamen's corruption in pronouncing the word "purser," the officer who issued the grog rations.

Pusser's Rum can also be called Nelson's Blood, we are told, because of the following legend: This same rum was used to preserve the body of Admiral Nelson for shipment home in a wooden keg after the Battle of Trafalgar. However, when the keg was opened, all the rum had vanished and telltale holes punched in the barrel revealed why: canny sailors, familiar with how good the liquor was, had drained it for their own consumption.

If you care to learn more about the subject, you can buy a book titled *Nelson's Blood*, by James Pack, in the company store that Pusser's maintains on Tortola. (For a complete catalog of T-shirts, Staffordshire decanters, pocketknives, humorous brass plaques, and the like, write **Pusser's Company Store,** Box 626, Road Town, Tortola, British Virgin Islands, West Indies.)

As for the rum itself, you can obtain it in most U.S. liquor stores as well as in Tortola. The last time we inquired of our regular mainland supplier, prices ranged from $11.95 a fifth up to $49.95 for a 1 3/4-liter bottle, 95.5% proof. For ourselves, we're more impressed by the handsome packaging than by the liquor itself. But you may well disagree. Browse for spirits at **The Fort Wine & Spirits Store** at Road Harbour, below Fort Burt (tel. 4-2388 or 4-2584), and in Virgin Gorda, **The Wine Cellar** (tel. 5-5250).

WATCHES

Here again, if you're going to St. Thomas or another freeport, you'd probably do better shopping for watches there. But take a look at what **Little Denmark** on Main Street (tel. 4-2458) has to offer just in case.

SPECIAL SITUATION: If you're in the market for a tummy tuck, nose job, or any other type of surgical embellishment, look up Robin Tattersall in his Arabian Nights–style headquarters dominating the harbor, known alternately as the Purple Palace or the Bougainvillea Clinic. An Olympic yacht racer who came to the islands from the Mother Country two decades ago as government medical officer, Tattersall left public service, took over the failed purple hotel, and has since built up a solid clientele of plastic surgery patients. The rooms are attractive, the swimming pool capacious and Tattersall's methods, we are told, uniquely effective in that they result in a minimum of swelling and bruising. This is, however, strictly second-hand hearsay not from personal experience, and in no way an endorsement. If you're planning repairs and improvements to your physiognomy, prudence would seem to dictate further research.

A virtue much admired among the British Virgin Islands descendants of Quaker colonists is that of discipline and self-denial. Typical of the restraint which Tortolians expect is the notice placed in the old *Tortola Times* some years back by the local dentist, whose name, truly, was Doctor A. E. Hurt:

"Doctor A. E. Hurt, Dental Surgeon, will close his office Thursday, 7th of April, through Monday, 11th of April. We hope all persons having toothaches during this period will defer suffering until a later date."

In this same spirit, any of you suffering from an uncontrollable urge to indulge in the ultimate shopping spree might do well to defer your desires until you get to a bigger and busier Caribbean casbah.

USEFUL ADDRESSES

The Ample Hamper: Village Cay Marina (tel. 4-2494 or 4-2784).

Bonkers Gallery: Main Street, Road Town (tel. 4-2535).

Carousel: Tropical Aisle Shopping Center, Wickham's Cay (tel. 4-2442).

The Cockle Shop: Main Street, Road Town (tel. 4-2555).

Collectors Corner: Village Cay Marina (tel. 4-3550).

Coral Creations: Main Street, Road Town.

Courtyard Gallery: center of Road Town (tel. 4-2455).

Crown Jewelers: Tropic Aisle Shopping Center, Wickham's Cay (tel. 4-3399).

Flaxcraft Jewelers Ltd.: off Main Street, Road Town (tel. 2892).

The Fort Wine & Spirits Store: Road Harbour, Tortola (tel. 2388 or 4-2584).

Little Denmark: Main Street, Road Town (tel 4-2458).

Ooh La La Gift Shop: the Town Square, Road Town (tel. 4-2433).

Past And Presents: Main Street, Road Town (tel. 4-2747).

Pretty Things: Main Street, Road Town (tel. 4-2892).

Pusser's Company Store: Road Town (tel. 4-2469).

Rite Way Food Markets: Branches at Pasea, Main Street, Lower Estate, and Macnamara.

Shipwreck Shop: Main Street, Road Town (tel. 4-2587).

Sunny Caribee Herb & Spice Company: Wickham's Cay, near Road Town (tel. 4-2178).

Turtle Dove: Flemming Street, Road Town (tel. 4-2211).

The Wine Cellar: The Shopping Center, Virgin Gorda Yacht Harbour, Virgin Gorda (tel. 5-5250).

Zenaida: the Town Square, Road Town (tel. 4-2134).

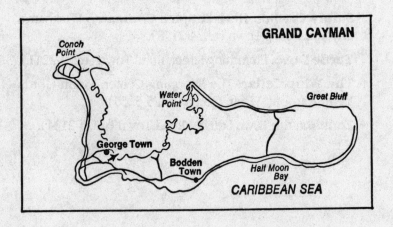

THE
CAYMAN
ISLANDS

THE CAYMAN ISLANDS AT A GLANCE

GOVERNMENT TOURIST OFFICE: Cayman Islands Tourism Department, Government Administration Building, George Town, B.W.I. (tel. 95358).

CURRENCY: The rate of exchange fluctuates slightly. As a rule, one Cayman Islands dollar (C.I.$1) equals about US$1.25. The Cayman dollar is divided into a hundred cents, with 1-cent, 5-cent, 10-cent, and 25-cent coins and $1, $5, $10, $25, $40, and $100 notes.

OFFICIAL HOLIDAYS: New Year's Day (or should New Year's fall on a Sunday, the day after), Ash Wednesday, Good Friday, Easter Monday, Day of Tree Planting by School Children (also known as Discovery Day, third Monday in May), the Monday after the Saturday designated as the Queen's Birthday, Constitution Day (first Monday in July), the Monday following Remembrance Day (November), Bank Holiday (November), Christmas Day, Boxing Day (December 26)—or when Christmas Day falls on a Saturday, the following Monday; if it falls on a Sunday, the holiday is celebrated the next Tuesday.

STORE HOURS: In theory, 8:30 a.m. to 5:30 p.m. In slow times, shops may open at 9 a.m. and close at 5 p.m.

LOCATIONS: For the addresses and telephone numbers of the shops, consult the alphabetical list at the end of this chapter.

No income, sales, or inheritance taxes whatsoever are levied here. King George III supposedly granted this amnesty two centuries ago, in perpetuity, after the islanders saved his son from the 18th-century Wreck of the Ten Sails, off Grand Cayman's Gun Bay.

Today's legislators have extended a new set of enticements to the international financial community. As a result, these tiny islands (New York's borough of Brooklyn has 10% more land than all three Caymans put together) now have full employment, low inflation, a booming economy—one bank for every 35 residents, 45 insurance companies, and 17,700 other corporations and firms. They also boast one of the best standards of living (some say THE best) in the Caribbean. Salaries are among the area's highest: a good secretary earns around US$24,000 a year.

So solvent are the Caymans (a British Crown Colony), in fact, that when Prime Minister Thatcher faced problems in the Falkland Islands, the islanders sent her an unsolicited donation of $40 for every man, woman, and child on Grand Cayman, Little Cayman, and Cayman Brac—a half a million dollars all told.

Under these serendipitous conditions, it's no wonder that ample capital has been available to create not one but several elegant shopping complexes on Grand Cayman.

Anchorage Centre on Harbour Drive, one of the fanciest, features ceilinged rooms, patios, walkways, and generous roof overhangs.

Cayman Falls on West Bay Road is Caymanian in style as well, with cedar wood and lattice panels, natural local rocks rough-cut by local stonemasons. The grounds are dotted with waterfalls, fountains, pools, walkways, and shaded sitting areas.

The many other clusters of emporiums include **Kirk Freeport Plaza**; twenty shops in **Elizabethan Square**; **Coconut Place**; **Tropic Center**; and the newest, as of presstime, **Seven Mile Shops** on West Bay Road.

Chanel, Lalique, Guerlain, Baccarat, Val St. Lambert, Waterford, Sèvres, Wedgwood, Royal Copenhagen, Christian Dior—you'll find all these and much, much more in the many boutiques and emporiums of the Caymans. And the savings can be impressive.

As examples, government spokesmen will cite you such bargains as:

A Rolex watch: U.S.$7,000 on the mainland versus U.S.$5,000 in the Cayman Islands

"Stoke-on-Trent," a five-piece setting of Anysley china, $106 in the U.S., U.S.$55 in the Caymans

A Waterford crystal goblet, "Lismore," $32 in the U.S., $21 in the islands

A Wedgwood five-piece china setting in "Agincourt Green," $125 on the mainland, $73 in George Town.

These and other savings are attributable not only to the duty-free situation but also, spokesmen say, to the fact that European manufacturers take into account the high cost of distribution in the United States. And because, the explanation continues, the Europeans do good business with Americans at home, they cut prices in the Caribbean to stimulate sales to travelers in the islands.

Browsing is by no means confined to imports. Well-heeled collectors will find locally fabricated jewelry of heirloom quality; old coins salvaged from the 325 wrecks scattered about the surrounding reefs, some dating back to the 1700s; outstanding sculptures and tableware fashioned of black coral; woodcarvings and the inevitable assorted straw work and souvenirs.

Grand Cayman claims to have the only turtle farm in the

world, and here you will find (at the **Cayman Turtle Farms Shop**, North West Point, in West Bay—tel. 93893/4) all sorts of objects fashioned from various parts of the animal, from the oils Polly Bergen made famous in her cosmetics to jewelry, turtle soap, ornamental boxes, and the like. Of the farm's usual inventory of about 15,000 specimens, many are released to their natural wild habitat. (One tagged specimen showed up at Cedar Key, Florida.) Less than five percent are slaughtered to provide food.

With a view to protecting this endangered species, United States laws have prohibited the importation of anything made from turtle since 1978. Efforts are now underway to exempt Caymanian products, manufactured as they are from the cultivated variety. Inasmuch as the United States' Caribbean Initiative is committed to encouraging island industry, especially when it produces needed protein as in this case, hopefully an exception will soon be made for items bearing the Caymanian Certificate of Origin.

Another well-known local product, as might be expected from a nation descended from pirates, buccaneers, and shipwrecked sailors, used to be the Caymanian hammock. Connoisseurs call it an engineering marvel—but try to find one these days! The most recent hammock chase turned up just one specimen: made in Honduras, sold at the **Gaelic Gift Shop**! (Elizabethan Square—tel. 97386).

The Caymans are well known among numismatists and philatelists. In some years in fact the sale of stamps has contributed over 12% of total island revenue.

When the Cayman group separated from the Jamaican monetary system and introduced its own currency in 1972, Stuart Devlin of the Royal Mint was commissioned to design the coins. They include a crayfish, a Cayman schooner, a hawksbill turtle, and the Cayman thrush found only in these islands.

In 1983, the royal visit of Queen Elizabeth and Prince Philip was commemorated with three new coins. A $50 gold piece bearing portraits of the royal couple flanked with the legend "Royal Visit" was struck by the Royal Mint in London. The C.I.$5 denomination depicts the royal coat of arms; the $2 piece features the Cayman parrot, the $1 piece a pineapple, and the 50-cent piece a morning glory blossom. To acquire any of these, drop into the nearest bank.

The Post Office's **Philatelic Bureau** does a brisk business with both local and overseas collectors. The Caymans achieved some small measure of fame as the only nation to issue a stamp in the denomination of one farthing. The larger denominations, featuring such Caymanian symbols as the royal poinciana, islanders making rope, or the Cayman thrush, are prized by philatelists.

ARTS AND CRAFTS

Heritage Crafts Ltd., on Shedden Road on the George Town waterfront (tel. 97093), displays paintings by local artists, along with handmade soft toys, woodcarvings, macramé, embroideries, and whatever local crafts are available. So does **Viking Gallery**, on the waterfront at Webster's Warehouse, South Church Street (tel. 94090).

The Amazing China Turtle in the Anchorage Shopping Centre (tel. 94514) also handles local crafts and emphasizes handmade dolls.

The Grand Cayman Craft Market on Cardinal Avenue (tel. 92195) may be worth your time if you're looking for straw hats, baskets, hammocks, and assorted rustic offerings.

Bear in mind, with zero unemployment and high wages, the incentive for islanders to sit on the beach and weave, crochet, or whatever diminishes perceptibly. As perhaps befits this prosperous isle, the residents are at their best working with luxury raw materials (see the section on Jewelry).

Out on the island, driving to the east end and north side:

Carey Hulstone in South Sound purveys carved acrylic, black coral, and assorted miscellany. In the other direction—in and towards East End—you'll find **Wreck View Shop**, the **Pirates Cave Gift Shop** (Bodden Town), and a woodworking operation.

CAMERAS

As indicated elsewhere, only you know whether the equipment you find here represents a worthwhile savings over what you would have to pay at home. To find out for yourself, you might want to investigate some of the following:

Cayman Camera, cayside on the waterfront in George Town (tel. 95326), features accessories as well as such cameras as Minolta and Pentax. Vivitar lenses and strobes for most makes are on hand. Ask Bob Henning, an able lensman with considerable know-how, to demonstrate the stock and answer your questions.

Camera Art in the McTaggart Building, corner of Jennett and Edward Streets (tel. 94143), handles Olympus, Kodak, Nikon, and Canon, among others; also does processing and portraits. If you have a special need, ask for Patrick Broderick, the photographic director.

Undersea Photo Supply at The Falls, West Bay Road (tel. 74686), sells Nikon, Oceanic, Nikonos, Fuji, Oceanic, Ikelite—along with T-shirts, shell jewelry, diving gear, wet suits and masks. If you'd prefer to rent equipment rather than to buy, you might check with them.

CHINA, CRYSTAL, AND HOME FURNISHINGS

One of the most unusual creations is cutlery with handles hand-carved out of black coral and combined with 14-karat gold and sterling silver. A 97-piece set was presented to Prince

Charles and Princess Diana as the Cayman Islands' wedding present. Most certainly one-of-a-kind. Find these at **Black Coral**, 1107 South Church St. (tel. 97156), or **Midas Goldsmiths**, Jack & Jill Building on Fort Street in the heart of George Town (tel. 94706). The candelabra are also exquisite. Be prepared, however, to pay as much as $10,500 for an eight-piece place setting.

Insofar as European crystal and china are concerned, the choice is wide. Some shops display considerable variety, others may have just a few pieces. But on the chance that these just might be the very brands you have in mind, herewith a more or less comprehensive rundown of possible sources:

Artifacts Ltd. on Harbour Drive on the waterfront (tel. 92442) includes English Staffordshire, Bilston, and Battersea enamel among its selection of silver, china, and antiques.

Aristocrat Jewelers, also on Harbour Drive on the waterfront (tel. 92491), beyond Cardinal Avenue, features Aynsley china and Capodimonte, Swarovski crystal, and Zaphir figurines.

The English Shoppe on Harbour Drive on the waterfront (tel. 92457) carries the opalescent, paper-thin Irish Belleek dishes and serving pieces, also Edinburgh crystal with the thistle design.

Kirk Freeport Center, Albert Panton Street, George Town (tel. 97477), offers probably the best volume in terms of top brands: Lalique, Rosenthal, Coalport, Minton, Haviland, Daum, Wedgwood, Royal Copenhagen, Bing & Grøndahl, Baccarat, Hadeland, Kosta Boda, Orreförs, Atlantis, St. Louis, Schott, Zwiezel, Nachtman, Val St. Lambert, Hoya and Hutschenreuther, Waterford, Sèvres, Swarovski, Hummel, Lladrò, Royal Doulton, Royal Crown Derby, Herend, Arzaberg, Villeroy and Boch, Midwinter Heinrich.

House of Merren on North Church Street (tel. 92961) adds china and crystal pieces to its displays of underwater gear, patent medicines, hardware, shoes and groceries. A one-stop shopping center, in other words.

Margaret's Boutique, Harbour Drive (tel. 92633), affiliated with The English Shoppe on the George Town waterfront, has Limoges. You may spot some crystal here as well.

Treasure Cove's three shops, one on either side of Cardinal Avenue and one at the Grand Caymanian Holiday Inn (tel. 92783), carry a considerable variety of luxury accoutrements: Wedgwood, Royal Worcester, Aynsley, Beswick, Spode, Royal Doulton, Stuart, Waterford, and the Royal Brierley which Queen Elizabeth favors. Here also you'll find the Spanish Lladrò figurines.

Viking Gallery, Webster's Warehouse, South Church Street (tel. 94090), also features the Lladrò line, and crystal as well.

FASHIONS

Scottish Shetlands, Israeli knits, Irish linens, Thai silks, Hawaiian cottons, Indonesian batiks, Guatemalan ponchos, Mexican huaraches, Icelandic sweaters, Chinese hand-embroidered jackets, West Indian fabrics, Liberty of London silk scarves—you will spot all these here. For ourselves, to date, we have no fabulous fashion finds or spectacular savings to report. You may well be more successful. Certainly there's no shortage of places to canvas:

Arabus Ltd. in the West Wind Bulding in George Town (tel. 94022) handles upscale European fashions, for both men and women.

Bettina's Boutique in the Seven Mile Shops, West Bay Road (tel. 98125), stocks leather shoes from Italy and Spain along with sportswear for both sexes.

Bridget's Fashions and Fragrances in Freeport Plaza, Harbour Drive (tel. 92699), was formerly known to affluent visitors as Brenda's, *the* place to pick up your Bleyles and other name brand luxuries. The store's merchandise and name have changed, but you still should find satisfying browsing at Bridget's. Ask, for example, to see those romantic soft Hawaiian satin cottons that look as right in the West Indies as they do in the Pacific.

Caymandicraft, South Church Street on the waterfront (tel. 92405), handles Liberty of London fabrics and ready-made fashions, along with mohair stoles and rugs, Indonesian batik, Scottish woolens, and Irish linens.

The **Gaelic Gift Shop**, Elizabethan Square (tel. 97386), spotlights tartans as well as linens.

Cayman Curio Shop, North Church Street (tel. 92272), has Mexican and Guatemalan ponchos, also those south-of-the-border straw shoes that feel especially comfortable in warm weather.

Calypso Boutique, in the Viking Gallery on Harbour Drive, features sportswear for men and women, exotic fabrics, caftans, handpainted skirts and tops, embroidered blouses, Oriental jackets (also embroidered).

Ruth Clarage (see fuller entry in Jamaica chapter) has a store on South Church Street on the waterfront (tel. 92108). Specializes in original West Indian designs.

Kirk Freeport Plaza I and II on Cardinal Avenue in the heart of George Town (tel. 97477), has Pringle cashmere sweaters.

Le Classique in Elizabethan Square (tel. 97121) concentrates on footwear and leather accessories. Among the labels you will recognize are Roland Pierre, Charles David, Sergio Zelcer.

PaceSetter in the Seven Mile Shops on West Bay Road (tel. 92489) carries haberdashery aimed at uppercrust, fashion-conscious males (for feminine frippery under the same management, see next entry).

Temptations in the Seven Mile Shops on West Bay Road (tel. 95600) a sibling of PaceSetter, handles a wide assortment of creative styles, with an on-site seamstress to assure custom fit.

Other possibilites include the **Mica House Boutique** in the Jack Dittman Building on Fort Street in George Town (tel. 92607); **Haymart** at Elizabethan Square (tel. 98125), and **Bettina's Boutique** in the Seven Mile Shop, West Bay Road (tel. 98125).

FOOD

Turtle meat is the local trademark and until the advent of tax shelters, turtles were virtually the islands' raison d'être.

When Columbus first sighted the archipelago in May of 1503, the shores were crawling with turtles, so many of them, in fact, that he named the trio of islands "Las Tortugas," The Turtles.

The deserters from Cromwell's army in nearby Jamaica, the Irish and Scottish sailors shipwrecked on the 325 vessels still visible under water, and especially the buccaneers hiding from the Royal Navy, soon built up a brisk business raising turtles to sell to the mariners plying these waters. Not only was the turtle meat flavorsome and high in nutrition, it also provided the early seafarers a convenient source of food with a minimum of care: keep a load of turtles on deck, on their backs so they can't get away, and slaughter them when necessary.

Turtle-raising continues to this day. The **Cayman Turtle Farm**, North West Point, West Bay (tel. 93893/4), is presumably the only such operation in the world. When you visit the farm, you'll see hatchlings anywhere from six ounces up to 600-pound denizens, and turtle soup for sale. The fact that this operation not only produces turtle meat for local consumption but has been successful in establishing a second-generation crop qualifies it as a proper, if unique, farm. Enjoy a taste of the crop while on-island, but don't invest in take-home turtleania unless you've checked with U.S. Customs in advance and made sure your purchases won't be confiscated.

If you can find it, Otto Watler's dark brown Cayman honey is another culinary collector's item, made in the southeast community of Savannah in Grand Cayman (not the state of Georgia). Mr. Watler only produces 18 barrels of honey a year, however, so it may not always be available.

As for imports, several supermarkets are well stocked with canned delicacies including Brazilian hearts of palm, French foie gras, Chinese mangoes, Korean ginseng, Chilean clams, Indian Bombay duck, Szechuan peppercorns, Hong Kong fish sauce, English Bisto gravy, Twining's Prince of Wales tea. To find your own favorites, scan the shelves of one or more of the following:

By-Rite at Eden Center; Walkers Road; Trafalgar Square (tel. 92345)

Coconut Place Liquor and Deli at Coconut Plaza on West Bay Road (tel. 74442)

Fosters Food Fair on Airport Road and at Coconut Plaza (tel. 95155)

Kirk Plaza on Shedden Road (tel. 94358)

House of Merren, North Church Street, near Seven Mile Beach (tel. 92961)

Gaelic Gift Shop, Elizabethan Square (tel. 97386), has Scottish shortbreads

JEWELRY

The Caymans excel in this department. Dennis Smith, who has been manufacturing jewelry in Grand Cayman longer than most anyone else, combines diamonds, pearls, gold doubloons from the first colonies in the New World, and other artifacts, to put together necklaces most definitely not duplicated elsewhere. Not cheap (prices begin around $1500), but a pleasure to behold. View the selection at **Smith's** of Cayman, on Fort Street (tel. 92733).

Sculptor Bernard Passman, who created the gold and coral cutlery set for Prince Charles and Princess Diana, does exquisite things with coral, interpreting its natural shape into pins, pendants, and other fine designs. Find many of them on display at **Black Coral**, 1107 South Church St. (tel. 97156).

On Fort Street visit **Midas Goldsmiths** (tel. 94706); they also make jewelry to order. Bear in mind, incidentally, that because of conservationist restrictions on the harvesting of coral in the Caymanian waters, much of the coral you will see in jewelry and otherwise fabricated is imported from other areas.

Mitzi Mercedes Ebanks' **Coral Art Collections** in the Old Fort Building in George Town (tel. 97805) is another worthy stop. Although just 23 years old, this young artist has been complementing the Caymanian coral with diamonds, pearls, shells, and semiprecious gems to produce imaginative pieces, no two alike, since she was fourteen.

Mitzi started out selling dockside to the cruise ships. Soon she was doing so well she launched her own full-scale business. Now she and another jeweler not only keep the local outlet provided with up to two thousand pieces, they also wholesale internationally. If you don't see what you're looking for, ask Mitzi about making something especially for you.

Miguel Powery in the Seven Mile Shops also makes outstanding black coral jewelry (**Jewels of the Sea** is the name of his enterprise, tel. 98033), and **Casio** (in the Seven Mile Shops, West Bay Road) features some as well, hand-crafted by local artisans. **Ruth Clarage** (on South Church Street—tel. 92108) carries black coral too.

Should none of these local creations strike your fancy, alternatives abound: if you favor imported elegance in haute couture parures, for example, you will not be disappointed. **Kirk Freeport Plaza I and II**, Cardinal Avenue (tel. 97477), exhibits fiery Greenfire emeralds; lustrous Mikimoto pearls; black, pink, and red coral pieces; and the ever-so-rare conch pearls. Here, too, you will find the well-known Lapponia of Finland line, plus a wide assortment of other 14-karat and 18-karat gold and gemstone creations.

Treasure Cove shops (on Cardinal Avenue and in the Grand Caymanian Holiday Inn—tel. 92783) also carry jewelry; as do the **Gaelic Gift Shop** (Elizabethan Square—tel. 97386), **The Viking Gallery** (South Church Street—tel. 94090), **Margaret's Boutique** (Harbour Drive—tel. 92633) and **Soto Freeport Store** branch on the waterfront (Soto Freeport Building—tel. 74444). (Caution: Those ivory pieces could mean trouble going through U.S. Customs.) Some items are on sale also at the **Caymania** shop branch in the Anderson Square Building (tel. 94520).

There are as well, less expensive adornments to be had on Grand Cayman. Bright, perky ceramic fish, seahorses, and other tropical motifs at **Ruth Clarage's**, Old Church Hall, South Church Street (tel. 92108), are attractive and islandy and can be had for $10 or so.

Coconut shell jewelry is sold at the **Cayman Curio Shop**, North Church Street (tel. 92272). Necklaces, bracelets, and earrings made of sea shells show up here and there from time to time. In general, these do not, however, strike us as exhibiting such exceptional originality as to warrant tracking down to any specific shop. On the other hand, in your travels you may encounter some pieces that are appealing to you. If so, so much the better.

LINENS

Nothing much is locally made. But quite a few shops do

bring in table linens, some most luxurious, from abroad. Among them:

The Amazing China Turtle at the Anchorage Shopping Centre (tel. 94514)

Heritage Crafts Ltd. on Shedden Road (tel. 97093)

Kirk Freeport Center at Albert Panton Street in the middle of George Town (tel. 97477)

Viking Gallery on South Church Street (tel. 94090)

PERFUMES AND COSMETICS

Island merchants speak of 40% savings, perhaps even more, on Patou's Joy, with equally impressive price breaks on other French perfumes. Note, however, that the American products will not be such bargains, and indeed, you would be well advised to price your favorite scent at home or on board your cruise ship before investing too heavily. Sample prices at this writing: Oscar de la Renta three-ounce spray, $32; one ounce of Joy eau de toilette spray, $29.50; Charlie Cologne Spray, $3.40 to $12; Chloë, $26 for three ounces of cologne spray.

Kirk Freeport Center, Albert Panton Street (tel. 97477), has the largest selection, over thirty fragrances, but other shops also handle perfumes and in some cases cosmetics. So if you don't find what you are looking for at first, try:

Caymania in the Anderson Square Building, in the Dittman Building, and at the Airport (tel. 94520) (they handle Esteé Lauder and Orlane cosmetics as well)

City Duty-Free in the Anchorage Shopping Centre and at the Airport (tel. 94595)

The English Shoppe on Harbour Drive (tel. 92457)

Gaelic Gift Shop at Elizabethan Square (tel. 97386) offers a change-of-pace item—Irish perfume

Margaret's Boutique on Harbour Drive (tel. 92633) stocks French scents

SPIRITS

Caymanians have not developed their own commercially popular brew. **The Wine Cellar Ltd.** at Selkirk Plaza on West Bay Road (tel. 96062) handles both wholesale and retail; proprietors Bob and Jeanne Brenton will deliver your order if you phone them. For the best prices, however, you should wait until you get to the Airport and make your duty-free buys just before departure.

WATCHES

With price tags as much as $2000 lower than the same luxury timepiece would cost at home, these are worth considering. Should you have a specific name brand in mind, here are some of the places where you might locate it:

Aristocrat Jewelers, on Harbour Drive (tel. 92491): Seiko

The English Shoppe, Harbour Drive (tel. 92457): Citizen, Delma, Felca, Orbit, Pulsar, Rodania, Tiara, and Universal Genève

Kirk Freeport Plaza II, Cardinal Avenue (tel. 97477): Baume & Mercier, Concord, Corum, Ebel, Heuer, Les must de Cartier, Mido, Movado, Omega, Oris, Patek Philippe, Piaget, Rolex, Raymond Weil, Swatch, Tissot

SPECIAL CATEGORY

Throughout their history, the Cayman Islands have been inextricably involved with the ocean. Even the motto on their national coat of arms comes from the 24th Psalm of David: "For He hath founded it upon the seas."

Thus it is not surprising to find here an extraordinary collection of old coins. Some may have fallen into the water out of the pockets of drunken sailors climbing aboard their ships; others were retrieved by divers, from the many shipwrecks floundering upon the surrounding reefs. And many are for sale—at such prices as $850 for one.

Among the more fascinating stories is one concerning the haul made by a diving boat. According to the people at **Artifacts Ltd.**, Harbour Drive (tel. 92442), which has the coins for sale, this is what happened:

One summer day three years ago, divers working on the ancient wreck of the *Vliegenhart* winched aboard their craft a wooden pine chest some 36 inches in length; one of three such boxes, they surmise, used to transport trading monies to the New World from the Old one. Traces of linen and rope bindings were still evident.

Inside the coins were found held in place by blocks of peat, the packaging materials used during the 1700s. Included were several thousand silver pieces-of-eight, minted in Mexico City and known as cobs. The denomination was eight reales, and the shapes were designed to reflect the weight equal to their silver worth.

Also retrieved, the story continues, were 2,000 gold ducats minted in Holland, dated 1729, when very few were circulated in the Netherlands; these were specifically for the export trade.

The Royal Coin Cabinet in The Hague was asked to scrutinize the find and reported the coins machine-made by a screw press, on planchets which were hand cut. Artifacts Ltd. calls these "excellent examples," and notes three dies as having been identified as used on the coins. Numismatists who are better able than we to evaluate their significance and authenticity can acquire these talismans, with numbered certificates, from Artifacts on the waterfront.

Pieces of Eight on Fort Street (tel. 97578) features coins from the treasure ship *Concepcion.* You can buy the verified doubloons in silver or gold, mounted or unmounted, reales from $100.

Smith's on Fort Street (tel. 92733) offers an imposing range of Spanish gold doubloons and reales, as well as some rare Greek, Roman, and Egyptian pieces.

Things are moving very rapidly in the Cayman Islands. There are now 30 tennis courts. Ultra-elegant new hotels— including the Grand Pavillion Hotel and Beach Club, and a 240-room Hyatt Regency on the Britannia Golf Course. Trafalgar House PLC has plans for a $100-million development, including a 252-room hotel at Double Head. Other developments are either contemplated or in the works.

With *Skindiver* magazine calling the islands "the Superbowl of Scuba," underwater addicts are zeroing in from all points of the compass.

Seven world records in a single year in deep-sea fishing are attracting more and more anglers also.

In fact, things generally have become so lively that it has become necessary to install a third traffic light on Grand Cayman.

There are reasons for the islands' increasing popularity. Crime is down 20%, with not a single murder reported last year. Drug laws are among the Caribbean's toughest. There's an outstandingly attractive new airport. A college accredited in Washington, D.C., is authorized to award both bachelor's and master's degrees among the indigenous population. There's a reassuring record of longevity: many Caymanians are reported to survive to a hale and hearty 115 years, in some cases even longer.

Still, modern times and tourist development have not yet completely swallowed up the archipelago; the total number of residents remains comfortably at 18,000 for all three Caymans.

Perhaps you'd better hurry on down, before it's too late.

USEFUL ADDRESSES

The Amazing China Turtle: Anchorage Shopping Centre, George Town (tel. 94514).

Anchorage Shopping Centre: Harbour Drive, George Town.

Arabus Ltd.: West Wind Building, George Town (tel. 94022).

Aristocrat Jewelers: Harbour Drive, George Town (tel. 92491).

Artifacts Ltd.: Harbour Drive, George Town (tel. 92442).

Bettina's Boutique: Seven Mile Shops, West Bay Road (tel. 98125).

Black Coral: 1107 South Church St., George Town (tel. 97156).

Bridget's Fashions and Fragrances: Freeport Plaza, Harbour Drive, George Town (tel. 92699).

By-Rite: Eden Center; also Walkers Road; Trafalgar Square, West Bay Road, West Bay (tel. 92345).

Calypso Boutique: David Millers, corner Mary and North Church Street, George Town (tel. 97840); also at Viking Gallery on Harbour Drive.

Camera Art: McTaggart Building, Box 1312, George Town (tel. 94143).

Carey Hulstone: South Sound.

Casio: Seven Mile Shops, West Bay Road.

Cayman Camera: Harbour Drive, George Town (tel. 95326).

Cayman Curio Shop: North Church Street, George Town (tel. 92272).

Caymandicraft: South Church Street, George Town (tel. 92405).

Cayman Falls: West Bay Road, Seven Mile Beach.

Caymania: Dittman Building, Fort Street, George Town; Airport; Anderson Square, George Town (tel. 94520).

Cayman Turtle Farm Shop: North West Point, West Bay (tel. 93893/4).

City Duty-Free: Anchorage Shopping Centre, George Town; Airport (tel. 94595).

Coconut Place: West Bay Road, Seven Mile Beach (tel. 74487).

Coconut Place Liquor and Deli: Coconut Plaza, West Bay Road (tel. 74442).

Coral Art Collections: Old Fort Building, George Town (tel. 97805).

Elizabethan Square: Elizabethan Square, George Town (tel. 95511).

The English Shoppe: Harbour Drive, George Town (tel. 92457).

Fosters Food Fair: Airport Road, George Town (tel. 95155); Coconut Plaza, West Bay Road.

Gaelic Gift Shop: Elizabethan Square, George Town (tel. 97386).

The Grand Cayman Craft Market: Cardinal Avenue, George Town (tel. 92195).

Haymart: Elizabethan Square, George Town (tel. 98125).

Heritage Crafts Ltd.: Shedden Road, George Town (tel. 97093).

House of Merren: North Church Street, George Town (tel. 92961).

Jewels of the Sea: Seven Mile Shops, West Bay Road (tel. 98033).

Kirk Freeport Center: Albert Panton Street, George Town (tel. 97477).

Kirk Freeport Plaza I and II: Cardinal Avenue, George Town (tel. 97477).

Kirk Plaza: Shedden Road, George Town (tel. 94358).

Le Classique: Elizabethan Square, George Town (tel. 97121).

Margaret's Boutique: Harbour Drive, George Town (tel. 92633).

Mica House Boutique: Jack Dittman Building, Fort Street, George Town (tel. 92607).

Midas Goldsmiths: Jack & Jill Building, Fort Street, George Town (tel. 94706).

PaceSetter: Seven Mile Shops, West Bay Road (tel. 92489).

Pieces of Eight: Fort Street, George Town (tel. 97578).

Pirates Cave Gift Shop: Bodden Town (no phone).

Ruth Clarage: Old Church Hall, South Church Street, George Town (tel. 92108).

Seven Mile Shops: West Bay Road, Seven Mile Beach.

Smith's: Fort Street, George Town (tel. 92733).

Soto Freeport Store: Grand Caymanian Holiday Inn; Soto Freeport Building, George Town; and Airport (tel. 74444).

Temptations: Seven Mile Shops, West Bay Road (tel. 95600).

Treasure Cove: Cardinal Avenue and Grand Caymanian Holiday Inn, George Town (tel. 92783).

Tropic Center: George Town.

Undersea Photo Supply: The Falls, West Bay Road (tel. 74686).

Viking Gallery: Webster's Warehouse, South Church Street, George Town (tel. 94090).

The Wine Cellar Ltd.: Selkirk Plaza, West Bay Road (tel. 96062).

Wreck View Shop: East End.

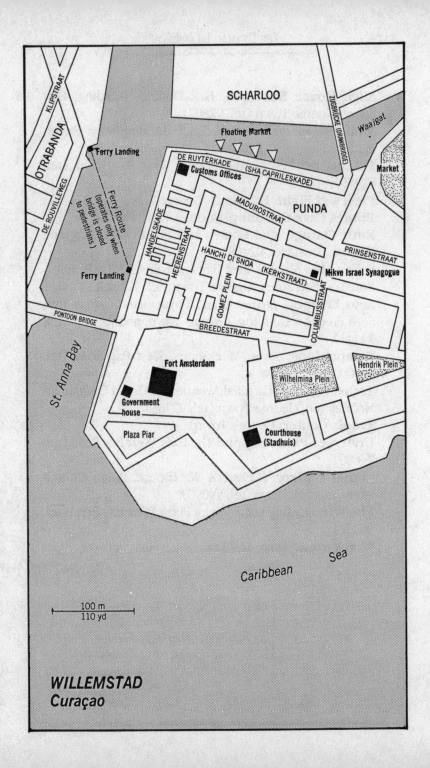

SCHARLOO

Floating Market

OTRABANDA

KLIPSTRAAT

DE ROUVILLEWEG

Ferry Landing

Ferry Route
(operates only when
bridge is closed
to pedestrians.)

Ferry Landing

ZUGBRÜCKE (DRAWBRIDGE)

Waaigat

Market

DE RUYTERKADE

Customs Offices

(SHA CAPRILESKADE)

MADUROSTRAAT

PUNDA

HANDELSKADE

HEERENSTRAAT

HANCHI DI SNOA (KERKSTRAAT)

GOMEZ PLEIN

PRINSENSTRAAT

Mikve Israel Synagogue

COLUMBUSSTRAAT

PONTOON BRIDGE

BREEDESTRAAT

St. Anna Bay

Fort Amsterdam

Wilhelmina Plein

Hendrik Plein

Government
house

Plaza Piar

Courthouse
(Stadhuis)

Caribbean   Sea

100 m
110 yd

WILLEMSTAD
Curaçao

CURAÇAO

CURAÇAO
AT A GLANCE

GOVERNMENT TOURIST OFFICE: Curaçao Tourist Bureau, Schouwburgweg z/n, Willemstad, Curaçao (tel. 677122).

CURRENCY: US$1 equals 1.77 Netherlands Antilles florin (NAf) for banknotes. A check is worth more—1.79 NAf.

OFFICIAL HOLIDAYS: New Year's Day, Carnival Monday, Good Friday, Easter Monday, Coronation Day (April 30), Labor Day (May 1), Ascension Day, Flag Day (July 2), Christmas Day, Boxing Day (December 26).

STORE HOURS: Monday through Saturday from 8 a.m. until noon and from 2 to 6 p.m. Some merchants open on Sunday and holidays when cruise ships are in port. For specifics as to which ones, phone 613918.

LOCATIONS: For the addresses and telephone numbers of the shops, consult the alphabetical list at the end of this chapter.

In the words of Christopher Isherwood (*The Condor and the Cows*): "Curaçao...the long, barren island, shaped like a ship hit broadside by a gale...seems to be listing. On the west, the land slopes up gently to a central range of sharp-peaked hills; on the east, it falls steeply away to the shore. Almost no vegetation and hardly any houses, until you round the cape and see Willemstad. The toy-like prettiness of the town makes you gasp. It is absurdly gay; orange, crimson, scarlet, parrot green and canary yellow. I don't know if this architecture is typical of the Caribbean, but it is extremely individual: ridiculous little classical porches, window-frames decorated with bold slapdash festoons of color, an air of mock grandeur, of high spirits, and something of the decor of the Russian ballet."

Located 38 miles north of Venezuela, flanked on the east by Bonaire and on the west by Aruba, Curaçao's capital, Willemstad, is indeed one of the most charming small cities in the entire Caribbean, a multicolored, sun-drenched miniature beauty whose architecture—not typical Caribbean as Isherwood speculates—in fact might have been lifted intact from its Dutch fatherland.

St. Anna Bay divides the municipality in two. It is the main drag, albeit a watery one, traversed by several thousand ocean-going ships each year. The non-webfooted cross this busy 515-foot-wide waterway on the Queen Emma Pontoon Bridge (advertised by the Tourist Board as being the longest in the world, which it certainly is not), or on free pedestrian ferries which dart back and forth during the 7,000 times yearly that Emma opens to accommodate the visiting liners. Most of the shops are located on the Punda, the eastern section, rather than on the Otrabanda (the other side).

Also on the Punda flank is the Floating Market, where sloops and schooners zip over from Venezuela and Colombia in the morning, tie up fender to fender near the market to offer fruits, vegetables, and spices under makeshift awnings of tattered sails and flour sacks. The local agora at harborside housed in a large, modern, air-conditioned building purveys island plants, and occasionally some handcrafts.

Willemstad was an established center of commerce long before the American Revolution. As early as the 17th century, Willemstad was emerging as a crossroads of trade between the old and new worlds because of location, weather, and a superb natural harbor. Peter Stuyvesant served as governor of the Dutch settlement here before becoming governor of New Netherlands, of which New Amsterdam (now New York City) was the capital.

Almost half of the island's total population of 165,526, composed of no less than 50 different nationalities, live in Willemstad. The remainder are scattered about the countryside in more than 100 small, nondescript villages. The rolling hills reach a maximum elevation of 1,220 feet at the peak of St. Christoffel Berg near the northwest tip.

You'll recognize the taxis by the sign on their roofs and the "TX" on their license plates. You can usually get a cab on the Otrabanda side of the bridge; however, there are taxi stands at the hotels or at the Airport (tel. 681220) or you can call for a dispatch cab (tel. 684574 or 684575). For forays into the Cunucu (which is Papiamento for "Outback"), there are government-operated buses.

Most Curaçaoans are quadrilingual: they speak Dutch, Spanish, English, and Papiamento with equal expertise, and as a people rank among the world's more talented philologists. They can also claim credit for inventing the first new language in modern times, Papiamento—the only "broken talk" to graduate from primitive patois to full written, academic status. The plays of Molière are among classics presented in Papiamento; the daily newspaper appears in Papiamento. Check your phone book—it is probably written in Papiamento too. All classes of society speak and write fluently this tongue based upon the Portuguese spoken by 17th-century slave dealers—*papear* in Portuguese means "to gibber." The Dutch added their dollop; so did the Spanish, English, and Africans; and by 1732 the grammar was pretty well fixed. Americanisms have made their way into the lexicon too: *payday, watch out,* and *okay* are now considered bona fide Papiamento.

Although not as insurmountable as Basque, the Papiamenton accent (all words seem to run together), combined with the choice of imagery, makes the language unfathomable to the average neophyte: *Pushi chikitu sa nister,* for example, means "Little pitchers have big ears"—except that the literal translation reads, "Small kittens sneeze." *Ceru chikitu mester baha pa ceru grandi* translates into "Respect your elders"; literally, "Small hills must bow for big mountains." *Ta taha pa huma* equals "No smoking"; *Gradici* is "To thank"; *Bai drum* means "Go to bed"; and *Mi ta sinti bo falta* is Papiamento for "I miss you."

Islanders are fiercely proud of this native tongue, and speak it widely among themselves. From the fluency with which we've heard children chatter Papiamento, this lingua franca seems slated to remain a permanent part of Caribbean culture.

If there's a linguist on your gift list, you might want to pick up a Papiamento-English dictionary at any one of the fifteen bookstores in town. But not to worry, everyone will converse with you in English.

ARTS AND CRAFTS

Your best bet in this area is to head straight for the **Curaçao Museum**, a handsome 19th-century structure on Van Leeuwenhoekstraat in Otrabanda near the pontoon bridge (tel. 623777), which once served as a military hospital for yellow fever patients. Most of the top local painters exhibit here. If a particular artist strikes your fancy and your interest is serious,

Verele Engels, the curator, can probably arrange an appointment for you to meet and discuss purchases. One of the better-known talents, José Capricorn, teaches in the art academy (and sells his canvases from $500 up).

Another possible source for local art is **Gallery RGN**, at 20 Keukenstraat, Wilhelminaplein, 2nd floor. The gallery features paintings, sculptures, wall hangings, and ceramics, some of it local but most of it from elsewhere. It closes when the owners go on buying trips, so write ahead to see if they will be open during your visit (Box 489, Willemstad, Curaçao, Netherlands Antilles).

Insofar as local crafts are concerned, probably the standout would be the handmade dolls representing characters out of local folklore. **Obra di Man** (the Curaçao handcraft foundation) (tel. 612220) maintains four outlets: 57 Bargestraat; the Gomezplein kiosk; Landhuis Brievengat, and at the Airport. Management guarantees no made-in-Taiwan ringers: "Only Obra di Man can guarantee you NOT IMPORTED handcraft goods. Our articles are all HANDMADE." These include wall hangings, tote bags, straw goods, ceramics, driftwood carvings, baskets, clay pots, and the above-mentioned dolls.

CAMERAS

Palais Hindu, at 29 Heerenstraat (tel. 611769), carries Canon, Leica, Minolta, Minox, Nikon, Olympus, Pentax, Yashica, plus lenses, flashes, pocket cameras, and other accessories by Vivitar. Their hi-fi line includes Akai, Panasonic, and Sony. To determine how much, if anything, you can save by buying here requires careful checking on your part of the lowest U.S. price you can get, and also a comparison of the year and model number.

El Louvre, at 76 Fokkerweg (tel. 614002), carries photographic equipment.

CHINA, CRYSTAL, AND HOME FURNISHINGS

The fifty-year-old firm of **Spritzer & Fuhrmann**, at the corner of Gomezplein and Breedestraat (tel. 612600), should probably be your first stop. You'll know it by the melodious carillon bells on the buildings, each named after a famous diamond, harmoniously chiming out the time. Toby jugs, Val St. Lambert goblets, Royal Copenhagen, Royal Doulton, Swarovski, Camusso, Lalique, Waterford, and Orreförs crystal, Christofle silver, Lladrò figurines—in short, just about all the top names in luxury china, crystal, and silver are represented here.

Kan Jewelers, also operating for the past half-century, purvey their Rosenthal china and crystal and flatware from headquarters in a restored 18th-century gabled building at Number 44 Breedestraat (tel. 612111). Kan commits to 20% to 30% savings over U.S. pricetags.

The New Amsterdam Store, on Breedestraat (tel. 612437) carries Chinese cloisonné, and Delft-blue China—as well as Lladrò from Spain. So does **Penha & Sons** at the corner of Heerenstraat and Breedestraat (tel. 612266). Find Hummel figurines at **The Yellow House** (La Casa Amarillo) on Breedestraat (tel. 613222).

FASHIONS

If there are any extraordinarily gifted local designers plying their trade in Curaçao, we have not found them. There are good buys to be had on a wide variety of European fashions, however, along with—for the Venezuelan and local trade—a fair amount of American merchandise as well.

J. L. Penha & Sons, occupying the oldest building in Willemstad, at the corner of Heerenstraat and Breedestraat (tel. 612266), for example, features Lanvin, Dior, and Liz Claiborne among feminine fashions. For men, Penha carries

D'Gala, Papillon, Dior, Lanvin, Givenchy, Eminences—and Ralph Lauren and Levi's. Penta traces their mercantile history back to 1708.

Scarves and ties can be had at **Gandelman Jewelers**, 35 Breedestraat (tel. 611854), along with Gucci bags and wallets.

The **New Amsterdam Store** branch on the corner of Gomezplein (tel. 612437) carries Courrèges and Chemise Lacoste of Paris men's shirts. There's an extensive collection of sportswear, including Adidas, Nike, and Puma. Upstairs you will find some interesting feminine cotton fashions from Turkey; Triumph and Aubade lingerie, Fink and Traicos dresses, hand-embroidered and crocheted blouses, swimwear from Aquasuit of Italy, Gottex and Gideon Oberson of Israel. Shoes by Bally, Ferragamo, Linia Lidia, and Mario Bologna. (Incidentally, this is one of the shops that does not close for noon siesta.)

El Continental, 24-26 Heerenstraat, has some smart styles in ladies' cashmeres.

Boolchand's, at 4B Heerenstraat (tel. 612798) also carries cashmere sweaters.

For haute couture, trendy pace setters browse the boutiques. Among our favorites: **Edicta Boutique** at 2 Breedestraat (tel. 611397); **Aquarius** (we've spotted Cardin, Courrèges, and Ted Lapidus there) at 11 Breedestraat (tel. 612618); and **Jackie's Boutique**, 23 Wilhelminaplein (tel. 613329).

FOOD

Traditional Curaçao cuisine is lively, exotic, and heavily oriented to Holland's one-time Eastern colonies. Some of the exotic condiments with the jaw-breaking names are discoveries you may want to add to your own culinary repertoire. For hors d'ouevres, try *saté* (bamboo-skewered beef bits dipped in a tangy sauce). You can buy cans of the sauce to take home. Try also *kroepoek oedang* (shrimp broth mixed with cassava, which you deep-fry—some are pink in color, rather like a blushing potato chip). House of Parliament sauce—crushed red-pepper paste in medium, hot, and very hot—and other Dutch delicacies we scoop up by the double handful, for gifts and for ourselves.

The pièces de résistance, though, are the cheeses. The Dutch make dozens of varieties, but Edam and Gouda lead the popularity parade, with 250,000 tons going to about 100 countries.

Gouda, a rich mix encased in yellow-gold rind, gets its creamy texture from its almost 50% fat content. At one to three months, it is soft and subtle. Old Gouda, up to a year old, is dry and sharp. Edam, recognizable by its bright red rind, was once made from whole milk, but now appeals to calorie-watchers with its lower fat content.

Dutch gourmets have long contended that only in the Friesland provinces of their country could a proper Edam be created. And government tests proved them right. Cheese confected from milk from the same cows and under identical conditions in other parts of the Netherlands definitely lacked that special Edam flavor.

This Is the Way We Cook, a regional cookbook featuring the epicurean secrets of some of the area's outstanding hostesses, has a marvelous recipe for *keshi yena*, involving a whole four-pound Edam scooped out and filled with delicacies, then baked. Other novelties included in the book (available at any Curaçao bookstore) are *nasi goreng* (involving fried rice and other ingredients), rabbit with coconut, iguana soup, onion custard, and roast lamb Passaat. This last one is hard to make without one essential ingredient—the trade winds fanning the meat-filled frames 2½ or 3 feet to windward of the coal. The Passaat (trade wind) permeates the meat with the special flavor and aroma of the coal. On a less arcane note, there is also a fine recipe for *ertwensoep* (Dutch pea soup).

Curaçao gastronomy is as cosmopolitan as its population: Sephardic Jews from Latin America, Spain, and Portugal contributed the zest and tang of southern condiments; the Dutch added their own robust food style, accented with off-trail Indonesian grace notes; and the Western African slaves topped off the whole with their own saucy seasonings.

Panino Delicatessen, 23 Hanchi di Snoa (tel. 616629) open from 8 a.m. to 7 p.m. Monday through Saturday, carries Edam and Gouda cheese—along with Dutch chocolates and Italian cappuccino.

Much of the local elite does its shopping at **Toko Zuikertuintje** (The Sugar Garden), a supermarket built around the original 17th-century Zuikertuinintje Landhuis—which is all the address you need (tel. 671288). You'll enjoy free tea or coffee in the self-service tea shop located on the porch, and you will find on the supermarket shelves all sorts of Dutch and European products. The same shopping complex includes a number of boutiques as well.

JEWELRY

Lest you think **Spritzer & Fuhrmann** don't take their jewelry business seriously, note they keep fully equipped goldsmith and watchmaking workrooms on the top floor of their main shop on the corner of Gomezplein and Breedestraat (tel. 612600). The assortment of diamond and gold jewelry is impressive, and covers a wide price range: anything from a small gold signature pin up to dazzling bracelets, pendants, and brooches priced in the five figures. In case of any problem—or if you did not have all the time you wanted to spend at their shops in Curaçao—the company maintains a branch in Manhattan at 5 East 57th Street, 4th floor.

Kan Jewelers, 44 Breedestraat (tel. 612111), claim 50-plus years in the business, with three generations having been members of the Amsterdam Diamond Exchange. Kan designs its own 14- and 18-karat gold pieces, and also handles precious and semi-precious stones and cultured pearls.

Gandelman Jewelers, 35 Breedestraat (tel. 611854), claim to be the only manufacturing jewelers in the Dutch Antilles. They make their own rings, chains, bracelets, and earrings, offering duty-free certificates on original pieces, enabling you to bring your purchases in under the special Caribbean Basin Initiative exception.

If you like gold filigree, Fechi Regales at **Fechi** (**Curaçao Gold & Gem Centre**), 1 Schimarukuweg (tel. 614698), is your man. Fechi (he goes by the one name) learned from his father and other old-world craftspeople how to handle the delicate hair-thin strands of gold. His pieces sell for $12 to $1,400. Fechi has a one-page sheet of sample styles; perhaps if you write him in advance he might send it along.

LINENS

You may find your own source, but as far as we're concerned, our best luck has been to hit the **New Amsterdam Store** (branches at Gomezplein and on Breedestraat, tel. 612437) when they are having one of their frequent (and for real) sales. Visually, this emporium will not make your heart beat faster. In fact, you may well find that the ambience leaves something to be desired. But dig in, persist, search, and we'll be very surprised if you don't come away with some very satisfying bargains. We certainly have—and are still enjoying them.

PERFUMES AND COSMETICS

These are popular, widely stocked items in Curaçao; you'll have no problem finding your favorite brand.

The Yellow House (**La Casa Amarilla**), on Breedestraat (tel. 613222), soon to celebrate its first century in business, is the exclusive distributor for Brigitte Bardot, Cartier, Carven, Charles Blair, Christian Dior, Dana, Dunhill, Fabergé, Folies Bergère, Fumée, Galanos, Givenchy, Guerlain, Hermès, J. L. Scherrer, Pacoma, Philippe Venet, Pierre Clarence, Piguet, Nina Ricci, Rochas, Sonia Rykiel, Tour Eiffel, Van Cleef & Arpels, Yardley, and Yolene. Cosmetics are big here: find Lancaster, Dr. Payot, La Prairie, Roc, Stendhal, among others.

J. L. Penha & Sons, 1 Heerenstraat (tel. 612266), for their part, have the rights to Lanvin, Chanel, Jean Patou, Yves Saint Laurent, Grès, Paco Rabanne, Myrurgia, Oscar de la Renta, Giorgio, and Chloë. In cosmetics, they handle Lancôme and Clinique—as well as Estée Lauder and Ultima II for local and South American consumption, which prompts a note of caution: savings on American-made fragrances are mostly insignificant. You will find worthwhile bargains mostly on those items produced in Europe.

One of our happiest discoveries in Curaçao is an unpretentious local all-purpose product distilled by the famed Curaçao liqueur people, and known as **Alcoholado Glacial**. Refreshing, cooling, it serves as a skin refresher, balm for aches and pains and mosquito bites, makeup remover—it's good for almost everything except as a cure for the common cold. Find it in drugstores, supermarkets—all over the place—in two versions: streamlined, silvertopped Aquamint, the color of the Caribbean Sea, and the one we prefer, the less fancy, green Alcoholado Glacial, the bottle decorated with a penguin and scented with the distinctive Curaçao orange. If memory serves, we paid about $3 at most for our last 16-ounce bottle. Friends of both sexes to whom we have given either variety beg for more.

As to how the formula evolved, apparently Curaçao suffered a scarcity of soap after World War II. A scientist from the Dominican Republic with the pithy name of Doctor Pop began to experiment with available materials in an effort to produce soap for the Curaçao Laboratories. During this experimentation, he developed the lotion which was to become Alcoholado Glacial. It became an instant success in the Caribbean. In 1960, Curaçao Laboratories began to export the concentrate. While not recommended today as a substitute for soap, you may find it a most agreeable addition to your cosmetics collection.

Spirits

All the upscale liqueurs and a good many fine vintages are available from Curaçaoan purveyors of wines and spirits. But the Number One locally made take-home item has to be **Curaçao, C O C** (Curaçao of Curaçao). Imitated all over the world but never duplicated, its secret lies partly in the well-guarded family formula. More important is the crucial ingredient—a green, lemon-sized, unattractive, wizened, singularly ill-flavored little fruit known as *Citrus aurantium curassuviensis* and cultivatable only in Curaçao. Transplanted to other soils, the seed produces handsome, plump, proper oranges—useless for the production of the liqueur. Orange peel from Haiti, Florida, or California sells for rock-bottom price; Curaçao's Senior Distillery will pay ten times more for the home-grown variety when it can get it. A blend of alcohol, secret spices, and 3 orange skins per fifth (not 24 as some fact sheets incorrectly state), this aromatic ambrosia comes in green, orange, or clear, but tastes the same regardless of the color. For information about touring The Curaçao Liqueur Distillery at **Chobolobo**, the 17th-century landhuis where the liqueur is made, phone 678450.

Amstel began bottling beer in Curaçao in the '60s and allegedly is the only firm to use desalinated seawater as a main ingredient. Whatever the process, it works: in the second and third year of production, Curaçao Amstel had already won two first prizes in a row at Paris and Brussels brewing exhibitions. Amstel allows visitors to tour its **plant** also. Call 612944 for specifics.

For something to take the top of your head off, try a dram of genever, a Dutch aqua vitae so powerful we couldn't find mention of the proof; veteran indulgers judge it to be around 160!

WATCHES

Patek Philippe, Audemars Piguet, Vacheron et Constantin, L. I. Chopard, Nivada, Seiko, Piaget, Corum, Tissot, Mido, Swiza—these are all at **Spritzer & Fuhrmann's** main store at Gomezplein and Breedestraat (tel. 612600), along with a complete watch-servicing department.

Gandelman Jewelers, 35 Breedestraat (tel. 611854), handles Baume & Mercier, Raymond Weil, Citizen, Gucci, and Heuer's underwater chronometers.

Kan Jewelers, 44 Breedestraat (tel. 612111), has Rolex, Les musts de Cartier, Girard Pérregaux—and Longine's.

Try **El Continental, Inc.**, 24-26 Heerenstraat, for Universal. As a rule of thumb, obviously, the more expensive the purchases, the bigger the savings—as a rule of thumb! Before committing any sizeable sum, consider phoning your favorite jeweler (if you did not bring a price list with you) and see what he will charge you for the same timepiece.

Whoever dubbed England a nation of shopkeepers could just as well have applied the phrase to Curaçao. Retailers in its 200-odd establishments have been playing this game for a very long time—in many cases for generations. They know exactly what they are doing, and how best to go about doing it. You are, in short, dealing with consummate pros.

In making your own shopping forays, bear that in mind. Compare prices, on-island and with the U.S., on as many items as at all possible. Scrutinize labels and quality. Generally, keep your wits about you. Among the mostly above-board merchants, you could run into a slippery one here and there.

In that connection you will do well to arm yourself with a copy of *Curaçao Holiday!* In continuous publication for over a quarter-century, frequently updated, it can be a valuable aid in helping you to separate the wheat from the chaff. Get it free of charge from the Curaçao Tourist Board office at Plaza Piar (tel. 613397 or 611967).

USEFUL ADDRESSES

Aquarius: 11 Breedestraat (tel. 612618).

Boolchand's: Kohinoor, 4B Heerenstraat (tel. 612798).

Curaçao Museum: Van Leeuwenhoekstraat (tel. 623777).

Edicta Boutique: 2 Breedestraat (tel. 611397).

El Continental, Inc.: 24-26 Heerenstraat.

El Louvre: 20 Scharlooweg (tel. 61402); branch at 76 Fokkerweg.

Fechi (Curaçao Gold & Gem Centre): 1 Schimaru-kuweg (tel. 614698).

Gallery RGN: 20 Keukenstraat, Wilhelminaplein.

Gandelman Jewelers: 35 Breedestraat (tel. 611854).

Jackie's Boutique: 23 Wilhelminaplein (tel. 613329).

J. L. Penha & Sons: 1 Heerenstraat (tel. 612266).

Kan Jewelers: 44 Breedestraat (tel. 612111).

New Amsterdam Store: 14 Gomezplein (tel. 612437); 29 Breedestraat; one other branch.

Obra di Man: 57 Bargestraat; Gomezplein kiosk; Landhuis Brievengat; International Airport (tel. 612220).

Palais Hindu: 29 Heerenstraat (tel. 611769).

Panino Delicatessen: 23 Hanchi di Snoa Straat (tel. 616629).

Spritzer & Fuhrmann: Gomezplein (tel. 612600); Plaza store; plus four other branches.

Toko Zuikertuintje: 395 E. D. Roosevelt Weg (tel. 671288).

The Yellow House (La Casa Amarilla): Breedestraat (tel. 613222).

DOMINICA

DOMINICA
AT A GLANCE

GOVERNMENT TOURIST OFFICE: Dominica Tourist Board, Cork Street, Roseau, Dominica, W.I. (tel. 809/449-2351).

CURRENCY: The Eastern Caribbean dollar is the official currency, although U.S. dollars are widely circulated. US$1 equals about EC$2.65.

OFFICIAL HOLIDAYS: New Year's Day, Carnival (ten days before Lent), Good Friday, Easter Monday, Labor Day (May 1), Pentecost Monday, Emancipation Day (first Monday in August), National Day (November 3), Christmas Day, Boxing Day (December 26).

STORE HOURS: 8 a.m. to 1 p.m. and 2 to 4 p.m. daily, except Saturday, which is a half-day. Closed Sundays.

LOCATIONS: For the addresses and telephone numbers of the shops, consult the alphabetical list at the end of this chapter.

F or people who enjoy the prospect of boiling lakes, bubbling sulfur springs, hundreds of roaring, tumbling rivers, the only extensive Forest Primeval in the Antilles, towering, almost mile-high peaks, Dominica is a real thrill: a lush, misty, beckoning 305-square-mile Bali Hai.

For shoppers interested in made-in-the-island acquisitions, Dominica is a gold mine. Do not fail under any circumstances to visit **Tropicrafts, Ltd.**, on Turkey Lane (tel. 2747), next to the Banana Marketing Corporation and the New Chronicle newspaper offices.

Sister Bertine and Sister Laura, of the Belgian Missionary Order of the Immaculate Heart of Mary, began Tropicrafts shortly after World War II to provide employment for the women whose husbands were away fishing. Six years ago the enterprise was sold to Rosalind Volney. And it has not missed a beat.

The nuns began their enterprise with rugs. And these still constitute the heart of the business. Workers shape the individual sections, a few no larger than a half dollar, into some of the most regionally inventive floor coverings since the Persians invented the art. The lacy, graceful shapes look ever so light, cool, and tropical.

The dried khus-khus grass of which they are made wears like iron (the Jamaicans make a famous perfume out of their khus-khus), and the airy grace of the mats can become the focal point of any summer residence in the States. We sometimes wonder if the good sisters realize how much pleasure they have afforded those of us who have enjoyed these floor coverings in our homes over the years. In our opinion, this may well be one of the finest handcrafts in the entire Caribbean.

About forty Dominicans living in the mountains gather the grass, harvest it, then put it on the roads for cars to run over, This makes the grass more flexible and easier to handle. Next it is wound into big balls of twine and delivered to the 25 girls who make up the mats. Using 8-inch needles threaded with damp strips of banana bark, the girls take about a week to put together a 9-by-12-foot rug.

Other items available at Tropicrafts include handbags in all sizes and shapes, dolls dressed in the local "Robe Douette" festive costume, and wonderful straw hats. The "Lady Di" model is particularly popular. There is also one named after the previous American ambassador Sally Shelton, who ordered them by the dozens.

The pocketbooks are priced from $3. Rugs can fetch as much as $300. If you would like to check out some patterns in advance, write to Mrs. Volney at Tropicrafts Ltd., Box 97, Roseau, Dominica, West Indies, and ask her to send you a catalog. Needless to say, your purchase can and will be shipped if you like.

The **Crafts Center** at the Carib Reserve fabricates extraordinary handbags, using traditional Indian methods, including covering one of the two layers of straw with earth. You'll find these, along with some of the Marinica Pottery connoisseurs prize, at various Roseau outlets. Try:

>**The Home Industries Cooperative** at Old Market Square (tel. 3207) or
>**Caribana Handcrafts**, 31 Cork St., Roseau (tel. 2761).

Dominican manufacturers manage to mimic the opulence of the French hard-milled soaps so effectively it's hard to tell the difference between theirs and the Gallic variety. Look for the name Ava Beauty Soap, manufactured by Dominica Coconut Products, Ltd.—and unless the price has gone up since we stocked up six weeks ago, be prepared to pay no more than 75¢ (U.S.) for the boxed two cakes.

Dominica also produces a marvelously juicy, flavorsome

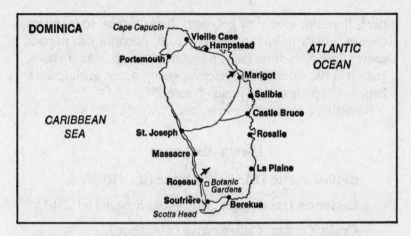

little lime so outstanding that Roses' Lime Juice maintained plantations and processing operations here for years. You can still find the Roses' Lime Juice, along with the usual West Indian complement of chutneys, hot sauces, jams and jellies, in various supermarkets on the island.

Dominican rums include D Special Rum, dark or light, Red Cap, and, as an added starter, Blended Soca Rum. All are produced at Belfast Estate by **Belfast Estate Ltd.** (tel. 1101). There is also Macoucherie Rum, made at the **Macoucherie Distillery** (tel. 6224).

All in all, for a comparatively pastoral island, Dominica produces a surprising variety of goods. To determine just how extensive, we asked local government authorities to identify them. That this comparatively remote and relatively sparsely populated country could engage in such a wide variety of manufacturing activities, as their response indicated, might impress you as much as it did us. Herewith the official list:

"Sorrel, wine, brandy, essence, coconut punch, rum, garments, gloves, bathroom rugs, bedroom slippers, travel luggage bags, screen-printed blouses and shirts, macaroni, chow mein, pastaroni, noodles, mattresses, louvre glass, corrugated steel sheets, wooden furniture, shampoo, placemats, fruit

179

peel, lime oil, aloe vera gel, bags, hats, purses, soap, guava cheese, guava jelly, candles, bay rum, coconut oil, pepper sauce, Café Noir, lime juice, passionfruit juice, leather shoes, jeans, cocoa, Vaseline™, cigarettes, spring water, refrigerators, fans, wood paints—and prefab houses!"

Something, in short, for everyone.

USEFUL ADDRESSES

Belfast Estate Ltd.: Belfast Estate (tel. 1101).

Caribana Handcrafts: 31 Cork St., Roseau (tel. 2761).

Crafts Center: Carib Reserve (no phone).

The Home Industries Cooperative: Old Market Square, Roseau (tel. 3207).

Macoucherie Distillery: Macoucherie (tel. 6224).

Tropicrafts Ltd.: (Box 97) Turkey Lane, Roseau (tel. 2747).

DOMINICAN
REPUBLIC

DOMINICAN REPUBLIC AT A GLANCE

GOVERNMENT TOURIST OFFICE: Dominican Republic Tourist Office, Calle César Nicolás Pensón, corner of Rosa Duarte, P.O. Box 497, Santo Domingo, Républica Dominicana (tel. 688-5537).

CURRENCY: The Dominican peso (RD$) is the official unit of currency, and you get about RD$2.80 to RD$3.20 to US$1. The currency changing must be carried out at special exchange banks (*bancos de cambio*).

Warnings: (1) Lest you succumb to the persuasive blandishments of sidewalk moneychangers offering you many more pesos for your greenbacks, remember: If caught you could be sent to jail, and while in practice this is unlikely, you could receive counterfeit bills.

(2) Don't reserve a fistful of local tender for spending on duty-free shopping at the airport, because those shops won't accept it—they only take credit cards, traveler's checks, or non-Dominican currency.

OFFICIAL HOLIDAYS: New Year's Day, Three Kings Day (January 6), Day of Our Lady of La Altagracia (January 21), Duarte's Birthday (January 26), National Independence Day (February 27), Movable Feast (60 days after Good Friday), Restoration Day (August 16), Day of Our Lady of Las Mercedes (September 24), and Christmas.

STORE HOURS: From 9 a.m. until 12:30 p.m. and from 2 to 5 p.m., six days a week.

LOCATIONS: For the addresses and telephone numbers of the shops, consult the alphabetical list at the end of this chapter.

As a shopper's mecca, the Dominican Republic is something of a sleeper, and one of the great discoveries in the Caribbean: birthplace of Oscar de la Renta (who still has a home here); the prime source of fine amber in this hemisphere; and the site of one of the most exciting arts and crafts complexes in the world. Because it is so fabulous, we begin with this extraordinary center about an hour's drive from the capital:

Altos de Chavón: A Special Category

A decade or so ago, the late Charles Bluhdorn, head of Gulf + Western at the time, conceived the idea of building on his company's 3,000-acre sugar plantation at La Romana a Renaissance-style Italian village that would reflect the sensibilities and substance of the era when Christopher Columbus first landed in the Dominican Republic.

Within this setting, Mr. Bluhdorn envisioned a center for training local artists and stimulating international enthusiasm for the country's cultural heritage. Under the sensitive and skillful direction of Bluhdorn's young daughter, Dominique, in less than a decade it has become a major center for the visual and performing arts in the Caribbean.

Film director Dino de Laurentiis, a frequent guest at what was then Gulf + Western's Casa de Campo resort (now owned by Costa Sun Hotels), suggested the project be entrusted to designer Roberto Copa, who created sets for Fellini and Visconti.

Location: Atop a fertile plateau with a 700-foot drop, overlooking the Chavón River, five miles from the elegant Casa de Campo resort. The construction was done entirely by local workers, entirely by hand, from local stone, wood, and iron.

Ambience: Spanish/Mediterranean architecture so impressive it is impossible to conceive how Copa achieved his magical masterpiece without ever using a written plan! One visitor, overwhelmed, described Altos de Chavón as "not just a place, it's a religious experience."

Swallows swoop over the village, egrets and blue herons linger about the premises. And it is not unusual, at dusk, to share the view with a flock of yellow butterflies. In sum: the most traveled or jaded visitor cannot help but see what the enthusiastic traveler meant and be enchanted.

Within the 14-acre complex a learning program has been established for 200 resident students who study with 18 artists-in-residence recruited from around the world. These professionals teach arts and crafts, weaving, pottery, fabric printing, silkscreening, and sculpture. Alastair Reid, for example, spent three months teaching writing. Other experts conduct classes in dance, design, and music. Each painter-teacher leaves behind a canvas to hang in one of the three art galleries in the complex. The Altos de Chavón School of Design has a two-year program, is an official extension of the Parsons School of Design, and is accredited for students to transfer to Boston's Museum School of Fine Arts, Philadelphia's College of Art, and other members of the National Association of Colleges of Art and Design.

You can buy the finished wares of the craftspeople at the following shops in Altos de Chavón, all of which may be reached by telephoning 682-9656, ext. 3212:

Atelier: One-of-a-kind jewelry made with amber, larimar (Dominican turquoise) and coral

Bougainvillea: Ceramics, leather, silkscreening, weaving, and embroidery

Everett Designs: Features amber pieces handset in gold and silver

El Mercadito: A local market featuring ethnic foodstuffs and household goods

Macramé Chavón: Placemats, belts, bags—assorted items of macrame

Oscar de la Renta/Freya: Oscar de la Renta's own line of tropical fashions

Qui' Avon: Hand-embroidered shirts, blouses, assorted sportswear. Prices run anywhere from $375 for a 16-inch sculpture to $11 for beer and coffee mugs. Store hours vary. Phone ahead to consult the concierge.

If you're an arts-and-crafts junkie, you could do worse than check into the ten-room La Posada Inn nestled in the center of the village itself (tel. 682-9656, ext. 2312). Once you've satiated your shopping urge, you have seven restaurants to choose from, a magnificent 5,000-seat amphitheater featuring everything from Frank Sinatra to the Caracas Symphony and the Taino Museum, displaying one of the most complete collections of quality cultural artifacts in the Caribbean. And for golf, tennis, and beaching, the shuttle bus will run you the three miles over to Casa de Campo.

In the event you can't make it to Altos de Chavón, you will see at least some of the artists' wares in the capital at giftshops in the **Santo Domingo Sheraton** (365 Avenida George Washington—tel. 685-5151) and the **Hotel Santo Domingo** (Avenida Independencia—tel. 532-1511), as well as **Ambiente Decoraciones** (Avenida Independencia), **Tienda Unica** (Calle Pasteur), and **Tienda Patapoof** (Plaza Criolla).

If there were to be a Miss Congeniality contest among Caribbean cities, Santo Domingo ought to win hands down. Whether taking a shopping break at one of the people-watching sidewalk cafés on the broad seaside boulevard known as the Malecón while savoring a slab of sumptuous

Dominican prime beef or strolling through the beautiful restorations in the old colonial section of town, you'll find the majority of the million Santo Dominicans among the warmest and friendliest of people.

It is pleasant, too, in the face of Yankee-go-home sentiments sometimes encountered elsewhere, to note that this city's grandest avenue is named after George Washington; its second handsomest thoroughfare, Sarasota, honors Santo Domingo's sister city in Florida.

The first permanent settlement of Europeans in the New World, the Dominican Republic claims more "America's firsts" than you can shake a Baedeker at: first city hall, first monastery, first mint, first paved street, first cathedral, first college, first hospital in the hemisphere. Some of the 300 15th-century buildings still standing need work. But much of the facelifting is apparent, for example, in the Alcazár, the palace Indians spent four years building for Christopher Columbus's son Diego, using nothing but hand tools—it's the jewel in the restoration diadem. To shop this city is an aesthetic pleasure, whether or not you buy so much as a pin.

ARTS AND CRAFTS

Dominicans are rightfully proud of their cultural heritage, and it remains vibrant today. To form your own assessment, several galleries in Santo Domingo offer a representative cross-section of local and foreign paintings:

Arawak, 104 Avenida Pasteur (tel. 685-1661)
Auffant Gallery, Calle El Conde
Candido Bido Gallery, 9 Avenida Mella
Casa de Teatro, 14 Arzobispo Meriño
El Greco Gallery, Avenida Tiradentes
Imagen, Avenida Pasteur
Otero Gustavo, Avenida Mejía Ricart

Rosa Maria, 7 La Atarazana
Takker Guitti, 3 Arzobispo Meriño

Galería de Arte Nader (Nader Gallery), 9 La Atarazana (tel. 566-6300), is an offshoot of Mr. Nader's Haitian enterprise, one which, quite frankly, we avoided for some years because of the hard-sell, casbah-like ambience. We were wrong. True, atmosphere is a bit rough-and-ready, and some of the offerings might strike you (as they did us) as less than outstanding. But mixed in with these are some interesting entries.

In the area of crafts, the Dominican Republic excels. Last year the prestigious New York Gift Show featured the works of 35 different Dominican producers: amber and larimar jewelry, ceramics, belts, hats, handwoven carpets, cushions, wooden toys, handbags, necklaces, and embroidered dresses were among the exhibits.

A decade ago, the Dominican Development Foundation, a private non-profit agency, created Planarte, a program providing technical, financial, and administrative assistance to artisans in more remote areas of the country as well as in the capital. In the **Bastidas Store**, in the Ozama Fortress in the heart of the colonial old city on Calle Las Damas, you will find ceramics, leather, dolls, papier mâché, wood carvings, and jewelry. If you get to Puerto Plata on the North Coast, by all means visit the **Planarte Factory** there, situated in an old tobacco warehouse on Calle John F. Kennedy. The director is German-born Heinz Meder; his assistant is Suzanne Coanboy, a Boston Peace Corps volunteer.

Other possibilities: **El Conde Gift Shop** at 25 Calle el Conde; the **Bishop's Basket** at the Episcopal Church, 63 Calle Independencia; **Novo Atarazana**, 21 La Atarazana (tel. 689-0582); **Artesanías Dominicanas**' two emporiums, at 24 Calle Tienda and on Avenida 27 Febrero.

For a totally unstructured, spontaneous expression of individual creativity, repair to **Mercado Modelo**, the National

Market, near the intersection of Avenida Mella and Santome. Here are sold wooden bowls, meringue scratchers, cowhorn and bone jewelry, and lots of replicas of the handcarved rocker presented to President Kennedy (they come unassembled, for you to put together yourself).

The predictable collection of souvenir-style trash is being hawked, and the Mercado is definitely on the taxi shill circuit. But withal, you'll see sturdy sandals, hand-carved coffee tables, and perhaps something you like. Haggle.

Be prepared for a real rat race: begging urchins, volunteer guides, and an eclectic cross-section of local society. Unless you're taxi driven, in which case your chauffeur will escort you, it might be easier and more comfortable to slip a likely youth a few pesos to run interference for you. Collectors of the fun, funky, and offbeat, fanciers of the so-bad-it's-good variety of "art," might note the carved coconut busts (we especially like the patriarch complete with hat, pipe, and stubble of beard), on sale for $15 or less. (We spotted ours at Stall 8—when you arrive there may be better ones elsewhere.)

Watch out for those roadside stone sculptures: dirt cheap ($10 or so buys the monster size), and some of them are amusing. But they break at a glance, despite their substantial appearance. And don't be misled into believing they are old, either. An enterprising con artist once bilked many an unsuspecting buyer out of imposing sums with his plausible talk of having dug up these primitive works in an ancient cave. Only when he began "discovering" antique artifacts on demand (i.e., "A statue of a seated man, about six inches tall, in white? Give me a week and I think I can find one for you") did customers begin to have their doubts. Whereupon the price of his objets d'art, along with those of legions of admiring imitators, plummeted—but only to the forewarned. Bear in mind that haggling with these vendors is also in order.

Since coming to the attention of cruise ships and other tourist interests, the town of Puerto Plata, population 45,000, has blossomed forth with a number of worthy enterprises. You can hire a guide to lead you through them for ten pesos or less—which could turn out to be a wise investment.

The **Tourist Bazaar Boutique** at 61 Duarte (tel. 586-2848) fills its capacious premises with paintings, woodcarvings, clothing, and other locally made articles. The reproductions of Taino Indian figures carved at the time of Columbus make interesting garden sculptures.

Ery's Gift Shop at 19 Avenida John F. Kennedy purveys all sizes and shapes of knocked-down, hand-carved rockers, including some for small fry.

Native Arts, a tiny tienda tucked within a mini-market on the road to Playa Dorada, carries excellent-quality ceramic ashtrays and vases, dolls, and plates.

CAMERAS

These are strictly free-port purchases: check the prices and goods at **Centro de los Heroes**, La Atarazana, and the shops in the **Sheraton, Embajador** and **Santo Domingo** hotels in Santo Domingo. Also, consider the duty-free airport shops. You'll not walk out with your purchase—pick them up upon departure at the airport or dock departure area. Whether or not Dominican Republic prices run less than you would pay at home you need to determine, either by consulting a discount catalog you may have been foresighted enough to bring along, or if you can, by making a quick call to a Stateside dealer.

A cluster of tourist-oriented giftshops in the handsome colonial **La Atarazana** section offers mixed merchandise, which we believe you might buy cheaper in the native market. Some of what is there, however, is worth a peek—you might turn up something appealing.

CHINA, CRYSTAL, AND HOME FURNISHINGS

Ceramic and wooden plates, bowls and trays, hand-carved

coffee tables and chairs, decorative items—the Dominican Republic produces these and more. As indicated above, look for them wherever crafts are featured: at Altos de Chavón, the markets, and the shops previously mentioned. For imported crystal, china, and the like, inspect the stock in the duty-free enclaves.

FASHIONS

Oscar de la Renta, who, after a long and distinguished career, remains one of the world's hottest designers, was born and raised in Santo Domingo—as just plain Oscar Renta, local gossips report. The noble "de la," they say, came later.

Be that as it may, by whatever name, this talented Dominican began at the top and has remained there, an alumnus of Balenciaga, Lanvin-Castillo, and Elizabeth Arden. His masterful legerdemain with line, color and texture is too celebrated to need belaboring here. Whether in classic shapes or on glamorous, splashy beaded creations, the inimitable touch is unmistakable. To see de la Rentas on the designer's own home ground, visit the **Freya Boutique**, Centro Comercial Naco, 3 Avenida Tiradentes (tel. 566-6300). The best haute couture in the country is generally to be found here, along with Oscar de la Renta designs. Open from 9 a.m. to 1 p.m. and from 3 to 7 p.m.

In Altos de Chavón, as we mentioned earlier, you will find an Oscar de la Renta boutique. You might even run into him. He built a villa on the Casa de Campo property.

Dominican women are gifted seamstresses; in fact, some famous designers from elsewhere send their sketches to be made up in the Dominican Republic. As yet, however, this talent has not made itself very accessible to visitors. If you plan on being around awhile, keep asking: the social director in your hotel, sales person—whoever seems likely. On one trip we did find smart European imports, including lovely embroidered Spanish shawls at an emporium called **María Cristina**, Fantino Falco. At **Farah**, 55 Avenida de Lope de Vega, we saw good-looking handpainted clothes, and were told that Farah will work out individual designs with clients according to her own ideas, provided they're prepared to pay prices that begin at over a hundred dollars. Should you wish to phone in advance for information, the María Cristina number is 562-2790. Reach Farah via 566-4774.

One item we definitely plan to scout on our next foray is something featured in at least one fancy stateside catalog as a "Higuero." Known in the Dominican Republic under the name *Crescentia Cujete*—what we would call a gourd—the six-inch sphere is intricately carved and handpainted to serve as an evening bag. We saw it in black-and-gold as well as hot pink, and the U.S. price was listed as $80. If you find a source for Higueros before we do, please let us know—and tell us, if you will, how much you saved.

FOOD

Supermarket buys? Routine items that we take for granted bear awesomely high price tags. On the other hand, besides the obvious bargain on that fine honey-colored sugar, locally produced comestibles include a wide variety of inexpensive tropical treasures prized not only by the Caribbean community but by many roving gourmets: guava shells for topping with cream cheese (as "Caribbean fruit compote," this dessert fetches a king's ransom in some of the trendy new West Indian restaurants in Manhattan); mouth-watering jams, jellies, and fruit pastes (mango, guava, cashew nut) are available too. Also look for pineapple marmalade and Dominican-made extracts (mint, vanilla, pineapple). And do not fail to try the crispy *galetas*, known in the States as Cuban crackers. Tangy island-made mustard, indigenous black beans, and spicy salami are tempting also.

One staple we invariably load up on is lively, gusty local seasoning: a taste-teasing mélange of garlic, vinegar, umpteen herbs, and who knows what else, guaranteed to zing up the dreariest most-anything. Whether you buy Sasodon, Ellas, or another local brand, you'll find yourself administering dollops of it to soups, stews, curries, whatever needs that elusive *je ne sais quoi* to bring out the flavor. And should you wish to experiment with Dominican recipes, Estrella Betances de Pujadas of the Ladies Guild put out a cookbook a few years ago with English on one side, Spanish on the other (the proceeds earmarked for the mentally retarded). Hopefully the book will be still in print by the time you get to Santo Domingo.

Dominican coffee is indeed "mountain grown." Duarte Peak and La Pelona in the Central Cordillera rise to heights over 10,000 feet. Under a selected listing by one of the better gourmet coffee houses in America, the Dominican bean— medium and flat—is praised as giving good body with plenty of yield. For optimum flavor, the experts recommend a dark roast. Unlike the Jamaican Blue Mountain variety, which is so expensive, this coffee can be had at regular prices in any Dominican supermarket. Our favorite market is the mammoth **Supermercado Nacional** on Avenida John F. Kennedy, a self-contained shopping center in itself.

JEWELRY

This is a top Dominican Republic item. Not only does the country claim the largest gold mine in the Caribbean, at Cotui, it is also probably the most productive source of top-quality amber in this hemisphere. And local designers are extraordinarily talented in knowing how best to use it.

Take time to learn a little about this truly unique substance, and we believe you will find it fascinating. **Artesanías Dominicanas** (write to Post Office Box 177-2, Santo Domingo, República Dominicana) has prepared an excellent two-page takeout on this exotic substance. Meanwhile, herewith just a few trivia tidbits about amber: warm to the touch whereas all other gems are cold; related geologically to diamonds; verifiably 30,000,000 years old. We are told that Moses broke amber at the rite of the Tabernacle to release its fragrant aroma in sacred offering.

Some Greeks believed amber to be the petrified tears of the gods, others considered it solidified sunshine. The Roman historian Pliny reported 1,900 years ago that a small piece of amber cost more in the marketplace than did a slave. So valuable was it considered that Romans dyed their hair to match their amber. One of the first gifts Christopher Columbus reports receiving in the new world was an amber necklace presented to him in Hispaniola by an Indian prince.

Amber continues to be valuable, but in the Dominican Republic it is not necessarily expensive. Mining amber is still a young (less than 50 years old) operation, one undertaken primarily as a cottage industry; you can buy a genuine piece for as little as $5. The most common shade is a yellow referred to as "transparent gold." Put it under fluorescent—or, better still, phosphorescent—light however, and it reveals tones of violet, red, opalene, and the rarest blue. This variety comes mostly from the Los Cacaos mine, where pieces of the solidified resin are embedded in blue glauconite clay.

The most expensive of all ambers, regardless of their color however, are those pieces that contain fragments, or even whole bodies, of prehistoric insects. The fly, or spider, crawled into the sticky resin trickling down the trunk of a now extinct mimosa-like tree, and the resin held fast, hardening into a translucent coffin. Nineteen of the 26 orders of insects as well as spiders and mites have been found in Dominican amber.

Where best to shop for your amber? A knowledgeable American living in Santo Domingo first steered us to the little house in the residential section where **Ambar Marie** holds forth (19 Rosa Duarte—tel. 682-7539), on the basis that most fashionable locals buy their amber here, and we believe it. The "solidified sunshine" piece we bought from Ambar Marie long ago remains, with the newer necklace acquired at Altos de Chavón, among our treasured possessions.

We passed the word among our journalistic colleagues, they in turn told their readers. But success has not spoiled Ambar Marie. The series of showcases and silk-lined trays in the living room of the modest cottage still contain top-quality specimens in every conceivable shade and setting, from $20 or so right up to the stratosphere. (Ask to see the collector's items; these are put away for safekeeping.)

Taller de Ambar on Calle el Conde in the old city is another recommended stop, as is the **Colon Gift Shop** across from the cathedral of Santa María la Menor in the plaza. Opposite the Alcázar, scout **Zodiac**, on Calle Arzobispo Novel.

Puerto Plata, as behooves a city in the heart of the amber belt, has a museum that traces the history of amber and houses 200 exhibits. Find the **Museum of Dominican Amber** at 61 Duarte (tel. 586-2848); admission is one dollar.

There is no charge to tour the Puerto Plata open market, where one table after another offers amber in all shapes, sizes, and colors—and haggling is acceptable.

Warning: Wherever you buy your amber, check it out. Although the real thing is inexpensive, unscrupulous rogues still find it profitable to substitute a most realistic-looking plastic imitation for the real thing. In some countries they have even been caught smearing the plastic beads with pine resin to mimic the incense-like fragrance of real amber and disguise the chemical odor of the plastic. Rub the stone briskly and then smell it; usually you'll detect its pleasant aroma. Or, after rubbing it energetically with wool or felt, try to pick up a dime-sized bit of Kleenex with the so-called amber. If the tissue clings firmly to the substance as if magnetized, fine. If not, you're being had.

Ten or 15 years ago, the Dominican Republic began producing jewelry using a new stone, a turquoise-like substance called larimar, combining from the name of young *Lari*ssa Mendez, who is credited with discovering it, and *mar* (the sea) where she first saw the stone at the water's edge.

Designers combine larimar with silver, sometimes gold, and frequently with the ivory of wild boar's tusks. Given the restrictions on importing ivory into our country, it is possible that any sizeable collection of these pieces might lead to more or less extended discussions with your friendly border inspector. The house of **Mendez** (Calle Arzobispo Novel) is said to belong to the family of the discoverer, Larissa. Whether or not they are related, the merchandise in Mendez, amber as well as larimar, is usually worth your consideration.

You will find other materials utilized in Dominican jewelry—black and pink coral and the shells of the conch, for example. In Puerto Plata, look in on **Harrison's**, 14 Avenida John F. Kennedy, and **Macaluso's**, 31 Calle Duarte.

PERFUME AND COSMETICS

Your principal source for perfume and cosmetics will be the previously mentioned duty-free shops. However, when visiting the supermarkets, stop at the soap and drug sections. Many of these carry the distinctive Alcoholado Glacial (see entry in the Curaçao chapter), fine hard-milled soaps made on the island of Dominica or imported from Spain, and refreshing West Indian bay rums and lemony colognes.

SPIRITS

Again, if you're looking to acquire that one bottle U.S. Customs allows you to bring in tax-free in the form of Johnnie Walker, Courvoisier, or another familiar liquor, you'll need to patronize the duty-free sector. If you're interested in sampling the *vin du pays*, for Dominicans, that would be, without question, Brugal Rum. There is also Brugal Anejo, Siboney Reserva Especial, and Bermudez 1852, so named because the distillery was founded in that year. For something extra special, the top of the line, either sipped as a liqueur after a meal or on the rocks, or with a dash of soda any time, treat yourself to the Bermudez Don Armando. It glides down with the same smoothness as Barbados Mount Gay Sugar Cane Brandy. This mild-tasting, mellow potion, with the wallop of an exploding firecracker once it bottoms out, is of such quality as to rival most of the hemisphere's fine rums. It's really that good. Find it in the supermarkets, priced at about what you might pay for Jack Daniels at home.

WATCHES

Again, whatever bargains are to be had you'll find in the free-port shops.

A Final Note: Unless you're Spanish-speaking or adept with the phrase book you really should carry with you at all times, communicating can be a problem. Except for such difficulties, we believe you will find the Dominicans as hospitable folk as you will meet anywhere. They do squabble among themselves, and some hot heads DO resort to physical force to settle their differences, but when it comes to receiving guests in their country, as long as the guests tend to their own affairs, behave with a minimum of shouting and arguing, they will go all out to make them welcome.

In case the language barrier becomes insurmountable and/or you need help, the U.S. Chamber of Commerce, with headquarters in the Hotel Santo Domingo Sur (tel. 533-7292) is a member of the United States Chamber of Commerce. The American Consul, Dudley Sipprelle, has offices in Calle César Nicolás Pensón (corner of Calle Leopoldo Navarro).

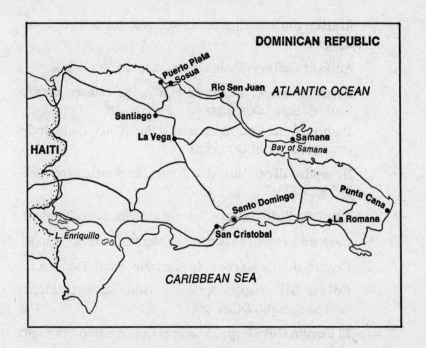

USEFUL ADDRESSES

Altos de Chavón: La Romana (tel. 682-9656, ext. 2312).

Ambar Marie: 19 Rosa Duarte, Santo Domingo (tel. 682-7539).

Ambiente Decoraciones: Avenida Independencia, Santo Domingo.

American Consulate: U.S. Embassy, on Calle César Nicolás Pensón (tel. 346-0013).

Arawak: 104 Avenida Pasteur (tel. 685-1661).

Artesanías Dominicanas: 24 Calle Tienda and Avenida 27 Febrero, Santo Domingo.

Atelier: Altos de Chavón, La Romana (tel. 682-9656, ext. 2312).

Auffant Gallery: Calle el Conde, Santo Domingo.

Bastidas Store, Planarte: Calle Las Damas, Ozama Fortress, Santo Domingo.

Bishop's Basket: Episcopal Church, 63 Calle Independencia, Santo Domingo.

Bougainvillea: Altos de Chavón, La Romana (tel. 682-9656, ext. 2312).

Candido Bido Gallery: 9 Avenida Mella, Santo Domingo.

Casa de Teatro: 14 Arzobispo Meriño, Santo Domingo.

Centro de los Heroes: La Atarazana, Santo Domingo.

Colon Gift Shop: opposite Santa María la Menor Cathedral, Santo Domingo.

El Conde Gift Shop: 25 Calle el Conde, Santo Domingo.

El Greco Gallery: Avenida Tiradentes, Santo Domingo.

El Mercadito: Altos de Chavón, La Romana (tel. 682-9656, ext. 2312).

Embajador Hotel Casino: Avenida Sarasota, Santo Domingo (tel. 533-2131).

Ery's Gift Shop: 19 Avenida John F. Kennedy, Puerto Plata.

Everett Designs: Altos de Chavón, La Romana (tel. 682-9656, ext. 2312).

Farah: 55 Avenida de Lope de Vega, Santo Domingo (tel. 566-4774).

Freya Boutique: 3 Avenida Tiradentes, Centro Commercial Naco (tel. 566-6300).

Galería de Arte Nader (Nader Gallery): 9 La Atarazana, Santo Domingo (tel. 688-0969).

Harrison's: 14 Avenida John F. Kennedy, Puerto Plata.

Hotel Santo Domingo: Avenida Independencia (tel. 532-1511).

Imagen: Avenida Pasteur, Santo Domingo.

Macaluso's: 31 Calle Duarte, Puerto Plata.

María Cristina: Fantino Falco, Santo Domingo (tel. 562-2790).

Mendez: Calle Arzobispo Novel, Santo Domingo.

Mercado Modelo: Avenida Mella, Santo Domingo.

Museum of Dominican Amber: 61 Calle Duarte, Puerto Plata (tel. 586-2848).

Native Arts: Puerto Plata Road, near Playa Dorada.

Novo Atarazana: 21 La Atarazana, Santo Domingo (tel. 689-0582).

Oscar de la Renta/Freya: Altos de Chavón, La Romana (tel. 682-9656, ext. 2312).

Otero Gustavo: Avenida Mejía Ricart, Santo Domingo.

Planarte Factory: Calle John F. Kennedy, Puerto Plata.

Plaza Criolla Shopping Center: opposite the Olympic Center on 27 de Febrero.

Qui' Avon: Altos de Chavón, La Romana (tel. 682-9656, ext. 2312).

Rosa Maria: 7 La Atarazana, Santo Domingo.

Santo Domingo Sheraton: Avenida George Washington, Santo Domingo (tel. 685-5151).

Supermercado Nacional: Avenida John F. Kennedy, Santo Domingo.

Takker Guitti: 3 Arzobispo Meriño, Santo Domingo.

Taller de Ambar: Calle el Conde, Santo Domingo.

Tienda Patapoof: Plaza Criolla, Santo Domingo.

Tienda Unica: Calle Pasteur, Santo Domingo.

Tourist Bazaar Boutique: 61 Duarte, Puerto Plata (tel. 586-2848).

U.S. Chamber of Commerce: Hotel Santo Domingo Sur, Santo Domingo (tel. 533-7292).

Zodiac: Calle Arzobispo Novel, Santo Domingo.

GRENADA

GRENADA
AT A GLANCE

GOVERNMENT TOURIST OFFICE: Grenada Tourist Bureau, the Carenage, St. George's, Grenada (tel. 2279 or 2001).

CURRENCY: The official currency is the Eastern Caribbean dollar (EC$), tied to the U.S. dollar. EC$2.65 = US$1.

OFFICIAL HOLIDAYS: New Year's Day, Independence Day (February 7), National Day (March 13), Good Friday, Easter Sunday, Monday, and Tuesday, Labor Day (May 1), Pentecost, Corpus Christi (Thursday after Trinity Sunday); Emancipation Day (first Monday in August); Thanksgiving Day (October 25, in recognition of U.S. intervention); Christmas Day, Boxing Day (December 26).

STORE HOURS: From 8 a.m. to 4 p.m. daily, Monday through Friday, with a lunch break from 11:45 a.m. until 1 p.m. Saturday is a half day, with shops open only from 8 a.m. until noon.

LOCATIONS: For the addresses and telephone numbers of the shops, consult the alphabetical list at the end of this chapter.

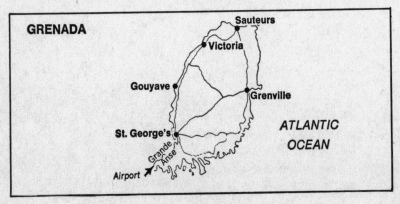

Grenada may not be the most sophisticated shopping center you'll ever visit, but it will certainly be among the loveliest. Less than 90 miles north of Venezuela and Trinidad, this oval-shaped island, 21 miles long and 12 miles wide, rises to a peak of 2,756 feet. Mount St. Catherine and other mountains cover four-fifths of the territory, swelling streams and creeks to river size, which then plunge and tumble seaward, creating misty cascades that spume into deep cool pools.

St. George's, the main settlement, the capital, and a superb port, almost completely surrounds the crater of a quiescent volcano that has remained inactive for at least 120 years. About 10,000 people live within the city; but it's one honey of a town.

Solidly built multi-level buildings, punctuated with lush tropical green patches, tumble down to the blue of the harbor where sailboats twist and turn, bob and curtsy on their way to the sea. Money is short, with the result that many of the buildings could use paint, and some scars of past disorders remain. But St. George's has little of the honky-tonk appearance a few old West Indian hands complain is creeping over certain shopping meccas to the north. It has rightly been rated by many as the most photogenic port in the West Indies.

English is spoken, the rhythmic, special Caribbean variety. Out in the countryside you might hear patois: a French graft on an African support, grown on British territory. Another Gallic legacy is the fact that over 60% of the people are Roman Catholic.

Grenada's tourist industry, a mainstay of the economy, has suffered some tough times during the 1980s. But now that the military presences, both Cuban and American, are no longer in the headlines, visitors are coming back—in force. Twenty-one percent more chose to vacation in Grenada during 1986 than in the same period in the previous year.

Projected coming attractions include a new golf course, additional hotel rooms, and more marinas. But, overall, government guidelines call for no structure higher than a coconut palm tree. Undoubtedly new and intriguing boutiques will spring up along with the other developments. Meanwhile, Grenada's established emporiums offer plenty of fruitful foraging.

ARTS AND CRAFTS

The Yellow Poui Art Gallery, on Young Street at the top of the hill (tel. 3001), is a good place to begin. The brainchild of Jim Rudin, an artistically oriented half Afro-American, half East Indian with New York Museum of Modern Art experience, it serves as a focal point for Grenada's burgeoning artistic talent.

Here you will find wall hangings, woodcarvings, quality photographs, and antique maps priced up to $150, and some ingratiatingly sly and witty primitive paintings by Canute Caliste.

A native of Carriacou, an island off Grenada, and compared by some to Grandma Moses, Caliste produces canvases sparkling with humor, filled with mermaids, devils, biblical observations, and with his personal political statements. They are also arresting to look at—and amazingly inexpensive to acquire: $15 should buy you a respectably sized (about 12-by-18 inch) one.

Bosco Holder, brother of Geoffrey Holder, also exhibits and sells his paintings here, but be prepared to pay $500 at the least for his; they go to $1,500. Good to know: The Yellow Poui offers you the hospitality of its courtyard to relax, rest, sip a cold drink, or even pause for a game of chess.

Do also drop by **Tikal** on Young Street (tel. 2310), or its branch boutique in the Spice Island Inn. Jeanne Fisher, the interior designer who runs these two emporiums, selects stock with a trained eye that reflects her own international background (she was born in Mexico City, educated in the States). You will find mahogany wood carvings of local motifs (armadillos, turtles, and the like), island maps and prints—a cross-section, in fact, of arts and crafts, chosen with expertise and good taste.

Among standouts are the so-called "thread poems." In their lore, purpose, and general thrust, these fine-stitched appliquéed one-of-a-kinds are the Grenadian equivalent of a family quilt. Each one tells a different story. Prices begin at around $20 for the smallest, about eight inches square. Here too, a variety of soft-sculpture dolls in the island idiom and other locally fashioned merchandise, of which more later. Tikal also features some antiques, Oriental imports—whatever finds Jeanne Fisher happens to ferret out on her regular buying trips overseas.

For a representative cross-section of local artisanry, **Grencraft**, the retail outlet of the Grenada National Institute of Handicrafts, is your best bet. An autonomous part of the Ministry of Education and Culture, the Handicraft Institute is involved in research, development, production, training, and, increasingly, the actual sale of local works. It is also mandated to upgrade the quality of what is made on Grenada and its dependent aits.

In the short time it has been in existence, Grencraft has managed to stimulate the islanders' interest in crafts as an important reflection of their cultural heritage. The head office and showroom are located on Melville Street in St. George's (tel. 2655); there is also a store at the airport. The production center is at Tanteen in St. George's.

Grencraft showcases a dozen different craft disciplines, among the most popular of which are wall hangings made of burlap appliquéed with bright Arawak Indian designs. These sell for under $12. Sculptures are on sale here as well, along with a wide variety of other articles made of tropical wood.

205

As of last year, Grencraft claimed to be the largest retail outlet for exclusively local handcraft in the Caribbean. Stock occasionally runs low, and after a series of cruise ships have visited the port, shelves can be pretty bare, but by and large, Grencraft deserves your attention.

CHINA, CRYSTAL, AND HOME FURNISHINGS

Grencraft (details above) is developing a line of island-made mahogany and red-cedar chairs, along with other furniture, both in modern and Victorian design.

Tikal (Young Street—tel. 2310) features ceramic cups, plates, serving dishes, and the like created by Grenadian artisans, and huge salad bowls made of mahogany roots, priced from about $25 to $75.

For Waterford, Wedgwood, and other imported luxuries, have a look at **The Gift Shop**, in the Grande Anse Shopping Centre (tel. 4408). Because of Grenada's membership in the Commonwealth, prices can be attractive.

FASHIONS

Look for tie-dyed dresses in **Grencraft** on Melville Street (tel. 2655), or **Tikal** on Young Street (tel. 2310). There too, Tahitian-style pareos, and for men, ties imported from the Orient.

If not sold out by the time you get there, Tikal carries 100% batiste wrap-around fabric lengths with African designs, which Jeanne Fisher can have made up for you into cover-ups, sundresses, or other casual wear within a week or so.

You might, if you're in the neighborhood, check out a little shop on Halifax Street across from the market called—if we read our scrawled notes correctly—**E.M. Fashion**. The imports from Paraguay, though not cheap (over a hundred dollars), are striking: all linen, hand-embroidered, plus some items brought in from the United Kingdom as well. One of the more distinctive articles for men on sale here is a garment invented in British Guyana, but adopted throughout the Caribbean. One West Indian Parliament even went so far as to rule it officially acceptable for business attire. As the name suggests — shirtjack — it combines the features of both, but being short-sleeved and lightweight it is considerably cooler.

The Dolphin in the Grande Anse Shopping Centre was recommended to us on a recent visit, but too late for us to investigate.

FOOD AND DRINK

Grenada is of course known as the "Spice Island," indeed bills itself as "the only spice-producing area in the Western Hemisphere."

One thing is certain: in Grenada and its two dependent islets of Carriacou and Petit Martinique, there is no shortage of aromatic plants, leaves, fruits, and nuts.

In the showrooms of **Grencraft** on Melville Street (tel. 2655), as well as those of **Spice Island Perfumes, Ltd.** at the Carenage between the LIAT airline office and the telephone company (tel. 2006); in supermarkets, at the airport, and in various locations throughout the island, you can pick up locally grown spices by the double handful. Nutmeg, cloves, cinnamon sticks, allspice, mace, tonka beans, West Indian bay leaves, Grenadian cocoa—some are unavailable in our own supermarkets, but all are available fresh in Grenada.

The Marketing Board on Young Street (tel. 3191) carries nutmeg syrup, honey spices, candies, cocoa, and other assorted Grenadian gourmetry.

Grencraft also handles homemade candies, jams, jellies, and one Grenadian condiment our larder is never without— namely, that special hot sauce. Glowingly orange as a ripe pumpkin, hot as a laser beam, it sells in most groceries and shops for a dollar or so. Through the years our own preferred Grenada brand was Panks Little Devil Pepper Sauce; on recent trips, we have been unable to find it.

Other gastronomic goodies we have scooped off supermarket shelves from time to time have included Buckfast tonic wine made by the Benedictine Monks of South Devon, England (28 proof no less); Trinidad mustard; Glasgow seasoning; bitter chocolate; and, especially, that lively Grenada chutney. Tulong tea is another delicacy grocers can't always keep in stock.

Grenada has a wide range of teas of its own, brewed from the leaves of bushes, vines, and trees grown on its hillsides. Folk medicos prescribe the various herbs, known as "bush tea," as effective remedies for specific ailments:

> **Petit Baume**, **Sugardish**, and **Santa Maria** combat colds and coughs
> **Bois Canot** functions as a soporific, as does the avocado leaf
> **Corille** is prescribed for high blood pressure
> **Lemon Grass** fights fever, tastes good besides
> **Black Sage** is said to clean the blood
> **Guava** is prescribed for stomach pains, cramps; it also acts as a vermifuge.

You may run into an odd-looking greenish potion identified as sea moss that tastes vaguely like seaweed. Although ostensibly valued as a refreshing taste quencher, its real worth, according to the coconut grapevine, is as an awesome aphrodisiac—so awesome, in fact, that too much of a good thing has been known to land those who ingested excessive amounts in the local hospital.

The aforementioned **Spice Island Perfumes, Ltd.**, which sells handpicked and sorted air-dried packages of these nostrums, also purveys some just-for-the-taste-of-it combination teas, including one flavored with citrus peel, spices, and bergamot essence. Another is flecked with small accents of dried Grenadian ginger, and a refreshing blend of lemon grass and lemon essence. At a dollar or two for the teas, the same for spices (around $5 for the seven spice assortment), these make great gifts for members of the bridge club, Girl Scout troop, or any other collection of people you'd like to remember.

As to local culinary specialties, Grenada has not yet become industrialized to the point of canning or otherwise preserving the ingredients.

To savor on the spot the broadest possible cross-section of Grenadian gourmetry, make reservations (which are essential) for a meal at **Mama's**, on Lagoon Road. Telephone her at 1459. You will dine in Mama's home, be served by her family—and pay around $13.50 for an 18-to-24-course feast.

To give you a rough idea of what you may expect, a recent dinner for four at Mama's consisted of: callaloo and lobster soup; turtle, lambi, lobster salad and two other salads; breadfruit balls, tannia cakes, chicken, mixed dumplings, baked breadfruit with cheese topping; baked plantain, stewed fish, fish salad, rice, beans, pig souse, dasheen, baked banana, steamed callaloo; topped by chocolate cake, coconut ice cream, assorted fresh fruit, and coffee.

To find out what you can buy locally in the way of culinary exotica, we suggest looking at **Food Fair** market on the Carenage in St. George's (tel. 2588). There is also a Food Fair in the Grande Anse Shopping Centre (tel. 4573).

JEWELRY

Years ago Scottish immigrants moved to the island of Bequia north of Grenada, to establish a whaling industry. Because the waters surrounding Bequia are fairly shallow, whales came from afar to feed on these flats.

In addition to the New England saltboxes that the whalers

built, causing some prose poets to call Bequia "the Cape Cod of the tropics," they left behind another legacy—the art of scrimshaw, a special way of carving whale tusks, bone, shells, and wood. Scrimshaw work is highly prized, and highly priced as well, the world over. You may find Grenadian versions from time to time in Grenada, probably at **Tikal** on Young Street (tel. 2310). Prices range from $36 up.

On display also here and there—Tikal and **Grencraft** (Melville St., tel. 2655) are likely hunting grounds—are coral bracelets, necklaces, and the like priced from $9 or so up to $25. The more intricate, elaborate pieces naturally cost more.

PERFUME AND COSMETICS

Grenada's **Spice Island Perfumes, Ltd.** at the Carenage (tel. 2006) ranks number one in this department. Founded by a prominent local family, the Bullens of Carriacou, the on-site manager, Mario Bullen, is skilled in the finer points of fragrance. The resulting line of products is one of the most comprehensive being manufactured in the Caribbean.

Essences of jasmine, ylang ylang, and frangipani, along with accents of spice and citrus, underlie many of the feminine perfumes and the array of male scents currently available. More are constantly being tested, so new varieties may well be on hand by the time of your visit.

You can acquire 50 milliliters of Island Flower, Jacaranda, Frangipani, Fancy Lady, or Wild Orchid for around $11. The masculine products—Spice and Vetyver, for example—cost about the same.

Natural extracts, constituted of oils and waxes drawn from the local trees, bushes, and flowers, are also available at Spice Island Perfume, to mix with your own scents for a distinctive new fragrance, to combine with pure alcohol to produce your individual eau de cologne, or to dab on a light bulb to perfume a whole room.

Extracts come packaged in either glass jars or handmade mahogany containers, for $5 and $7, respectively. Choose from Jasmine, Frangipani, Bitter Orange, Patchouli, Ylang Ylang, or assorted spices.

You'll find outstanding potpourri here also, fetchingly presented either as the "spice lady" island doll or, for Christmas, a Santa Claus as well as a Georgian house you can hang on your Christmas tree. All are priced around $5.

Perfumed body oils include the naturally scented monois, based on coconut oil, flavored with spice, sweet root, rosemary, thyme, lavender, and mint. Take your pick, at $5 per bottle. The concentrated bath oil is $4.

The firm's Carriacou Sun Products include tanning lotion, a protection preparation, two tanning oils, and an after-sun emulsion. The most complete selection of all this merchandise, obviously, is at the Carenage headquarters. You will, however, find some of the items on sale elsewhere, including at the airport, **Grencraft**, and sometimes even on board cruise ships when they are in port.

SPIRITS

The celebrated drink of Carriacou is a white rum of awesome strength called jackiron, recommended by its proponents because, they say, it will never give you a headache the next day. What they neglect to add, according to one beleaguered imbiber, is that you may well have no head either.

Author Frances Kay puts it this way: "There is a completely distinctive attribute of jack which, as far as I know, no other drink has. ICE DOESN'T FLOAT IN JACK, IT SINKS! When you first see those frightened ice cubes huddling on the bottom of your glass, it shakes you." HANDLE WITH CARE!

The Grenada variety is more mellow, only around 80 proof, and goes by the name of Clark's Court. It costs under $4.50 the

211

bottle. Special to Grenada is a liqueur known as De La Grenade. Flavored with nutmeg and a variety of other spices, it also is 80 proof, and costs just $7.50 or so. The De La Grenade rum punch runs about $5. You'll spot both the liqueur, the rum, and the punch in most shops, including the supermarkets.

You might also want to visit an ingratiating escale known as **The Best Little Liquor Store**, in the heart of the Carenage. Owner Geoff Thompson is a leading native-born Grenadian businessman. His attractive blond wife, Gillian, serves as Executive Director of the Hotel Association. You'll enjoy meeting them even if you don't walk off with a bottle.

A final suggestion: if you become as captivated with Grenada as most of us do, try to buy, beg, or borrow a copy of Frances Kay's out-of-print but totally delightful book entitled *This—Is Grenada*. This 128-page labor of love is full of information, is enchantingly readable, and can contribute much to your enjoyment of the Isle of Spice. The author covers history, language, music, food, drink—almost anything and everything anyone might possibly want to know about this beautiful Bali-Ha'i.

And the facts are brightened with delightful dollops of commentary. Consider, for example, these entries, in the chapter on the ornithological population. Reportedly two hitherto unrecorded species, they would seem guaranteed to cause considerable twittering among bird-watchers:

Red-Eyed Rumsipper. *Tourist Alcoholus flammeur.* 68 inches. Plumage generally brilliant. Feathers on head scanty and mostly gray. Noisy and conspicuous. Call a loud *rumpunchrumpunchrumpunch.*

White-Breasted Mansnatcher. *Craft. Homograbula albifrons.* 64 inches. Legs and throat generally brown, in startling contrast to white breast. Never seems to come to rest. Call a raucous *who-he, who-he.*

Frances Kay describes her adopted homeland skillfully, knowledgeably, but most especially with love.

"This is a magic island," she writes, "an island with green mountains rising, tier on tier, from white beaches into the clouds. An island whose capital is a town of rainbows and bells. An island where almost every house has a view, and one of the favorite occupations is comparing them. An island so beloved by the sea that, with some 80 miles of coast, it has more than 65 bays. An island which steals your heart when the trade winds bring the smell of spice and the sound of blown conch shells as fishing boats return."

Now if they could only bundle all that up and sell it to us, wouldn't *that* be the ultimate take-home trophy.

USEFUL ADDRESSES

The Best Little Liquor Store: The Carenage, St. George's (tel. 2198).

The Dolphin: Grand Anse Shopping Centre, Grand Anse.

E.M. Fashion: Halifax Street, St. George's.

Food Fair: The Carenage, St. George's (tel. 2588); also at Grand Anse Shopping Centre, Grand Anse (tel. 4573).

The Gift Shop: Grand Anse Shopping Centre, Grand Anse (tel. 4408).

Grencraft: Melville Street, St. George's (tel. 2655); plus branch at the airport.

Mama's: Lagoon Road, St. George's (tel. 1459).

The Marketing Board: Young Street, St. George's (tel. 3191).

Spice Island Perfumes, Ltd.: The Carenage, St. George's (tel. 2006).

Tikal: Young Street, St. George's (tel. 2310); plus branch at Spice Island Inn, Grand Anse Beach.

The Yellow Poui Art Gallery: Young Street, St. George's (tel. 3001); plus branch in the country (tel. 2121).

HAITI

IMPORTANT NOTICE

As of presstime, Haiti founders in yet another series of tribulations, probably the worst ever—which is saying a great deal for this proud but beleaguered nation. Many, if not most, touristic experts consider it at the very least unpleasant, at the most unsafe, to vacation in this, the oldest black republic in the hemisphere, at this particular time. Our own view, and especially our hope, based on 20 years' experience with this indomitable country, is that Haiti will bounce back.

In that spirit of wishing for the best, we include this, one of the most inventive and talented islands of the Caribbean, in this book. By the same token, however, we must point out that it is of *paramount importance* that you check with the State Department Caribbean desk, the airlines serving Haiti—every possible source of information—before taking off. We pray they will give you an all clear signal, not only for the sake of the Haitians, who so desperately need your patronage, but for the extraordinary discoveries the wondrously gifted people have to offer you.

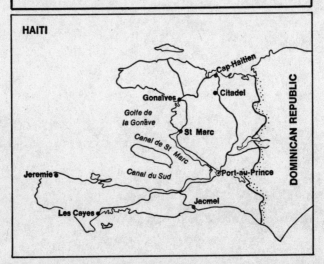

The world's oldest black republic, one of the most hauntingly beautiful islands in the Caribbean, Haiti is also about the unluckiest. On top of generations of economic misery comes first, the catastrophically bad publicity concerning the country's association with AIDS, soon followed by a State Department advisory to tourists to stay away from Haiti because of political chaos.

However the latest crisis resolves, the aftermath is bound to make prospective visitors think twice about picking this vacation destination above all others. Nevertheless, to omit Haiti entirely from this Guide would be unconscionable. Some day, somehow, conditions must stabilize so that visitors may once again savor the vibrant, exuberant creativity exhibited in the articles made for sale by these most gifted and indomitable of people.

As of this writing, you can buy some Haitian products either by mail to a Stateside address, or through American sources. We pray that by the time you read these lines the country will have opened up, enabling you to go and shop for yourself for many more, right at the source.

In the meantime, herewith a quick bird's eye mercurial view of likely addresses, with more than the usual caveats given the mercurial situations. Given the uncertainties, we have confined listings only to those enterprises which in the past have seemed to be able to withstand the test of turbulent times, while still serving visitors well.

ARTS AND CRAFTS

The number one treasure is art. Every second Haitian fancies himself another Grandma Moses, and the profusion of offerings is bewildering. You will find paintings for sale on your hotel walls, in the streets, at various shops, in galleries, in dirt-floored huts. Some of it is very good, most of it is interesting.

Haiti's fame as a center of primitive art goes back a few years. But the present product is considerably more sophisticated, and, as a result, might be more lasting in value. Nuns in Port-au-Prince who have been holding classes in anatomy and draftsmanship might be responsible for some of the more impressive results, but more likely they are due simply to logical evolution.

You will see Haitian art decorating the walls of opulent expatriates in Switzerland; the American Embassy in India at one time had a Haitian mural occupying a place of honor; chic Manhattan galleries display Haitian collections. One happy collector informs us that according to one published estimate, Haitian paintings have on occasion appreciated as much as 300% in a year.

In Port-au-Prince, the capital, the number of dealers we've seen writing checks to Issa's Galleries would seem to make his twin establishments close to tops (Issa has also exhibited at Parke Bernet in New York). Issa El Saieh (17 Avenue de Chili and in town at 9 Rue Bonne Foi) left Bethlehem for Haiti, went into retailing, and when his private collection of art outgrew his home, opened a gallery next to it. Issa is not bound by regular hours. He will receive you as cheerfully on a Sunday morning as any other time. Of the over a hundred artists he represents, many work on the Avenue de Chili premises, with proper brushes and canvas which Issa suplies.

For busy shoppers, Issa also stocks a cross-section of woodenware, carved door panels, metal sculptures, some wild cotton rugs.

If you have someone special on your list you'd like to impress with a truly original gift (or merely wish to pamper yourself), here's a thought. Issa can arrange to have the likeness of your choice incorporated into a sizeable painting, for 25% over its regular price, working from a color photograph. The range: from $75 upward.

Centre D'Arts at 58 Rue 22 September 1957 is an important stop for art lovers (some of the hand-painted wooden boxes we acquired there have tripled in price). **Galerie Monnin**, at 11 Rue Lamarre in Petionville, and 17 Laboule, on the Kenscoff road is another highly regarded operation.

In Cap Haitien, **Flamingo Gallery** is a cooperative owned by local artists. **Marassa Gallery**, also represented in Port-au-Prince, is recommended by knowledgeable Cap Haitians.

As for crafts, every municipal market, every street corner—the whole of Haiti is one gigantic arts and crafts fair. Straw and metal work, woodcarvings and utensils, handwoven fabrics, embroideries—you name it, they make it. And the Casbah philosophy of commerce is prevalent. If the back room sculptor quotes $50 for the coffee table that catches your eye, argue him down to $30. A tray priced $8 is happily handed over for $4. By and large, for amateur hagglers, the final price equals about half the original asking price.

A dedicated second generation American Baptist missionary couple, Wallace and Betty Turnbull, run one of the best all-around, and especially, a hundred percent hassle-free source of crafts in all Haiti. Look for them in Fermathe, atop a 4,500-foot eminence a half hour's drive from Port-au-Prince. Theirs is also an inspiring story of American dedication and competence.

Wallace and Betty's parents founded the mission forty-three years ago, with Mrs. Turnbull teaching a few women to sew and embroider and selling the results out of a trunk in her living room.

Today the young Turnbulls' **Mountain Maid Self Help Outlet** provides incomes for over 1,300 families that might be otherwise unemployed. They produce, for sale, woodcarvings, ceramics, outstanding furniture, embroidered fashions and table linens, leatherware, jewelry, handwoven cottons, and wrought iron.

A tearoom at the mission even purveys, along with American-style sundaes, burgers and fries, orders of escargots "to go," a feature Betty Turnbull tells us she believes makes the mission Tea Terrace unique in the fast-food business. Proceeds from this, and the Flower Shop, support the crafts project. All profits from those sales go to the artisans themselves.

The mission, occupying land once owned by a renowned witch doctor, also encompasses a 100-bed hospital, 50-bed tuberculosis sanitarium, and mobile medical units. The mission has established 200 churches with 30,000 members, 180 schools providing 25,000 children with nutritious hot lunches daily. The Turnbulls offer three-year courses in auto mechanics, electrical installation, carpentry, tailoring, weaving and other practical skills.

Wallace Turnbull traveled to Israel to study agricultural methods there. On his return he initiated a comprehensive agricultural program at the mission to teach farmers to conserve their soil, and upgraded their animal stock by importing from the U.S. superior quality breeding animals to service them. The Turnbulls have also sponsored poultry and rabbit farms. In addition, a hundred of their charges have been established raising cut flowers. A half a million seedlings are distributed free each year for reforestation.

As for the retail side of the mission, if you will write ahead to **Mountain Maid Self Help Project**, Betty Turnbull will see that you get a copy of their 33-page catalog. Primitive in the extreme, with drawings which at best can be described as "basic," you will still get some idea of what is available and for how much.

Mountain Maid is excellent about filling special orders. We send away to them regularly for hand hemstitched, hand cross-stitched, cocktail and/or tea napkins in red, white, and green drip-dry cotton. At fifty cents apiece, six of them make an attractive Christmas remembrance—especially if you ask Betty either to use Christmas tree motifs or stitch Merry Christmas next to the design.

The official address is Box 1386, Port-au-Prince, Haiti, W.I., (telephone 011/509-74043). But we correspond with the Turnbulls c/o Mountain Maid — MFI, Beckett Ramp Hangar #18, P.O. Box 15665, West Palm Beach International Airport, West Palm Beach, Florida 33406.

Another likely source for arts and crafts: **Carlos** (Alexander Guerin, Cite de l'Exposition). You may have visited the branch in St. Thomas. Some offerings, such as nutcrackers in the shape of feminine thighs, are not calculated to win any design prizes, but the woods are of good quality and you just might find the painting you've been looking for here. **Nader's Gallery** (2 Rue de Bonne Foi) is another possibility, so is the shop in the Episcopal School, next to Cathedrale Sainte Trinite in downtown Port-au-Prince. Visit the Le Caille **Mahogany Factory** only if your sales resistance is supersolid.

In Cap Haitien you will find a branch of Carlos and a retail outlet of the Baptist Mission called the **Cohaga Shop**. Not to be missed: the shop in the Haitian Art Museum of the College St. Pierre, Place des Heros, Champ de Mars. At the **Mahogany Factory** you can watch articles being made. **Guy Benjamin** shop is an outlet for the Factory.

CHINA, CRYSTAL, AND HOME FURNISHINGS

Carlos may have some Limoges and Royal Copenhagen china. Look also at La Belle Creole and Versailles. Basically however, your best buys in home furnishings consist of what is made in Haiti.

At **Mountain Maid**, for example, a tropical hardwood salad bowl of rich swirling grain, natural finish, 12 inches in diameter, costs $15, including the salad serving fork and spoon. We've seen carved door panels at Issa's Gallery for well under $20 apiece.

Our two dozen mahogany dinner plates came from **The Salvation Army** workroom on Avenue François Duvalier (look for the sign "Centre des Handicapes Armee du Salut"). Variety is not extensive, but what the 46 handicapped workers (most of them blind or deaf mute) do make, they assemble with care. Periodically, the Army also has issued a catalog. (You know, of course, to place wood purchases in your home freezers as soon as you get home to kill stowaway insects.)

For Haitian fabrics, try **Cano**, 21 Boulevard Harry Truman downtown.

FASHIONS

Haiti has a way of stashing away hugely talented designers, usually working at home, on an obscure side street, the exact address carefully guarded from outsiders by regular resident patrons. Longtime visitors will remember Madame Celestin, for example (on the road to Petionville behind the reservoir). Madame was a wizard with hand embroidery, inspired in the use of crochet, and could take a Simplicity pattern and make it perform like a Balenciaga toile. Or Paris-trained Yolande Monta, who whipped up fantastic originals from her tiny boutique near the Red Carpet for like $50. Whether either or both are still in business, or who the current Madame Celestin or Yolande might be is not clear at this moment of crisis. But when, hopefully, it is over, and Haiti is once again able to receive visitors calmly, keep asking.

Whether or not you hit pay dirt in that area, you should discover several boutiques worth browsing. Ex-Connecticut Yankee Sue Seitz took up moonlighting from her duties running the Oloffson Hotel to join forces with a Haitian aristocrat. Together they opened a sleek, clever, and a mite pricey, stateside-type boutique called **Bagaille** on Rue Pan Americaine in Petionville. Another emporium with a similar, but not identical name, **Bagatelle**, also on Rue Pan Americaine, is also a possibility.

We've had good luck at Helene Clerie Delaquis's **Helene**

Shop (67 Rue Pan Americaine), both in well-made prairie-type denim skirts and for to-order embroidery: bring her the blouse or skirt or whatever and she'll have the work done to your specifications for $20 or so.

Pierre Cole is a third generation tailor, experienced in the States, perhaps a bit extreme for conservative males unless you can persuade him to mute the styling. For ladies, however, he does great blazers, meticulously put together with all the right stitching and reinforcements, for $50 or less. it needs saying that M. Cole serves primarily a hometown clientele, is not oriented towards the tourist trade, and is rather shy. But he has good fashion sense and charges very fair prices.

When we first approached Lucienne Liautaud 15 years ago about mentioning her in print, she was not all that wild about the idea of publicity. Since then other writers have followed suit and revealed her whereabouts as well (on Aviation Avenue near the Salvation Army showroom). Nevertheless, Madame Liautaud, who exports hand-crocheted fashions to the top shops in the U.S., remains gracious to visitors who phone for an appointment in advance at 2-3716.

Amidst the flotsam and jetsam at Carlos's you can find the best straw pocketbooks to be had in Haiti, some sporty denims and unbleached muslin designs, and a comfortable patio for lounging and refreshments. Around the corner, Cite de l'Exposition, you may spot some nice linens at **Jacqueline's**.

Mountain Maid boy's western shirts are $6.50, ladies' embroidered backwrap skirts of denim or permanent press blend, $11. Hand crocheted blouse, $6, crocheted baby dress, $4, baby skirt, $3.

FOOD

Amidst the Heinz and Gerber jars at Port-au-Prince supermarkets you will find homemade Haitian peanut butter known as Mamba: no additives, no preservatives, but lustily seasoned and delicious. Madame Rene Malary puts up a preserve called simply Gelee under the brand Carm (Preparation Soignee guaranteed on the label). Composed of what fruit or fruits we haven't a clue, but melt in the mouth it does. Haitian pound cake is also uncommonly flavorsome. So, alas, is the crackling crisp-on-the-outside, mostly-fluffy-on-the-inside bread. As for that rich, full-bodied, assertive Haitian homegrown coffee, coffee experts J. Gill Brockenbrough, Jr., and Peter Coe, authors of the book *Coffee,* rate it "Medium bean, good roast, heavy bodied with good aroma." As to its availability, they rank it next to "Rare."

JEWELRY

We were pleased, but not surprised, to spot at one of the most prestigious of Caribbean and South American expositions of upscale goods in Miami, a display featuring the jewelry of **Pericles**. Using various tones and textures of copper, Pericles creates chokers, pendants, rings, and body mail of great talent and originality. Pieces begin at $10, go all the way up into the hundreds. A standout: the necklace composed of two dozen 112-year-old two centime coins.

You'll find bits and pieces of Pericles at **Carlos**, the airport shop, here and there about town. But nothing to approach the assortment laid out in his own little showroom at 46 Rue Geffrard, Port-au-Prince. Moreover, his pieces have not been lacquered, as a result of which those in some of the boutiques tend to tarnish and look somewhat seedy. But if you cannot get to his atelier, take a second look at what Pericles creations you do locate. An admiring New York artist we know calls Pericles the Cellini of the Caribbean. You might tend to agree.

LINENS

You'll see lots of the home-embroidered variety in your travels through Haiti; often the quality of the fabric leaves something to be desired. On the other hand, we've been washing and drip-drying our Mountain Maid place mats for ten years with no problem whatsoever.

PERFUME AND COSMETICS

Sue Seitz teamed up with the Key West Fragrance and Cosmetic Factory to found the **Haiti Perfume Factory**, 21 Rue Pan Americaine, Petionville. There they put in prepared scents, as well as sales girls trained to show you how to blend your own individual combination best suited to your chemistry. Offerings to consumer include such piquant scents as patchouli (grown in the islands and said to be the favorite of high-class Parisian call girls), narcissus and nutmeg, also West Indian in origin. The various lotions and skin creams are lavishly high in content of the tropical aloe. We also acquired here some of the clearest, purest alcohol ever (made from oranges, the clerk told us) with which to blend our own perfume oils at home.

SPIRITS

The limey soil of Haiti's sugar-growing area resembled that of France's Cognac district, and the double-distilling process of making rum parallels the Gallic method of confecting brandy. Barbancourt rum is made direct from cane juice and not from molasses. The result is mellow, fragrant, smooth as silk.

You're welcome to tour the **Barbancourt** headquarters on the outskirts of Port-au-Prince where drinks are on the house and unlimited. Barbancourt rum comes in one Star, three Star, and five Star grades, plus a limited edition, "Reserve du Domaine." Oenologist Alexis Lichine calls Barbancourt "one of the fine rums of the world." *Food and Wine* agrees: "The most outstanding dark rums we've encountered."

Named Barbancourt also, but not to be confused with the above-mentioned distillery, **Jane Barbancourt** liqueurs include all sorts of exotica—mango, hibiscus, and papaya are among the 18 varieties. (Our favorite: coconut.) Stop by the reconstructed *fabrique* known as Jane Barbancourt castle en route to Kenscoff and see for yourself. The operation goes back a long time—to 1765, as a matter of fact, when Jane Barbancourt's ancestor Louis Barbancourt left Bordeaux and came to Haiti while it was still the French colony of St. Domingue.

Incidentally, those orange peels you see drying along the streets are exported to France for the preparation of Grand Marnier. Haitian oranges are also used to make Cointreau.

———————

At press time, these roughly are some of the options you might enjoy exploring in Haiti. Hopefully by now the turmoil will have ended. All we can do is hope so, and indicate in the broadest terms the best bets as per our most recent investigation, while at the same time asking you most earnestly to keep us advised of any later developments.

Haiti is a mysterious, mercurial, miracle of a country—brooding, elemental, utterly and endlessly fascinating, and, too often, dogged with misfortune.

But if the political horizon does look clear when you plan your Caribbean trip, please do try to slip this special country into your itinerary.

JAMAICA

JAMAICA
AT A GLANCE

GOVERNMENT TOURIST OFFICE: Jamaica Tourist Board, New Kingston Office Complex, 79-81 Knutsford Blvd., New Kingston 5, Jamaica (tel. 929-8070).

CURRENCY: The official monetary unit is the Jamaican dollar (J$), known locally as a "Jay." Recently it has been valued at about J$5.70 to US$1 but the relationship between the two currencies is too volatile to nail down precisely at this time. Verify the latest rate of exchange with any bank.

Local law requires that you make all purchases and pay all bills in Jamaican dollars. You must obtain this currency either at a bank or at one of the specified *change bureaux* situated at the airports and the hotels.

Should you be tempted to deal in the black market or on a street corner (which is of course illegal), bear in mind that upon departure you will need a receipt for the money exchanged in order to convert it back into your own tender. In fact, it is recommended that in order to have proper documentation you produce identification when making bank transactions and when converting Jamaican dollars back into U.S. dollars. Taking Jamaican money off-island is prohibited.

OFFICIAL HOLIDAYS: New Year's Day, Ash Wednesday, Good Friday, Easter Monday, Labor Day (May 23), Independence Day (first Monday in August), National Heroes Day (third Monday in October), Christmas Day, Boxing Day (December 26).

STORE HOURS: These vary from city to city. In Ocho Rios, for example, stores have longer hours than in Montego Bay. As a general rule, however, most businesses operate from 8:30 a.m. until 4:30 p.m., Monday through Friday. Some shops close on Saturday; others are open until noon.

LOCATIONS: For the addresses and telephone numbers of the shops, consult the alphabetical list at the end of this chapter.

This Isle is a marvelous fertile Isle, and is as a garden or store house for diverse parts of the maine. It is full of plaine champion ground, which in the rest of the Indies we have not seen. It aboundeth in beeves and Cassava, besides most pleasant fruits of diverse sorts. We have not found in the Indies a more pleasant and wholesome place.
—Sir Anthony Sherley (1597), in Richard Hakluyt, *Principal Navigations...of the English Nation, 1590–1600.*

Jamaica is a happy hunting ground for bargain hunters on two levels: (1) A bumper crop of appetizing specialties exclusive to this country, and (2) duty-free imports from around the world. Things Jamaican to quicken the pulse of enthusiastic browsers include bags, cigars, coffee, carvings, ceramics, cutwork, costume jewelry, embroideries, exotic gourmetry, paintings, rugs, rum, sandals, sculptures, straw in infinite variety—to name just a few.

Among import finds scooped up from across the seven seas you will find French perfumes, English china, Irish crystal, Japanese cameras, Swiss watches, Oriental pearls, and many more served up for your delectation.

There are custom-made skirts, blouses, dresses, shorts, slacks, suits and jackets, ingeniously engineered accessories, novel jewelry, and excellent island cologne for men and women.

Little leaguers score with native toys, musical instruments, and play-clothes galore.

As with all the islands, but especially here, anything even remotely resembling a complete survey of the retail picture within the space allowed is out of the question. There is just too much to cover. Once over lightly, herewith some suggestions:

A Note About Prices and Availability: Conditions change rapidly in all merchandise marts, but nowhere is it apparent more than in Jamaica. For instance, last May we brought home a couple of unusual bird-feeders then available on every street corner for a couple of dollars. When we returned in December, loaded with requests from friends who admired them, not one was to be found in all of Jamaica.

Prices are equally volatile, with rum up 20% within weeks. As one philosophical clerk put it, "The only thing that comes down in Jamaica is the rain." So if you will, bear that in mind

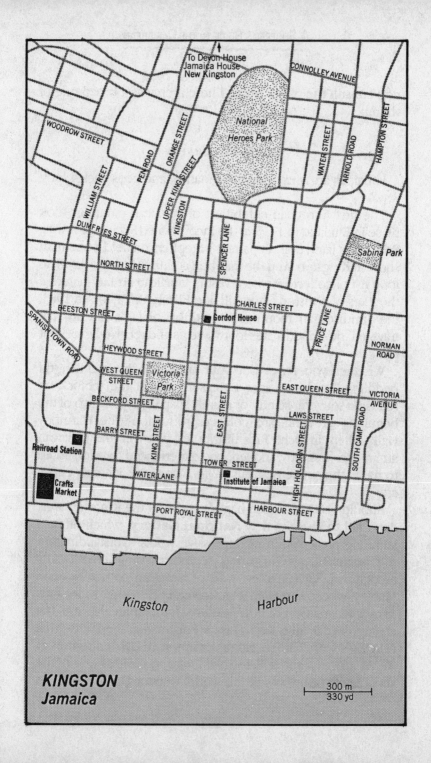

To Devon House
Jamaica House
New Kingston

CONNOLLEY AVENUE

WOODROW STREET

National
Heroes Park

WATER STREET

ARNOLD ROAD

HAMPTON STREET

WILLIAM STREET

PEN ROAD

ORANGE STREET

UPPER KING STREET

KINGSTON

SPENCER LANE

DUMFRIES STREET

Sabina Park

NORTH STREET

BEESTON STREET

CHARLES STREET

PRICE LANE

Gordon House

SPANISH TOWN ROAD

HEYWOOD STREET

NORMAN ROAD

WEST QUEEN STREET

Victoria Park

EAST QUEEN STREET

VICTORIA AVENUE

BECKFORD STREET

EAST STREET

LAWS STREET

SOUTH CAMP ROAD

BARRY STREET

KING STREET

HIGH HOLBORN STREET

Railroad Station

Crafts Market

WATER LANE

TOWER STREET

Institute of Jamaica

PORT ROYAL STREET

HARBOUR STREET

Kingston   Harbour

KINGSTON
Jamaica

300 m
330 yd

and consult the prices quoted herein only as a broad rule of thumb.

ARTS AND CRAFTS

Jamaican art is exciting, imaginative, and goes back a long way.

The first European exhibition of Jamaican paintings took place in England in 1775, at the Incorporated Society of Artists. Four years later, portrait painter J. Stephenson held a one-man show in Kingston. And the tradition continues to this day. The long list of collectors who invest in Jamaican art has included the likes of Winston Churchill and Elizabeth Taylor. In 1983, the Smithsonian mounted an exhibit of Jamaican art that traveled the United States for two years and received excellent notice.

Whether you ferret out your own budding genius still peddling "yard art," spot a treasure amidst the schlock on roadside souvenir stands, or merely snap up a set or two of the beguiling greeting-card color reproductions the Harmony Hall Gallery in Ocho Rios distributes, you will find Jamaican art an excellent buy. Indeed, one experienced traveler, asked to name the single best buy in Jamaica, unhesitatingly chose art.

Should you perchance happen to be in the Kingston area, don't fail to visit the new **National Gallery**, which offers a stunning presentation of impressive works. Outstanding are the powerful, awe-inspiring sculptures of internationally recognized Edna Manley, wife of Jamaican patriot Norman Manley, whose son Michael followed in his father's footsteps as a charismatic political leader. Memorable also are the creations of Mallic Reynolds, a Pocomania shepherd (that religion's word for leader) ranked by such U.S. authorities as *Art In America* and a *New York Times* art critic as one of the six greatest primitives in the world. Curator David Boxer, an art historian, alumnus of Cornell and Johns Hopkins, and an artist in his own right, deserves great credit for his work in assembling this display.

Look for Jamaican art in Kingston at the **Bolivar Gallery**, 10 Grove Road, Kingston 10; the **Frame Gallery**; the **Upstairs Bookshop and Downstairs Gallery** on Harbour Street; and the **Mutual Life Gallery.**

In Montego Bay, art dealers and serious collectors head for Elizabeth DeLisser, at the **West Indian Gallery of Art** on Church Street, near the Parish Church. The DeLisser family is prominent in Jamaica, its members pioneering in the hotel business and in fashion design.

In the event you don't happen to find what strikes your fancy at Mrs. DeLisser's establishment, you might give **Ky Ann Walker** a call at 952-2065. Ms. Walker, who once operated her own art gallery, now does special shows involving antiques, prepares occasional special exhibits, and frequently accompanies interested buyers to Kingston, where she knows the major artists.

In Ocho Rios, **Harmony Hall**, four miles east of town on the main road to Oracabessa, is probably your best bet (tel. 974-4222). A Victorian house over a hundred years old, Harmony Hall was once part of a pimiento estate. At one time it was the Methodist Manse, later a private residence. Five years ago, renovation began, involving exposing the original stonework and replacing intricate gingerbread fretwork; upon its completion, the Prime Minister cut the ribbon on the Harmony Hall complex.

Harmony Hall displays the works of outstanding Jamaican artists (including, on occasion, a number of those selected by the Smithsonian Institution for its Traveling Exhibition of Jamaican Art). You will also find for sale a changing assortment that might feature alabaster carvings, handmade wooden Annabella Boxes (they come with a brief history), one-of-a-kind antiques, figurines, lutes, prints, posters, and, for less than $3 the set, some delightful prints based on the diary Queen Victoria supposedly kept on an incognito visit she made to Jamaica. Our favorite shows the Queen, in full regalia, on waterskis. There is even a book devoted to the escapade.

In **Port Antonio,** for watercolors and original works of art, visit the **gallery** located near the Trident Hotel, 2½ miles east along the coast toward Frenchman's Cove.

Among those whose works you should keep an eye out for in your travels:

Albert Huie—born in Falmouth, Jamaica, featured in the Smithsonian traveling exhibition, his work is impressionistic in feeling, and occasionally rather reminds some observers of Van Gogh. You might also find him at his own studio in Kingston at 107 Constant Spring.

Allan Zion is a member of the Jamaican "Intuitive School," represented by Kapo, Brother Brown, and Albert Artwell. Zion's canvases depict country life on the island in a mood somewhat reminiscent of a Grandma Moses primitive combined with Haitian joie de vivre.

Eve Foster chooses subjects similar to Zion's, but treats them with more detail and more sophistication. Now and then you might even get a remote feeling of Dali from some of her canvases.

Should originals of any of these artists exceed your price range, you will find full-color, good-quality reproductions at the above-described **Harmony Hall**, at **Things Jamaican** at the Montego Bay Airport (tel. 952-1936), and here and there on the island at various other shops. They come assembled eight to the package, cost about 25¢ apiece—including the envelope.

CRAFTS

Island artifacts indicate that over three centuries ago, less than 20 years after the British took possession of Jamaica, at least one artist was creating handsome wig holders, combs, and other objets d'art out of expertly polished tortoise shells adorned with intricate carvings of banana, cocoa, cactus, and cashew.

The line separating arts from crafts, often arguable, is especially so in Jamaica, where an estimated 40,000 wood-carvers, weavers, and other artisans produce some uncommonly interesting creations. Some of what is offered for sale is, or borders on, the tacky when it comes to motif and finish. But look twice, and you should be rewarded.

If you take the time to examine bags labeled on one side "Souvenir of Jamaica," you will find that on the reverse side the "straw lady" may have embroidered flowers or local scenes with considerable skill and taste.

Certain woodcarvings sold at the 50-odd roadside stands lining the way from Montego Bay to Ocho Rios, and going for $10 and less, are exceedingly well executed. There are those, of course, that are quite simply ghastly insofar as subject and finishing is concerned. But seldom is the workmanship inept, which is the more unusual given the shortage of proper carving tools. Frequently, all the carver has for chisels are flattened nails. Occasionally a generous tourist will send instruments along after he gets home, to the delight of the artist. If you have any to spare, by all means pass them on to those in charge at Things Jamaican (see below).

To market and distribute the output of island artisans, the Jamaican government has established an operation known as **Things Jamaican:** leather goods, ceramics, wood, straw, embroidery, and handwork are the main categories of its production. Devon House at 26 Hope Rd. in Kingston (tel. 929-6602) is one of the major outlets for the operation. There is a very small, crowded showroom at 44 Fort St. in Montego Bay (tel. 952-5606), a little Things Jamaican boutique at the Montego Bay Airport (tel. 952-1936), as well as one at The

Kingston Airport (tel. 924-8556). For more information about the operation of Things Jamaican, write them at Things Jamaican, Bumper Hall Road, P.O. Box 60, Kingston 14.

Also worth a visit if you are in Kingston is the cooperative known as **Special Things**, 29 King St. (tel. 922-5873), Mrs. Amy Marsh Brown, Manager.

In 1687, the Duke of Albemarle, then governor, brought with him from England his personal botanist and physician to sketch the local flora (he collected over 800 varieties). Accurate identification of medicinal plants was an essential part of a doctor's practice—and to a degree, still is. Today's islanders know their vegetation and how to put it to good use.

High in the Blue Mountains, the Watsonia lily leaf is boiled, dried, and plaited into hats and bags. There are hammocks made of designs inherited from the Arawak Indians; cups made of coconuts; calabashes etched with drawings of plants and flowers, a custom dating back 300 years. As pocketbooks, you'll see them advertised in upscale Stateside catalogs for $80.

One of the more interesting aspects of island crafts has to do with a trunkless plant bigger than a man, with fan-shaped leaves and long stems shooting up from the ground, known as the Jippi-Jappa. From its straw, island women weave most of their hats, mats, baskets, and bags, while men choose its wood for their carvings. From mahogany and lignum vitae Jamaicans fashion plates, bowls, and carved figures. Others create free-form furniture out of tree roots.

An important first stop to scan the variety of offerings available in various disciplines is the **crafts market**, which also constitutes the social and economic nerve center of most every island community, large and small. Bargaining between buyer and seller is expected, often spirited, but much better humored these days than heretofore.

In Kingston, Courtesy Cops are stationed throughout the market to arbitrate any disputes. Theoretically there are officers to monitor the markets in Montego Bay and Ocho Rios as well, but we failed to see any on our last swing through. There is no rule of thumb as to how much the vendors will slice off the original asking price. From our own experience, we'd say 15% to 20% would be about par for the course.

Some visitors prefer to hire one of the youths offering their services as escorts to do their bargaining for them in the market, and at the same time ward off too-pushy hustlers.

CAMERAS

Camera purchases can be tricky, so take care. Double-check the U.S. price lists, and as a rule don't expect to save more than 20% (not counting what you would pay back home in sales tax).

A catalog such as that put out by 47th Street Photo (67 West 47 Street, New York, NY 10017—tel. 212-260-4410) or other such outlet is useful to study and clip. You might well find prices there as good as those in Jamaica.

In certain instances there are sizable savings to be had—as much as 40%, for example, on the Nikon L35AF, according to one satisfied buyer. He reports having seen it (a) listed in the United States at $179; (b) obtainable at a cut-rate shop for $139, and (c) on sale at **Chulani Shops** (see below) for $109. Another contented client tells of paying $92 for an Olympus XA11 priced $149 up North, selling on the American "gray market" at $111.

Accessories such as filters, lenses, and the like are well worth investigating. As to whether you will find better buys on other islands, generally speaking, with the possible exception of Sint Maarten, costs run pretty much the same up and down the chain. Wherever you buy, make every effort to verify that the article is genuine, of current model, and in working order, not a second.

Here is where you should find the widest selection of photographic equipment on Jamaica:

Casa de Oro at the Pineapple Place Shopping Centre (tel. 974-2577) in Ocho Rios, and at the Holiday Village Arcade, Rose Hall, in Montego Bay (tel. 953-2600), carries Canon, Minolta, and Vivitar lenses

Chulani Shops at Pineapple Place in Ocho Rios (tel. 974-2421) and 44 City Centre in Montego Bay (tel. 952-2158) carries Nikon, Minolta, Canon, and Olympus

La Belle Créole at 36 City Centre, Montego Bay (tel. 952-3502), has Canon, Minolta, and Vivitar lenses

Holiday Inn Duty-Free Shop at the Rose Hall Holiday Inn, Montego Bay (tel. 953-2503), stocks Canon, Minolta, Nikon, Olympus

CHINA, CRYSTAL, AND HOME FURNISHINGS

During the underwater exploration carried on by the Institute of Jamaica more than twenty years ago, many beautiful pewter utensils were uncovered, extraordinarily well preserved for 275 years under 15 and 20 feet of sand and mud.

One especially interesting line exclusive to Jamaica and to be found nowhere else are antique reproductions based on the artifacts uncovered in the sunken city of Port Royal. Look for them at **Things Jamaican** at Montego Bay Airport (tel. 952-1936); Kingston Airport (tel. 924-8556); at Devon House, 26 Hope Rd., Kingston (tel. 929-6602); and 44 Fort St., Montego Bay (tel. 952-5605).

Apparently the citizens of 17th-century Port Royal used a variety of spoons—some Dutch, some English, some local. There were three pewter-makers in the town, as well as six goldsmiths and one ivory turner. After the Institute of Jamaica digs, impressions and molds were made of these spoons. Things Jamaican then created copies in leadless pewter alloy similar in composition to that which English pewterers used for export during the reign of William and Mary.

You will find rattail spoons, a William and Mary spoon featuring the monarchs' heads, spoons with pied-de-biche handles, "splay-footed lion rampant" spoons, a rum-measuring jigger known as a baluster, and a Tudor-Rose seal. Packaged in a leather pouch made from special split calfskin tanned in Jamaica, a serving spoon is a good and interesting value at $5 or so.

Knives have handles made of pewter and lignum vitae hardwood. Some flaws—pitmarks, scratches, and other imperfections—in the originals have been left purposely in the molds, because the originals were used articles when buried, before being reclaimed from the ocean.

In ceramics, Things Jamaican has duplicated plates, beer mugs, chocolate pots, and onion bottles all in the Bristol-Delftware the early settlers used—a primitive imitation of Chinese Ming porcelain, with grace notes from the Restoration and from the period of William and Mary. Today's versions, when available, are all hand-painted by local artists.

As for contemporary imports, longtime Jamaica visitors who have not been back for a few years will note smaller stocks and less extensive arrays of expensive luxury items for one very good reason—merchants have difficulty in obtaining the foreign currency necessary to make their purchases overseas. The exchange rate that Jamaican banks quote their customers depends on a unique system of auctioning off, once or twice a week, whatever foreign currency is available. Quotas are allotted for those imports requiring exchange, and the banks must stay within those limits; they cannot give out more foreign monies than the quotas allow.

There are other factors also to keep in mind. As we noted earlier, the climate of international shopping in general has changed—the rapid fluctuations in currency values make today's bargain invalid tomorrow; the increased mobility of the American public, to whom dashing off to London or Paris for a weekend of shopping is no longer unheard of; the ease of ordering by toll-free phone... all these elements inevitably have affected Jamaica's in-bond shopping.

But there is good news also. Duty-free shopping in Jamaica is much simpler now than it used to be. No more red tape, airport delivery, or any other roadblocks. You walk into the store, pay for your purchase (in Jamaican dollars, since all purchases must be paid for in local currency), and walk out with it.

You will find Baccarat, Lalique, and other fine crystal in Jamaica—only in smaller quantities and with less selection than in the past. But at least one Jamaican merchant guarantees that prices on these brand names are higher in Europe than in the Caribbean, and claims duty-free tariffs are the same in both areas. This is hard to verify, with currency values changing from day to day as they do.

For buyers who don't plan on going abroad any time soon, the comparison between overseas and Caribbean rates is less relevant than the contrast to what they would pay for the same merchandise at home. As a rule, a 35% savings is the figure most often quoted (plus the eliminated U.S. sales tax). Sometimes that figure can be higher. We found one piece of Baccarat, featured in a top-drawer American catalog at $195, on sale in Montego Bay for $85. A place setting of Wedgwood listed at $120 in the U.S. was being sold in Jamaica for $60.

The handmade Hungarian Herend china much in style in the United States these days is often a good buy: a pattern featured by one famous Texas-based emporium for $220 costs $142 the place setting in Jamaica. Irish Belleek china is equally attractively priced.

You will find the better-known brands represented as follows:

Americana Shops at Coconut Grove and Ocean Village

Shopping Centers in Ocho Rios (tels. 974-2414 and 974-2248, respectively): Royal Doulton, Wedgwood, Aynsley, Coalport, and Royal Worcester

Bijoux at Casa Montego Hotel Arcade, Montego Bay (tel. 952-3277): Wedgwood, Minton, Royal Doulton, Royal Albert, and Aynsley

Carousel at 24 King St., Kingston (tel. 922-6802): Royal Doulton, Minton, Wedgwood, Aynsley, and Royal Albert

K. Chandiram Ltd. at the Jamaica Pegasus Hotel, 81 Knutsford Blvd., New Kingston (tel. 926-3690): Minton, Wedgwood, Royal Doulton, Aynsley, and Royal Albert; consult the Useful Addresses list for other branches

China Craft at Holiday Village Arcade, Rose Hall, Montego Bay (tel. 953-2404): Wedgwood, Minton, Royal Doulton, Royal Albert, and Aynsley

Chulani Shops at Half Moon Club, Montego Bay (tel. 953-2053); Pineapple Place Shopping Centre, Ocho Rios (tel. 974-2421): Kaiser and Belleek; consult the Useful Addresses list for other branches

Hemisphere Shops at the Americana and Sheraton Hotels, Ocho Rios (tels. 974-2151 and 974-2201, respectively); Wyndham New Kingston Hotel, 85 Knutsford Blvd., Kingston (tel. 926-5430); Wyndham Rose Hall Beach Club, Montego Bay (tel. 953-2715): Wedgwood and Coalport; for other branches consult the Useful Addresses list

India House at 60 King St., Kingston (tel. 922-2951); 51 St. James St., Montego Bay (tel. 952-5844); and Rose Hall Holiday Inn, Montego Bay (tel. 952-2485): Wedgwood, Minton, Royal Doulton, Royal Albert, and Aynsley

FASHION

According to Jamaican author Morris Cargill, "Our women,

as soon as their economic situation permits them to care for their clothes and diet, are quite unusually beautiful."

And that they are. With a special instinct for what's right to wear in their island setting. Jamaican women walk slowly, heads and shoulders erect, skirts swinging from their hips, and local designers create clothes to accommodate their distinctive look and bearing.

Young women are trained in embroidery, cutwork, appliqué, and crochet, some by instructors straight from Paris. As a result, you can pick up handmade garments, lavishly decorated, for as little as $15 or $20.

We found several lovely examples in the **Special Things** cooperative, 29 King St. in Kingston (tel. 922-5873), but you will spot hand-embroidered, appliquéed, or cutworked garments in the craft markets, at roadside stands, and at most corner boutiques. Jamaican designer **Frances Keane**, at 125 Hagley Park Rd., in Kingston (tel. 923-7350), is known for her use of cutwork.

Other Kingston designers of note: **Norma Sosa,** 2a Suthermere Rd., Kingston 10 (tel. 926-6262) and **Melanie**, in Sunshine Plaza, Kingston.

Elizabeth Jean, a tiny little mart in Montego Bay's Beachview Arcade (at least one slick national magazine has featured one of her confections on the cover), had a couple of bargains when we were last there. The work on one white linen dress, at just a little over US$100, was superb. There are crocheted swimsuits, sundresses, off-the-shoulder blouses—the stock changes with the times. *Note:* Elizabeth Jean, as with many interestingly stocked emporiums, is not much for window-dressing. Do not, however, be put off by an unpretentious storefront.

Sasha has just one shop, at the posh Tryall Golf and Beach Club a short drive from Montego Bay (tel. 952-5110), but if you are out that way, by all means drop in.

Two of Jamaica's most successful fashion operations were

created by American expatriates who chose to live in Jamaica. Ruth and Dick Clarage fell in love with the island virtually at first sight, forsook successful Stateside careers to build new lives in their personal paradise, and in so doing added considerable luster to the escutcheon, and the economics, of Jamaica.

Mouth-watering Ruth Clarage fabrics produced on the island present a colorful kaleidoscope of Jamaican charms. Lacy bamboo branches, banana leaves—these and other tokens of the distinctive West Indies experience adorn crisp yardage made into blouses, skirts, shorts, hats, swimwear, dresses long and short. Whether you favor the classic, carefully casual look that belongs in patrician resorts on either side of the ocean, or are on the lookout for very young clothes full of pep and pizzaz, you should find something you like here. Ruth Clarage's typically tropical, painstakingly constructed collection, originally a 100% personal operation, and now enhanced by the addition of an able pro lured away from the New York fashion district, includes cool caftans, wrap skirts, and perky sun hats in the $30 to $70 price range.

With leftover scraps and snippets of their own yard goods, the Clarage-factory workers fashion a variety of small gift items, accessories, aprons, dolls, and a clever gimmick consisting of a set of three folding traveler's trays.

You will have no problem locating a **Ruth Clarage** branch—there are seven of them: in Kingston at the Wyndham New Kingston Hotel, 85 Knutsford Blvd.; in Montego Bay at the Casa Montego Arcade (tel. 952-2282), the Montego Bay Freeport Shopping Centre (tel. 952-3278), the Holiday Village Shopping Centre (tel. 953-2579), and the Half Moon Club (tel. 953-2211); in Ocho Rios, at Pineapple Place Shopping Centre (tel. 974-2658), and Ocean Village Shopping Centre (tel. 974-2874). One commentator referred to the Ruth Clarage look as the Caribbean successor to Lilly Pulitzer. In certain respects, you may agree.

In Port Antonio, Errol Flynn's widow, **Patrice Wymore,** combines working the pimiento and coconut plantation known as the Errol Flynn Property with a **boutique** in the Trident Villas and Hotel, 2½ miles east of Frenchman's Cove.

Find fashions also in the shopping plaza in downtown Port Antonio, in Dragon Bay, in the San San area.

FOOD AND DRINK

The motto on Jamaica's national coat of arms reads "Out of many, one people." Nowhere is the resulting explosive creativity more evident than in the cosmopolitan culinary mix of Jamaican gastronomy. Cassava bammy cakes; ginger cookies called *bullas;* sparkling-clear, aromatic logwood honey; Jamaican cane sugar, glistening cocoa-brown, its caramel-like flavor lingering enticingly on the tongue; saucy, sophisticated curry powder blended on-island by connoisseurs in the Indian community; flaming local hot sauces, some triple-potent, others country-style piquant...These are just a few of the temptations that await you on supermarket shelves. And the prices are incredibly low.

Jamaica Hell Fire, for example, made from sun-ripened Capsicum peppers with the Blue Mountain pimiento and sugarcane vinegar, packs four times the wallop of its nearest Stateside equivalent. It sells for around 75¢ the five-ounces. Plaza, the brand name for a zesty sauce paysanne, costs about the same, as does a bottle of the Jamaican's own variety of browning liquid. Empire curry powder, a skillfully sweet-and-spicy combination, can be had for about $1 the six-ounce package.

For sweet tooths, there's the strong, assertive "Miracle" guava jelly at under $1 for 12 ounces; fluffy coconut-drop candies, at 20¢ a bag; superb quality hand-dipped coconut and chocolate clusters by Highmark at $6 or so per pound.

All in all, for adventurous epicures this land is hog heaven.

In supermarkets, in tiny hole-in-the-wall convenience stores, in mom-and-pop corner groceries, and also in some of the tinier boutiques catering to visitors, culinary collectors will find an eclectic assortment of savory exotica, canned or packaged, to take home. And some are steeped in tradition.

Callaloo, for example, the pungent tropical green leaf essential to the preparation of any truly fine, proper Caribbean pepperpot, is traditionally the plant of romance. Feed it to a reluctant suitor and according to calypso lore he'll find himself unable to resist proposing marriage. (The jumbo-sized can shouldn't cost more than $1. For the romantic miracles it's supposed to perform, it is cheap at the price.)

Ackee, the subtly flavored, brilliantly scarlet fruit which, with codfish, constitutes the national dish, traces its ancestry all the way to Africa. The seeds came to Jamaica on a slave ship more than two centuries ago. Captain Bligh of *Bounty* fame took an ackee back from Jamaica and introduced it to Europe, and the scientific community named it after him (*Blighia sapida*). Ackee grows elsewhere in the Caribbean, but is said to have originated here. Some food professionals compare the flavor of ackee to scrambled eggs; others say the taste is like celestial chestnuts.

As for the famed breadfruit, legend and history mix in the tale of its introduction to Jamaica. At one point, the planters were said to object to raising food for the slaves on land that could be more profitably used for cane cultivation. Therefore, according to accounts, they dispatched Captain Bligh to Tahiti, aboard the good ship *Bounty,* to fetch breadfruit seedlings, which could grow in areas not suitable to raising cane. But something unexpected happened to Captain Bligh along the way—namely, the famed 1789 mutiny. Three years later Bligh tried again, this time aboard the H.M.S. *Providence;* he finally succeeded in delivering 800 breadfruit trees to Jamaica, some of which are still standing. (Nor only is breadfruit still a staple of Jamaican diet, but its leaves, when applied to the forehead, are said to relieve headache and hypertension. Cabinet-makers use the wood to make furniture.)

The Arawak Indians, Jamaica's earliest residents, were the first to discover and cultivate the root of cassava, a snowy-white farinaceous root of considerable gastronomic versatility. The African slaves who succeeded them adopted cassava as their own. Conquistadores plying the Spanish Main, who used Jamaica as a supply depot, loaded up on cassava because it kept for so long and so well.

Today as then the cassava bammy is a local favorite—a sort of West Indian English muffin. Serve it hot, toasted, slathered in butter or cheese, either with a meal or with drinks, and you will find the flavor both distinctive and delicious. You should have no problem finding bammies—The Flower Hill Cassava Project, in association with the St. James Land Authority, produces a superior variety known as Western Bammies. Even the tiniest commissary (such as the one tucked between the Montego Bay Club and Beechview Hotel on Gloucester Avenue in Montego Bay) keeps a regular supply.

As to the various ways to prepare these and other savory Jamaican gastronomic novelties you may collect in your travels, one of the best sources is a small, inexpensive (less than $3) compendium by Leila Brandon entitled *A Merry-Go-Round of Recipes From Jamaica*. It has proved so popular that it is still in print more than 20 years later. From this book you will learn how to confect a cloud-like ackee soufflé; ways to stuff breadfruit with piquant combinations of meats and condiments; formulas for whipping up toothsome desserts with names like Pinch-Me-Round, Guava Crisp, Mango Delight, or Pineapple Fantasy. And in the process you will also acquire a strong sense of what Jamaican cuisine, as cosmopolitan as its population, is all about.

As a matter of fact, you could do worse than to arm yourself with Mrs. Brandon's book before you do your browsing, and with it in hand scan the grocery shelves to locate the ingredients she mentions. All are not necessarily West Indian —Mrs. Brandon calls for Quaker oats, Crisco, whatever she feels does the job best regardless of where it comes from. Nor are all the entries themselves self-consciously "native." Included are beef Wellington, various ducks with l'orange, and some wine-based recipes, as well as a range of other Continental classics favored by worldly hostesses. But, when her book specifies "wet sugar," these are no-substitutes-please requirements!

According to the Schweppes company, only Jamaican ginger provides just the right zing for their tonic water. Several other local spices are also distinctive and of superior quality. You'll find them mixed in with the French's mustard, Spice Island peppercorns, and other conventional U.S. staples, products which are part of most every Jamaican household as well.

But if you can carry just one Jamaican spice home, it probably should be the pimiento known also as allspice. Not to be confused with what we think of as pimientoes, the Jamaican version is a dark, reddish-brown seed with the happily combined aroma of cinnamon, cloves, and juniper.

Among the recipes calling for pimiento are those for soups, pickled meats, and some desserts—anything calling for a musky, elusive flavor. Medicinally the pimiento is said to help upset stomach and neuralgia.

Pepper elder is used in preparing the celebrated *jerk pork*. Supposedly pepper elder prevents fatigue. It is employed in rural areas in conjunction with pimiento leaves for embalming! Presumably it keeps the cadaver intact for up to three days.

For a more complete assortment of strictly Jamaican herbs and plants, many of them fetchingly packaged in calico with line-drawing labels, shop **Devon House** at 26 Hope Rd. in Kingston (tel. 929-6602); the **Things Jamaican** branch at the Montego Bay Airport (tel. 952-1936—see also Useful Addresses list); the minute, combination tour office and commissary called **Sweet Jamaica**, located opposite Casa Blanca on

Gloucester Avenue in Montego Bay; the **Under the Rainbow** branch in Montego Bay; **Living Wood Shop** in the Ocean Village Shopping Centre of Ocho Rios (tel. 974-2601). Several of these shops also stock cookbooks, liqueurs, ceramics, and sometimes fresh fruits in season. Supermarkets and gift shops also carry Jamaican spices and comestibles.

Look as well for the various recipe postcards—the finished dish in living color on one side, the recipe on the other. Mail them home in place of the cliché sunset scene, or keep them for yourself—at 20¢ or so apiece, you can afford to do both.

The most famous of all Jamaican spice creations, Pick-a-Peppa sauce, is in all probability on sale right now no farther away than your own corner grocery store. Conceived in 1921 by one Jamaican gourmet named Norman Nash, acquired by another Jamaican, Kee Chow, it is distributed in 49 countries, with an especially loyal following among New Orleans restaurateurs and the California movie colony. Composed of onions, raisins, mangoes, tomatoes, tamarind, vinegar, small red Jamaican peppers, and 21 Jamaican spices, Pick-a-Peppa contains no artificial preservatives, colorings, or chemicals. Although the firm does no advertising whatsoever, word-of-mouth huzzahs for this tingle-on-the-tongue elixir are such you needn't bother hauling it home; it's available there already. On the other hand, if you feel like journeying up to the mountain factory at Shooters Hill near Mandeville, you will probably be given a free bottle (which retails in town for 75¢ or so), and perhaps even given a draft of chilled local Red Stripe Beer to accompany it.

If for some arcane reason a frosty stein of hearty Red Stripe doesn't strike your fancy, Jamaica provides a wide variety of alternative thirst quenchers. Nectars of tangerine, mango, tamarind, and soursop not only make refreshing drinks but also convert into intriguing sherbets and ice creams. While you're in the supermarkets, pick up a tin or two to try when you get home.

Jamaican ginger beer, combining the celebrated fresh local ginger with equally choice Jamaican honey, the previously mentioned wet sugar, and assorted other secret weapons, is another collector's item (see p. 44 of the above-recommended Mrs. Brandon's recipe book).

"Sweet Cup," based on the unlikely combination of grapes and custard, may be an acquired taste. But one local product towers above them all. On this there can be no question. Nowhere in the world will you find a finer, more sought-after coffee than the Blue Mountain variety.

In 1728, five years after a young French officer smuggled the first coffee shrub from Paris's Jardin des Plantes to Martinique, Jamaica's governor, Sir Nicholas Lawes, picked off some berries from the Martinique plants for his own Jamaica estate.

Although its lowlands produced a most palatable coffee, it soon became evident that at Jamaica's up-to-7,000-foot elevations, the richer soil and cooler temperatures brought out the best in the beans.

Years of government supervision and scientific cultivation have made Blue Mountain coffee a connoisseur's prize. It's the champagne of coffees, in a class with Dom Perignon bubbly and Beluga caviar. Blue Mountain sells the world over at prices up to $30 a pound—when you can find it. Affluent Japan alone buys half the annual crop for use in that country's 100,000 coffeehouses, as coffee is fast catching up with tea as a Japanese favorite. As a result, canny Japanese investors have been snapping up controlling interest in almost 90% of the best Jamaican coffee properties.

Even with an optimum 100 boxes of beans for each of the 45,000 acres under cultivation—one to two pounds per plant—Jamaica's moist, fertile uplands, jungle-lush and rich with the variety of forest life, cannot keep up with the demand.

When the six-foot bushes blossom in spring, the contrast of

berries in five different stages of development, green new ones and deep-red ripe ones accented by white blossoms, all at the same time, is a sight to behold.

Up in the Blue Mountains it takes beans almost a year to mature from flower to red berry. It is this longer incubation period, resulting from the combination of altitude, temperature, and the nature of the soil, that produces the uniquely rich bean known as Blue Mountain. The Jamaican Coffee Board, founded over 30 years ago to ensure highest standards, puts its seal on each bag to certify that the Blue Mountain contents were grown at the right altitude, dried by natural sunlight and not artificial means, and roasted and put up under government supervision. Mechanical harvesters are never used, because only the most thoroughly ripened berries are picked, requiring judgment calls on the part of pickers who, their baskets slung over their shoulders, harvest from July into fall. As for the final brew itself, the dark vigor and vitality of taste is so pervasive, you are almost sorry to swallow it. There is no bitter aftertaste, no oily coating, only exquisitely balanced, totally satisfying, intoxicatingly exotic flavor.

As of this writing, Blue Mountain coffee can be bought in a variety of on-island locations. If you're touring, you might drop in at the source, such as the Pine Grove coffee plantation halfway to the mountain crest at where you can buy 12 varieties of the local crop for $7.50 the pound. **Things Jamaican, Devon House, Sweet Jamaica, Living Wood,** and other gourmet-style emporiums mentioned (see Useful Addresses list) feature the precious beans, attractively packaged.

At the risk of horrifying the purist, we confess to acquiring Blue Mountain coffee in instant form, decaffeinated as well, and enjoying it very much indeed. The trick is to add the coffee to water when it is at a galloping boil (not the reverse), bring it to a quick second boil, then remove it from the fire instantly.

As to where to do your shopping for coffee and groceries, consult, as the saying goes, the Yellow Pages to find the market closest to you. (Like most other West Indian islands, Jamaica indeed has Yellow Pages.)

If you don't have a phone book handy, herewith a few suggestions.

In Kingston, try the **Allied Food Store** at 1 Tobago Ave. (tel. 926-4811), **Family Pride Supermarket** in Havendale Plaza (tel. 925-7925), **Food Town** at 30 Dunrobin Ave. (tel. 925-6090), or **Best Buy Supermarket** at 69 Waltham Park Rd. (tel. 923-7325).

In Montego Bay, try **Under the Rainbow** or any one of the in-and-near-town marts such as **Hometown** in Overton Plaza Shopping Centre or the cheerful little **Holiday** market opposite the Rose Hall Holiday Inn.

In Ocho Rios, visit **Family Food Supermarket** (tel. 974-2901) or the previously mentioned **Living Wood Shop** (tel. 974-2601), both in the Ocean Village Shopping Centre.

JEWELRY

India House at 51 St. James St., Montego Bay (tel. 922-2951), features Mikimoto, the inventor and Cadillac of cultured pearls, at $100 per inch. Directly across the aisle, in the same establishment, lustrous Majorca pearls sell for $1 per inch. According to the clerk who showed us both types, the difference is so immediately apparent "a galloping horseman can tell the difference."

Maybe so—if his name is Van Cleef or Arpels. To our nonprofessional eye, those luminous substitutes, made in Majorca in a painstaking and complex process involving layer upon layer of fish scales, are handsome adornments in their own right.

If you are looking for arresting silver and 18-karat gold jewelry, try among others, the following shops, grouped according to location.

In Falmouth:

Chulani Shops, Trelawny Beach Hotel (tel. 954-2151)

In Kingston:

Bijoux, 7 Dominica Drive (tel. 926-4784)
Carousel, 24 King St. (tel. 922-6802)
India House, 60 King St. (tel. 922-2951)
Swiss Stores, corner Harbour and Church Streets (downtown) (tel. 922-8050); Pegasus Hotel, New Kingston (tel. 926-3690, ext. 552); Kingston Airport (tel. 938-6023)

In Hanover:

Chulani Shops, Round Hill Hotel, eight miles from Montego Bay (tel. 952-5150)

In Montego Bay:

Bijoux, Casa Montego Hotel Arcade (tel. 952-3277)
Casa de Oro, Holiday Village Arcade, Rose Hall (tel. 953-2600)
Chulani Shops, Half Moon Club (tel. 953-2053) and Wyndham Rose Hall Beach Club
Holiday Inn Duty-Free Shop, Rose Hall Holiday Inn (tel. 953-2503)
India House, St. James Street (tel. 952-5844) and Rose Hall Holiday Inn
Swiss Stores, Casa Montego Arcade (tel. 952-3087), Half Moon Club (tel. 953-2520), and the Wyndham Rose Hall Beach Club

In Ocho Rios:

Americana Shops, Coconut Grove Shopping Centre (tel. 974-2414) and Ocean Village Shopping Centre (tel. 974-2248)

Casa de Oro, Pineapple Place (tel. 974-2577)
Chulani, Pineapple Place (tel. 974-2421)
Nancy's, Pineapple Place
Swiss Stores, Ocean Village Shopping Centre (tel. 974-2061)

Necklaces, rings, and other precious and semi-precious pieces are what is known in the trade as "blind items," meaning merchandise on which firm price comparisons are virtually impossible. As anyone who has had appraisals made knows, one "expert" can value a stone at a price up to 35% more or less than that estimated by another, equally competent expert. So it makes sense to shop primarily for what appeals to you; buy for pleasure rather than profit.

Insofar as local specialties are concerned, black coral is featured in Jamaica, as it is in several other Caribbean islands. In the Holiday Village Shopping Center, the **Blue Mountain Gems Workshop** (tel. 953-2338) features a collection by Mike O'Hara using stones found in the riverbeds of the Blue Mountains. Here again, the question of value is subjective—up to you. What you are willing to pay is what the purchase is worth. (Blue Mountain creations can also be seen at **Blue Caribe Gems**, 9 Via Mizner, Worth Avenue, Palm Beach.)

Jamaica excels in costume jewelry, with at least two lines worth at least a second look. The first combines the natural resources of the sea with the imagination of one of Jamaica's many famous local beauties: a former Miss World with the tongue-twisting name of Cindy Breakspear Tovares Finson. Wisely Ms. Breakspear Tovares Finson chose a more manageable moniker for her jewelry, calling it simply Italcraft. Italcraft has maintained an emporium at Twin Tree Plaza in Kingston, but you will also spot selections of the line in most of Jamaica's finer boutiques.

Tryall Golf and Beach Club in Hanover Parish (tel. 952-5110)

Twin Gates Plaza and **Devon House**, 26 Hope Rd.,
Kingston (tel. 929-6602)
The Bay Line, Gloucester Avenue, Montego Bay
Wyndham Rose Hall Beach Club, Montego Bay
Round Hill, Montego Bay
Americana, Harmony Hall Art Gallery, Ocho Rios
Trident Hotel, Port Antonio
Eden II Resort, St. Ann's Bay

You might even spot some Italcraft in Bloomingdale's in
New York; the first shipment reportedly sold out in two days.

Prices hover around $50 or so. Designs in belts, chokers,
and ropes are bold combinations of oversized shells, multicolored braid, and bright-colored beads. They are distinctive,
clearly not off an assembly line, and conversation-piece
additions to a smart summer wardrobe.

The other collection you might want to examine is the
brainchild of the Princess of Liechtenstein, who started the
first ceramic jewelry operation in Jamaica. Ruth Clarage took
over from the Princess, giving it her own sprightly imprimatur.
At the **Ruth Clarage** shops (see Useful Addresses list), you
will now find the bright baubles some shoppers scoop up by
the handfuls: sea-life bracelets and pins; earrings in the form
of parrots swinging on their perches, or seahorses, starfish—
motifs vary from season to season. But the theme remains
cheerful and Jamaican, prices from under $10.

Undoubtedly you will ferret our your own finds as you
wander through the native markets, the roadside stands, and
the various shopping centers. A Kingston firm has produced
some handsome pieces made from, believe it or not, coconut
shells. Every now and again someone comes up with an
interesting selection of small shell jewelry. Island women
produce some strange and occasionally wonderful things by
stringing together beads with names like Lucky Beans,
Woman's Tongue, Elephant Ear, and Job's Tears. Keep a sharp
eye out. Chances are excellent you will be rewarded.

LINENS

Tablecloths, placemats, these and other linens, like jewelry, come under the heading of "blind items," in that direct price comparisons between two pieces, identical in the United States and Jamaica, are virtually impossible.

Jamaica does hold a certain advantage over U.S. retailers in that buyers from that country have been free to shop the manufacturers in the People's Republic of China for decades, during times when it was forbidden to import goods from there into the United States. And during those years the Jamaican retailers forged enduring relationships with their suppliers. They know who are the best.

Therefore you will find some worthy pick-up items: embroidered hot-roll servers for $1.50 or so; handsome handkerchiefs and guest towels in the same range; hand-crocheted placemats, $3 and $4; a tablecloth and matching napkins for under $20. Here again the shortage of foreign exchange has limited the volume and variety of imports to a certain extent. But there are still many good buys to be had.

In addition to the imports, Jamaica itself has been developing its own skills in embroidered linen. West Indian girls grow up handy with needle and thread, but talented European instructors also have been brought into the trade schools to perfect and professionalize their inborn talents. Unfortunately, the high price Jamaicans have to pay for quality imported linen when they can get it greatly increases their overheads thereby hampering the workers' ability to capitalize on what has been tremendous improvement in their skills in recent years.

Devon House at 26 Hope Rd. in Kingston (tel. 929-6602) exhibits a cross-section of current offerings. Those featuring tropical designs such as breadfruit or banana leaves are especially striking.

Allsides Embroidery Workroom, at 22 Parkington Plaza,

Half Way Tree area, also in Kingston (tel. 926-8963), is another possible source.

In Montego Bay, scout **Things Jamaican** at 44 Fort St. (tel. 952-5605).

Try also the following shops in Kingston:

Bijoux, 7 Dominca Dr., New Kingston (tel. 926-4784)
Carousel, 24 King St. (tel. 922-6802)
K. Chandiram Ltd., 7 Dominica Dr. (tel. 926-4784)

In Montego Bay, stop by:

Bijoux, Casa Montego Hotel Arcade (tel. 952-3277)
Casa de Oro, Holiday Village Arcade, Rose Hall (tel. 953-2600)
China Craft, Holiday Village Arcade, Rose Hall (tel. 953-2404)
India House, 51 St. James St. (tel. 952-5844) and at Rose Hall Holiday Inn (tel. 952-2488)
La Belle Créole, 36 City Centre (tel. 952-3502)

In Ocho Rios, check out:

Americana Shops, Main Street (tel. 974-2911); Coconut Grove Shopping Centre (tel. 974-2414); Ocean Village Shopping Centre (tel. 974-2248)
Casa de Oro, Pineapple Place (tel. 974-2577)
Nancy's, Pineapple Place (no phone)
Things Unique, 9 Lincoln Plaza (no phone)

PERFUME AND COSMETICS

Oscar de la Renta, Chloë, Joy, Opium, Anais-Anais—the latest scents are on sale here, and on these you will save a bunch. Unlike some of the other bounty you'll be looking at, perfume is not a blind item; shop your hometown department store and compare.

Again, because of the foreign-exchange problem, you will not find huge quantities of stock. Nevertheless, merchants select what they do handle with discernment. And fragrances, as indicated earlier, whether domestic or imported, rank close to the top of the list when it comes to good buys in the Caribbean. As for home-brewed Jamaican products, these rate among the finest. At $10.50 or so for two ounces of local cologne, it's worthwhile to experiment.

Benjamins of Jamaica are known for their scent Khus-Khus, the word for a local grass called vetiver in the international perfume trade. Musky, sensual, it comes in various strengths: perfume, toilet water, eau de parfum, and cologne.

Parfums Jamaica's headliner, White Witch, is lighter, more floral in tone, as is Forget-Me-Not, named after the tiny wild flowers growing in the mountain plateaux. Other Parfums Jamaica scents you might like to try include Jackie and Jeunesse.

For men, Benjamins of Jamaica offers Cacique, with ambitious claims as to what its "warm, earthy" product can do: "It invades a women's senses and touches where nothing else can...Unmistakably male..."

Parfums Jamaica's masculine alternative makes equally seductive promises: "She'll think of you as bold, yet sensitive. Confident, yet understanding. Discover Pirate's Gold and explore the treasures of intimacy..."

What's more, to scale these heights won't cost much. The sum of $10 or so buys a good supply of either the His or Her scents. Final perfumes on sale in virtually every hotel, every luxury boutique, every shopping complex.

For more matter-of-fact males who merely want a refreshing all-purpose cologne or aftershave, **Royall Jamaica Lyme** combines sugarcane alcohol and fresh limes with various oils in secret proportions, then ages the result in vats at the Royall Jamaica Lyme factory in Bogue, Montego Bay. Find Royall Lyme just about anywhere and everywhere.

Among the assorted items being peddled on various street corners is a milky white liquid known in Jamaica as "Single Bible." Whether the magic elixir does in fact perform the anti-aging miracles attributed to it or not, the juice of this tropical plant has earned attention worldwide under the name of aloe vera.

Benjamins of Jamaica also manufacturers Khus-Khus Suntan Lotion and Suntan Oil, using pure coconut oil with sunscreen.

If you're into different kinds of soaps, 50¢ or so will buy a bath-sized (5.2 ounce) cake of pure castile toilet soap with olive oil, made in Kingston. No brand name, just look for the black-and-gold wrapper in any supermarket or minimart. There is also a dressier, top-quality Dominican coconut-oil package of two cakes for about 75¢. The brand name is Ava.

SPIRITS

"A friend and brother to one alone in the dark, a warm blanket on a chilly night, an excitement in the cheek and an inspirer of bold and brave deeds."

Thus did Sir Henry Morgan, Governor of Jamaica and a buccaneer of some repute, describe the mystique of rum. Jamaica's affinity for that special *vin du pays*, from golden dark sweet to pale light dry, dates back at least three centuries to the early days of British colonialism. And, to a degree, even before that—to the era of Spanish conquistadors. Invented in the West Indies, this extract from the cane has developed from a brash and bracing seaman's ration to the suave base for exotic tropical cocktails, punches, sours, daiquiris and "doubloons," "bamboozles" and "beady-eyed birdies," "tropical itches" and "Caribbean coolers."

Jamaica claims to have initiated its own special production process of such quality that Jamaica rum is the richest in world classifications of sugarcane liquor.

Of Jamaica's nine rum distilleries, **Appleton Rum** is the oldest and largest. It has been in operation for 150 years, harvesting nearly 220,000 tons of cane from its own 11,000-acre plantation, between December and June each year. Appleton disciples contend that only in the Black River, where Appleton Estate is located, can the ideal fermentation process occur.

First the thick, syrupy molasses is separated from the crystal sugar extracted from the crushed cane. Then special seaweed yeast induces the molasses, thinned with water into a "wash," to ferment into rum. Each gallon and a half of molasses yields a gallon of liquor. Slow distillation in old copper pots boils off the alcohol in the rum, leaving the water behind. The clear 80-proof product is then put into four-gallon casks for four to twenty years of aging.

On average, 2% of the contents of each barrel evaporates each year—except in Jamaica where 6% disappears. Whimsical workers submit that the reason three times as much rum vanishes from the Appleton establishment as elsewhere is because the angels claim a larger share; they know where the best is made, they say. Rum blends to be presented as dark get a caramel coloring; white rums pass through activated charcoal. Different vintages of varying characters and ages are "married" to produce the proper blend.

Jamaicans use this brand of fire water for far more than drinking. They spike their stews and sauces with it, as well as desserts, the same way other cultures employ wine. A spoonful in salad dressing, barbecue sauce, or over a fruit cup, keenly sharpens the flavor.

Pork takes especially well to a rum flame just before serving, and chicken marinated in a rum-ginger-soy sauce reflects the delicate exotic rum taste. Leila Brandon's *Merry-Go-Round of Recipes* (see entry under "Food") provides a whole gamut of rum-based formulas: babas, soufflés, parfaits, trifles, etc.

Rumona, a special Jamaican coffee-rum liqueur, brings rich afterglow to ice cream, cake frosting, puddings. Combined with whipped cream and "wet sugar," it easily rivals (some say even surpasses) the delights of traditional Irish coffee. Tia Maria, also a coffee liqueur, is even better known abroad than Rumona.

Up in Mandeville, in the hill districts, one C. P. Jackson back in 1929 produced a seedless, heavily juiced fruit known as **Ortanique**, a name compounded of orange, tangerine, and the word "unique." An excellent cordial is made from this fruit. Coconut milk is the basis for another fine liqueur, as is ginger. Count on spending $10 or so for a bottle of any of these.

One of the most interesting lines of cordials, Old Jamaica Liqueurs, winner of several international gold medals, is the brainchild of a transplanted Scottish intellectual named Ian Sangster. The author of two books—*Jamaica: A Holiday Guide*, and *Sugar and Rum of Jamaica*—Dr. Sangster came to the island to become director of the Sugar Industry Research Institute, a position he still holds.

Dr. Sangster's award-winning libation is produced in a hamlet called "World's End," which is located on a steep side of the Blue Mountains. Sangster's Old World Jamaica Wild Orange is presented in a facsimile of the 17th-century ceramic rum flagon. Wade of Great Britain fabricates today's version. Each decanter is numbered as part of a limited series. The original is on display in the Institute Of Jamaica.

You can pick up a bottle of run-of-the-mill Jamaican rum in any supermarket or tavern, but not for pennies. Count on paying at least $5 per fifth. For more sophisticated purchases, either domestic liqueurs or your favorite brand of imported spirits, check the following emporiums.

In Kingston:

Bijoux, 7 Dominica Dr. (tel. 926-4784)
Carousel, 24 King St. (tel. 922-6802)
Little Liquor Store, Kingston Airport (tel. 924-8037)

In Montego Bay:

Bijoux, Casa Montego Hotel Arcade (tel. 952-3277)
India House, 51 St. James St. and the Rose Hall Holiday Inn (tel. 952-2485)
Montego Duty-Free Liquor Store, Montego Bay International Airport
Ship'n Shore, the little sundry shop adjoining the Montego Bay straw market, also carries some native cordials
Sweet Jamaica Ltd., Gloucester Avenue

Best buys are, of course, at the well-stocked airport duty-free counters.

WATCHES

As is clear from the proliferation of full-page watch ads in our own country, quality watches are among the hottest merchandise in the current market. One Fifth Avenue jeweler reports sales 25% ahead of last year. Cartier increased their advertising budget 20% to keep up with the demand, and the editor of *Jewelers' Circular Keystone*, a trade publication, tells the *New York Times* he has never seen anything like it.

Among the many reasons given for the watch boom is that prices of 18-karat gold timepieces have not really kept pace with the soaring metal costs. Regardless of whys, watches are in fact an important acquisition that many investors are making these days.

Whatever your preferred brand, chances are you will not only find it in Jamaica, but at a considerably reduced price— some merchants say 40% under U.S. prices. As suggested elsewhere in these pages you could do worse in a purchase of this magnitude than to phone home and check the cost there first before committing yourself. As to where to find what, here are a few likely sources:

In Kingston:

Bijoux, 7 Dominica Drive (tel. 926-4784): Bulova, Citizen, Raymond Weil

Carousel, 24 King St. (tel. 922-6802): Bulova, Citizen, Raymond Weil

K. Chandiram, Ltd., 7 Dominica Dr. (tel. 926-4784): Bulova, Citizen, Raymond Weil

Swiss Stores, corner Harbour and Church Streets (downtown) (tel. 922-8050); The Mall, Constant Spring Road; Pegasus Hotel, New Kingston (tel. 926-3690, ext. 552); Kingston Airport (tel. 938-6023): Omega, Patek-Philippe, Rado, Rolex, Tissot

In Hanover, try:

Chulani Shops, Round Hill Hotel (tel. 952-5150)

In Montego Bay:

Bijoux, Casa Montego Hotel Arcade (tel. 952-3277): Bulova, Citizen, Raymond Weil

Casa de Oro, Holiday Village Arcade, Rose Hall (tel. 953-2600): Borel, Cartier, Corum, Seiko

Chulani Shops, 44 City Centre (tel. 952-2158); 10 North Lane (tel. 952-5170); Half Moon Club (tel. 953-2053): Ebel, Girard-Pérregaux, Porsche, Seiko

Hemisphere, Wyndham Rose Hall Beach Club (tel. 953-2715): Ebel, Girard-Pérregaux, Seiko

Holiday Inn Duty-Free Shop, Rose Hall Holiday Inn (tel. 953-2503): Ebel, Girard-Pérregaux, Seiko

India House, 51 St. James St. (tel. 952-5844), and at the Rose Hall Holiday Inn: Bulova, Citizen, Raymond Weil

La Belle Créole, 36 City Centre (tel. 952-3502): Borel, Cartier, Corum, Seiko

Swiss Stores, Ltd., Half Moon Club (tel. 953-2520) and Casa Montego Arcade (tel. 952-3087): Omega, Patek-Philippe, Rado, Rolex, Tissot

In Ocho Rios:

Americana Shops, Main Street (tel. 974-2911); Coconut Grove Shopping Centre (tel. 974-2414); Pineapple Place (tel. 974-2351); and Ocean Village Shopping Centre (tel. 974-2248): Seiko

Casa de Oro, Pineapple Place (tel. 974-2577): Borel, Cartier, Concorde, Corum, Movado, Seiko

Hemisphere Shops, Americana Hotel (tel. 974-2151) and Sheraton Hotel (tel. 974-2201): Ebel, Girard-Pérregaux, Seiko

SPECIAL CATEGORY

For the inveterate smoker who cannot or will not kick the habit, Jamaican cigars, recognized as among the world's best, are an inexpensive and appreciated gift. When faced with political turmoil, makers of the world-renowned H. Upmanns and Montecristos left Cuba, taking their traditions and expertise to the Canary Islands and Jamaica. These destinations already had a tradition of cigar-making, established a century earlier by the celebrated Machados dynasty.

From the rolling fields of tobacco plants around Colbeck Castle to the connoisseur's cheroot, each step in production is a ritual. A hollow bamboo rod inside each pile of leaves contains a thermometer, which experts watch with an eagle eye as the fermentation begins to determine proper aging.

Each cigar is handmade, with an inner and outer wrapper, deftly packed to ensure even burning. The smooth, aromatic, and full-flavored end product sends the most demanding puffer into transports of joy. Count Bill Cosby among the celebrated smokers who are seldom without their Jamaican stogie. "Royal Jamaica" is one of the accepted standard bearers, but many other brands are good, including those sold loose in the supermarkets for a quarter or so apiece.

As a perhaps more handsome alternative, pick up a dozen or so of the island's own stately, durable anthurium blossoms—$6 or so for 12 at the **Ocean Village Florist**, Ocean Village Shopping Center, a little higher in Montego Bay. The last time we checked with the U.S. Customs Service as to importing these, they replied, in the island vernacular, "No problem."

Finally, one note of caution: plan your Jamaica shopping excursion carefully and well in advance. The stores are widely-scattered, are not, by and large big on outer trappings, and there are an awful lot of them. So unless you plot your course wisely and with foresight, you risk running out of time (and or steam) before you even get to some of the very best shops.

And that, you had better believe, would be one everlasting, flamin' shame!

Useful Addresses

Allied Food Store: 1 Tobago Ave., Kingston 5 (tel. 926-4811), and additional locations.

Allsides Embroidery Workroom: 22 Parkington Plaza, Kingston 10 (tel. 926-8963).

Americana Shops: Main Street, Ocho Rios (tel. 974-2911); Coconut Grove Shopping Centre, Ocho Rios (tel. 974-2424); Ocean Village Shopping Centre, Ocho Rios (tel. 947-2248); Pineapple Place, Ocho Rios (tel. 974-2351).

The Bay Line: Gloucester Avenue, Montego Bay.

Best Buy Supermarkets: 69 Waltham Park Rd., Kingston 10 (tel. 923-7325), and additional locations.

Bijoux: 7 Dominica Dr., Kingston (tel. 926-4784); Casa Montego Hotel Arcade, Montego Bay (tel. 952-3277).

Blue Mountain Gems Workshop: Holiday Village Shopping Center, Montego Bay (tel. 953-2338).

Bolivar Gallery: 10 Grove Rd., Kingston.

Carousel: 24 King St., Kingston (tel. 922-6802).

Casa de Oro: Holiday Village Shopping Center, Rose Hall, Montego Bay (tel. 953-2600); Pineapple Place Shopping Centre, Ocho Rios (tel. 974-2577).

China Craft: Holiday Village Shopping Center, Rose Hall, Montego Bay (tel. 953-2404).

Chulani Shops: 44 City Centre, Montego Bay (tel. 952-2158); Half Moon Club, Montego Bay (tel. 953-2053); Pineapple Place Shopping Centre, Ocho Rios (tel. 974-2421); Montego Bay Airport (tel. 952-2377); and other branches throughout the country.

Devon House: 26 Hope Rd., Kingston (tel. 929-6602).

Elizabeth Jean: Beachview Arcade, Montego Bay.

Family Food Supermarket: Ocean Village Shopping Centre, Ocho Rios (tel. 974-2901).

Frame Gallery: Kingston.

Frances Keane: 125 Hagley Park Rd., Kingston (tel. 923-7350).

Harmony Hall: 4 miles east of Ocho Rios on the road to Oracabessa (tel. 974-4222).

Hemisphere Shops: Wyndham Rose Hall Beach Club, Montego Bay (tel. 953-2715); Montego Bay Airport (tel. 952-1747); Wyndham New Kingston Hotel, 85 Knutsford Blvd., Kingston (tel. 926-5430).

Holiday Inn Duty-Free Shop: Rose Hall Holiday Inn, Montego Bay (tel. 953-2503).

Hometown: Overton Plaza Shopping Centre, Montego Bay.

Huie, Albert: Studio, 107 Constant Spring Rd., Kingston.

India House: 60 King St., Kingston (tel. 922-2951); 51 St. James St., Montego Bay (tel. 952-5844); Rose Hall Holiday Inn, Montego Bay (tel. 952-2485).

Italcraft: Twin Tree Plaza, Kingston.

K. Chandiram Ltd.: 51 St. James St., Montego Bay (tel. 952-2630); Rose Hall Holiday Inn, Montego Bay (tel. 953-2706); 7 Dominica Drive, Kingston (tel. 926-4784); Jamaica Pegasus Hotel, 81 Knutsford Blvd., New Kingston (tel. 926-3690).

La Belle Créole: 36 City Centre, Montego Bay (tel. 952-3502).

Little Liquor Store: Kingston Airport (tel. 924-8037).

Living Wood Shop: Ocean Village Shopping Centre, Ocho Rios (tel. 974-2601).

Melanie: Sunshine Plaza, Kingston.

Montego Duty-Free Liquor: Montego Bay Airport.

Mutual Life Gallery: Kingston.

Nancy's: Pineapple Place, Ocho Rios.

National Gallery: Roy West Building, Kingston.

Sosa, Norma: 2a Suthermere Rd., Kingston (tel. 926-6262).

Ocean Village Florist: Ocean Village Shopping Centre, Ocho Rios.

Patrice Wymore's boutique: Trident Villas and Hotel, 2½ miles east of Frenchman's Cove.

Port Antonio Art Gallery: Near Trident Hotel, 2½ miles east on the coast road toward Frenchman's Cove.

Royall Jamaica Lyme: Bogue, Montego Bay.

Ruth Clarage: Pineapple Place Shopping Centre, Ocho Rios (tel. 974-2658); Ocean Village Shopping Centre, Ocho Rios (tel. 974-2874); Casa Montego Arcade, Montego Bay (tel. 952-2282); Montego Bay Freeport Shopping Centre (tel. 952-3278); Half Moon Club (tel. 953-2211); Holiday Village Shopping Centre, Montego Bay (tel. 953-2579); Wyndham New Kingston Hotel, 85 Knutsford Blvd., Kingston.

Sasha: Tryall Golf and Beach Club, Hanover Parish, Montego Bay (tel. 952-5110).

Ship'n Shore: at Montego Bay straw market.

Special Things: 29 King St., Kingston (tel. 922-5873).

Sweet Jamaica: Gloucester Avenue, opposite Casa Blanca, Montego Bay.

Swiss Stores: Pegasus Hotel, New Kingston (tel. 926-3690, ext. 552); Kingston Airport (tel. 938-6023); The Mall, Constant Spring Road, Kingston; Corner Harbour and Church Streets, Kingston (tel. 922-8050); Half Moon Club, Montego Bay (tel. 953-2520); Casa Montego Arcade, Montego Bay (tel. 952-3087); Ocean Village Shopping Centre, Ocho Rios (tel. 974-2061).

Things Jamaican: Montego Bay Airport (tel. 952-1936); Devon House, 26 Hope Rd., Kingston (tel. 929-6602); 44 Fort St., Montego Bay (tel. 952-5605); Kingston Airport (tel. 924-8556).

Things Unique: 9 Lincoln Plaza, Ocho Rios.

Under the Rainbow: Ocean Village Shopping Centre, Ocho Rios (tel. 974-5158); branch also in Montego Bay.

Upstairs Bookshop and Downstairs Gallery: Harbour Street, Kingston.

Walker, Ky Ann: Montego Bay—call for appointment (tel. 952-2065).

West Indian Gallery of Art: Church Street, Montego Bay.

MARTINIQUE

MARTINIQUE
AT A GLANCE

GOVERNMENT TOURIST OFFICE: Martinique Tourist Office (Office Départemental du Tourisme), Boulevard Alfassa, along the waterfront of Fort-de-France, Martinique (tel. 71-79-60).

CURRENCY: The French franc. How many equal one U.S. dollar depends on the rate of exchange at the time you visit. On average, you can figure, very roughly, at six and one half to one. Bear in mind that paying for your purchases with traveler's checks will net you a discount—how much depends upon the rate the individual shop uses in calculating the exchange.

OFFICIAL HOLIDAYS: New Year's Day, Easter Sunday, Easter Monday, Labor Day (May 1), Ascension Thursday, Whit Sunday, Whit Monday, Bastille Day (July 14), Schoelcher Day (July 21), Assumption Day (August 15), All Saints' Day (November 1), Armistice Day 1918 (November 11), Christmas Day.

STORE HOURS: About 9 a.m. to 12:30 p.m. and 2:30 p.m. to 6 p.m.—more or less—Monday through Friday. Saturday is a half day, open mornings only.

LOCATIONS: For the addresses and telephone numbers of the shops, consult the alphabetical list at the end of this chapter.

Make no mistake about it, Martinique is French to its fingertips. An integral, official part of a European nation, it enjoys a status equivalent to full statehood in the U.S.

Napoleon's Josephine was a Martiniquaise. Cole Porter found the beguine here and immortalized it in his own composition. All in all, Martinique—the second-largest island (Guadeloupe is number one) between Puerto Rico and Trinidad is quite a charmer.

Fort-de-France, the chief metropolis and economic center of Martinique, rises above the harbor like a pastel layer cake. An amphitheater of hills majestically backdrops the port, which is located in the middle of the island on the Caribbean coast. Over 100,000 of the island's 350,000 inhabitants make this city their home.

The town square, a mini-park known as La Savane, constitutes Fort-de-France's social center. Small boys play their after school football on this lawn; vendors hawk iced cane juice and sticks of sugarcane; lissome local belles stroll gracefully along the walks in the cool of the evening. An elaborate white marble statue of Empress Joséphine pointing regally in the direction of her girlhood home across the bay dominates the square of the town. Napoleon III presented the statue of his grandmother to Martinique in her honor.

French and Créole—and not much else—is spoken here. English is far from the universal language! More and more desk personnel, cab drivers, and shop clerks are studying English. But to be on the safe side, you had better carry along that French phrase book and brush up on your sign language.

The Créole vocabulary and pronunciation can be traced back to the days of Louis XIII, with cadences softened and streamlined by succeeding waves of Africans. There is no subjunctive; no passive verbs exist; the infinitive serves most

271

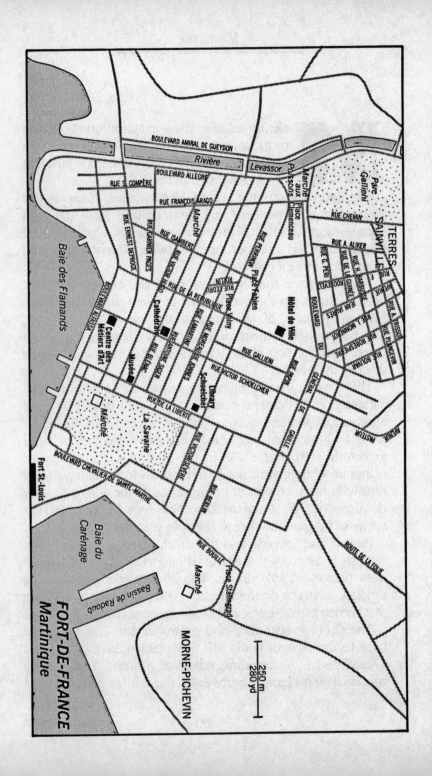

FORT-DE-FRANCE
Martinique

Baie des Flamands

Baie du Carénage

Bassin de Radoub

Fort St-Louis

BOULEVARD AMIRAL DE GUEYDON

Rivière Levassor

BOULEVARD ALLÈGRE

RUE S. COMPÈRE

RUE FRANÇOIS ARAGO

Marché

RUE GARNIER PAGÈS

RUE ERNEST DÉPROGE

RUE ISAMBERT

RUE PERRINON

Place Fabien

RUE VICTOR HUGO

RUE DE LA RÉPUBLIQUE

RUE REDOUTE DU MATOUBA

Place Volny

BOULEVARD ALFASSA

Centre des Métiers d'Art

Cathédrale

Musée

RUE BLÉNAC

RUE ANTOINE SIGER

RUE LAMARTINE

RUE MOREAU DE JONNES

Library Schoelcher

RUE DE LA LIBERTÉ

Marché

La Savane

BOULEVARD CHEVALIER DE SAINTE-MARTHE

RUE VICTOR SÉVÈRE

RUE BERLIN

RUE BOUILLÉ

Place Stalingrad

Marché

MORNE-PICHEVIN

Hôtel de Ville

RUE GALLIENI

RUE VICTOR SCHOELCHER

RUE PERRIN

BOULEVARD DU GÉNÉRAL DE GAULLE

Marché aux Poissons

Place Clemenceau

Parc Gallieni

RUE CHEMIN

TERRES SAINVILLE

RUE A. ALIKER

RUE G. PÉRI

RUE H. BARBUSE

RUE DE LA GUINÉE

RUE J. MONNOT

RUE ROBESPIÈRE

AVENUE JEAN JAURÈS

AVENUE ROOSEVELT

RUE A. TRISSOT

RUE PLANGEVIN

RUE BOLIVAR

AVENUE PASTEUR

ROUTE DE LA FOLIE

250 m
280 yd

purposes. Oddly enough the traditional Créole hardly ever employs the intimate *tu* and *toi* form; *ou* is "you," *zott* is "you all." Genders are pretty well eliminated also; islanders have been known to indicate sex by referring to mother cow or father cow. Just about every Martiniquais you meet nowadays will speak orthodox French as well. But if you should hear dialogues incomprehensible to you, take heart. It's not your command of the language that's slipping—they're speaking Créole.

Merchandise prices fluctuate widely, depending on the rate of exchange and specific comparisons are too volatile to quote in depth here. Suffice it to say, canny shoppers who have worked both sides of the Atlantic report that not only do the Fort-de-France tariffs compare favorably with those of Paris, sometimes they run even lower. But for your own benefit, verify and compare the charges yourself with the information you brought along, or, failing that, via a last-minute phone check.

ARTS AND CRAFTS

For a generation the mayor of Fort-de-France was a surrealist poet—Aimé Cesaire. Christopher Columbus declared Martinique to be "the best, richest, the sweetest, the evenest, the most charming country in the world." This in 1502, by which time the Admiral of the Ocean Seas had seen enough islands to know a winner when he saw one. Pissarro and Gauguin both lingered to paint in Martinique (unfortunately, virtually all the pictures Gauguin did were destroyed in the eruption of St. Pierre).

Other artists of varying abilities, major and minor, have attempted to capture the bewildering beauty of the island not only on canvas, but in a variety of mediums. Island talents such as Joseph René-Corail, Jean-Joseph Dumas, and the painter Alexandre Bertrand, studied in Paris, Nice and Vallauris, then returned to Martinique to revitalize and preserve their native forms of creative expression. Through them, and the disciples they inspired, the workshops and cooperatives they created, there occurred an important rebirth of local crafts. The rekindling of artistic enthusiasm is expressed in the Centre Des Métiers D'Art of Fort-de-France (in English it is called the Caribbean Art Center), located on the bayfront boulevard facing the government Tourist Office. (The Center also has a branch at Sainte-Anne's.)

The founders of the Center were committed to preserving the originality and authenticity of the craftsmen's sources of inspiration and at the same time developing new means of expression, all derived from local folklore or everyday existence. The result is a true theme of genuine, specifically Antillean creativity, one that does not play down its African origins but on the contrary emphasizes the distinctive ethnic and cultural mix that is Martinique.

One of its most distinctive artforms is the patchwork tapestry wherein island scenes, characters, and slices of island life are depicted through skillful combinations of fabric colors and textures designed as wall hangings. Some of them are of museum calibre. The cutting of the cane, a cock fight, a fishing scene—whatever strikes the stitcher's fancy provides the subject matter.

In some cases the actual composition may be sketched by a name artist—René-Corail was perhaps the most famous one to create them—and then executed by young workers at a cooperative. The tapestries are considered *objets d'art* and are priced accordingly. Although you can acquire one for considerably less than you would have to pay for a handmade Appalachian quilt, the wall hangings still do not come cheap: count on spending at least $50 minimum for a good one.

Other interesting creations bearing the René-Corail imprint are the figures made of supple wire covered with felt, then costumed and positioned to constitute a faithful re-creation of contemporary life. René-Corail also has done ceramics.

The Center's assortment of dolls is extensive, from one actually known as a barbie (Bébé Barbie) to the earth mother, Gran' Berthe. They wear the traditional Madras costume with neckerchief, and some have hand embroidered skirts.

Local sculptors fashion works from mahogany and other tropical woods and create distinctive carvings and flowerpots from the roots of tree ferns. Occasionally on exhibit at the Art Center are rustic tables and footstools made of wood without removing the bark, with legs either of such wood or of wrought iron.

The Art Center features pottery; the Martinique equivalent of a Hawaiian muumuu known here as the "boubou"; and the customary collection of seed necklaces, and objects made from bamboo, tortoise shell, and coconut. Remember that tortoise-shell objects are frowned upon by the U.S. Customs. Don't scoff, incidentally, if you find carved calabash gourds made into pocketbooks. We have a clipping from a U.S. catalog advertising a particularly handsome one of these for $80!

On a somewhat loftier plane, you will note an extensive collection of gold jewelry at the Art Center. Some pieces have won awards in Paris. But especially, they occupy a unique place in the hearts and minds of the Martiniquais—not only because of their decorative aspect but also due to the security, both financial and emotional, the various pieces represent. In earlier days, this jewelry was part of the family patrimony, an anchor to windward for when times were hard.

There were "grains of gold" necklaces, *colliers forcat* ("prisoner's necklaces"), hornet's nests, caterpillars, and other fancifully named styles. The most popular, *collier chou* ("darling's necklace"), is inspired by the French phase, *mon petit chou,* "my little cabbage," or sweetheart.

Unless you happen to hit the Art Center the day after six cruise ships have cleaned out stock, no single shop really offers the variety and quality to be found under that one roof. Merchandise changes, obviously, from month to month and depending on the whim of the artist. *Tip:* You'll find clean, modern restrooms on the ground floor here and the friendly staff seems more than happy to have you use the facilities.

Insofar as straw and/or wickerwork is concerned, Martinique claims to have preserved, in the district of Morne-des-Esses among just a few families, the original Carib Indian technique of basket-weaving, of treating and weaving the local leaves. The three distinctive shadings are achieved the old-fashioned original way: beige by boiling, light brown by exposure to the sun, and black by dipping in a special mud. When in Morne-des-Esses look for an emporium known as **La Paille Caraïbe**.

Open markets and small souvenir shops here and there also sell crafts. We've heard of, but not visited, **Le Carbet** at 55 Rue Blenac (tel. 71-26-46) and **Les Pieces** in the Cluny Shopping Center. Stock is said to include paintings, straw work, fabrics, books, and records of the area. Also **Arts Caraïbes** at 38 Rue Ernest Deproge (tel. 60-40-08) and **Caraïbe Artisanat** at the Bellevue Shopping Center (tel. 60-33-83).

For strictly fine arts—paintings, watercolors, etc.—check with the hotels as to dates and times of scheduled exhibits. You may also find a small gallery or two tucked away here and there.

CAMERAS

Cameras are not, insofar as we can determine, one of Martinique's better buys.

CHINA, CRYSTAL, AND HOME FURNISHINGS

For discerning, quality merchandise, **Roger Albert**, main branch at 7 Rue Victor Hugo (tel. 71-71-71), has the finest selection, the fairest prices, and among the best track record in the Caribbean: forty years of uninterrupted service. We've been shopping and recommending this firm for almost two decades to travel guide readers and several million newspaper subscribers. During this time we have had but a single complaint. It was justified—and rectified instantly. One lone criticism has appeared in print, possibly the result, satisfied patrons speculate, of not enough homage, concrete or otherwise, paid to the writer.

There has to be a reason why Patek Philippe, Baccarat, Chanel, Cartier—the makers of the finest merchandise—choose to place their good name and reputation in Martinique in the hands of Roger Albert. It's because they trust him.

As a result of this prestige, Roger Albert shops can be much too busy at times, as hectic as the floor of the most frantic Commodities market. We understand Monsieur Albert is working on streamlining the sales process. Hopefully, improvement is on the way. Meanwhile, if the crowds become too overwhelming, leave the main branch store and head for the satellite store in either Dillon (tel. 70-63-63) or Cluny (tel. 73-23-23) suburban shopping centers. Both Dillon and Cluny offer a number of other browsing opportunities as well.

Whatever location you choose, the Roger Albert stock is outstanding. Cristalleries Lalique, whose creations grace the illuminated foundations at Rond Point on the Champs-Elysées and the mansions of the President of France and other international personages, are available here—at mind-boggling savings. One delighted moneybags reports paying $333 for a Lalique cat he fancied at Roger Albert, only to find it featured back home at $1,000.

Other Roger Albert bargains include the Lalique swan at $1,409 versus $2,125 in the States; a vase selling for $1,350 up north priced $897 here; a Baccarat Massena glass at $46.90 versus $70 on the mainland; the Cartier gold and stainless steel Santos watch. $1,100 as opposed to $1,550; the Santos lighter, $145 contrasted to $210 in the U.S. (the

U.S. prices, incidentally, do not include the various taxes).

Besides investigating the big names, note some perhaps lesser-known finds. Have a look, for example, at Bayel crystal. Founded by a Venetian master-glassworker over three centuries ago, this lustrous, limpid line, known also as Cristalleries de Champagne, could rank as one of your happiest shopping discoveries. Quality is first-rate (lead content exceeds 27%). Bayel is one of a handful of firms selected to set the tables of the Paris Ritz. Samples have even appeared at the White House and U.S. Embassies abroad—and the *prices are very low.* For example, the Bourgeoir Sicile candlestick priced at $11 or the Munich fumé ashtray, $21.40.

Cost differentials on such items as wine glasses or salad plates may not be quite as spectacular as the crystal feline. But study your stateside price list and compare—or when contemplating a large purchase, phone home. On the whole, we have found Martinique prices on French imports among the lowest in the Caribbean.

Cadet Daniel, at 72 Rue Antoine Siger (tel. 71-41-48), traces its origins as a commercial house in Fort-de-France all the way back to 1840, specializing in top-of-the-line tableware along with other goods. Among the names you will recognize: Limoges, Sèvres, Daum, Baccarat, and Christofle.

Au Printemps, at 10 Rue Schoelcher (tel. 71-38-66), probably should be put on your itinerary. It is one of the few department stores in the Caribbean worth shopping, and it includes china and crystal in its inventory.

If your decor features antique maps or vintage bibelots of one sort or another, browse **La Malle des Indes** located in the Cluny Shopping Center in the Fort-de-France suburb of Schoelcher (tel. 71-39-85).

Ceramics are produced locally on Trois-Ilets by the **Poterie des Trois Ilets** (tel. 76-03-44).

Beaufrand, long a fixture in purveying quality furnishings for home and table, has gone out of business.

FASHIONS

Imported neckties, Hermès scarves, fancy handbags, dainty French lingerie—these are among the many fashion accessories at **Roger Albert**. (Lacoste shirts, the Parisian ones, on hand here also.)

Shoes, if European lasts fit your foot, can be a good buy in Martinique. Bally, Charles Jourdan, Cardin—you'll find a good selection of these and other name brands at such establishments as **Maison G. Celma** at 47 Rue Lamartine and 23 Rue Blenac (tel. 70-18-81), and **Siniamin,** 7 Rue Antoine Siger (tel. 71-53-20).

Chaussures Reinette, at 80 Rue Antoine Siger (tel. 70-24-91), has a satisfied local clientele.

In the strictly-for-fun, fantasy price range, **K Dis** (formerly **Prisunic**), at 99 Place Fenelon (tel. 70-11-75), 13 Boulevard du Général de Gaulle (tel. 73-14-65), and at the Cluny Shopping Center (tel. 70-03-81), offers all sorts of possibilities. One of our more uninhibited flights of fancy led to the acquisition of a lipstick-red patent-leather "cartable" (schoolchild's bookbag), firmly reinforced on a fixed frame, with lots of pockets and zippered compartments—an ideal carryall/briefcase/totebag which cost $3.50 fifteen years ago and is still very much in use.

Mammouth, in the Cluny Shopping Center, and **Monoprix**, in the Dillon Shopping Center (tel. 60-31-31), handle similar miscellaneous, low-cost items.

As for clothes, Caribbean designers in general do have a special knack in creating fashion for their own climate and lifestyle, and these we collect with enthusiasm in most islands. However, so far we have not made the right connection in Martinique.

Obviously, the many boutiques large and small doing business not only in Fort-de-France but tucked here and there throughout the islands must have a lot going for them, else they would not prosper. Hopefully you will locate in one or more of them just what you are looking for. We have not.

To assist you in your efforts, therefore, we asked the knowledgeable, government-selected liaison between Martinique tourism and U.S. reporters, guide writers, and other media to provide us with the names of those shops which seem to appeal to the most tourists, so that we might pass them on to you. Herewith his comments:

"For *haute couture* and resortwear, there are dozens of boutiques dotting downtown Fort-de-France. These places, which look as though they've been transplanted from the Riviera or the side streets of Paris, frequently go unnoticed by tourists since they *are* tiny. Their size is a plus, however. Each can be checked out in a matter of minutes, and on-the-spot alterations at many are free.

"Some boutiques, like **Santalia** on Rue Lamartine, are *prêt-a-porter* (ready-to-wear) shops that have been in business for many years and carry fashionable sportswear from Paris and Côte d'Azur designers. Other spots, like **Mounia**, at 32 Rue Perrinon (tel. 73-77-27), are somewhat newer but also carry top names: Claude Montana, Angelo Tarlazzi, Dorothee Bis, and Yves Saint Laurent. YSL is an especially appropriate label at Mounia since the boutique is owned by and named for a Martiniquaise who made her mark as a top Saint Laurent model.

"Young Martinique designers have also been presenting their own collections this year. They usually show every Thursday in their respective shops in Fort-de-France. The most prominent *haute couture* name is Yves Gerard; for ready-to-wear, the names are Daniel Rodap, Monique Louisor, and Gilbert Basson, whose label is 'Gigi.'

"In fashion-conscious Martinique, a new crop of boutiques seems to blossom each season, although some like **Gisele** at 14 Rue Victor Hugo (tel. 71-38-67) and **Mahog-Annie** at 6 Rue Blenac (tel. 73-88-35) have been around awhile. A word of caution, however. Even though the owners are often as fetching as the names they give their shops, they aren't always English-speaking, so if your French is rusty, bring along a phrase book or pocket dictionary. *The American Express International Traveler's Pocket French Dictionary and Phrase Book* fits the bill.

"The above places are mostly for women, but shops like **Prune**, at 72 and 109 Rue Lamartine (tel. 60-34-87 and 73-41-87), also carry fashions for men. Exclusively for masculine clients are **Borsalino** at 54 Rue Victor Hugo, **Via Veneto** at 35 Rue Victor Hugo, and **Aventure** at 17 Rue Victor Hugo (tel. 72-55-32 and 73-37-73), **Valentino** on Rue Perrinon, and **Jack** at 28 Rue Moreau de Jonnes (tel. 73-85-25 and 60-61-39)."

Madras, made into headscarves and kerchiefs, skirts, and shirts, etc., is virtually the official fabric of the French West Indies. Buy it 'most anywhere. But bear in mind that (1) it is made in India, not in Martinique, and (2) the genuine article bleeds—i.e., fades. It's supposed to, granted. And remember that it must always be washed separately.

FOOD AND DRINK

Martinique food, *ça va sans dire,* is just plain terrific! Whether you opt for the suavest of haute cuisine à la française, or choose the gutsy, sensual Créole fare, Martinique has matchless epicurean experiences to offer you.

How much of all this can you take home? On gourmet items from *la metropole,* the sky's the limit. Soufflés in a pouch, tiny jugged hare in a tin, a cassoulet to kill for (also canned), containers of huge Parisian mushrooms, fruits in cognac, woodsy black truffles, succulent snails—every conceivable delicacy, and a lot of even more delicious everyday sustenance is on sale at prices not much higher than your corner supermarket charges for canned corned beef hash or chicken fricassee.

You can pick up some comestibles at the **French Farm** at

Lamentin Airport (tel. 70-12-34). However, time permitting the **K Dis**, **Mammouth**, and **Monoprix** markets mentioned above are your best source.

Allow yourself plenty of time to wander through aisle after aisle filled with one temptation after another. And be sure to consult your pocket dictionary where labels do not clearly identify contents. To anyone who complains about not being able to read these, locals who travel but don't read English are quick to relate their own problems, such as lugging home from the U.S. a large can enticingly adorned with a platter of fried chicken, but which, when opened, turned out to be Crisco. The American packager, they contend, should have made it clear that the chicken was the *RESULT*, not the *CONTENTS*.

While in the markets, do not fail to meander into the department displaying what we in our country usually refer to as kitchen gadgets: all sorts of very portable choppers, graters, shredders, salad tossers. The kind of culinary collectors' items that cost the earth in our own gourmet departments back home, go for very little here. Sturdy, good-looking, bone-handled serrated table knives, casseroles, knife rests—there's a wide range of miscellany.

Obtaining Créole gourmetry, however, can present a problem. If anyone is canning sea urchin soup, stuffed crab backs, or other local delicacies, we have not found such specialties packaged for sale yet. In the hamlet of Bezaudin, not far from Sainte-Marie, one Madame Nogard puts up preserves and also purveys home-grown spices in a little market known as **Ella** (tel. 75-30-75). Madame Laurent de Meillac, at **Habitation Durocher** (not pronounced as in the baseball celebrity), processes the livers from her flock of 1,500 ducks into highly prized confections selling from $6 for a small quantity, to $50 for the half-pound foie gras terrine made with armagnac that is presented in a Poterie de Trois-Ilets ceramic container.

But can you get these through U.S. Customs? The last time we tried to bring in some tinned foie gras the inspectress made such a fuss muttering about meat products, etc., that we vowed never to try it again. And while on the subject of pitfalls, beware of vendors offering vanilla beans on street corners; those beans could well be "previously used"—recycled!

COFFEE

For the second most valuable commodity traded in the world today (oil rates number one), popular as a bracer, social stimulant, and general all-around picker-upper, we have Martinique to thank. Therefore, some background may be in order.

The Arabs, who discovered coffee, guarded the secret weapon jealously for a thousand years. But once the word spread to Westerners, so did the desire for a source of supply. The first coffee tree relocated from Arabia to the Netherlands provided cuttings for what became the great coffee plantations of the Dutch East Indies.

One of the original sample trees sent to Amsterdam was presented to France's King Louis XIV. And it is from this one plant, which His Majesty received in 1714, that virtually all the coffees of the Caribbean and South and Central America descend.

Because in 1723 a young French army officer by the name of Gabriel Mathieu de Clieu, assigned to serve in Martinique, took along with him to his new post one lone coffee plant, sharing with it his slight water ration on the ocean trip over.

Once in Martinique, the horticulturally inclined soldier installed the coffee plant amidst some protective thorn bushes, and the rest—you guessed it. By the end of the 18th century, Martinique had almost twenty million healthy coffee trees. The governor of Jamaica made off with one of them, to introduce to his own country what has now become a world-famous strain. And soon other islands began to follow suit.

Unfortunately, coffee is no longer a main crop in Martinique. Coffee professionals, in fact, describe its availability as "limited." This is to be deplored, considering the high marks given by professional tasters to the "Fine Green" variety, who described it as a "long, thick bean with lots of light skin in the roast. The favorite of Colonial America. Delicate bouquet and good body."

If you find a source, please share it with us.

JEWELRY

French—therefore Martinique—law requires that only 18-karat gold be used in the manufacture of jewelry for sale. This of necessity raises the price on the one hand; on the other hand you may still save because of the lower manufacturing cost and smaller markup.

Basically, however, here as elsewhere it is a mistake to look for price savings on blind items such as jewelry. With the exception perhaps of classic chains that you may have priced in advance, a direct comparison—such as in the case of perfume, china/crystal, or watches—is impossible. Buy what you like because you like it and not for investment purposes.

Among shops you might scout to look for baubles imported from Europe as well as the bangles and beads made on the island are:

Roger Albert Shops at 7 Rue Victor Hugo (tel. 71-71-71); the Cluny Shopping Center (tel. 73-23-23); and in the Dillon Shopping Center (tel. 70-63-63)

Albert Venutolo, 13 Rue Victor Hugo (tel. 72-57-44)

L'Or et l'Argent, 32 Rue Victor Hugo (tel. 70-10-58)

Montaclair, 37 Rue Victor Hugo (tel. 71-59-16)

Cadet Daniel, 72 Rue Antoine Siger (tel. 71-41-48)

La Gerbe d'Or, 60 Rue Isambert (tel. 71-41-21)

284

Thomas de Rogatis, 24 Rue Antoine Siger (tel. 70-29-11)

And look again also, at **Centre des Métiers d'Art**, Rue Ernest Deproge (tel. 70-25-01). We've seen some handsome pieces there.

While at Roger Albert, inspect his "Articles de Paris" section. Not technically jewelry, perhaps, but certainly decorative luxury accessories: Dupont and Cartier lighters, pens and pencils, from $52 to $309.

LINENS

We have stocked up on cheerful hemstitched sheets and outsized shams at **K Dis** (all three branches) and **Mammouth**, Cluny Shopping Center, that absolutely refuse to wear out.

Au Printemps at 10 Rue Schoelcher (tel. 71-38-66) usually carries those amusing and good-quality French kitchen towels with recipes inscribed on them, as well as other towels decorated with sprightly art. As for tablecloths, napkins, or other heirloom-quality linens, however, Martiniquaises don't seem to produce much of that sort of handwork. Or if they do, we have not found a source.

PERFUME AND COSMETICS

These represent a top buy in Martinique, with French fragrances frequently priced lower than in France itself.

As indicated earlier, the extreme volatility of exchange rates results in constant price changes—sometimes as much as 25% in a single month. By and large, however, merchants claim they regularly run at least 10% under such competitors as the U.S. Virgin Islands.

With all these qualifiers very much in mind, as of presstime, herewith a few examples: one ounce of Paco Rabanne's Calandre, $129.90 with tax in New York is only $53 at Roger Albert; Chanel No. 5, $162.37 the ounce in New York, less than half that—$79—in Martinique; Yves St. Laurent's Opium, $184.02 in the U.S., $101 in Fort-de-France. Shalimar, $146.13 in the U.S. versus $80 in Martinique.

Noting, once again, that the rate of exchange could raise or lower the following quotations by 25%, perhaps even more, compare these prices with those your home boutiques are charging:

	New York Retail*	Martinique: Roger Albert Retail†
Shalimar (Guerlain)	$146	$ 80
Joy (Patou)	200	134
Calandre (Paco Rabanne)	130	53
Chanel No. 5 (Chanel)	162	79
Opium (Y. Saint-Laurent)	184	101
Van Cleef (Van Cleef)	120	108
Bal A Versailles (Jean Desprez)	150	94
L'Air du Temps (Regular) (Nina Ricci)	120	67

   *The U.S. prices quoted include sales taxes.
   †Martinique prices reflect the 20% discount for paying by traveler's checks.

On cosmetics, savings can be equally impressive.

Take, for example, the status-symbol line of Clarins, made of pure plant extracts, and not always readily available everywhere:

	New York*	Martinique: Roger Albert†
CLARINS:		
Crème Multireductrice	$21.00	$16.80
Crème de Soins	13.50	10.80
Beaume Yeux aux Plantes	8.50	6.80
Doux Nettoyant	6.00	4.80

On other products the following savings can be effected:

LANCÔME:

Progrès Intensif Rides	$25.25	$20.20
Nutribel (jar)	15.25	12.10
Bienfait du Matin (jar)	13.50	10.80

ORLANE:

B-21 Crème BioEnergic	43.75	35.00
Extrait Vital	43.75	35.00

GERMAINE MONTEIL:

Suplegen Night Crème	30.50	24.40
Acti Vita Anti Rides	32.50	26.00

   *Sales taxes included.
   †Reflects the 20% traveler's check discount.

SPIRITS

At the time of the cane harvest, some romanticists say the island of Martinique has a special scent: the fragrance wafting over the countryside is precisely that of a freshly opened bottle of good rum!

According to André Simon, dean of wine and spirit writers and founder of the International Wine and Food Society, Martinique's manufacture of rum is distinctive because only here (and in Haiti) is the liquor distilled directly from the fermented juice of the sugarcane and not by the more economical method of using molasses. The procedure is said to date all the way back to the earliest historian, a 16th-century priest named Père Labat. Because of the method of preparation, the result—according to Paris-born Simon—is a more aromatic rum, a favorite of such regulars as Ernest Hemingway.

Islanders will tell you that the best brand of rum in the world is the one you have in your glass! One school of thought holds that the reason the rums from the St. Pierre region taste so good is that the water with which they are made is filtered through the rich, mineral-laden soil around the slopes of the volcano.

"Petit punch," the national drink, bears no resemblance to a martini in the making, yet according to certain devotees it somehow manages to create the soul-soothing, nothing-quite-like-it-effect martini drinkers enjoy. Every connoisseur swears that his or her particular method is the only proper way to make an authentic punch. Herewith our effort at consensus:

To one part cane sugar syrup (preboil a little more sugar than water together) add five parts white rum, two ice cubes, and a dash of West Indian—repeat, West Indian—green lime. Squeeze some of the juice into the glass, then drop the rest of the tiny fruit into the drink. Purists will wax apopleptic—according to them lime RUINS vintage rum! Nevertheless, with or without lime, a good Martinique rum is, quite simply, *merveilleux.*

The sixteen distilleries of *Le Syndicat des Rhums de la Martinique* welcome visitors from January to July to watch the procedure and taste the result. One of them, the St. James Distillery, supposedly the Hemingway favorite, even invites you to come to its **Musée du Rhum** at Sainte-Marie, any day, any month.

You will pay $7 for a liter of Depaz dark; Clement dark, $6 or so per fifth; Bally runs roughly the same. Sample—and if you like, buy—at **La Case à Rhum**, 5 Avenue de la Liberté (tel. 73-73-20), or **Boutique du Rhum**, 41 Rue Victor Hugo (tel. 74-42-20). Or you could leave this purchase until your departure at the airport. On other, imported liquors, you will find few bargains; taxes are stiff.

WATCHES

At the risk of belaboring the obvious, once again: check the costs at home before making a sizeable investment. And if the price list you brought does not include the specific (and presumably expensive) purchase you are contemplating, verify the U.S. price tab via a telephone call to the dealer of your choice.

Roger Albert (see list at end of chapter for branches) carries Patek Philippe, Omega, Piaget, Seiko, and Cartier. A Cartier gold and steel Santos, the small model, currently retails for $950. The Omega Seamaster Titane fetches $548.70 at this writing, the Constellation Chronometer, $915. Seikos begin at $57.50.

Take these figures to your local jeweler and compare. We'll be most surprised if you don't find the Martinique numbers very attractive indeed.

SPECIAL CATEGORY

Martinique was originally named *Madinina*, "the Isle of Flowers," and with reason. Pre-Columbian plants, clumps of orchids, blazing anthurium, flaming bird-of-paradise blossoms—Martinique has them all. Some say it's because of the richness of the volcanic soil, others credit the many rivers.

Whatever the reason, this is indeed a hospitable climate for flowers, and their cultivation is a growing industry. On one of the most agreeable afternoons we have spent in Martinique, a friend took us to the anthurium farm in the hills beyond Fort-de-France, where acres upon acres of gorgeous blooms are groomed for international export. One of the great pluses about the anthurium and the birds-of-paradise is that they travel well and last up to three weeks.

Maurice Lubin in Saint-Joseph (tel. 77-61-92) specializes in packing blooms for export. **Lelia Flor**, at 106 Rue Victor Sévère (tel. 71-38-28), is another florist offering world-wide delivery service, open seven days a week. Or if you prefer, pick up a dozen anthuriums and take them with you. U.S. Customs are used to flower-bearing returnees and will wave you through with no problem.

If you'd like a more permanent memento of your trip, pick up some local records of beguine, quadrille, or other Martinique music at your hotel, at **Chez Jojo** (Cluny Shopping Center, Schoelcher), at **George Debs** (Cluny Shopping Center, Schoelcher), **Le Carbet** (55 Rue Blenac), or **Hit Parade** (55 Rue Lamartine).

USEFUL ADDRESSES

Albert Venutolo: 13 Rue Victor Hugo (tel. 72-57-44).

Arts Caraïbes: 38 Rue Ernest Deproge (tel. 60-40-08).

Au Printemps: 10 Rue Schoelcher (tel. 71-38-66).

Aventure: 17 Rue Victor Hugo (tel. 72-55-32 and 73-37-73).

Borsalino: 54 Rue Victor Hugo (no phone).

Boutique du Rhum: 41 Rue Victor Hugo (tel. 74-42-20).

Cadet Daniel: 72 Rue Antoine Siger (tel. 71-41-48).

Caraïbe Artisanat: Bellevue Shopping Center (tel. 60-33-83).

Centre des Métiers d'Art: Rue Ernest Deproge (tel. 70-25-01).

Chaussures Reinette: 80 Rue Antoine Siger (tel. 70-24-91).

Chez Jojo: Le Patio de Cluny, Cluny Shopping Center, Schoelcher.

Ella: Bezaudin, Sainte-Marie (tel. 75-30-75).

French Farm: Lamentin Airport (tel. 70-12-34, ext. 1148).

George Debs: Le Patio de Cluny, Cluny Shopping Center, Schoelcher.

Gisele: 14 Rue Victor Hugo (tel. 71-38-67).

Habitation Durocher: Mme. Laurent de Meillac, prop., Lamentin (tel. 51-14-47).

Hit Parade: 55 Rue Lamartine (tel. 70-01-51).

Jack: 28 Rue Moreau de Jonnes (tel. 73-85-25 and 60-61-39).

K Dis (Prisunic): Cluny Shopping Center (tel. 70-03-81); 99 Place Fenelon (tel. 70-11-75); 13 Boulevard du Général de Gaulle (tel. 73-14-65).

La Case à Rhum: 5 Avenue de la Liberté (tel. 73-73-20).

La Gerbe d'Or: 60 Rue Isambert (tel. 71-17-21).

La Malle des Indes: Le Patio de Cluny, Cluny Shopping Center, Schoelcher (tel. 71-39-85).

La Paille Caraïbe: Morne-des-Esses.

Le Carbet: 55 Rue Blenac (tel. 71-26-46).

Lelia Flor: 106 Rue Victor Sévère (tel. 71-38-28).

Les Pieces: Cluny Shopping Center, Schoelcher.

L'Or et l'Argent: 32 Rue Victor Hugo (tel. 70-10-58).

Mahog-Annie: 6 Rue Blenac (tel. 73-88-35).

Maison G. Celma: 47 Rue Lamartine and 23 Rue Blenac (tel. 70-18-81).

Mammouth: Cluny Shopping Center, Schoelcher.

Maurice Lubin: Saint-Joseph (tel. 77-61-92).

Monoprix: Dillon Shopping Center (tel. 60-31-31).

Montaclair: 37 Rue Victor Hugo (tel. 71-59-16).

Mounia: 32 Rue Perrinon (tel. 73-77-27).

Poterie des Trois-Ilets: Trois-Ilets (tel. 76-03-44).

Prune: 72 and 109 Rue Lamartine (tel. 60-34-87 and tel. 73-41-87).

Roger Albert: 7 Rue Victor Hugo (tel. 71-71-71); Cluny Shopping Center (tel. 73-23-23), and Dillon Shopping Center (tel. 70-63-63).

Santalia: Rue Lamartine.

Siniamin: 7 Rue Antoine Siger (tel. 71-53-20).

Thomas de Rogatis: 24 Rue Antoine Siger (tel. 70-19-11).

Valentino: Rue Perrinon.

Via Veneto: 35 Rue Victor Hugo.

MONTSERRAT

MONTSERRAT
AT A GLANCE

GOVERNMENT TOURIST OFFICE: Montserrat Tourist Board, Church Road, Plymouth, Montserrat, W.I. (tel. 2230).

CURRENCY: The Eastern Caribbean dollar is the official currency. US$1 equals about EC $2.65.

OFFICIAL HOLIDAYS: New Year's Day, St. Patrick's Day, Good Friday, Easter Monday, Labour Day (first Monday in May), August Monday (first Monday in August), Discovery Day (November 11), Christmas Day, Boxing Day (December 26).

STORE HOURS: 8:30 a.m. to 4 p.m. weekdays, except Wednesday, when the shops close at 12:30 p.m.

LOCATIONS: For the addresses and telephone numbers of the shops, consult the alphabetical list at the end of this chapter.

In case you wonder about the shamrock on top of Government House, and why St. Patrick's Day is celebrated as an official holiday, Irish settlers populated this island more than 350 years ago. At one time there were 3,000 Irish families living in Montserrat. Traces of Erin can still be seen in the light-skinned, red-headed moppets splashing in mountain streams. Immigration officials may stamp your passport with an official Montserrat three-leaf clover.

On the island of Montserrat you will find nature at her extravagant, luxuriant best: green, *green*, GREEN hillsides; rampant beds of brilliant blooms; roaring mountain streams; and towering craggy peaks.

As for the capital—although Plymouth retains much of the ambience of the old-time West Indies, the infusion of visitors and well-heeled part-time residents has prompted a number of enterprising pioneers to open ateliers and shops on the island.

Warning: Do not purchase articles made of turtle shell or goatskin; U.S. Customs inspectors will likely seize them.

ARTS AND CRAFTS

Island watercolors and paintings go for $20 to $60 at **The Sugar Mill** on Parliament Street, in Plymouth (tel. 2343). The shop also sells Montserrat dolls and other locally crafted items.

The Trade Winds on Parliament Street (tel. 2004) displays various coconut crafts, from $5 up, along with stained-glass wall hangings for $30.

The Red Cross Society Workshop for the Blind, near University Center in Plymouth (tel. 2699), produces a large variety of island-made reed, rush, straw, and fiber items. Table mats cost $3, dolls $5 and $7. Here also you will find needlepoint rugs and wall hangings.

Dutcher's Studio, at Olveston, outside Plymouth (tel. 5253), makes tiles, pottery, Christmas tree ornaments, serving dishes, and assorted other items, many of them to order. It was at Dutcher's Studio that we first saw the sprightly ornaments made from liquor bottles (wind chimes, etc.) that are now on sale in many outlets. These run from $3 to $40 here. The ceramic dolls made at the studio with movable arms and legs, dressed in island costumes, begin at $15.

Carol's Corner at the Vue Pointe Hotel in Old Towne (tel. 5210) features an upscale craft collection—along with cookbooks and sportswear. One of the more popular items is the collection of stationery handpainted in Montserrat: a packet of ten cards with matching envelopes begins at around $6.

China, Crystal, and Home Furnishings

Other than the duty-free collection at the **Et Cetera Shop** in Wapping, outside Plymouth, you'll not find a great deal in the way of china or crystal on Montserrat. But there are very interesting locally fabricated home furnishings.

Montserrat's outstanding contributions to homes beautiful here and abroad involve three categories: fabrics, for upholstering as well as for draperies, bedspreads, and the like; a very special kind of floor covering; and some remarkable handcrafted furniture.

The **Montserrat Sea Island Cotton Company Limited** workroom, at George and Strand Streets in Plymouth (tel. 2557), produces a most attractive fabric made from the sea island cotton grown and processed in Montserrat. The material is dyed in a range of colors and color combinations. The most sought-after shade, however, is the creamy off-white natural, untouched variety. This government-owned operation will make draperies, table covers and napkins, bedspreads— whatever you require—to your specifications and you can purchase additional yardage to match. If you only want a small sample to take home, the table mats can be had for $10.

You may spot some ceramics to your liking there as well. But bear in mind, before you load up on any of the leather items, to find some way to make sure they are not goatskin.

Out at the Industrial Estate, you'll see still more top-quality sea island cotton at the **Spinning Plant** (tel. 2825) or the **Hand-Weaving Studio** (tel. 2915), both owned and operated by the government also. Here too: various designs of place-mats, tablecloths, and baby blankets.

As for rugs, those produced by **Tapestries of Montserrat** in Wapping, outside Plymouth (tel. 2520), warrant a special stop on your itinerary. Each rug and wall-hanging is tufted by a single artisan; there is a choice here of literally hundreds of colors and patterns. The heavier carpets are backed with finest jute, bonded with latex for additional cushioning and non-skid quality. The same method is used to confect totebags—and these are washable. (**Carol's Corner** at the Vue Pointe Hotel, tel. 5210, also carries them.) Count on paying $90 or so for the rugs and tapestries, depending on size, color, and complexity of design. The totebags begin at $6.

Montserrat's third claim to fame in furnishings is largely attributable to an extraordinarily gifted craftsman known as Dr. Felix. At **Felix's Furniture** in Richmond, across from the Montserrat Museum (tel. 2860 or 2679), you will find chairs, tables, desk, doors, beds, dressers, all made by hand, gleaming with the special polish Dr. Felix created himself. A mahogany cocktail table costs $33; a mahogany three foot door, $125; a mahogany armchair and sofa, $800; a mahogany bed with attached headboard, $200.

Interested in smaller wood items? The above-noted **Tapestries of Montserrat** includes original signed woodcarvings in its inventory, as does the **John Bull Shop**, on Old Fort Road in Wapping (tel. 2520). The latter also offers a variety of other interesting merchandise gathered from diverse sources by the discerning American couple who own it.

FASHIONS

Find dresses, blouses, skirts, belts, and stoles, all fashioned from Montserrat sea island cotton, at **Montserrat Sea Island Cotton Company Outlet** in Plymouth (tel. 2557). The belts cost about $10, dresses start at $40, go up to $75 for some of those made to order.

You can buy off the rack at **Celeste Fashions** on Upper George Street in Plymouth (tel. 5210), but many prefer to choose their own style and cloth and have beach caftans, skirts, or whatever sewn to their specifications. You can have something simple stitched up in sea island cotton for as little as $12. The fine imported silks, brocades, and chiffons, however, run from $8 a yard and up.

Sunny Limited at Fort Barrington outside Plymouth (tel. 3271) specializes in embroidered dresses, blouses, and table linens. The dresses and shirts being at $22.

Riley's Rainbow on George Street near the square, Plymouth (tel. 3454), features fashions made from its own batik and tie-dyed fabrics. Here, too, you can specify made to order.

O.R. Kelsick, on nearby Parliament Street (tel. 2561, 2562, or 2888), caters to the needs of local residents, purveying fabrics and cosmetics, among other items.

FOOD

In addition to rugs and wall hangings, **Tapestries of Montserrat** at Wapping, outside Plymouth (tel. 2520), carries a line of locally made jellies, jams, spices, and packed condiments.

Riley's Rainbow on George St. (tel. 3454), mentioned previously as a spot for fashion, is also a place to shop for locally made jam and mango chutney.

For bottled Montserrat lime juice, as well as locally

298

produced honey and condiments, visit the **Wade Inn Gift Shop** in town on Parliament Street (tel. 2881).

JEWELRY

The Unique Gift Shop, on George Street in Plymouth (no phone), specializes in jewelry—gold, silver, shells—some of it made on Montserrat.

By all means, try the **John Bull Shop** over the bridge in Wapping (tel. 2520), and **Carol's Corner** at the Vue Pointe Hotel (tel. 5210).

SPIRITS

Until cane cultivation began to phase out, Montserrat produced an unbottled, unbranded rum—dubbed "plastic" by the locals, for reasons we never quite understood, but apparently someone thought the liquid looked like a transparent drop cloth. At any rate, the stuff was so walloping strong that one experienced island barkeep used to measure the proof with an alcoholometer before serving: he then added water in proportion to his estimate of your capacity to handle the jolt. Now, alas, the lethal grog is a collector's item.

But the formula with which some mixologists softened the impact—a secret mixture of herbs, spices, and other aromatics—survives. You'll find the elixir bottled under various names—Perks Punch, most frequently—purveyed here and there around Plymouth, at the **Wade Inn Gift Shop** on Parliament Street in Plymouth (tel. 2881) for sure.

Montserrat may not have the glitz and glamour to cater to Cadillac tastes, but what it does offer is quite precious: A friendly, scenic retreat.

Will it last? For the moment, most Montserratans share the view of the veteran taxi driver who once told us while driving us to the airport, "I hope no big chain decides to come in here and improve us too much."

Amen!

USEFUL ADDRESSES

Carol's Corner: Vue Pointe Hotel, Old Town (tel. 5210).

Celeste Fashions: Upper George Street, Plymouth (tel. 5210).

Dutcher's Studio: Olveston, outside Plymouth (tel. 5253).

Et Cetera Shop: Wapping, outside Plymouth.

Felix's Furniture: across from the Montserrat Museum, Richmond (tel. 2860 or 2679).

Hand-Weaving Studio: Industrial Estate, Plymouth (tel. 2915).

John Bull Shop: Old Fort Road, Wapping, outside Plymouth (tel. 2520).

Montserrat Sea Island Cotton Company Limited: George and Strand Streets, Plymouth (tel. 2557).

O.R. Kelsick: Parliament Street, Plymouth (tel. 2561, 2562, or 2888).

Red Cross Society Workshop for the Blind: University Center, Plymouth (tel. 2699).

Riley's Rainbow: George Street, Plymouth (tel. 3454).

Spinning Plant: Industrial Estate, Plymouth (tel. 2825).

The Sugar Mill: Parliament Street, Plymouth (tel. 2343).

Sunny Limited: Fort Barrington, outside Plymouth (tel. 3271).

Tapestries of Montserrat: Wapping, outside Plymouth (tel. 2520).

The Trade Winds: Parliament Street, Plymouth (tel. 2004).

The Unique Gift Shop: George Street, Plymouth.

Wade Inn Gift Shop: Parliament Street, Plymouth (tel. 2881).

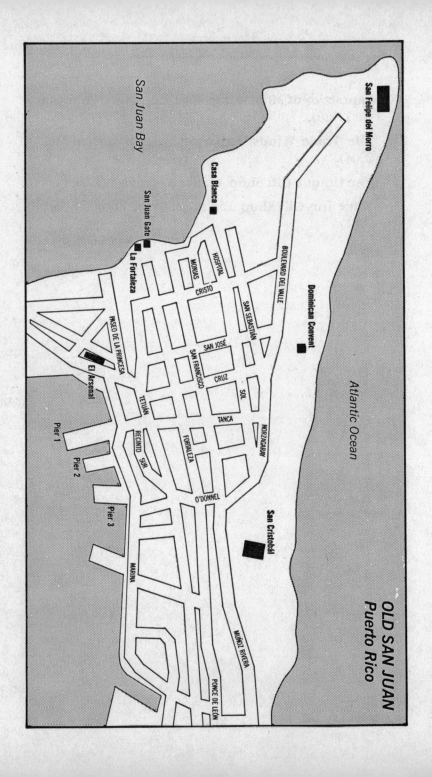

OLD SAN JUAN
Puerto Rico

Atlantic Ocean

San Juan Bay

San Felipe del Morro

Casa Blanca

San Juan Gate

La Fortaleza

Dominican Convent

HOSPITAL

MONJAS

CRISTO

BOULEVARD DEL VALLE

SAN SEBASTIÁN

SAN JOSÉ

SAN FRANCISCO

CRUZ

SOL

PASEO DE LA PRINCESA

El Arsenal

TETUÁN

TANCA

NORZAGARAY

San Cristóbal

Pier 1

Pier 2

Pier 3

RECINTO SUR

FORTALEZA

O'DONNEL

MARINA

MUÑOZ RIVERA

PONCE DE LEÓN

PUERTO RICO

PUERTO RICO
AT A GLANCE

GOVERNMENT TOURIST OFFICE: Puerto Rico Tourism Company, 301 San Justo at Recinto Sur, Old San Juan, Puerto Rico, 00902 (tel. 721-2400).

CURRENCY: The official currency is the U.S. dollar.

OFFICIAL HOLIDAYS: New Year's Day, Three Kings' Day (January 6), Eugenio María de Hostos's Birthday (January 11), Lincoln's Birthday (February 12), Washington's Birthday (February 22), Abolition of Slavery Day (March 22), José de Diego's Birthday (April 16), Good Friday, Memorial Day (May 30), U.S. Independence Day (July 4), Luís Muñoz Rivera's Birthday (July 17), Constitution Day (July 25), José Barbosa's Birthday (July 28), Labor Day (first Monday in September), Columbus Day (October 12), Discovery Day (November 19), Veterans' Day (November 22), Thanksgiving Day (last Thursday in November), Christmas Day, Boxing Day (December 26).

STORE HOURS: Most shops are open from 9 a.m. until 6 p.m. Monday through Saturday, with hotel shops staying open longer at night—and on Sundays. Many other emporiums also operate extra hours, and on the Sabbath, on cruise ship days.

LOCATIONS: For the addresses and telephone numbers of the shops, consult the alphabetical list at the end of this chapter.

Whehen Luís Muñoz Marín set his fellow Puerto Ricans to building a tourism complex over thirty years ago, he had another objective besides the obvious one of cashing in on the coming Caribbean boom. Muñoz Marín aimed to upgrade the image often projected by the mainland media, which pictured the typical Puerto Rican as a barefoot, unshaven little fellow debarking in New York, making tracks for the nearest welfare office.

As we came to realize during the three years we lived in Puerto Rico, this characterization, however it might have applied in certain instances in the past, is far from the truth about the people on this island today. Puerto Ricans have great creativity and enormous pride in their heritage and national identity. The combination of these factors results in some of the richest, most professionally made local products to be found in the entire Caribbean.

Puerto Rico does not have freeport status, nor does it offer cut-rate, bargain-basement pricing. But for shopping with a flair, it offers extraordinarily fruitful grounds to forage. Naturally, since the Commonwealth is a part of the United States, there is no duty on anything you acquire here.

Your first priority, if possible before you leave home, is to secure copies of two essential guides. One, *Qué Pasa?*, is yours free from the Puerto Rico Tourism Company, 1290 Avenue of the Americas, New York, NY 10104 (tel. toll free 1-800-223-6530, or 212-541-6630). This glossy, almost-hundred-page compendium provides maps and a good rundown on stores, plus all sorts of other useful information.

Additional specifics on the shopping scene are contained in a publication called *Walking Tours of San Juan*. Send $5 to Caribbean World Communications, Walking Tours of San Juan Book, First Federal Building, Office No. 301, Santurce, Puerto

Rico, 00909, and your copy will be sent airmail. If you can wait until you are in San Juan, you'll pay half that. Published by a veteran U.S. journalist who has lived in Puerto Rico for about thirty years, the information it contains is generally both accurate and comprehensive.

Shopping combines the old and the new in and around San Juan. **Plaza Las Americas**, off the Las Americas Expressway in Hato Rey, with its 192 shops, is described as the largest shopping center in the Caribbean.

The **Plaza Carolina**, a 25-minute drive from city center off Route 3 in the Carolina section of San Juan, features 160 stores filled with imported European cosmetics and fashions, shoes, musical instruments, and other temptations.

Most fun to browse, however, is the seven-block shopping area of the ancient city, known as Old San Juan.

ARTS AND CRAFTS

ARTS

The fact that Luís Muñoz Marín was not only Puerto Rico's first elected governor but a poet of considerable note gave a special impetus to the government's nurturing and encouraging of local talent, in both fine arts and the crafts.

The **Institute of Puerto Rican Culture**, conceived during the Muñoz Marín years, serves as a catalyst and motivator for young islanders exploring all the disciplines. Housed in an exquisitely restored 500-year-old Catholic monastery at 98 Norzagaray, in the heart of Old San Juan, the Institute presents exhibits and sales of native art and handcrafts on the premises.

It's open daily from 8 a.m. to 4:30 p.m. To find out what is being featured at the time of your visit, call 724-0700.

Although obviously you will find talent scattered throughout the Commonwealth, much of the art community is concentrated in the capital city of San Juan.

If you are interested in acquiring a Puerto Rican work of fine art, you will find a number of dealers on the island to accommodate you:

Galería Coabey, at 101 San Sebastían, Old San Juan (tel. 723-1395), operates from 10 a.m. to 5 p.m., Monday through Saturday. Specializes in paintings and graphics.

Galería Diego at 51 María Moczo, Ocean Park (tel. 728-1287), is open Monday through Wednesday and on Friday, from 10 a.m. to 6 p.m., on Thursday from 10 a.m. to 9 p.m., and on Saturday from 10 a.m. to 1 p.m.

Galería Espiral at 68 Navarro, Hato Rey (tel. 758-1078), is open Monday through Friday from 9 a.m. to 6 p.m., and on Saturday from 9 a.m. 2 p.m.

Galería Liga de Arte at Plaza de San José, Old San Juan (tel. 722-4468), is open Monday through Saturday from 8 a.m. to 4 p.m.

Galería Palomas at 207 Cristo, Old San Juan (tel. 724-8904), is open Monday through Saturday from 10 a.m. to 6 p.m.

Galería W. Lablosa at 312 San Francisco, Old San Juan (tel. 724-6393), is open Monday through Saturday from 9:30 a.m. to 1 p.m. and from 2 to 5:30 p.m.

Galería San Juan, at 204 Boulevard del Valle, Old San Juan (tel. 722-1808), is open Tuesday through Saturday from 10 a.m. to 5 p.m. American-born Jan D'Esopo, the artist in charge, also exhibits works by other young Puerto Rican talents.

Galerías Botello, at 208 Cristo, Old San Juan (tel. 723-2879), is open Monday through Saturday from 10 a.m. to 6 p.m.

Another Galerías Botello branch at the Plaza Las Americas shopping center in Hato Rey (tel. 754-7430) is open Monday through Thursday and on Saturday from 10 a.m. to 6 p.m., and Friday from 10 a.m. to 9 p.m.

Connoisseurs who have shopped the handsome two-century-old one-time Spanish aristocrat's mansion which is now

Galerías Botello (Calle Cristo branch) include Laurance Rockefeller, Deborah Kerr, and Mike Wallace. The roof rests on rafters hewn from the local ausubo tree—wood so hard it bends the nails aimed at penetrating the beams. Old bricks brought over as ballast in the sailing ships constitute the floor. Under the stairs, there's the little oubliette most colonial dons built into their island haciendas: for storing wine when times were peaceful, as a refuge during attacks by hostile raiders.

The most recent addition to the art scene, Isabel Vasquez's **Galería Costa Azul**, is housed in a former supermarket on the corner of Sol and Cruz Streets in Old San Juan. Señora Vasquez has plans to make it a center of information about Puerto Rican artists and art, featuring poetry, music, the dance, and theater as well as the visual arts.

Among the names to look for in the various art galleries are Roberto Moya and Ramiro Pazmino for oils; ceramists and sculptors Jaime Suárez, Lorraine de Castro, Raúl Acero, and Augustín Andiono. Puerto Rico also really excels in the production of fine prints. Guided by an autonomous governmental agency known as the Division de Educación de la Comunidad, pioneers achieved international recognition for creating silkscreen posters and for raising printmaking to an art form.

If you fancy graphics, duck into the **Galería Colibrí** at 158 Cristo, Old San Juan (tel. 725-2840). You will find strictly graphics: lithographs, serigraphs, woodcuts, etchings, some locally done, others imported.

Puerto Rico is also known for developing another specialty, one distinctly its own, in the area of primitive or *naif* art. For three centuries native sculptors have been creating talisman "saints," locally called *santos*. Santos are probably the island's most enduring cultural expression, said to be the only one in the Caribbean not influenced by vaudoo (voodoo), obeah, or other non-Christian strains.

Catholic prelates originated the art when they were unable

to bring into Puerto Rico a sufficient quantity of religious objects, so they taught the residents to make their own. Every proper Puerto Rican family has at least one santo, handed down from one generation to the next, as were those of New Mexico. The santos of New Mexico are almost unobtainable, even to museums. Canny collectors foresee the same situation developing in Puerto Rico before too long.

New York City's Cooper Union brought the first exhibit of Puerto Rican santos to the United States a generation ago. Other museums—the Smithsonian Institution included—began to snap them up; then individual collectors followed their lead. The Puerto Rican government filmed a motion picture on the subject that won first prize at the Venice Film Festival in the 1960s. A New York private dealer then sponsored a santos exhibit, which gave further impetus to the vogue. The overall result has been a wholesale, gold-rush stampede throughout the Commonwealth in search of authentic antique santos.

Traditionally, the choice of a patron saint usually involved a favor. If a physical ailment was cured, the saint was decorated with a silver ex voto representing the part of the anatomy he restored to health: arm, leg, torso, head, etc. One statue of St. Joseph, supposedly a specialist in mammalia, was found adorned with no less than twenty-seven bosoms.

St. Cecilia helped with eye problems. St. Ramon eased childbirth, and his santos are, in fact, shaped to be clutched in hand during labor. Husband-hunting, the specialty of St. Anthony, was broadened to include providing satisfactory sexual relations as well. When things aren't going well in this department, local lore handed down from the elders suggests you turn your St. Anthony santo upside down, spank him smartly on the backside, and stand him in the corner until the situation improves. One San Juan dealer likes to tell of a none-too-intellectual British rock star who bought a St. Anthony, and upon being told his function, indignantly told the dealer, "Listen, mate. You take care of your own love life. I can handle mine without a saint."

Much prized is the Virgin of Montserrat, patron of newlyweds, whom some islanders credit with at least two miracles: a child lost for two weeks was reported found in the care of a spiritual-looking lady with a black face (the Montserrat Virgin, carved of ebony, is often called the Black Virgin); and a cane-cutter who, while being charged by a bull, was purportedly saved when the Virgin ordered the beast to its knees.

The Three Kings, though not true saints, are among the most popular santos because they symbolize generosity; Puerto Ricans love nothing more than gift-giving.

Vintage santos, usually from 8 to 20 inches high, are carved of capap or cedar, and cost from $50 up to $1,000—or sometimes a good deal more.

If you only have time to visit one repository, go to sculptor-painter Angel Botello's historic colonial mansions, Galerías Botello, at 208 Cristo (mentioned above). Besides the paintings on display, you will find a fine selection of santos.

A refugee from the Spanish Civil War, this discerning septuagenarian scouted other Caribbean sites before locating permanently in Puerto Rico. Once smitten by the antique santos concept, he spent over thirty years scouring the countryside for choice specimens. At one time, his collection numbered 10,000; he has sold about two thirds of those, but there remain many fine pieces.

The best-known modern santero, Carlos Vasquez, lives in Ciales in the north-central region (and will receive you). Other santeros can be found in Camuy, Jayuya, and Ponce.

CRAFTS

Puerto Rican crafts represent the blending of three cultures: that of the original inhabitants, the Taino Indians; of the

European immigrants, Spanish especially; and of the African slaves.

Ceramics of today, for example, still use Taino designs. The island's favorite musical instrument, the *cuatro*, is derived from the Spanish lute of the 16th century, the period when Spaniards first invaded the New World. The high-toned cuatro is fashioned from special native guaraguao and yagrumo woods. The Institute of Puerto Rican Culture sponsors cuatro-performing contests, instrument design competitions, and lessons. You can visit "cuatristas" (those who produce cuatros) in Cídra, Humacao, Corozal, and Utuado.

The festive masks still used to celebrate special holidays evolved from those African slaves brought over from their homeland during the 1500s. Today's artisans make their masks of wood, ceramics, metals, grass, fish scales, coconut, and a huge variety of other local materials. Once a year, residents of the northern coastal town of Loíza Aldea celebrate the day of their patron saint, Santiago Apostol (St. James the Apostle), parading through the streets in costumes and brightly painted masks. The best-known maskmaker here is Castor Ayalo. But in other parts of Puerto Rico, where masks are used for decorative purposes, they may differ from those of Loíza Aldea.

Regardless of where they originate, you'll find a wide assortment on sale in various San Juan locations: one of the main outlets, **Centro de Artes Populares** (Center of Popular Arts) is located at the Dominican Convent next to the five-century-old San José church at Plaza San José on Cristo Street, where three generations of Ponce de Leon's family worshipped. Ponce de Leon himself was buried here for a time.

The wares at the Center are well designed and well priced: bamboo salad-servers and hand-embroidered cocktail napkins, baskets, pottery—these and other changing offerings are all likely candidates for your Gifts-Under-$10-List.

Even if you don't buy here, stop at the office anyway.

Personnel can steer you to a hundred different artisans around the island who welcome visitors to their ateliers. You can also obtain here directions to the hammock makers in San Sebastián; the cuatro crafters in Utuado; the basketweavers in Jayuya; the santos carvers in Ponce; and the mask designers in Loíza Aldea in the north. Or you can telephone the Center at 724-6250 for details. It is open Monday through Saturday from 10 a.m. to noon and from 1 to 5 p.m.

Across the street from Pier 3 on the waterfront in Old San Juan, the municipal crafts center, **La Plazoleta del Puerto** (tel. 722-3053) offers visitors a fine opportunity to view some of the island's artisans at work. At one time or another we've watched a silkscreen printer, a landscape painter, a ceramist, a ragdoll maker, a hammock maker, needleworkers, and creators of various musical instruments (including the cuatro). The artisans' shops are open daily from 9 a.m. to 6 p.m.

The Condado Convention Center (center El Centro), in the Condado section, holds an artisans' market every Saturday and Sunday afternoons from noon on.

Puerto Rican Arts and Crafts, 204 Fortaleza, in Old San Juan (tel. 725-5596), is open daily except Sunday from 10 a.m. to 6 p.m. If you have something specific in mind, telephone to ask if they have it.

Visit **Mercado Artesanía Puertorriqueña** (Hermandad de Artesanos), at Muñoz Rivera Park, Puerta de Tierra, Old San Juan (tel. 757-6365), is open Sundays only, from 9 a.m. to 5 p.m.

Mercado Artesanía Carabali at Sixto Escobar Park, Puerto de Tierra, Old San Juan (tel. 722-0369), operates daily from 9 a.m. to 5 p.m.

In the Bayamón section of San Juan, **Artesanos Unidos de Bayamón**, Parque Central, functions Sundays only from 10 a.m. to 4 p.m.

Usable either indoors or out, produced in every size and color, from traditional net-stretchers to swing chairs, they range in cost from $50 up. Find them at—among other locations—**The Gentle Swing**, 156 Cristo, Old San Juan (tel. 724-6625), or at Stall 9 in La Plazoleta del Puerto (Puerto Rican Crafts Center), directly across from Pier 3 on the Old San Juan waterfront (tel. 722-3053).

In La Plazoleta del Puerto also, at **El Gelechal**, in Stall 5 (tel. 722-3053), you will find lamps and chairs made from the handsome dark caoba wood. Juan Ramírez's hanging chairs carved out of caoba sell for about $800 apiece here. But bear in mind, it takes Señor Ramírez almost a year to complete a single chair.

To see the more contemporary style-setter known as the HAMOK chair, winner of *Industrial Design Magazine*'s Designer's Choice Award six years ago, one of eleven pieces of furniture so honored in the entire world, The Gentle Swing is your best bet. If you're planning to do any touring, and are interested in seeing artisans at work, ask at the Popular Arts Center near San José Church for the addresses of hamaqueros in San Sebastian and Yabucoa. Some of the most skilled work in these areas.

What do Muhammad Ali, Jimmy Carter, Greta Garbo, and the king of Saudi Arabia have in common? Each of their homes features at least one **V'Soske** carpet, handmade in Puerto Rico. So do the mansions of the Rockefellers, the Fords, and the Firestones. The Museum of Modern Art has at least two in its permanent collection, and Frank Lloyd Wright donated one to the Dallas Museum of Art. At one time the White House had five V'Soskes.

A half a century ago a Polish immigrant named Stanislav V'Soske developed a special technique of tufting wool yarns through a strong cotton base, using a needle that could produce varying densities and heights of pile. Thus the designer was freed from the restrictions imposed by the warp and the weft of the traditional carpet loom.

Thousands of color formulas are on file in the V'Soske

laboratories, with more shades being developed daily. One order required sixty-five shadings of yellow, from the palest to the deepest. Most V'Soske carpets are crafted to order; the designer sends the pattern to the customer for approval first. Do not plan on scooping these up by the gross unless you're a two-time state lottery winner: prices begin around $5,000. The address for the central office of V'Soske Shops is Route 155, Intersection Route 670, in the community of Vega Baja, some 30 miles outside San Juan (tel. 858-2600).

Extremely old, once considered lost, the art of tinwork has been rediscovered. **Rafael Valentín Reyes** hand-manufactures tin lamps at his headquarters in Utuado in the central mountainous region of Puerto Rico. But you may also find his work on sale at the various San Juan craft shops and fairs cited above, including La Plazoleta del Puerto on the waterfront in Old San Juan.

There too, look for Stall 2, where **M. Rivera** creates and sells miniature reproductions of old island landmarks. Show him the house of your choice, he'll duplicate it, handcarved and painted on wood. Senor Rivera also sells papier-mâché items, from bottles to lamps, handmade by local artists. If you plan to be in town long enough and are interested in the medium, you can enroll in a class with Rivera and experiment yourself with papier-mâché.

Collection de Charm, Stall 7, La Plazoleta del Puerto (tel. 722-3053), features stained glass, attractive handmade stoneware, small bowls and vases. These sell for under $15 as a rule, the mugs for $5 or so less than that.

Amparo Porcelain Inn, at 53 Cristo in Old San Juan (tel. 722-1777), carries distinctive hand-painted porcelains. Founder Señora Eaves earned this shop considerable acclaim by hand painting Limoges and other fine chinas in designs distinctly her own: house plaques and/or numbers, apothecary jars— one Christmas she made and sold 1,200 different hand-painted tree ornaments. They are expensive, but one of a kind, and made to your order.

Casa Joscar Art Shop, 109 Fortaleza, Old San Juan (tel. 724-6339), has ceramics also, along with some antiques and miniatures.

Frances del Toro Porcelains, Condado Beach Arcade, 1351 Ashford Ave., Suite 2C, Condado section (tel. 722-1857), is another possibility.

For wooden dinner plates, papier-mâché, ceramics—the assortment changes from one year to the next—have a look at Don Roberto, 205 Cristo in Old San Juan (tel. 724-0194). Bob Smith, the New Mexico art professor who founded this house, is no longer in charge. But the last time we were there the current management seemed to us to be doing a fine job of maintaining Bob's original standards.

Los Artesanos, Urbanización Industrial Julio N. Matos, Barrio Martin Gonzalez, in the Carolina section (tel. 752-9800), is open daily except Sunday from 8 a.m. to 5 p.m.

Browse through **Artesanía Camui**, on Route 3, at the 15-kilometer mark in Canóvanas. It is open daily except Sunday from 8:30 a.m. to 6 p.m.

Or try the **Beachcomber**, on Route 304 in the town of La Parguera. Its hours are daily from 8 a.m. to 6 p.m.

Enjoying San Juan, 153 Tetuán, Old San Juan, sells crafts daily except Sunday from 10 a.m. to 5 p.m.

If you are especially interested in cuatros, head for an establishment called **Olé** at 105 Fortaleza in Old San Juan (tel. 724-2445). Handmade cuatros range from $15 to $50 here.

At certain times of the year there are special festivals at which local artisans bring out their best offerings.

Watch for the Annual Ceramic Festival in San Juan in October; the Crafts Fair in the city of Mayagüez in early December; the Vieques Fold Festival on the island of Vieques in February; Crafts Fair in the town squares of Ponce and Cayey in March. In May, weavers will display their skills at the Isabela Weaving Festival. July is the big annual National Crafts Fair held at City Plaza in the town of Barranquita.

Cameras

Puerto Rico is not *the* place to buy camera equipment—as islanders, who acquire theirs in New York, will tell you.

China, Crystal, and Home Furnishings

Although Puerto Rico does not promote itself as duty-free, at least one customer reports finding Baccarat, Lalique, and St. Louis crystal priced as advantageously in San Juan as in St. Thomas and Hong Kong. Among the more promising locations for china, crystal, and the like:

Ambiance, Condado Beach Arcade, 1055 Ashford Ave., Condado section (tel. 724-6426), for top-of-the-line imported porcelain, crystal, and china. Quality is first-rate, selections discerning.

Casa Cavanagh, an offshoot of the original St. Thomas emporium founded by Virginia and Jere Cavanagh, soon developed a life of its own. It now has its own character. Imports include china, crystal, specialties from Europe and the Far East along with other local products as well. Shop Casa Cavanagh, either at its original 202 Cristo St. location in Old San Juan (tel. 725-3520) or in the Plaza Las Americas shopping complex (tel. 753-0133).

If these locations disappoint you, try also:

Bared & Sons, located at the corner of Fortaleza and San Justo, Old San Juan (tel. 724-4811)

Albanese, 311 Fortaleza, Old San Juan (tel. 722-1261)

José E. Alegría & Associates, at 152–54 Cristo, carries antiques along with fine arts. No bargain basement this—but it doesn't cost anything to look. The lovely old Spanish-style building opposite the small piazza in front of El Convento would be worth seeing even if it were empty, which it most certainly is not. The lower floor dates to 1523; the top story was added a century later.

But although you may well duplicate the happy experience of the satisfied shopper referred to earlier by finding your favorite Lladrò, Wedgwood, or whatever, interestingly priced, when it comes to treasures for the home, Puerto Rico's most distinctive offerings are those created locally, in its own workshops.

Christopher Columbus first discovered Puerto Rican crafts in the form of a hammock made by the Taino Indians. To this day, shops and artisans purvey hammocks to lie on, sit on, even to swing in. Originally conceived by the Taino Indians as the simplest means of achieving personal comfort and relaxation, Columbus saw the "swinging nets," as they are sometimes called, made very much the way today's versions are: by hand, of pure cotton, on either a mechanical loom or a vertical frame. The "hamaqueros" who create these handwoven designs usually take two to three days to complete a piece.

FASHIONS

Balenciaga, whom many consider the greatest couturier of the century, was Spanish. So is Oscar de la Renta, by way of the Dominican Republic. You will find that same Spanish flair in the work of many of Puerto Rico's name designers. In the past few years, their collections have been shown in a hundred major world cities.

Fernando Peña, dean of Puerto Rican couturiers, is not an islander by birth. But he has been practicing his art in Puerto Rico for twenty years or more. As one enchanted señorita once told us mischievously, "Fernando can park his pincushion under my sewing machine *any* time!" At present, Senor Peña parks his pincushion at 1409 Avenida Ponce de Léon, San Juan (tel. 725-0607) and 1400 Magdalena in Santurce (tel. 724-7539). And although he still manufactures his clothes in his factory in Puerto Rico, the maestro himself recently moved to

Miami in order to nurture his growing Stateside clientele at the various branches of Neiman Marcus, Saks Fifth Avenue, and other smart shops throughout the United States.

Born in Spain, educated in Nova Scotia (his father was a Cuban diplomat), Peña grew up in Europe and North America. One of his first exposures to fashion, at age seven, was visiting Coco Chanel's boutique with his mother while she was having a suit made. From there, the young designer literally worked his way up, starting off sweeping floors at Balenciaga. Peña specializes in elegant sewn-to-size ball gowns, but he also sometimes does superbly simple resort linens, carefully confected under the master's watchful eye.

Milli Arango, 450 Sagrado Corazón, Santurce (tel. 728-5308), conjures up delicate feminine frippery that seems to retain its fashion relevance forever. Our chum Freck Hart, Travel Editor of the *San Juan Star*, wears a lavishly embroidered two-piece white linen dinner suit that envious colleagues invariably covet.

Luis Fuentes, 353 San Francisco, San Juan (tel. 724-4750), as well as 669 Fernandez Juncos, in the Miramar section of Santurce (tel. 724-2234), has been around a long time, pleasing local residents especially with realistically priced, pretty party clothes.

Carlota Alfaro, 1850 Loíza, Santurce (tel. 724-0613), is on our list for next time, along with highly recommended David Fernandez, 1646 Volga Street, in Río Piedras (tel. 767-1912).

A Note of Caution: Unless you've shopped a lot in European couture houses, the comparatively small stock on hand in many of these establishments may disappoint you. This is because most luxury-bracket shoppers are regulars, who know that they can have what they like in size 6 made up to their size 12, and choose the color for it, at minimum if any extra charge. Thus sometimes the cupboards can look pretty bare. So although you certainly can walk out wearing anything that strikes your fancy, do look through all the sizes; just because that irresistible pink linen is not in your size doesn't mean you can't have another one, made to fit.

Occasionally the designers will add to their own creations ready-to-wear from higher volume manufacturers. In our view this is a mistake, in that the quality we have seen often cannot compare to their own. However, perhaps we just happened in on a bad day. Certainly we have thoroughly enjoyed the Christian Dior accessories we purchased from Fernando Peña years ago—in fact, we still use them.

Note Also: Be prepared for price tags in line with what you would pay for haute couture anywhere else. Maybe 10% to 15% less, but still in the several-hundred-dollar range.

Oddly enough, some of the best clothing bargains to be had in Puerto Rico come there from the United States mainland.

Polo Ralph Lauren Factory Store at 201 Cristo in Old San Juan (tel. 722-2136), offers reductions of up to 30% – 50% on men's, women's, and children's apparel and accessories. Some home furnishings as well.

The **Hathaway Factory Outlet** at 203 Cristo in Old San Juan (tel. 723-8946) sells its regularly $45 shirts for $18.50; the Jack Nicklaus Hathaway Gold Classic for $18; Hathaway for Her at $21 (regularly they retail for up to $65). In this same shop you can also pick up Christian Dior shirts for one half to one third off their usual price.

The **Bass Shoe Factory Outlet** also offers savings at its 206 Cristo headquarters in Old San Juan (tel. 725-3000).

If you're a browser, you could spend weeks prowling through the boutiques of Plaza Las Americas, around El Morro, and especially in the Condado, Santurce, and Isla Verde sections of Greater San Juan.

FOOD

Oranges from Spain, bananas from Africa, pineapple from the South Seas, sugarcane from India—Puerto Rico's breadbasket is international, a legacy of seafarers who berthed at the island for almost half a millennium. Under Spanish rule, no ship was allowed to sail for Puerto Rico without bringing along plants. Okra seeds came aboard the slave ships from Africa; the vanilla plant, which is really an orchid; the native yam, a lily, not a sweet potato; wild peanuts, eggplants, cassava—local raw materials are endless.

More than forty varieties of bananas now grow in Puerto Rico. As for the local pineapple, this is without doubt nectar for the gods. No other variety, including the Hawaiian for our money, can top the flavor of the blond, succulent, firm fruit grown here. Island papaya is delicious too, as are the occasionally available hearts of palm and mango. The guava paste, eaten with the fine local goat cheese or, if unavailable in your neighborhood, regular cream cheese, makes one of the world's fine desserts.

Thanks to a well-developed canning and packaging industry, you can take much of Puerto Rico's gourmetry home. Most U.S. Department of Agriculture restrictions pertain to palms and palm fronds. Otherwise, you should have no problem whatsoever bringing in all the delicacies you like. In case of doubt, inspectors maintain a regular booth at the airport to inform departing passengers and if necessary inspect their agricultural loot.

Pueblo supermarkets are dotted throughout the land, featuring the canned nectars of soursop, mango, and other tropical fruits. (The inscriptions are in Spanish, but you'll recognize the pictures on the label.) For the name of the store nearest you, telephone Pueblo headquarters at Campo Rico and Expreso in Loíza Carina at 757-3131.

320

Super Básico is another big chain. The executive offices are at Centro Commercial San Francisco in Río Piedras (tel. 758-5353).

Along with the fruit pastes, jellies and juices, the spices and marinades, you might pick up a jar or two of *Sofrito*. An aromatic blend of tomatoes, sweet peppers, onion, ham, coriander, and garlic, a spoonful or two of this mixture seldom fails to pick up the flavor of soups, sauces—almost anything seemingly lacking that intangible oomph.

Another staple in our larder is the *Sazón con Culantro y Achiote* packaged by the Goya Company. Labeled "Créole Seasoning," it too adds its West Indian accent to meats, salads, and is especially helpful with rice. Query **Condimentos de Puerto Rico Inc.**, P.O. Box 2728, Bayamón (tel. 787-6735), for further information.

Coco López cream of coconut, produced by Industrias La Famosa of Bayamón, was originally developed in the 1950s as a homogenized cream made from the meat of the coconut, strictly for use in preparing desserts, cake frostings, exotic dishes, and as an alternative to pumpkin pie for island Thanksgiving. Now, of course, it is probably best known as the key ingredient in piña colada rum drinks, which were invented, incidentally, by a Caribe Hilton bartender.

Puerto Rican coffee grows in high country similar to that favored by Juan Valdez. A large, handsome bean with strong body, good aroma, and a distinctive flavor, it works best with a slightly dark roast. Coffee connoisseurs in the States know it under the market name of Primero. The brand names to look for in Puerto Rico are Yaucono, Café Rico, Café Crema, and Rioja. You'll pay less per pound at any grocery in Puerto Rico than you would the the ordinary house blend in your home supermarket. *Caution:* Do not attempt to bring in the beans; only ground roasted coffee can be legally imported into the U.S.

JEWELRY

Rafaela Vegas Planas works in Stall 3 at San Juan's Plazoleta del Puerto (tel. 722-3053) and turns fish scales gathered from local fishermen into combs, earrings, and pins selling for under $5 apiece. Señora Vegas also purveys jewelry made from silver, coral, and abalone.

The community of Corozal is headquarters for artisans producing seed jewelry because of the abundance of brightly colored seeds in the area: the scarlet granate and the ivory camandula are the most popular. Islanders will tell you, tongue-in-cheek, that until American cows arrived on the island native herds had the consideration not to graze on the camandula seed. Despite the insensitivity of the Yankee bovines, camandula grass still grows abundantly along the rivers running through Corozal. Two of the best-known seed jewelers in Corozal are **Rafael Negrón** and **Felicita Padilla de Berrios**.

In the settlement of Orocodis, the Aviles family carves rings out of the ebony-colored corozo, which grows on a certain strain of palm; when corozo is combined with bone, the result is especially eye-catching.

To see a cross-section of these items, if you are in the Plaza Las Americas in Hato Rey, you might look in on **Régalos Toni** in the Main Arcade (tel. 753-8970).

In years gone by, sophisticated shoppers have bypassed homemade confections of seeds, fish scales, and the like as being "square," "corny," "gross," or "tacky"—the term depending on the generation. But in today's fashion climate, with emphasis on off-trail, one-of-a-kind handcrafts, these items may well be worth a second look. Especially for budget-watchers.

Insofar as diamonds, gold, and other fine jewelry are concerned, you will have difficulty even scratching the surface of all the offerings. The actual U.S. market value of the individual pieces is hard to pin down precisely, however, since a direct U.S.-to-Puerto Rico price comparison on the identical piece is difficult if not impossible. This is a judgment you yourself will have to make. As in so many instances, the wisest course is to buy what you like and can afford and not concern yourself too much as to whether you saved a few bob.

Reinhold Jewelers at 201 Cristo in Old San Juan (tel. 725-6878) has a reassuringly durable reputation for integrity and skill in the manufacture of custom-made pieces.

Ambiance, in the Condado Beach Arcade at 1055 Ashford Ave. (tel. 724-6426), is also very highly regarded.

Other top emporiums include:

Bared & Sons, corner of Fortaleza and San Justo, Old San Juan (tel. 724-4811)

Swiss Import Jewelry Company, 263 San Francisco, Old San Juan (tel. 722-5761)

Gold Extra, Inc., 250 San Francisco, Old San Juan (tel. 725-6670)

LINENS

Puerto Rico produces an interesting handmade bobbin lace, called *mundillo*, which is worked on a mundillo frame into bands of lace which appear on tablecloths, placemats, doilies, handkerchiefs, and collars.

El Imperio, at 209 San Francisco in Old San Juan (tel. 724-0221), has a good selection.

Aguadilla en San Juan, at 352 San Francisco in Old San Juan (tel. 722-0578), features an extensive selection of mundillo in the form of handkerchiefs, trimmings, and edges, sold by the yard or by the item. Here you can also stock up on the tools and materials to make your own lace: quality threads, bobbins, and instruction guides.

And with so much handwork involved mundillo does not come cheap. Wherever you buy yours, be prepared to part with from $25 to $65 for a representative piece.

PERFUMES

Quite honestly, prices on fragrances have always been so advantageous in St. Thomas, we've never even considered buying them in Puerto Rico. So we're not up on what possibilities exist. We may well have erred. At least one emporium, **La Fragrance** at Plaza Las Americas shopping center in Hato Rey (tel. 753-0506), is said to be worth a look, if only for the sheer volume and variety of the merchandise on hand.

SPIRITS

There's a saying in Puerto Rico that goes like this: "Let us give thanks for rum. It delights us and consoles us—and it keeps us."

And that it does.

Puerto Rico is the largest producer of rum on earth, accounting for 83% of U.S. rum sales alone. Three distilleries, including the world's largest, produce enough rum for six companies to sell under twelve brand names. The labels "Bacardi," "Don Q," and "Ronrico," among others, are so popular that island rums are served in every city in the world, making rum production the Commonwealth's *single most important source of tax revenue.*

Whether or not you consider the few dollars' saving on the one bottle you may bring home worth investing in rum, you should take in the free tour (with samples) of the **Bacardi Distillery** in Cataño (tel. 795-1560), a short ride from downtown San Juan.

Every day except Sunday (half day on Saturday), the Bacardi plant offers ½-hour tours through its 127-acre "Cathedral of Rum," which include a view of the stored rum, an explanation of the processing stages by winsome guides, a walk through the bottling plant and the nicely manicured grounds, a peek at the distillery's own museum, and a free sample tippling of the up to 100,000-gallon-a-day production.

Although you can usually arrange group land transport via your hotel for the 20-minute drive (about $5 per person), the leisurely scenic route by ferry is more fun, across San Juan Bay to Cataño; from there it's just a short bus ride to the distillery.

Puerto Rican rums claim to be lighter and drier than others because they are distilled at high proof. Also, Puerto Rican law specifies that all rum be aged at least one year; for gold rum, the requirement is three years and 175 proof; white rum must be 180 proof. This high required alcoholic content produces what Puerto Ricans claim is a purer final distillate than that of other liquors. Bourbon and rye, they contend, are distilled according to U.S. law at under 160 proof, which results in greater retention of impurities that can contribute to toxicity and to hangovers!

To evaluate the quality of rum, experts suggest the following procedure: Warm a sample tot by holding the glass in your hands. Sniff the rum. There should be no rawness or sharp odor. Pour some of it on your hands and rub them dry; there should be no residual aroma. Taste the rum. Sip, swallow, and wait. There should be no "bad impression" on the stomach, no metallic or astringent taste in the mouth.

And for those who cannot resist one sampling too many, a spokesman for the Puerto Rican Tourism Company suggests trying the traditional Puerto Rico hangover remedy: Rub a half a lemon under your arms!

Islanders are proud to remind their gringo brethren that rum, the oldest of all hard liquors, is also a traditional Yankee favorite. Rum primed the throat of Patrick Henry when he rose to make his famous speech before the House of Burgesses in Virginia. Rum was an important entry in George Washington's ledgers, which are still on view at Mount Vernon. Irving S. Cobb, writing of his favorite rum drink, the Tom and Jerry, describes it lyrically: "Then the first sip laved your throat with a velvety touch. Then the next soothing swallow fanned your middle system to a gentle simmer, and when you had emptied your tumbler and stepped forth, robust and unafraid, into the storm, you could feel the afterglow of that beneficial compound searching you all over."

As for the Puerto Ricans themselves, their national toast is more down to earth: *"Salud, pesetas, amor, y tiempo para gozarios,"* meaning, drink to "health, money, love, and the time to enjoy them."

WATCHES

Rolex timepieces are available at **Joyeria Riviera,** 205 Cruz in Old San Juan (tel. 725-4000).

Mido and Eterna watches are sold at **Joyeria R. Pascual,** 250 San Francisco, Old San Juan (tel. 723-0061).

Les must de Cartier has a boutique located at 1120 Ashford Ave. in the Condado section (tel. 722-2980).

If you don't find what you are looking for at any of the above establishments, try **Bared & Sons** at the corner of Fortaleza and San Justo in Old San Juan (tel. 724-4811), or the **Watch and Gem Palace,** 204 San José in Old San Juan (tel. 722-3867).

We assisted at the birthing of Puerto Rico tourism decades ago when we were residents of that island. Since then we've been first elated at its progress, then sharply disappointed. Now the pendulum has swung back your and our way, and for this year, you'll be hard put to find a more promising vacation destination, one which truly does have something for everyone.

Sporting facilities—boating, golfing, tennis—are of top quality. Night people will find sophisticated nightlife and government-regulated casino gambling. For exploring, there are outstanding targets. In the northwest corner of the island, for example, open to the public for the first time, Puerto Rico's Rio Camuy Caves, are rated one of the world's five most beautiful cave systems, featuring the world's third largest underground river. Throughout the area, Puerto Rico's Spanish ambience remains intriguingly foreign, yet reassuring, for you are always on American soil.

As for accommodations, the eclectic assortment includes facilities to suit every taste and pocketbook. The prestigious Hyatt chain, with the whole Caribbean from which to choose, elected to site its first West Indian beachhead—a $30-million investment—in Puerto Rico. The Hyatt Regency Cerromar pool alone is one of the wonders of the resort world: a third of a mile long—526 feet more than the Empire State Building is high—it features gorges, flumes, tunnels, subterranean Jacuzzis, fourteen waterfalls, four waterslides, a spiral chute with a 187-foot drop, and landscaped surroundings dotted with 30,000 tropical plants, 254 palm trees, and a lake populated with black swans and pink flamingos.

On the western edge of the central Cordilla mountain range, on a restored coffee plantation, an 1830 residence has been converted into a 21-room inn. Hacienda Juanita features swimming pool, tennis court, and a rustic dining room veranda overlooking a lush forest of flowering plants and trails leading to a waterfall. The original ausubo ceiling beams, from native trees, remain intact; antique tools used in the production of coffee decorate the living room walls. Sponsored by the government travel division, Hacienda Juanita is one of a series of country retreats modeled after the Spanish parador system. Each facility must be situated in a historic place or site of exceptional scenic beauty, whether in the mountains, at the beach, or on an offshore island; at high winter season, double rooms cost no more than $60 a night, meals $6.

Add to these lures the special pleasures of prowling the shops of extraordinary variety in setting and stock, and you will be hard put to find a more promising location for your Caribbean holiday.

USEFUL ADDRESSES

Aguadilla en San Juan: 352 San Francisco, Old San Juan (tel. 722-0578).

Albanese: 311 Fortaleza, Old San Juan (tel. 722-1261).

Ambiance: Condado Beach Arcade, 1055 Ashford Ave., Condado section, San Juan (tel. 724-6426).

Amparo Porcelain Inn: 53 Cristo, Old San Juan (tel. 722-1777).

Artesanía Camui: Route 3, 15-kilometer marker, Canóvanas.

Artesanos Unidos de Bayamón: Parque Central, Bayamón.

Bacardi Distillery: Cataño (tel. 795-1560).

Bared & Sons: Corner of Fortaleza and San Justo, Old San Juan (tel. 724-4811).

Bass Shoe Factory Outlet: 206 Cristo, Old San Juan (tel. 725-3000).

Beachcomber: Route 304, La Parguera.

Carlota Alfaro: 1850 Loíza, Santurce (tel. 724-0613).

Casa Cavanagh: 202 Cristo, Old San Juan (tel. 725-3520); Plaza Las Americas shopping center, Las Americas Expressway (tel. 753-0133).

Casa Joscar Art Shop: 109 Fortaleza, Old San Juan (tel. 724-6339).

Centro de Artes Populares: Dominican Convent, Cristo Street, Plaza San José, Old San Juan (tel. 724-6250).

Collection de Charm: La Plazoleta del Puerto, Stall 7, Marina Street, Old San Juan (tel. 722-3053).

Condado Convention Center: El Centro, between the Condado Beach and La Concha Hotels, Condado section, San Juan.

Condimentos de Puerto Rico, Inc.: Bayamón (tel. 787-6735).

Don Roberto: 205 Cristo, Old San Juan (tel. 724-0194).

El Gelechal: La Plazoleta del Puerto, Stall 5, Marina Street, Old San Juan (tel. 722-3053).

El Imperio: 209 San Francisco, Old San Juan (tel. 724-0221).

Enjoying San Juan: 153 Tetuán, Old San Juan (no phone).

Fernando Peña: 1409 Avenida Ponce de Léon, San Juan (tel. 725-0607); 1400 Magdalena, Santurce (tel. 724-7539).

Frances del Toro Porcelains: 1351 Ashford Ave., Suite 2C, Condado section, San Juan (tel. 722-1857).

Galería Coabey: 101 San Sebastián, Old San Juan (tel. 723-1395).

Galería Colibri: 158 Cristo, Old San Juan (tel. 725-2840).

Galería Costa Azul: Corner of Sol and Cruz Streets, Old San Juan.

Galería Diego: 51 María Moczo, Ocean Park (tel. 728-1287).

Galería Espiral: 68 Navarro, Hato Rey (tel. 758-1078).

Galería Liga de Arte: Plaza de San José, Old San Juan (tel. 722-4468).

Galería Palomas: 207 Cristo, Old San Juan (tel. 724-8904).

Galería San Juan: 204 Boulevard del Valle, Old San Juan (tel. 722-1808).

Galerías Botello: 208 Cristo, Old San Juan (tel. 723-2879); Plaza Las Americas shopping center, Hato Rey (tel. 754-7430.

Galería W. Lablosa: 312 San Francisco, Old San Juan (tel. 724-6393).

The Gentle Swing: 156 Cristo, Old San Juan (tel. 724-6625), or at Stall 9 in La Plazoleta del Puerto (Puerto Rican Crafts Center), directly across from Pier 3 on the Old San Juan waterfront (tel. 722-3053).

Gold Extra, Inc.: 250 San Francisco, Old San Juan (tel. 725-6670).

Hathaway Factory Outlet: 203 Cristo, Old San Juan (tel. 723-8946).

Institute of Puerto Rican Culture: 98 Norzagaray, Old San Juan (tel. 724-0700).

José E. Alegría & Associates: 152–154 Cristo, Old San Juan (no phone).

Joyería Riviera: 205 Cruz, Old San Juan (tel. 725-4000).

Joyería R. Pascual: 250 San Francisco, Old San Juan (tel. 723-0061).

La Fragrance: Plaza Las Americas shopping center, Hato Rey (tel. 753-0506).

La Plazoleta del Puerto: Marina Street, opposite Pier 3, Old San Juan (tel. 722-3053).

Les must de Cartier: 1120 Ashford Ave., Condado section, San Juan (tel. 722-2980).

Los Artesanos: Urbanización Industrial Julio N. Matos, Barrio Martin Gonzalez (tel. 752-9800).

Luis Fuentes: 353 San Francisco, San Juan (tel. 724-4750); 669 Fernandez Juncos, Santurce (tel. 724-2234).

Mercado Artesania Carabali: Sixto Escobar Park, Puerta de Tierra, Old San Juan (tel. 722-0369).

Mercado Artesanía Puertorriqueña: Muñoz Rivera Park, Puerta de Tierra, Old San Juan (tel. 757-6365).

Milli Arango: 450 Sagrado Corazón, Santurce (tel. 728-5308).

M. Rivera: La Plazoleta del Puerto, Stall 2, Marina Street, Old San Juan (tel. 722-3053).

Olé: 105 Fortaleza, Old San Juan (tel. 724-2445).

Plaza Carolina: Route 3, Carolina, San Juan.

Plaza Las Americas: off the Las Americas Expressway, Hato Rey.

Polo Ralph Lauren Factory Store: 201 Cristo, Old San Juan (tel. 722-2136).

Pueblo Supermarkets: headquarters at Campo Rico and Expreso, Loíza Carina (tel. 757-3131).

Puerto Rican Arts and Crafts: 204 Fortaleza, Old San Juan (tel. 725-5596).

Rafael Negrón: 16-7A Calle 3 Van Scoy, Corozal (tel. 797-8215).

Rafael Valentin Reyes: headquarters in Utuado; work available at various stalls in La Plazoleta del Puerto, Marina Street, Old San Juan.

Rafaela Vegas Planas: La Plazoleta del Puerto, Stall 3, Marina Street, Old San Juan (tel. 722-3053).

Régalos Toni: Main Arcade, Plaza Las Americas shopping center, Hato Rey (tel. 753-8970).

Reinhold Jewelers: 201 Cristo, Old San Juan (tel. 725-6878).

Super Básico: executive offices at Centro Commercial San Francisco, Río Piedras (tel. 758-5353).

Swiss Import Jewelry Company: 263 San Francisco, Old San Juan (tel. 722-5761).

V'Soske Shops: Route 155, Intersection Route 670, Vega Baja (tel. 858-2600).

Watch and Gem Palace: 204 San José, Old San Juan (tel. 722-3867).

SABA

SABA AT A GLANCE

GOVERNMENT TOURIST OFFICE: Saba Tourist Office, Windwardside, next to the Post Office, Saba, N.A. (tel. 2231).

CURRENCY: The official unit of currency is the Netherlands Antilles florin or guilder (NAf). US$1 equals 1.77 NAf. In addition, U.S. dollars are widely accepted.

OFFICIAL HOLIDAYS: New Year's Day, Good Friday, Easter Monday, Queen's Birthday (April 30), Labor Day (May 1), Ascension Day, Whit Monday, Armistice Day (November 11), Kingdom Day (December 15), Christmas Day, Boxing Day (December 26).

STORE HOURS: Monday through Saturday from 8 a.m. until noon and from 2 to 6 p.m.—for the most part.

LOCATIONS: For the addresses and telephone numbers of the shops, consult the alphabetical list at the end of this chapter.

Everything about Saba, including the shopping, is measured on the micro-scale: (1) its total land area is only 5 square miles; (2) the population numbers 1,046; (3) rentable rooms total about 25; (4) the 1,312-foot-long runway is the shortest this side of an Alaskan bush strip; (5) the only cross-island, handmade, 9-mile-long concrete road, so sharply curved that drivers must back-and-fill to negotiate the zigs and zags, in many places only accommodates one-way traffic; (6) the number of emporiums offering merchandise, all duty-free, to the tourist trade is less than a dozen at most.

As for the airport on this, the only inhabited beachless island in the Caribbean, both ends and one side of the strip drop straight into the water; sheer mountain peaks preclude any margin of error on the fourth side.

Of the five hamlets on Saba—The Bottom, Hell's Gate, St. John's, English Quarter, and Windwardside—The Bottom and Windwardside are your mercantile meccas.

Windwardside, perched at 1,622 feet on the crest of two ravines, offers magnificent vistas. Scuttling clouds may blot out parts of this lovely little village, but through the drifts you will make out phantom chimneys, ghostly houses, and smudged landscapes. If you're up to a two-hour hike, you can climb the steps to the top of Mount Scenery and back down.

Otherwise, wander by the neat cottages and their multi-colored gardens, with hillsides dropping directly down to the bluest sea in the world, under a cerulean sky dotted with cirrocumulus puffs that look to be miles high.

The **Island Craft Shop** in Windwardside will introduce you to the Saban specialty known as Spanish work, and will take special orders for the handmade tablecloths. **Saure Nickel Shop**, also in Windwardside, includes Saba lace in its stock of souvenirs. **The Yellow House,** Windwardside again (tel. 2234), is a branch of the Curaçao emporium of that name, and carries perfumes as well as some lingerie.

Well-known author Will Johnson tells how Spanish lace evolved: a century ago Mary Gertrude Johnson, the daughter of a prominent Saba family, was sent away to school in a Caracas convent. There the Venezuelan nuns taught her the delicate drawn threadwork that creates airy, lacy designs on linen garments, napkins, and scarves. Convents the world over used to teach drawn threadwork—a technique that resembles hemstitching—as well as the art of sewing a fine seam, to upper-class young ladies. Both skills were considered symbols of gentility.

Mary Gertrude brought the drawn threadwork craft home, passed it on to her fellow Sabans, and, by 1884, wives and daughters were sewing up a storm while their men were away. Fourteen years later, the ladies had become so skillful that Saba's Florence Every won honorable mention in an exhibition of women's handcrafts in The Hague. At the turn of the century, one Saban not only won first prize in a Copenhagen competition, but was invited by the Danish government to spend four months in that country to pass on her expertise to the Scandinavian girls.

Gradually, Saba women began to market their work. They compiled a mailing list of potential buyers by copying the names of U.S. firms from boxes of merchandise sent to Saba. The budding entrepreneurs would then send the company a letter explaining their craft and enclosing a price list—in the hope that some compassionate Yankee would post their communiqué on the office bulletin board, or otherwise spread the word. Their plan worked: by 1928 they were exporting 25,000 guilders' worth of needlework a year.

As the individual workers compiled their own client lists, addresses were kept strictly confidential; bitter feuds developed if anyone was even suspected of raiding a rival's roster.

Soon the women prevailed upon their country's high officials to assist them in their venture with endorsements. When American businessmen queried the Vice-Governor of Saba about the economic situation of the females who were soliciting orders from their employees, His Excellency would delicately suggest that the housewives could certainly "stand some help." Actually, many of the "lacemakers" ranked among the richest families on the island.

The Great Depression knocked The Bottom, to coin a phrase, out of the Spanish-work market, and the craft almost went into eclipse—until the building of the airport in 1963 opened the island to visitors. Since then Spanish work has been resumed, and last year the women sold $100,000 worth of placemats, hand towels, aprons, biscuit warmers, blouses, children's dresses, and other handmade articles.

Actually, a good number of the stitchers display their wares on their own front porches and will invite you in to have a look. Some bring their work to you on the street. Most of them use quality materials—good linen, proper thread—and price the results accordingly. If you have something in mind you'd like to have made to order, they can handle that as well.

You may also find something you like amidst the U.S. imports in the **Treasure Chest**, at Windwardside, more probably in the **Captain's Store** (tel. 2201), next to the Captain's Quarters Inn at Windwardside (look here also for paintings and original art, as well as goods from the Saba Artisan Foundation).

In The Bottom, the metropolis on the opposite side of the island, you will find the major shopping target on Saba, one of the United Nations' happiest success stories—the above-mentioned **Saba Artisan Foundation** (tel. 3260). Experts and professional designers planted the seed, and it has most certainly taken root. In the Foundation's workrooms, artisans are engaged in silkscreening the designs of tropical flora on silky cotton fabric, as well as in making distinctly Saban blowups of the Spanish work stitches. Buy the cloth already made up into accessories or clothing (the dresses cost under $50). Or buy it by the yard. Here too find Saba lace, local liqueurs, embroidered denim toppers, and some imports from the other Dutch islands—dolls, woodenware, coral. If you don't see what you like, query the manager, Max Nicholson. And if you want to call ahead, phone 3260.

"Saba Spice" completes the inventory of made-on-the-island take home treasures. A dozen "secret" ingredients—fennel seed, brown sugar, nutmeg, cloves, and cinnamon to name a few—are infused in a cask of 150-proof rum. Once properly aged, the elixir is bottled in discarded Dewars fifths, or whatever bottle comes handy, and is sold for about $6. Sipped as an after-dinner liqueur, the flavor may faintly remind you of ouzo.

Saba Spice was the subject of a small commotion at one point between Sint Maarten and Saba. Seems some sharpies on the Big Island decided to swipe the formula—which is not patented but rather handed down from mother to daughter (in this community, the distaffers are the mixologists)—and brew up their own version. The packaging was slick, the marketing professional. But, connoisseurs will tell you, it will never replace the Real Thing (among the objections: the imitators only use 80-proof rum). To sample authentic Saba Spice—and meet one of the island's most ingratiating pillars of local society—drop into the bar at **Scout's Place** at Windwardside (tel. 2205) between 11 a.m. and 1:30 a.m. A long, longtime Caribbean resident, expatriate of a prominent Ohio department store dynasty, Scout Thirkield logged time as a department head in St. Thomas's Continental Shop and as Resident Manager of the Caravanserai Hotel on St. Maarten; he headed up Captain's Quarters on Saba, and then founded his own unorthodox little hideaway—Scout's Place. Scout knows everyone who is anyone in the West Indies, has a special feel for the islands, and a wondrous, low-keyed sense of humor. If you want to make sure to catch him, phone ahead, 011-5994, to make sure he's not wandered off to Yugoslavia or some other exotic retreat for a change of pace. And when you do catch up with him, tell him we sent our usual best.

In the almost certain event you leave Saba longing to return, or at the very least, to know more about what some call "The Unspoiled Queen" or "The Green Gumdrop," be sure to look up Will Johnson's insightful book, *Tales from My Grandmother's Pipe.* A native-born Saban, educated in Curaçao, Mr. Johnson came home to become editor of the island paper, *The Saba Herald.* Eschewing the urban crush of either The Bottom or Windwardside, he and his wife, Lynn, live with their two children in a suburb known as The Level, population 250, on the mountainous outskirts of Windwardside.

USEFUL ADDRESSES

Captain's Store: Captain's Quarters Complex, Windwardside (tel. 2201).

Island Craft Shop: Windwardside.

Saba Artisan Foundation: The Bottom (tel. 3260).

Saure Nickel Shop: Windwardside.

Scout's Place: Windwardside (tel. 2205).

Treasure Chest: Windwardside.

The Yellow House: Windwardside (tel. 2234).

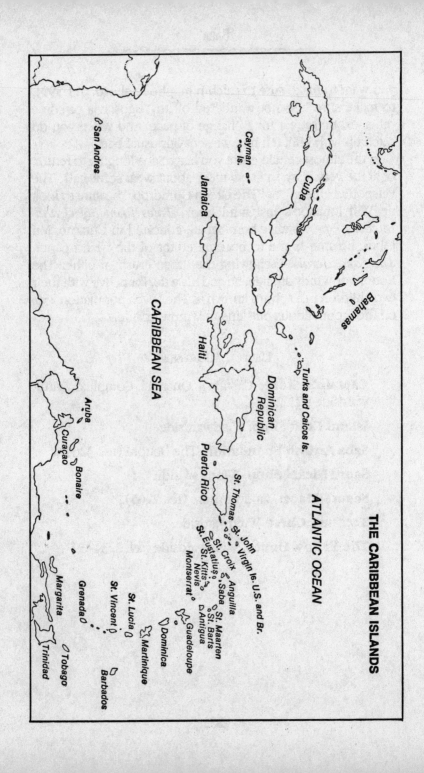

THE CARIBBEAN ISLANDS

ATLANTIC OCEAN

CARIBBEAN SEA

San Andres

Cayman Is.

Jamaica

Cuba

Bahamas

Turks and Caicos Is.

Haiti

Dominican Republic

Puerto Rico

St. Thomas

St. John

Virgin Is.–U.S. and Br.

St. Croix

Anguilla

St. Maarten

Saba

St. Barts

St. Eustatius

St. Kitts

Nevis

Antigua

Montserrat

Guadeloupe

Dominica

Martinique

St. Lucia

St. Vincent

Barbados

Grenada

Aruba

Curaçao

Bonaire

Margarita

Tobago

Trinidad

ST. BARTHÉLÉMY

ST. BARTHÉLÉMY
AT A GLANCE

GOVERNMENT TOURIST OFFICE: Office du Tourisme, Gustavia, St. Barthélémy, French West Indies (tel. 27-60-08).

CURRENCY: The French franc is legal tender, but American dollars are accepted everywhere. At what rate depends on where you make the exchange, when, and if you are using traveler's checks. When you buy, ask whether or not the establishment making the transaction grants the 20% allowance for traveler's checks.

OFFICIAL HOLIDAYS: New Year's Day, Mardi Gras, Ash Wednesday, Mid-Lent, Easter Monday, Labor Day (May 1), Ascension Thursday, Pentecost Monday, Bastille Day (July 14), Festival of St. Barthélémy (beginning August 24), honoring the island's patron saint, All Saints' Day (November 1), Armistice Day (November 11), Christmas Day.

STORE HOURS: Monday, Tuesday, Thursday, and Friday from 8 a.m. to noon and from 2 to 5 p.m. Wednesday and Saturday are half-days, from 8 a.m. until noon.

LOCATIONS: For the addresses and telephone numbers of the shops, consult the alphabetical list at the end of this chapter.

Although the biggest planes it can accommodate are 19-seaters, St. Barthélémy sports one of the most notorious airstrips in the West Indies. And on your first white-knuckle experience with the Gustav III Airport, appropriately called l'Aérodrome de la Tourmente, you'll see why. Narrowly bounded by a steep hillside at one end and the ocean at the other, some islanders suggest that to ensure collision-free landing and takeoff, approaching and departing visitors should pray to the white cross looming between the two seemingly inevitable peaks that flank the field. As if this weren't enough to chill your bones, a cemetery adjoins the strip.

On our first, bouncy crossing, one agitated passenger was heard to say to another who was perched on a case of scotch bound for St. Barths, "For Pete's sake, don't sit on it—open the box and pass some of that stuff around."

As for our companion, a young, first-time travel agent, his immediate question upon landing was, "How much is land selling for here these days? Because, obviously, I'm never going to get back on that bird again."

This little Gallic gumdrop has another claim to fame: with such part-time residents and visitors as David Rockefeller, Edmond de Rothschild, Christie Brinkley and Billy Joel (they met here), Beverly Sills, Liza Minnelli, Peter Jennings, and a whole flock of European counts, barons, and assorted bluebloods, this eight-square-mile isle has been called the Celebrity Capital of the Caribbean.

The French first occupied it, followed by the Knights of Malta. St. Barths also represents Sweden's first and last attempt to establish a New World outpost.

For almost a century, up to 1878, when by petition they rejoined the French orbit, St. Bartians were subjects of the Swedish crown. Because that government forbade the importation of slaves for sugar cultivation, St. Barths' 3,000 souls constitute the only predominantly white island population (about 95%) in the area. Despite Scandinavian occupation, they have retained the characteristics of their Norman-Breton ancestors in speech and in dress.

Gustavia, the cozy cove that constitutes the capital, port, and main shopping center, was named after Swedish King Gustav III. Sprightly, coquettish, her venerable buildings sparkling with fresh paint, Gustavia looks like a Gilbert and Sullivan stage set. Truly a sailor's snug harbor, this is one of the cleanest, brightest corners in the West Indies. Whenever the St. Bartian gets ten francs ahead, he embarks on *l'entretien* (maintenance). Either the hurricanes have been kind to Gustavia or the Swedes built extra strength into their structures, because many handsome ones still stand.

Excellent paved roads connect the beguiling villages that dot St. Barths: Lorient, Governor's Quarter, Corossol. Every so often on the side of the road notice a thick-walled, dome-topped brick oven. Through the years the local ladies took turns stoking it for community bread-baking.

You will find these to be frugal, tough, hardy, seafaring folk. The man rules his household with an iron hand, brooks no back talk from spouse or small one. "When I speak," explains one diminutive old-timer, "my wife has nothing to do but listen!" The family hammock traditionally has been reserved for the head of the house; and no one had better snooze in it without his permission.

With increased traffic with the outside world, and the younger generation bringing back different ideas from their forays into big-city life, some of the edges are blurring. But you will still see women wearing the distinctive *caleche* or *quiche-notte*—an enveloping sunbonnet some say was developed to ward off mashers seeking to steal a kiss. The men, especially the older generation, tend to wear nautical blues with either a sailor cap or their own distinctive island-made straw hat.

If you find the French spoken here differs from that to which you are accustomed, some scholars will tell you that is because this is classic 17th-century French, articulated exactly as it was in the days of Louis XIII, but colored with the regional accents of Normandy and Brittany.

Two minor misapprehensions might bear correcting: first, the preferred name for this island is not, as many self-appointed experts would have you believe, St. Barts—it's St. Barths. And if you're in the know, you say it the islanders' way, with the "th" pronounced as a hard "t."

Not that St. Barths is not a happy hunting ground for discriminating shoppers—especially affluent ones. Because of the uptown calibre of the clientele, perhaps, or due to considerable emphasis on quality—or both—this is not, you might say, the K-Mart of the Caribbean. But whether you shop the souks of beautiful downtown Gustavia or repair to the series of boutiques clustered in the St. Jean area, you will find more than enough to interest you.

ARTS AND CRAFTS

Although native sons or daughters have not yet distinguished themselves as major first rank painters, a number of talented artists living part or full time on the islands have captured with oils or with watercolor much of the Caribbean flavor.

Among the signatures to look for is that of Margot Ferra Doniger, a transplanted American who lived here for fifteen years, generally considered the island's best-known artist.

Alana Fagan and Claire Rentoul, also Americans, are popular for their watercolors as well as oils.

Pierre Lacouture, a native of Madagascar, produced a considerable body of work during his year-long stay in St. Barths.

Canadian David Jones specializes in depicting out-of-the-way corners of the island.

La Bruyère, from the mother country, concentrates on seascapes and sunsets.

From nearby St. Martin comes the outstanding primitive painter known by the single name of Richardson.

Since no full-fledged professional art gallery concentrates exclusively on showcasing these artists, you'll need to ask around—query your innkeeper, restaurateur, and helpful shopkeeper where to look. Postcard reproductions you will find in most shops.

St. Barths' famous straw craft, fashioned mostly by women, children, and oldsters, dates back a hundred years. Part of the secret lies in the raw material: dried leaves of the latania palm imported and planted near the settlement of Corossol by a French priest just before the turn of the century.

Sixty years ago another prelate, Père de Bruyn, brought in an expert Dutch milliner to teach his flock the trade of hatmaking. The resulting combination of fine raw material and professional training has created a finely made topper known as the St. Barths Panama hat.

Some time later, another instructor, this one French, passed on techniques for using straw for decorative as well as millinery purposes. But whether you are looking at hats, baskets, or any other type of work, you will note a standard of quality praised in mainland journals and not duplicated elsewhere in the West Indies.

These products are not bargain priced, because the procedure involved in producing them is time-consuming and complicated. First, the fan-shaped palm leaves are opened, cut, unfolded, and the fronds separated. Next, they spend fourteen days spread out to dry in the sun. At the first sign of rain, the latania must be taken in immediately; otherwise, it loses it elasticity and tone.

When it comes to the actual fashioning of the hat, mat, or handbag, this begins with any one of several types of braiding: the basic eleven-strand or the three-strand all-purpose variety;

the knotted braid, featuring continuous circles; the button braid, with intermittent loops; the hemstitch, using thin threads of straw in large designs; and finally, the saw-toothed edging type you'll see embellishing assorted articles, including hats and placemats.

The hamlet of Corossol is headquarters for the straw workers, who peddle their own wares there without benefit of middlemen.

In Gustavia, you will find St. Barths straw at **Smoke & Booze** on Rue du Général De Gaulle, **Colibri** on Rue du Bord de la Mer, and **Chez Joe** on Rue du Général De Gaulle. Chez Joe maintains an escale at the airport as well.

There is also **St. Barth Pottery**, on the road to St. Jean, whose products we are told are not only custom-made but will withstand the rigors of both dishwashers and microwaves.

CAMERAS

Making sure before purchasing to check your home store prices, you might look in on **Micro-Shop**, Rue du Roi Oscar II, Gustavia. Another possibility is the **Alma** branch off the Rue Couturier, in Gustavia (tel. 27-61-36). Also try the **Hi-Fi Center**, dockside in Gustavia.

CHINA, CRYSTAL, AND HOME FURNISHINGS

Because of the advantageous tax situation, St. Barths is in a position to offer French luxury items at a cost that is sometimes less than that in the mother country.

Bijouterie Carat, in Gustavia, carries Lalique, Baccarat, Waterford, and Swarovski.

Try also **Alma**, off the Rue Couturier, and **Vestibule**, on Rue de la République, both in Gustavia, for Sèvres crystal.

FASHION

Jean-Yves Froment is the big name here. His original designs, hand-blocked or silk-screened and signed, are featured in smart shops on both sides of the Atlantic, and are snapped up by visiting celebrities (such as French singer Charles Aznavour, who chose a jacket of Jean-Yves Froment fabric). You have a choice of buying by the yard or selecting from the ready-made collection. Enter the Jean-Yves Froment establishment in Gustavia from Rue du Général De Gaulle or from Rue du Roi Oscar II (tel. 27-62-11).

À la Calèche, brainchild of realtor Roger Lacour's attractive Westport, Connecticut, wife, Brook (and housed in the Lacour office building on Rue du Général De Gaulle), features gifts, cards, sports fashions, and swimwear from top houses. Should you decide to rent a villa or other short-term accommodations in St. Barths, the Lacours' **S.I.B.A.R.T.H. Real Estate** company represents most of the properties available. Write them at P.O. Box 55, Gustavia, St. Barthélémy (tel. 27-62-38). They also maintain a Stateside office in Newport, Rhode Island (P.O. Box 1435), with a toll-free number: 1-800/932-3222.

Other chic spots to scout for accessories and assorted frippery:

Stéphane et Bernard near Rue de la République, Gustavia, and at the new airport center
La Boutique sur le Quai on the Rue du Bord de la Mer, Gustavia
Le Bastringue on Rue de la France, Gustavia
La Romana on Rue Thiers, Gustavia, and in St. Jean

For collectors of regional fashions, the local feminine sunbonnet, known as a *calèche*, can be obtained ready-made or stitched to order for $10 or so. Choose from among several types—the *calèche à platine* is always white, as is the *calèche à batons,* which is based on a series of wooden twigs enclosed within the fabric and topped with a frilly ruffle; the *cape* is navy blue for everyday, black for dress. These hats are also sometimes called *quichenottes,* said to be derived from the phrase "kiss-me-not," because the protective headgear was supposedly a barrier against amorous English or Swedish outlanders.

FOOD

Whether St. Barths' growing prestige as a gastronomic mecca is the reason *New York Times* food expert Craig Claiborne visits there regularly and reports favorably on the cuisine, or whether the cuisine is so outstanding because of Craig Claiborne's influence is a matter for debate. In any event, the island is acquiring an impressive reputation for fine dining, with amateur and professional epicures gathering from various points of the compass to sample the wares of the thirty-six restaurants or to enroll in cooking classes conducted by well-known Parisian chefs.

Next to working in straw, the baking of bread is probably the most valued skill on St. Barths. The croissants or baguettes are made individually, by hand, in a special island way.

As for gourmetry to take home, you will find the shelves of food markets well stocked with Gallic imports. **Mammouth,** the ubiquitous supermarket chain, has a branch across the landing strip. Robust cassoulets in tins, powdered soufflés, and ingenious French kitchen gadgetry are featured, but the stock can run low on occasion. As a rule, however, you'll probably not want to leave empty-handed.

Le Comptoir, on Rue du Général De Gaulle in Gustavia, caters superbly to sophisticated gourmet tastes.

A stellar attraction, one most informed epicures label not to be missed: **La Rôtisserie** on Rue du Roi Oscar II (tel. 27-63-13).

Another prime target: **The Gourmet Shop** in Gustavia. We plan to check it out on our next trip.

JEWELRY

L'Hibis d'Or, at La Villa Creole on Baie de St. Jean, carries gold chains, bangles, pins, and rings.

Bijouterie Carat, in Gustavia, features Les must de Cartier, along with a good selection of Parisian 18-karat-gold jewelry.

The Shell Shop, on the Gustavia waterfront, offers gemstone and shell creations.

You will find other pieces especially of costume variety in other establishments in Gustavia and St. Jean.

LINENS

Shop **Alma** in Gustavia (tel. 27-61-36) for fancy cloths, placemats, and other home linens, some beautifully hand-embroidered and/or crocheted.

At **Vestibule** in Gustavia you may spot some of those country-style, French-farmhouse-print table accessories so much in vogue.

La Fonda on the Rue de la République in Gustavia includes Hermès leather goods and accessories.

PERFUMES AND COSMETICS

As you would expect on a French island, fragrances and cosmetics are big items, and at most advantageous prices.

Alma in Gustavia (tel. 27-61-36), carries perfumes.

La Boutique sur le Quai in Gustavia handles cosmetics.

In St. Jean, look up **L'Artisan Parfumeur,** oceanside, near the PLM Hotel Jean Bart.

Les Parfums de France, Rue du Général De Gaulle, Gustavia, as the name indicates, purveys fragrances—as well as laser treatment, massages, and sauna.

Privilege, on Rue de la République, Gustavia, features French cosmetics.

SPIRITS

Although it produces no special liquor that we know of, St. Barths acquired something of a reputation back in the days of Prohibition for its activities in what was euphemistically known as "import-export"—that is, smuggling spirits into the U.S.-held islands, and in some cases other areas as well, to avoid taxes. Nowadays, the island is acquiring some renown for the volume and variety of fine wines and liqueurs on sale, at prices knowledgeable oenologists tell us are most advantageous. To find out if you agree, scan the offerings at **Smoke & Booze** on the Rue du Général De Gaulle in Gustavia and at **La Cave de Saint Barthélémy,** between Lorient and Grand Cul de Sac at Marigot.

WATCHES

Bijouterie Carat in Gustavia carries Piaget.

Alma, also near the waterfront in Gustavia, handles imported watches. So do other emporiums here and there.

SPECIAL SUGGESTION

Do not leave St. Barths without picking up a copy of *Bonjour St. Barth!* This 126-page, closely written Baedeker, printed in both English and French, is a gold mine of interesting tidbits about this fascinating island. We learned a lot from reading it, and enjoyed every minute of the process. We believe you will also. If you don't find the book at **Le Select** on Rue du Général De Gaulle, try **À La Calèche** on the same street, **Alma** at dockside, or even L'Office du Tourisme.

USEFUL ADDRESSES

À la Calèche: Rue du Général De Gaulle, Gustavia (tel. 27-62-38).

Alma: Rue Couturier, Gustavia (tel. 27-61-36); fashion branch and Optiques branch, both at dockside, Gustavia.

Bijouterie Carat: two blocks from the waterfront, Gustavia.

Chez Joe: Rue du Général De Gaulle, Gustavia; branch also at Airport.

Colibri: Rue du Bord de la Mer, Gustavia.

The Gourmet Shop: Gustavia.

Hi-Fi Center: dockside, Gustavia.

Jean-Yves Froment: Rue du Général De Gaulle at Rue du Roi Oscar II, Gustavia (tel. 27-62-11).

La Boutique sur le Quai: Rue du Bord de la Mer, Gustavia.

La Cave de Saint Barthélémy: between Lorient and Grand Cul de Sac, Marigot.

La Fonda: Rue de la République, Gustavia.

La Romana: Rue Thiers, Gustavia; branch also in St. Jean.

La Rôtisserie: Rue du Roi Oscar II at Rue Lafayette, Gustavia (tel. 27-63-13); branches also in St. Jean and Pointe Milou.

L'Artisan Parfumeur: near PLM Hotel Jean Bart, St. Jean.

Le Bastringue: Rue de la France, Gustavia.

Le Comptoir: Rue du Général De Gaulle, Gustavia.

Le Select: Rue du Général De Gaulle, Gustavia.

Les Parfums de France: Rue du Général De Gaulle, Gustavia.

L'Hibis d'Or: La Villa Creole, Baie de St. Jean.

Mammouth: across from the airstrip.

Micro-Shop: Rue du Roi Oscar II, Gustavia.

Privilege: Rue de la République, Gustavia.

The Shell Shop: on the waterfront, Gustavia.

S.I.B.A.R.T.H. Real Estate: Gustavia, St. Barthélémy, F.W.I. (tel. 27-62-38; also toll free in the U.S., 1-800-932-3222).

Smoke & Booze: Rue du Général De Gaulle, Gustavia.

St. Barth Pottery: on the road to St. Jean, outside Gustavia.

Stéphane et Bernard: near the Rue de la République, Gustavia, and at the Airport.

Vestibule: Rue de la République, Gustavia.

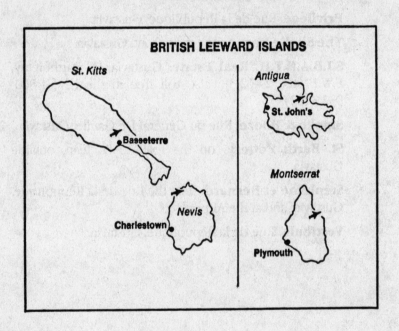

ST. KITTS-NEVIS

ST. KITTS-NEVIS
AT A GLANCE

GOVERNMENT TOURIST OFFICE: Church Street, Basseterre, St. Kitts, W.I. (tel. 465-2620 or 4040); Main Street, Charlestown, Nevis (tel. 465-5494).

CURRENCY: The Eastern Caribbean dollar is the official currency. US$1 equals about EC$2.65.

OFFICIAL HOLIDAYS: New Year's Day, Good Friday, Easter Monday, Labour Day (first Monday in May), Whit Monday, Queen's Birthday (second Saturday in June), Culturama in Nevis (end of July/beginning August), August Monday (first Monday in August), Prince of Wales's Birthday (November 14), Carnival (December 25 to January 1).

STORE HOURS: Monday through Saturday from 8 a.m. until noon and from 1 to 4 p.m., except Thursday, when shops close at noon. Closed Sundays.

LOCATIONS: For the addresses and telephone numbers of the shops, consult the alphabetical list at the end of this chapter.

Who will most enjoy what this area has to offer? First and foremost, the old Caribbean hands, those who know the West Indies from way back. Younger pilgrims will find their blood coursing just a bit faster at their first sight of the historic fortress at Brimstone Hill, of a stately sugar tower silhouetted against a sparkling clean sky, or of a sloe-eyed donkey munching hibiscus under a feathery palm tree, languidly watching the light-and-dark clouds play on the turquoise sea.

For lazing, loafing, daydreaming, rapping, ruin-rambling, exploring, and just plain battery-recharging, this area is very hard to beat. The beach is still clean, and for snorkelers, divers, and fishermen, the water shoals off into enticingly virgin territory. As for walking, hiking, and small-mountain climbing, this two-island nation offers enough of that to satisfy all save conquerors of Piutha Hiunchuli or other such crampon-and-piton-bearing ibexes.

Which is not to say that "progress" has not caught on in some respects, especially in St. Kitts. In the capital, you may encounter rambunctious tourists, radios blaring, and, as a result of such intrusions, some restlessness among the home folks. But compared to the highly developed tourist centers, St. Kitts-Nevis is still a very likely place to search out the ephemeral charm and low-keyed delights of old-fashioned West Indian ambience.

Although there is a casino, and group travelers do descend on St. Kitts, in terms of actual volume the island is reminiscent of Montego Bay back in the days when Charlie Morrow's single new 100-room hotel actually doubled the tourist capacity of the town; or of St. Thomas in those halcyon times when in the absence of any nightlife whatsoever, what after-dark activity did take place revolved around cozy gatherings at Bluebeard's and Blackbeard's Castles, Smiths Fancy, Contant, the Grand, and Higgins Gate.

357

Development in this three-year-old nation is still on a small enough scale—akin to portions of Jamaica and the Virgin Islands a decade or so ago—to make it possible to zero in on the countryside, to examine in more detail the rich history, the distinctive heritage, and the frequently awesome physical beauty.

In so doing, you'll be following in some pretty heavy footsteps. Christopher Columbus thought so much of this discovery of his that he named the larger island Saint Christopher after himself. No one refers to it so formally these days. It's St. Kitts, with no apostrophe. Alexander Hamilton was born on the sister island of Nevis. Horatio Nelson fell in love and married there. Philippe de Longvilliers de Poincy, known to most travelers for the tree (royal poinciana) named after him, headquartered in St. Kitts.

Although there are no huge emporiums or giant malls teeming with singleminded bargain-hunters, you can, we believe, ferret out from among the wares offered many original and interesting items.

ARTS AND CRAFTS

Spencer Cameron Art Gallery on the Bay Road in Basseterre (tel. 465-4047), established a decade ago by a pair of young British artists, provides mementos of the islands in whatever price range you choose, from a $5 lithograph to a $300 original oil. Exhibits include flower prints, photographic reproductions of 19th-century maps and engravings, note-paper featuring local scenes, original watercolors of the island at $35 unframed.

You might also stop by **Kassab's Art Gallery** in Fortlands, on the outskirts of Basseterre, to see what may have come in recently in arts or handcrafts.

St. Kitts-Nevis took every possible advantage of the expert advice and guidance offered by United Nations designers some years back, and, as a result, crafts are thriving. Whether you fancy ceramics, straw, leatherwork, coconut or wood carvings, you'll find plenty to choose from.

On Bay Road, east of the Treasury Building, Basseterre, the **Craft House Emporium** (tel. 465-3241) is headquarters for local output.

The Unique Boutique, on Frigate Bay Road, borders a field of lush sugarcane, and among island-made objects features art-on-leather.

Palm Crafts, on Princess Street, Basseterre, with a branch in Dieppe Bay at the Golden Lemon Hotel (tel. 465-2889), purveys articles made of shell and black coral, wall hangings, and baskets in various sizes and shapes.

Faoud Abourizk on Central Street in Basseterre mixes Caribbean handcrafts in with his stock of electronic equipment and jewelry.

Several other boutiques and shops include handcrafts along with their other lines of merchandise, among them:

David Coury & Company, College Street, Basseterre (tel. 465-2506)

Losada's Antiques & Things on Wigley Avenue in Fortlands (tel. 465-2216) offers for sale those handcrafts that meet the exacting standards of its discriminating proprietor, Ghislaine Cramer

Glendale Boutique, Central Street, Basseterre (no phone)

Lotus Gift Shop, Bay Road, Basseterre (tel. 465-2021)

In Nevis, head for the **Nevis Crafts Studio Cooperative,** Main Street, in Charlestown, and **Crafthouse Nevis**, also in Charlestown (tel. 465-5505).

CAMERAS

We've said it before, and it needs saying again: before

making any sizeable investment in photographic equipment, check the U.S. prices, by long-distance phone if necessary. Local operators are on duty 24 hours a day.

Try **Ram's Duty-Free Shop**, Liverpool Row (tel. 465-2145), or **T.D.C.'s Duty-Free Shop**, at the corner of Bank and West Square Street (tel. 465-2511), both in Basseterre.

CHINA, CRYSTAL, AND HOME FURNISHINGS

Belleek, Coalport, Porcelaine de Paris, Royal Copenhagen, Limoges, Bayel, Crown Staffordshire china, Val-St. Lambert crystal, Goebels, Sèvres—these are a few of the name-brand imports **A Slice of Lemon** offers you in its duty-free shops at the Palms Arcade, at The Circus in Basseterre, and at the Golden Lemon Hotel in Dieppe Bay (tel. 465-2889 and 7260). We have so far been unable to verify the stores claim that their prices run only 10% above U.S. wholesale. If you succeed in doing so, please let us know.

Have a special look at the collection of porcelain: some 30 pieces, all with black-on-white design depicting the famous 1776 Basseterre fire. (There's an account of the event inscribed on the other side.) Glazed by a photographic process, items include bar bottles, decorative plates and trinket boxes, various sizes of flasks. If you're in the market for imported silverplate—silver spoons, rattles, and the like—those come here from Holland.

Losada's Antiques & Things nestles in an elegant private home on Wigley Avenue near the Ocean Terrace Inn and the Fort Thomas Hotel (tel. 465-2216). The accent here is most definitely on quality, not only in china and crystal, but in fourposter beds and other antique furnishings, some of them heirlooms left over from the balmy days of the plantocracy.

At **Palm Crafts** in Basseterre (tel. 465-2860) note the carved and hand-painted wooden mirror frames, from $75 up; hand-cut-and-sewn fabric wall hangings; decorative carved animal figures; and some of the prized pottery—glazed or unglazed—from The Newcastle cooperative in Nevis. Ashtrays, flowerpots, candlesticks, and boxes range in price from under $5 to $15 or so.

Pottery has been a family tradition in the village of Newcastle for over a century. All the clay is dug locally, and thrown without additives. The pottery's distinctive red color comes from an iron-bearing rock on the island, which is crushed and hand ground to a fine powder. This is painted on the items, which are then hand burnished with a smooth stone to create a shiny finish. All Newcastle articles are fired on burning coconut husks. And if you are in Nevis, you are welcome to visit the **Pottery Cooperative**; one of the potters might even make something to order upon your request. Newcastle is just east of the airport.

T.D.C.'s Duty-Free Shop, at the corner of Bank and West Square Street in Basseterre (tel. 465-2511), offers you Wedgwood, Lalique, Lladrò, Baum, Waterford, and Royal Doulton.

Ram's Duty-Free Shop on Liverpool Row, Basseterre (tel. 465-2145), features Hummel figurines and Capodimonte.

In Charlestown, Nevis, **Crafthouse Nevis** (tel. 465-5505) features coconut straw made up into floor rugs at $1.75 per square foot, as well as doormats and placemats, also $1.75 apiece. From the coconut shell they manufacture jewelry, piggy banks, goblets, children's toys, and some beguiling birdfeeders.

The Sand-Box Tree, on Chapel Street in Charlestown, sells small and large antiques left from the colonial days of Nevis.

Several St. Kitts shops carry at least some china, glassware, and silver, among them:

John Gumbs Ltd., Bay Road, Basseterre (tel. 465-2370)
S.L. Horsford & Company, West Square Street, Basseterre (tel. 465-2616)

Lotus Gift Shop, Bay Road, Basseterre (tel. 465-2021)
Kassab's Art Gallery, Fortlands (no phone)

FASHIONS

Some of St. Kitts' most distinctive inhabitants are a strain of monkeys known alternately as vervet monkeys or *Cercopithecus aethiops sabeaus* depending on how technical you want to get. California research scientist Frank Irving decided St. Kitts was an ideal place to study the aberrant behavior of primates in their natural habitat. Within an unobtrusively enclosed test acre on the grounds of an old plantation south of Dieppe Bay, 200 Kittitian simians function in a society as similar as possible to their natural habitat.

As one of their experiments, Frank Irving and his wife, Pat, once threw a hand mirror into the monkey's yard. And guess what happened: the females of the species pounced upon it, fighting for possession. They preened and posed for the rest of the day. The males, on the other hand, showed no interest whatsoever. Which may or may not point up the fact that for its size, population, and number of tourists, still to reach potential, this nation has an extraordinary feel for fashion.

Probably the most famous fashion operation is that of **Caribelle Batik** (The Circus, Main Street, Basseterre—tel. 465-2905). Utilizing the traditional Indonesian technique of wax printing, a design is first sketched on West Indian sea-island cotton; then a mixture of molten bee and paraffin wax is applied with a tool known as a *tjanting*. Color is then added by either painting the cotton or dipping it directly into the dye, the wax insulating the areas not requiring color. This process is repeated as many times as the shadings and design require.

Purists point out that many so-called batiks are actually made these days by dipping big copper seals into wax, and then stamping them into the fabric—a much quicker, easier, and less expensive process than that of Caribelle Batik, where each piece is individually made. Which is one reason fine shops throughout the Caribbean carry the Kittitian batik in preference to other varieties.

Given the painstaking labor involved, prices offer very good value: wrap-around skirts, $35; button-down shirts from $10; beach wraps, $25; men's shirts from $10; shorts and bikinis, $20; children's dresses, from $10 to $18.

If you have the time, do drive out to the main Caribelle factory and shop at Romney Manor, on the road between Basseterre and Brimstone Hill (tel. 465-6253). Romney Manor is a magnificent 300-year-old sugar plantation. The view is fabulous: you can stop and look at the Carib petroglyphs en route (near Old Road Town), and thence continue on to Brimstone Hill.

In Nevis, the Caribelle Batik shop is in the Arcade, Main Street, Charlestown (tel. 465-5426).

If you like clothes made to order, investigate two shops located across from each other in Basseterre, **La Collage Boutique** (tel. 465-2072) and the **Glendale Boutique** (no phone), both on Central Street.

Both have secret weapons: seamstresses on hand who will make most anything to your specifications, often in as little time as a day or two. Prices vary according to how complicated the design is.

Glendale Boutique also carries handmade ready-to-wear clothes.

Spencer Cameron Art Gallery, Bay Road, Basseterre (tel. 465-4047), carries some ready-made fashions featuring their own art work.

Dandy Boutique on Fort Street in Basseterre (tel. 465-2258) includes St. Kitts–made Casino jeans in its assortment.

If you like Liberty of London fabrics, look for them at **David Coury & Company** on College Street in Basseterre (tel. 465-2506).

In your travels, keep an eye out for the label Southern Clothes. Manufactured in Nevis, for men and for women, each garment is seen to completion by one worker. Featuring bands of color and hand stenciling, these confections are not inexpensive—women's blouses run from $40 to $75, men's shirts are $37.50—but we're still enjoying a blouse we bought ten years ago. **Palm Crafts** (Princess Street—tel. 465-2860) and **A Slice of Lemon** (The Circus, Main Street—tel. 465-2889 and 7260) are likely Kittitian sources; on Nevis there's a Southern Clothes' retail shop in Charlestown.

The Sand-Box Tree on Chapel Street, Charlestown (no phone), is a good place in Nevis to shop Caribbean fashions for men and children as well as women.

FOOD

Ram's Duty-Free Shop (Liverpool Row, Basseterre—tel. 465-2145) features, along with its eclectic assortment of nonedible merchandise, an on-premises supermarket carrying a variety of local delicacies.

The **native open-air markets**, on Bay Road in Basseterre and off Main Street in Charlestown, are likely places to pick up homemade hot sauces, chutneys, and other tropical favorites (best days are Fridays and Saturdays).

The **Kittitian Kitchen** on Princess Street in Basseterre (tel. 465-2889), with an outlet at Dieppe Bay, is a treasure trove featuring: 24 local jams and jellies; five varieties of chutney made from mango, guava, papaya, or lime; spiced teas; West Indian seasoned salts made with island herbs and spices. For fun, they offer a West Indian Hangover Cure (an herbal tea) and an Arawak Love Potion (also an herbal tea).

In Charlestown, Nevis, visit **Caribbean Confections**—and while you are there, try their fruit ice creams.

JEWELRY

You may well pick up several pieces of shell, coconut, or other locally made items in any one of the craft shops. In addition, there are imports to look at:

Martin Kreiner at **A Slice of Lemon** (main store at The Circus, Basseterre—tel. 465-2889) puts considerable emphasis on jewelry, with interesting pieces ranging from under $10 up to $1,500. The designs originate with artists based in Yugoslavia, Denmark, France, England, and Portugal; they feature 14- and 18-karat gold, silver, and precious and semiprecious stones.

Heyliger Jewelry Store on Fort Street in Basseterre (tel. 465-2136) is an associate of Y. de Lima of Trinidad. Here you will find the charms, bangles, and other gold items reflecting the flora and fauna of the Caribbean, designed and manufactured in Trinidad.

While you are in **Losada's Antiques & Things** on Wigley Avenue, Fortlands (tel. 465-2216), ask to see what's new in the jewelry line. The proprietor, Mrs. Cramer, has a sharp eye for outstanding pieces of gold or silver.

LINENS

A length of Caribelle batik would make a stunning tablecloth as would some Liberty of London fabrics, all obtainable at the **Caribelle Batik** outlets—see Useful Addresses list.

You will also see hand-crocheted cotton cloths, placemats, and doilies in the handcraft shops, especially in Nevis. The **Nevis Crafts Studio Cooperative** on Main Street in Charlestown, Nevis (no phone), will make to order anything you have in mind and ship it as well.

T.D.C. Duty-Free Shop at the corner of Bank and West Square Streets, Basseterre (tel. 465-2511), features linens.

PERFUMES AND COSMETICS

In addition to stocking more than 100 fragrances with names such as Chanel, Guerlain, Paco Rabanne, Nina Ricci, and Yves Saint Laurent—at prices some shoppers report to be under those of competing resorts—**A Slice of Lemon** in The Circus at Basseterre and at the Golden Lemon Hotel in Dieppe Bay (tel. 465-2889 and 7260) has its own scent: Golden Lemon cologne. Spicy, citrusy, and suitable for either men or women, it comes in a half-ounce spray at $4.95, the four-ounce splash, $12.

The **T.D.C.'s Duty-Free Shop** (mentioned above) also handles perfumes.

The **Kittitian Kitchen** on Princess Street in Basseterre (tel. 465-2889) carries scented coconut oils (choose from tangerine, coconut bay, or coconut cinnamon) at $4.50 the bottle. Coconut soap, four to a package, costs $5.

SPIRITS

St. Kitts Carib beer is delicious, but other than that, the islands produce no spiritous beverage, so far as we know. If they do, **H & R Liquor Store** in the Bentels Building on Canyon Street, Basseterre, will have it.

WATCHES

Borel, Concord, Ebel, and Meerson watches are all on sale at **A Slice of Lemon,** The Circus, Basseterre (tel. 465-2889 and 7260); there's a branch also at the Golden Lemon Hotel in Dieppe Bay. (Ebel, as you may know, are the Swiss makers of Cartier timepieces.)

Ram's Duty-Free Shop on Liverpool Row, Basseterre (tel. 465-2145), handles Seiko and Citizen brands.

Heyliger Jewelry Store on Fort Street, Basseterre (tel 465-2136), also carries watches.

SPECIAL CATEGORY

Nevis was one of the first islands in the West Indies to issue stamps under its own name, back in 1861, and it continued to do so until 1903. Almost eight decades later, in June 1980, Nevis resumed this practice.

Visit the Philatelic Bureau off Main Street in Charlestown, and you will see a variety of colorful denominations: some depict the pineapple of hospitality, others tall ships; there is even a $5 stamp to commemorate the 1981 royal wedding of Charles and Diana. Under separate portraits of the Prince and Princess, there is the caption "Congratulations from the people of Nevis." (Charles visited these islands regularly before his wedding and was very popular.)

In St. Kitts, the Philatelic Bureau is on Bay Road, Basseterre.

USEFUL ADDRESSES

Caribbean Confections: Charlestown, Nevis.

Caribelle Batik: Romney Manor, between Basseterre and Brimstone Hill (tel. 465-6253); branches at The Circus, Main Street, Basseterre (tel. 465-2905), and in the Arcade, Main Street, Charlestown, Nevis (tel. 465-5426).

Craft House Emporium: East Bay Road, Basseterre (tel. 465-3241).

Crafthouse Nevis: Charlestown, Nevis (tel. 465-5505).

Dandy Boutique: Fort Street, Basseterre (tel. 465-2258).

David Coury & Company: College Street, Basseterre (tel. 465-2506).

Faoud Abourizk: Central Street, Basseterre (no phone).

Glendale Boutique: Central Street, Basseterre (no phone).

H & R Liquor Store: Bentels Building, Canyon Street, Basseterre.

Heyliger Jewelry Store: Fort Street, Basseterre (tel. 465-2136).

John Gumbs Ltd.: Bay Road, Basseterre (tel. 465-2370).

Kassab's Art Gallery: Fortlands, St. Kitts (no phone).

Kittitian Kitchen: Princess Street, Basseterre (tel. 465-2889); also outlet at Dieppe Bay.

La Collage Boutique: Central Street, Basseterre (tel. 465-2072).

Losada's Antiques & Things: Wigley Avenue, Fortlands, St. Kitts (tel. 465-2216).

Lotus Gift Shop: Bay Road, Basseterre (tel. 465-2021).

Nevis Crafts Studio Cooperative: Main Street, Charlestown, Nevis (no phone).

Newcastle Pottery Cooperative: Newcastle (just east of the airport), Nevis.

Palm Crafts: Princess Street, Basseterre (tel. 465-2860); branch at Golden Lemon Hotel in Dieppe Bay (tel. 465-2889).

Philatelic Bureau of Nevis: off Main Street, Charlestown, Nevis.

Philatelic Bureau of St. Kitts: Bay Road, Basseterre.

Ram's Duty-Free Shop: Liverpool Row, Basseterre (tel. 465-2145).

The Sand-Box Tree: Chapel Street, Charlestown, Nevis (no phone).

S.L. Horsford & Company: West Square Street, Basseterre (tel. 465-2616).

A Slice of Lemon: The Circus, Basseterre (tel. 465-2889 and 7260); branch also at Golden Lemon Hotel, Dieppe Bay.

Spencer Cameron Art Gallery: Bay Road, Basseterre (tel. 465-4047).

T.D.C.'s Duty-Free Shop: Corner of Bank and West Square Streets, Basseterre (tel. 465-2511).

The Unique Boutique: Frigate Bay Road, Basseterre.

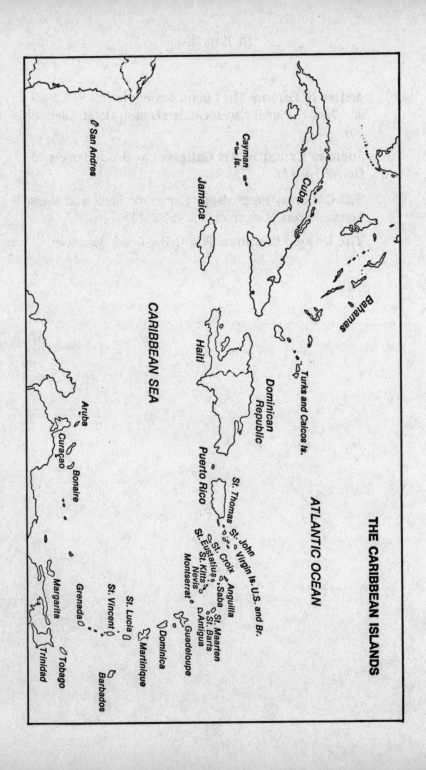

THE CARIBBEAN ISLANDS

ATLANTIC OCEAN

CARIBBEAN SEA

San Andres

Cayman Is.

Jamaica

Cuba

Bahamas

Turks and Caicos Is.

Haiti

Dominican Republic

Puerto Rico

St. Thomas
St. John
Virgin Is. U.S. and Br.
St. Croix
Anguilla
St. Maarten
St. Barts
Saba
St. Eustatius
St. Kitts
Nevis
Antigua
Montserrat
Guadeloupe
Dominica
Martinique
St. Lucia
St. Vincent
Barbados
Grenada
Tobago
Trinidad
Margarita
Bonaire
Curaçao
Aruba

ST. LUCIA

ST. LUCIA
AT A GLANCE

GOVERNMENT TOURIST OFFICE: St. Lucia Tourist Board, Sans Souci, and at the Pointe Seraphine Cruise Terminal, Castries Harbour, St. Lucia, W.I. (tel. 452-9568).

CURRENCY: The Eastern Caribbean dollar US$1 equals about EC$2.65.

OFFICIAL HOLIDAYS: New Year's Day, New Year's Holiday (January 2), Carnival (first week in February), Independence and Carnival Day (February 22), Labor Day (May 1), Corpus Christi Day, Queen's Birthday (second Saturday in June), August Bank Holiday (first Monday in August), Thanksgiving Day (first Monday in October), National Day (December 13), Christmas Day, Boxing Day (December 26).

STORE HOURS: Monday through Saturday from 8 a.m. to 4 p.m.—more or less, with Saturdays half days. Inquire when you arrive, especially about half day closings.

LOCATIONS: For the addresses and telephone numbers of the shops, consult the alphabetical list at the end of this chapter.

If Gauguin had seen St. Lucia before he headed for Papeete, he might have saved himself the trip.

Towering green-sloped peaks jut dramatically out of lambent peacock seas. Fluffy palms rim golden beaches. Sparkling mountain pools, giant tree ferns, bubbling streams, wild orchids—this island matches the sensual spell of the South Pacific—and then some!

Gros Piton (2,618 feet) and Petit Piton (2,415 feet), twin volcanic spires towering above the ocean at an abrupt 55-degree angle, just south of the town of Soufrière, rank among the top photographic targets in the Caribbean. The ocean floor plunges twice as precipitously: the 224-mile channel separating the island from Martinique drops to 4,500 feet in depth.

Of the island's infinite variety of birds, one species of bright parrot (*Amazon versicolor*) flies only over St. Lucia. A copious rainfall (up to 160 inches in the interior) brings forth fragrant jasmine, lacy lavender-centered flowers, waxy frangipani, spiky bird-of-paradise, and flaming anthurium. Of indigenous fauna (sparse) watch out for the deadly fer-de-lance snake—not often seen, fortunately, except in the virgin forests in the mountains.

Castries, the capital city, accounts for about a third of the island's total 120,000 population. Named after French Marshal de Castries, the town also went briefly under the euphoric name of Felicityville.

Of major importance is the recent completion of Castries' first duty-free port. These facilities are at Pointe Seraphine Cruise Terminal, which can accommodate any ship cruising the Caribbean today. Features also include an attractive courtyard shopping area offering duty-free brand-name crystal, china, electronic equipment, and perfume. Native crafts will be on hand, as well as some of St. Lucia's celebrated batik and silkscreened fabrics.

Customers will be required to present a passport or other document identifying them as nonresident.

ARTS AND CRAFTS

Minvielle & Chastanet, known locally as M & C, sponsors a Fine Arts Exhibtion. For dates and times, which vary, consult the St. Lucia Tourist Board (tel. 452-9568).

Year-round, you will find paintings and other works of art by local artists at the **Tapion Craft Center**, La Toc Road, Tapion. Prices are tempting: from under $30. In addition to paintings, the Tapion also purveys embroidered and straw work, pottery, and wooden ware.

Try also the **Artists Workshop**, La Clery. Ron Savory there does excellent framing too.

The work of sculptor Eudovic is known world wide. Since he likes to work with the natural bases of tropical woods, pieces tend to be rather large—and not inexpensive. The master does teach, however, and sometimes you can pick up good smaller offerings that will be easier to take home as well as costing considerably less. The **Eudovic Art Studio and Restaurant** is at Goodlands, Morne Fortune (tel. 452-2747).

Noah's Arkade, located on Bridge Street in Castries (tel. 452-2523), as well as branches at Soufrière and Rodney Bay, unabashedly goes in for souvenirs. Nevertheless, in picking through what might strike you as banal, you may well find something you'll thoroughly enjoy.

If you're a crafts freak, do not fail to prowl the **native open market** on Jeremie Street in Castries, especially for straw goods and rustic pottery. Uusally weekends are best.

CAMERAS

The local branch of **Y. de Lima** of Trinidad, located on

William Peter Boulevard in Castries (tel. 452-2898), has been representing Asahi, Pentax, Minolta, and other name brands for many years. Find branches also at Hewanorra International Airport (45 miles from Castries) and the Pointe Seraphine Cruise Terminal.

As always, before making an important purchase, check the price of your hometown distributor, who might be able to match or even better the offer.

CHINA, CRYSTAL, AND HOME FURNISHINGS

Mystique Gift Shop on Laborie Street in Castries (tel. 452-2632), with a counter at the new Seraphine Cruise facility, offers Hummel figurines, Limoges porcelain, Royal Doulton china, silver souvenir spoons for collectors, and assorted German and English tableware.

Look also at the wares on display at **Cox & Company, Ltd.**, a department store on William Peter Boulevard (tel. 452-2211), **Lanai Decorating and Home Furnishing** on Mongiraud Street (tel. 452-2572), and **J.Q. Charles, Ltd.** on William Peter Boulevard (tel. 452-2721), all in the heart of Castries.

For island-made rugs, try **Noah's Arkade** on Bridge Street (mentioned above) and the **Castries native market**. Prices begin at around $25 or so.

Bagshaws Studio and Workshop, a short and scenic trip to La Toc from Castries (tel. 452-2139), is justifiably one of the most celebrated silkscreening enterprises in the entire West Indies. Sydney Bagshaw, formerly with the *Reader's Digest* art department, founded this operation a generation ago with a combination of top-quality fabrics, colorfast pigments, sensible prices, and, most of all, just plain, old-fashioned talent.

One banana blossom, framed in cool green leaves, constitutes the focal point of a linen placemat. Brilliantly plumaged parrots dominate a wall hanging. Bright, well-tailored throw pillows make handsome additions to prep school or college dormitory rooms.

The decorator who set up our villa in Hilton Head was so enchanted with Bagshaws' placemats that she had twenty-four of them framed, to cover an entire wall of the den. Two of the wall hangings are permanently installed facing our beds.

Sydney died a couple of years ago, but his winsome daughter-in-law, Alice, has preserved his designs and maintained the business, keeping 99 artisans on the payroll.

The fabrics, many of which are special-ordered 59,000 yards at a time, are processed in the Bagshaws workshop, according to the special method Sydney developed: a formula for hard-edged silkscreening with "tight registration," so that not even a millimeter off is allowed when screens are overlapped. All the work is done by hand, and one design will have up to a dozen different colors, which means that twelve different screens have to be stacked one exactly on top of the other, the shades applied with rubber squeegees through many repetitions. Once the fabric is completed, the work moves on to individual St. Lucian homes for stitching.

Choose from seventy-five different beautiful designs of placemats—birds, flowers, butterflies, fish—all on 100% linen. And the cost? A mere $3.50 apiece! At this price, you can just imagine how many sets we have given as wedding presents. Very often, the brides have told us that they too have framed theirs. Considering these rates (the wall hangings are only $15), it is hard to think of a better-looking, less expensive, more easily packed purchase to take home, for yourself or for gifts.

You'll enjoy browsing around the spacious, garden-surrounded headquarters, but if time is short, visit the Bagshaws branch shop at the new Seraphine Cruise Terminal. And should you spot a slim, pretty blonde patrolling either of the premises, introduce yourself to Alice. If you're interested in either photography or scuba diving—or both—you've found yourself a soul sister.

FASHIONS

Bagshaws (see entry above) is a big name in this area. At least one writer referred to the late Sydney as "the Pucci of the Caribbean." Wrap skirts decorated with leafy bamboo ($35), men's sports shirts featuring tall ships under sail ($15 up), yardage for do-it-yourselfers ($15 for 2½ yards), totebags that double as conversation piece pocketbooks ($8)—be they for man, woman, or child, the clothes are superbly styled, properly made, and reflect a marvelously regional idiom.

Bagshaws' merchandise not only provides a beautiful botany lesson in Technicolor—it stands on its own anywhere in the world as quality fashion. We've had discerning travelers as far away from this hemisphere as Tunisia comment on the fact we are wearing what they recognize instantly as "a Bagshaws." If you have only time for one stop, we'd say make it to one of the two Bagshaws outlets (the only places you can buy Bagshaws' products).

Bagshaws is not St. Lucia's only fashion resource. The **Sea Island Cotton Shop** in the Voice Building on Bridge Street (tel. 452-3674) also produces its own creations on fabric, with emphasis on batik, and the workmanship is painstaking.

The ubiquitous **Ruth Clarage** operation is represented here as well (see the write-up in the Jamaica chapter under "Fashions"), at 14 Brazil Street in Castries and at the Hotel La Toc, 2½ miles south of Castries (tel. 452-1253), presumably at the Pointe Seraphine Cruise Terminal also. The fabrics used are bright, the styles simple and rather preppy. One fashion writer considers the Ruth Clarage look the successor to Lilly Pulitzer.

Other emporiums you might care to explore:

Marie-Claire Boutique at the St. Lucian Hotel, 6½ miles from Castries (tel. 452-8351)
Rain Restaurant and Boutique, Columbus Square, Castries (tel. 452-3022)
Coletta's, Mongiraud Street, Castries (tel. 452-3534)
Roma's Boutique, Columbus Square, Castries (no phone)
Island Connection, Mongiraud Street, Castries, and at the Halcyon Beach Club, Choc Bay—4 miles outside Castries

One of the most imaginative merchandise ventures on this island concerned an enterprising young Peace Corpsman some years back who parlayed a master's degree in business and an investment of $3.50 into a clothing industry supporting a number of cooperative owners.

Under the firm name of "Flour Power" (sic), they fabricated shirts, dresses, sunhats, and shorts out of flour-sacking tailored along American-made Levi lines. Founder Ronnie Savitz returned to the States, and we haven't seen any bona fide Flour Power labels of late, but imitations in varying degrees of worth have proliferated throughout the Caribbean since his departure. You might keep an eye out for these as you browse through such establishments as **Noah's Arkade** on Bridge Street (tel. 452-2523). But unless they're so fantastically low-priced that it's not important, scrutinize size, stitching, and the like before you buy.

St. Lucia has some first-rate men's tailors, and we've had excellent luck with slacks and shorts made to order for us there. However, this is still eminently a cottage industry, with individuals, known only to regular clients, working in their homes. Ask your waiter, chauffeur, chambermaid—better still, check with savvy locals who have their own clothes made to order.

Food

"Aunt Lucie" is the brand of choice for chutney, hot sauce, compotes, and delicious jams and jellies made of such tropical fruits as guava, mango, and pineapple. Aunt Lucie's headquarters are in Dennery, but you can pick up the products at any of a number of local supermarkets.

Best bet: **J.Q. Charles, Ltd.** on William Peter Boulevard in Castries (tel. 452-2721)—wide aisles, lots of cool breezes provided by ceiling fans, and air-conditioned storage for perishables.

Individual island cooks sell their wares at the **Castries native market**, Saturday is the big day, morning's the best time!

Jewelry

Monica Giraudy is the resident expert on this subject. And if she doesn't as yet have her operation at Pointe Seraphine fully functioning, give her a call at 452-8316, to find out latest specifics, and/or ask Alice Bagshaw. At one point Monica told us she was bringing in top quality Brazilian gems to sell at attractively low prices. Alice can probably also show you some of her pieces, and tell you about custom-design.

Y. de Lima of Trinidad maintains a shop on William Peter Boulevard (tel. 452-2898), selling the gold charms, bangles, and pins manufactured in the Port-of-Spain workrooms, much of it out of Guyana gold.

Maraj and Sons Company, Ltd. of Trinidad also maintains a branch here (Bridge Street, Castries—tel. 452-2640).

Tapion Craft Center on La Toc Road features jewelry locally fabricated out of shells, leather, and, as a novelty, bits of sulfur from the island's Soufrière volcano. We have been assured that the sulfuric odor has been duly removed!

LINENS

Apart from what's available at **Bagshaws** (see "China, Crystal, and Home Furnishings," above), St. Lucia provides you with no great linen buys that we know of.

PERFUMES

Shop for imported scents at **Cox & Company, Ltd.** (William Peter Boulevard, Castries—tel. 252-2211), **Mystique Gift Shop** (Laborie Street, Castries—tel. 452-2632), **Images** (Bridge Street, Castries—no phone), and the **Y. de Lima** duty-free shop at Hewanorra International Airport (tel. 452-2898).

St. Lucia Perfumes, Ltd., with a factory scenically located on Red Tape Lane next door to the Green Parrot Restaurant, Morne Fortune (tel. 452-3890) manufactures some very agreeable and fragrant products. And it won't cost you much to try them: $5 will buy 5 cc. of perfume ($13 the ounce). In the masculine line, toilet water can be had for under $5.

St. Lucia Bay Rum continues to have a loyal following. Most boutiques carry it.

SPIRITS

Denros Bounty is the Everyman rum. Distilled and manufactured on the island, it sells for $3 or so the quart. Admiral Rodney Rum is considered more refined, is aged longer, and costs maybe a dollar more per bottle. Both are available in all supermarkets and liquor shops.

J.Q. Charles, Ltd. (William Peter Boulevard, Castries—tel. 452-2721) and **Cox & Company, Ltd.** (William Peter Boulevard also—tel. 452-2211), among others, carry imported brands. There is also a duty-free liquor shopping center at Hewanorra International Airport.

SPECIAL CATEGORY

Longtime Caribbean regulars who remember **Minvielle & Chastanet, Ltd.** on Bridge Street as one of the finest department stores in the West Indies will find that Minvielle & Chastanet has a new owner: J.Q. Charles, Ltd. This store remains, however, a tempting target. Essentially oriented to the local population, the merchandise is most attractive and often priced well under that purveyed by the smaller competitors. Fabrics in particular are outstanding here.

John Compton, the thoughtful Prime Minister who has been leading this country for a generation, once made a statement that sums up the situation of all emerging nations discerningly. It should be required reading for every statesman in the West Indies.

"The theme of the Caribbean's colonial past is a history of stability in government. How can this tender and delicate fabric be preserved, unless we satisfy the aspirations of the people? But political freedom is not an end in itself. It is a tool which must be used to satisfy the needs of the people. It can be used like a waterfall, harnessed for productive channeling, or allowed to roll downhill, destroying everything in its wake. These islands can only preserve their political liberties if these liberties are translated into their economic well-being."

At the ground-breaking of the new multi-million-dollar port facility last year, the Prime Minister added another observation.

"We are late in this tourism race. We must therefore offer better value if we are to catch up. Trying to make a 'quick killing' will be self-defeating and is the surest recipe for failure. *Quality, price,* and *service* must be our watchword."

With the ongoing expansion and improvement of visitor accommodations, and with continued good leadership at the helm, St. Lucia seems indeed headed to epitomize the official motto which was in effect for so many decades: *Statio Haud Malefidia Carinis,* A Safe Anchorage for Ships. And one from which no discerning shopper need sail away empty-handed.

Useful Addresses

Artists Workshop: La Clery (no phone).

Bagshaws Studio and Workshop: just outside Castries, at La Toc (tel. 452-2139); branch at Pointe Seraphine Cruise Terminal.

Coletta's: Mongiraud Street, Castries (tel. 452-3534).

Cox & Company, Ltd.: William Peter Boulevard, Castries (tel. 452-2211).

Eudovic Art Studio and Restaurant: Goodlands, Morne Fortune (tel. 452-2747).

Images: Bridge Street, Castries (no phone).

Island Connection: Mongiraud Street, Castries, and at Halcyon Beach Club, Choc Bay, 4 miles outside Castries.

J.Q. Charles, Ltd.: William Peter Boulevard, Castries (tel. 452-2721).

Lanai Decorating and Home Furnishing: Mongiraud Street, Castries (tel. 452-2572).

Maraj and Sons Company, Ltd.: Bridge Street, Castries (tel. 452-2640).

Marie-Claire Boutique: St. Lucian Hotel, 6½ miles from Castries (tel. 452-8351).

Minvielle & Chastanet, Ltd: Bridge Street, Castries (phone St. Lucia Tourist Board, 452-9568, for information).

Mystique Gift Shop: Laborie Street, Castries (tel. 452-2632); branch also at Pointe Seraphine Cruise Terminal.

Noah's Arkade: Bridge Street, Castries (tel. 452-2523); branches also at Soufrière and Rodney Bay.

Rain Restaurant and Boutique: Columbus Square, Castries (tel. 452-3022).

Roma's Boutique: Columbus Square, Castries.

Ruth Clarage: 14 Brazil Street, Castries, and at Hotel La Toc, 2½ miles south of Castries (tel. 452-1253).

Sea Island Cotton Shop: Voice Building, Bridge Street, Castries (tel. 452-3674).

St. Lucia Perfumes, Ltd.: Red Tape Lane, Morne Fortune (tel. 452-3890).

Tapion Craft Center: La Toc Road, Tapion (no phone).

Y. de Lima: William Peter Boulevard, Castries (tel. 452-2898); branches also at Hewanorra International Airport and Pointe Seraphine Cruise Terminal.

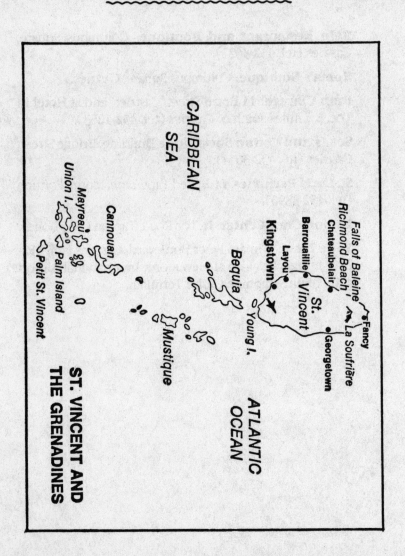

ST. VINCENT AND THE GRENADINES

ST. VINCENT AND THE GRENADINES AT A GLANCE

GOVERNMENT TOURIST OFFICE: St. Vincent Tourist Board, Halifax Street, Kingstown, St. Vincent, W.I. (tel. 457-1502).

CURRENCY: The Eastern Caribbean dollar is the official currency. US$1 equals about EC$2.65.

OFFICIAL HOLIDAYS: New Year's Day, St. Vincent and the Grenadines Day (January 22), Good Friday, Easter Monday, Labor Day (May 1), Whitmonday, Caricom Day (first Monday in July), Carnival Day (Tuesday after Caricom Day), Emancipation Day (first Monday in August), Independence Day (October 27), Christmas, and Boxing Day (December 26).

STORE HOURS: 8 a.m. to 1 p.m. and 2 to 4 p.m., Monday through Friday. Saturday is a half day, shops open from 8 a.m. until noon only.

LOCATIONS: For the addresses and telephone numbers of the shops, consult the alphabetical list at the end of this chapter.

S t. Vincent and its surrounding islands have never been at what you might call the forefront of big-time tourism—and therein lies much of their charm. Because of the privacy that the Grenadines afford, the likes of Lord Tennant, Princess Margaret, Dina Merrill, Racquel Welch, Mick Jagger, and other high-profile notables have taken to sneaking into St. Vincent and its satellite islands more and more often for tranquil, unpublicized hegiras.

No question about it, this is an area with a lot going for it. While much of the Caribbean huffs and puffs trying to keep pace with an exploding tourist trade, this archipelago with its center of St. Vincent—"Gem of the Antilles" as it is sometimes called (or in Carib Indian, *Hairoun*, meaning "Home of the Blessed")—could in the long run outlast the fancier, faster, flash-in-the-pan, skyrocketing mass-movement booms of sister spas.

St. Vincent's economic claim to fame as the arrowroot capital of the world faded for a while, because demand for this starch, even as baby food, was not exactly growing by leaps and bounds. Now, however, it turns out that arrowroot is an important base for the manufacture of paper used in computers, so things should continue to look up. Besides arrowroot, you will find much of interest to occupy your shopping time.

Arts and Crafts

St. Vincent Craftsmen, located at French's Gate in the northwest section of St. Vincent's capital city of Kingstown (tel. 458-4751), presents a cross section of crafts, and you may see some artisans at work producing woodcarvings, wall hangings, placemats, straw bags, baskets, ceramics, jewelry made of black coral as well as precious metals. This cooperative maintains a shop at the airport, and in several locations throughout the region, including one on the island of Bequia. If you're planning to tour St. Vincent, you might get a list of the branches it maintains either from its Kingstown headquarters, or through the tourist bureau.

Noah's Arkade on Bay Street in Kingstown (tel. 457-1513), handles a little of lots of miscellany: straw hats, bags, and mats, woodcarvings, handpainted postcards, locally made clothing. There's a Noah's Arkade branch on Bequia as well.

Handcrafts at the **Hibiscus** on James Street are worth investigating also.

One of the outstanding products of the region originate in Bequia, sometimes known as the Cape Cod of the tropics because of the New England–style saltboxes built by Scottish immigrants who came to harpoon the many whales feeding off the flats surrounding Bequia. As might be expected in a community of seafarers and shipwrights, model boats are a popular hobby.

The Bequians at **Sargent Brothers Model Boats,** Port Elizabeth, have been handcarving and finely finishing theirs for three generations. At one time you could provide a photograph or a sketch of your own boat and a model would be carved and shipped to you. We hear tell, however, that the younger generation is not as eager to carve to order nowadays. In any event, those boats already finished, with their colorful bottoms, white sails, and miniaturized gear, are well worth a second look.

CHINA, CRYSTAL, AND HOME FURNISHINGS

For truly fine, top-of-the-line china and crystal, the very best names in the world, you can hardly do better than to shop **Stecher's Jewellery Limited,** Bay St., Lot 19, in Kingston. A pillar of the Trinidad and Tobago commercial and social community, John Stecher and his comely wife, Sheila, have been contributing much honor and taste to their adopted Caribbean homeland ever since emigrating from Europe in the dark days just before World War II. Motion-picture stars, best-selling authors, and, especially, knowledgeable Caribbean regulars, do their buying either in the lovely emporium housed in the Cobblestone Inn, a converted warehouse, or at the smaller escale at the Arnos Vale Airport (both may be reached by phoning 458-4587). If what you need is not available in either location, rest assured it can be whisked over from Trinidad or St. Lucia for you.

To give you an idea of the scope of the Stecher operation, consider the name brands John represents: Aynsley English bone china, Hummel, Royal Doulton, Beatrix Potter animals, Wedgwood, Royal Crown Derby, Rosenthal, Royal Worcester, Belleek, Bing & Grøndahl, Royal Copenhagen, Havilland-Limoges, Swarovski crystal, Orreförs, Lalique, Baccarat, Waterford, Val St. Lambert, and Sèvres—to name a few.

Of more passing interest are the reproductions of sculpture and museum pieces, including copies of ancient Greek ceramic vases from various places—e.g. Corinth—and periods —e.g. the Minoan and the classical eras.

Stecher's does not go in for handcrafts, but when they spot a good piece of local copper work, or other creation that meets their standards, they carry it. If you plan any serious purchases along these lines, you can't afford to miss a visit here.

For locally made home furnishings—lacy khus-khus rugs, mahogany salad bowls, and the like—try **Hibiscus** at James Street in Kingstown (no phone).

FASHIONS

Batik Caribe, on the main street of town, Bay Street (tel. 456-1666), purveys hand-drawn, silk-screened, or tie-dyed pareos, sportswear, caftans. You can also buy the yardage and make your own, or specify the design of your choice and have whatever you like whipped up here in a couple of days or so.

Edwin C. Layne & Sons on Bay Street (tel. 456-1411) also carries batik, sent here from the plant at Walliabou, outside of Kingston.

Norma's Boutique on Egmont Street (tel. 457-1027) has earned her a loyal following for made-to-order fashions.

Dan Dan Boutique on Bay Street (tel. 457-1083) has its own following for made-to-order clothes. And here you can shop for the whole family.

For imported European—and American—clothes, check out **Charmaine's Boutique** on Sharpe Street in Kingstown (tel. 457-1952).

Most of the resorts maintain their own shops, for fashions and some crafts.

As for the other islands; Bequia has its own hand-painting and silkscreening operation, the **Crab Hole Boutique & Silk-Screen Factory** (tel. 458-3290). If you like, watch the work in process—and perhaps order something custom-stitched.

Another Bequia address you might look into is **Cinderella's Hideaway.**

Food

St. Vincent has no specialty distinctly and exclusively its own. But if you have not already stocked up elsewhere, you will find the usual complement of hot sauces, jams, jellies, chutneys, and assorted spices, either in the open market or at one of several supermarkets.

Jewelry

This is a specialty with **Stecher's** (see "China, Crystal, and Home Furnishings" section). The stock includes Mikimoto pearls, Georg Jensen silver, handmade charms in 18-karat or 14-karat gold, cameos, jade, enameled pieces, and precious stones.

Y. de Lima, the well-known Trinidad firm which advertises itself as "the largest manufacturers of gold and silver jewelry in the Caribbean," also maintains a St. Vincent shop on Bay Street in Kingstown (tel. 457-1681). If you collect regional pieces, this is the place to find them: hibiscus, orchids, all manner of tropical flora and fauna are reproduced in gold charms, pendants, or pins.

WATCHES

Patek Philippe, Audemars Piguet, Piaget, Cartier, Girard Perregaux, Jaeger Le Coultre, Universal Genève, Seiko, Heuer Chronographs, Delano, Ebel, Consul, Ernest Borel, Juvenia—these, among others—are all handled by **Stecher's**, discussed in detail above.

SPECIAL CATEGORY

If you're looking for a novelty item for your version of the man who has everything, herewith a valued St. Vincent contribution to our collection of mementos: a book by John L. Chapman, M.B.E., on the life of the island's famous Sylvester Consalves de Freitas, commonly known as Syl, or Live Wire.

This eccentric extraordinaire, of the kind some swear can only be found in the West Indies, came to St. Vincent as a mere sprout, seeking asylum after participating in a three-cornered tussle, during which one Bad John was disembowled with a knife. He proceeded to fame and fortune. A 5'4" dynamo who so loved to dance that he built four different clubs in which to indulge his passion, he is credited by his biographer with the following achievements—among others: "Introducing mechanical transport of estate produce;

replacing donkeys with motorcars; promoting sea transport between islands; playing a leading role in developing both silent and talking pictures; promoting professional pugilistics; operating a lime kiln; running a dry-goods store, a hotel, and a grocery; and creating the first land-development enterprise on the island."

Live Wire lived to be 75 (though he smoked 200 cigarettes a day); he died in 1967 and is buried on Dove Island, just off the main road, in a cross-shaped sarcophagus constructed to his own specifications: the coffin is standing upright and facing east. To quote one of his friends, "In death as well as in life, Syl was determined to be always on his feet." A thought to give pause to Frank Blair and all those purveyors of "think-ahead" plans for final resting places....

USEFUL ADDRESSES

Batik Caribe: Bay Street, Kingstown, St. Vincent (tel. 456-1666).

Charmaine's Boutique: Sharpe Street, Kingstown, St. Vincent (tel. 457-1952).

Cinderella's Hideaway: Bequia.

Crab Hole Boutique & Silk-Screen Factory: Bequia (tel. 458-3290).

Dan Dan Boutique: Bay Street, Kingstown, St. Vincent (tel. 457-1083).

Edwin C. Layne & Sons: Bay Street, Kingstown, St. Vincent (tel. 456-1411).

Hibiscus: James Street, Kingstown, St. Vincent.

Noah's Arkade: Bay Street, Kingstown, St. Vincent (tel. 457-1513); also branch on Bequia.

Norma's Boutique: Edgmont Street, Kingstown, St. Vincent (tel. 457-1027).

Sargent Brothers Model Boats: Port Elizabeth, Bequia.

Stecher's Jewellery Limited: Cobblestone Inn, Bay Street, Lot 19, Kingstown, St. Vincent (tel. 458-4587); also branches at Arnos Vale Airport and on Trinidad and St. Lucia.

St. Vincent Craftsmen: French's Gate, Kingstown, St. Vincent (tel. 458-4751); also branches at Old Country Ginnery, at Arnos Vale Airport, and on Bequia.

Y. de Lima: Bay Street, Kingstown, St. Vincent (tel. 457-1681).

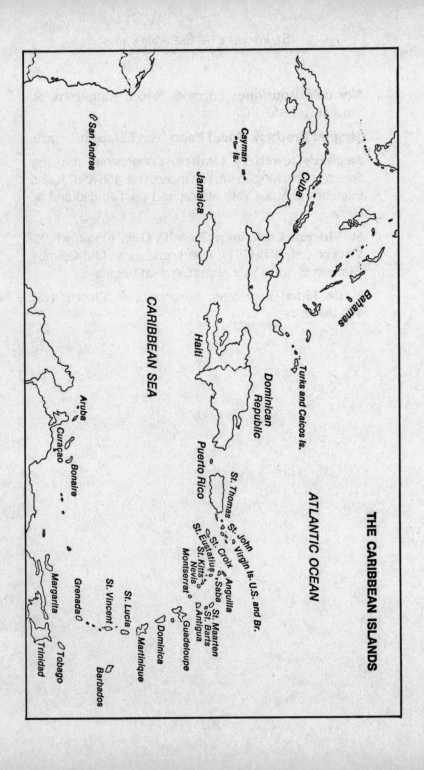

THE CARIBBEAN ISLANDS

ATLANTIC OCEAN

CARIBBEAN SEA

San Andres

Cayman Is.

Cuba

Jamaica

Bahamas

Turks and Caicos Is.

Haiti

Dominican Republic

Puerto Rico

St. Thomas
St. John
Virgin Is.-U.S. and Br.
St. Croix
Anguilla
Saba
St. Maarten
St. Eustatius
St. Barts
St. Kitts
Nevis
Antigua
Montserrat
Guadeloupe
Dominica
Martinique
St. Lucia
St. Vincent
Grenada
Barbados
Tobago
Trinidad
Margarita
Bonaire
Curaçao
Aruba

SINT
EUSTATIUS
(STATIA)

SINT. EUSTATIUS (STATIA) AT A GLANCE

GOVERNMENT TOURIST OFFICE: Sint Eustatius Tourist Bureau, 13 Emmaweg, across from the Fort in the Government House, St. Eustatius, N.A. (tel. 2219, ext. 15).

CURRENCY: The official unit of currency is the Netherlands Antilles florin or guilder (NAf). US$1 equals 1.77 NAf.

OFFICIAL HOLIDAYS: New Year's Day, Good Friday, Easter Monday, Queen's Birthday (April 30), Labor Day (May 1), Ascension Day, Whit Monday, Armistice Day (November 11), Kingdom Day (December 15), Christmas Day, Boxing Day (December 26).

STORE HOURS: Vary from shop to shop. (Consult Tourist Bureau for latest schedules.)

LOCATIONS: For the addresses and telephone numbers of the shops, consult the alphabetical list at the end of this chapter.

At one time up to 80 ships a day anchored off Sint Eustatius, loading merchandise to and from huge warehouses lined up two deep for almost two miles along the bay. In a single year 25-million tons of merchandise flowed in and out of this port.

An affluent upper-crust Scottish "lady of quality" visiting the island described its capital in her journal as one continuous marketplace "where goods of the most different uses and qualities are displayed before shop doors. Here hang rich embroideries, painted silks, flowered muslins, with all the manufactures of the Indies. Just by hang sailor's jackets, trousers, shoes, and hats. The next stall contains most exquisite silver plate, the most beautiful indeed I ever saw; and close by iron pots, kettles, and shovels." After inventorying more of the stock, including some elegant French gloves and English hose which she bought for herself, Janet Schaw concludes that "in every store you find every thing."

But that was then (more than 200 years ago)... and this is now. Today the chief attraction of this beguiling 8-square-mile Dutch land dot is as a lady with a long past. Its charming capital and sole town, tucked in the shadow of a great crater, borders a harbor that once accommodated 200 sailing vessels simultaneously. Oranjestad is now virtually deserted. And therein lies much of its lure.

Lovers of the West Indies who nostalgically remember the whole tranquil chain before developers took over should make an undelayed dash to this, one of the very last of the as-it-was, unspoiled, romantic pieces of real estate left. Soon this one too will change. But there is still time.

Now that Sint Eustatius, more commonly known as Statia, is no longer a major trading center, the island's chief claims to fame are: (1) its volcano, (2) its fetching anachronism of a capital, and (3) the fact that as the site of the first salute rendered the U.S. flag, Statia can be considered our nation's oldest friend.

There can be no doubt about the validity of the first two lures. Seismologists rank Statia's quiescent volcano, called "The Quill" (a corruption of the Dutch word *Kuil*, meaning "pit"), as one of the most beautiful, classic examples of a truncated cone with symmetrical concave sides in the Antilles. The 1,000-foot crater, 800 yards wide with precipitously steep inner walls, is an arborous and botanical wonderland. To horticulturally inclined pilgrims, it alone justifies any effort to reach the island.

Oranjestad, the only settlement, consists of Upper and Lower Town, twin preserved-in-amber anachronisms that are paradises for ruin-ramblers. One enthusiastic writer calls Statia "the Pompeii of the Caribbean."

Take a leisurely stroll through the lanes and paths and savor the historic remains as well as modest, still-standing 100-and 200-year-old structures.

As for Statia's third distinction, there is room for argument as to whether it was Statia or St. Croix in the Virgin Islands (then Danish) that made the first move. The expert we asked to untangle that historical vignette for us put it this way:

"Statia was the site of the first *official* salute given by a foreign power (the Dutch) to an armed warship (brigantine) flying the Grand Union flag of the 13 American Colonies. The salute was considered by the British to be an acknowledgment, and recognition, by the Dutch of the independence of the Colonies from England. The earlier salute rendered the U.S. flag on the island of St. Croix was made to a merchant ship, not a warship, and thus did not carry the international implications of the Statia action. More importantly, the local authorities gave continued aid and support to the American revolutionaries."

"Had it not been for this infamous island," Admiral Rodney wrote to Rear Admiral Sir Peter Parker, "the American rebellion could not possibly have subsisted." In a letter to his wife, the Admiral commented: "This rock has done England more harm than all the arms of her most potent enemies." Admiral Rodney sacked the island in retaliation in 1781, doing $20-*million* worth of damage. Affluence and prosperity disappeared in a matter of days, and so did most of what had been one of the busiest emporiums in the Caribbean.

You'll be hard put to overspend on Statia today. Shopping is not really where it's at any more. Number One take-home item: the rare, expensive, hard-to-find blue beads special to this island. Earlier in this century a cache of blue glass beads of various sizes and configurations was uncovered in a half-sunken ruin known as Crook's Castle near Lower Town. According to one theory, these are the beads slaves used for barter; they were brought over by the Ashantis and other African captives and were intended for distribution throughout the Caribbean. According to another version, Manhattan was purchased with blue beads exactly like these. Twenty years or more ago, you could buy them either as is or fashioned into attractive pieces of jewelry in several places. The last time we looked, however, there were none to be found.

If you're really interested in locating the blue beads, however, look up John May, your host at **The Old Gin House**, on the shore at Lower Town (tel. 2319), and ask him. If anyone can direct you to a source, it will be John. Actually, you'll not want to leave Statia without at least a visit to The Old Gin House anyway—unless you're lucky enough to be staying there. The food is superb, ambience agreeable, and the ocean lapping up on the black beach next to the terrace a rare, truly Caribbean, experience. Former Connecticut schoolteacher May and partner, Marty Scofield, a onetime New York J. Walter Thompson art director who logged time in Ethiopia before coming to Statia, have done a great job of converting the remnants of the old gin house into a comfortable caravansarai without sacrificing any of the atmosphere.

As to where to do your overall browsing, here are your options:

The **Mazinga Gift Shop** on Oranjestraat in Upper Town (tel. 2245) offers duty-free perfume and liquor, assorted woodcarvings, sometimes custom-designed jewelry as well. Open Monday through Saturday from 8 a.m. until 6 p.m.

The **Sint Eustatius Foundation Museum Gift Shop**, situated in the Doncker-deGraaff House on Oranjestraat, features postcards, books, some handmade local ceramics known as Statia Earth Jewelry—earrings, necklaces, a few occasional small pieces such as ashtrays. Check with the Historical Foundation (a very active, on-the-ball organization) for precise operating hours (Box 171, Sint Eustatius, Netherlands Antilles).

Golden Rock Artisan Foundation, on Rosemary Lane (tel. 2352), sells locally made articles composed of shells and wood. Also available here are fabrics and Spanish work from the Saba Artisan Foundation shop. The shop hours are 8 a.m. until noon and 1 to 5 p.m., Monday through Friday.

The **Henriquez Shop** on Heyligerweg offers clothing to resident clients.

Inevitably, as the numbers of home builders and short-term visitors rise, boutiques will proliferate and development will increase. But as of now, Statia is loaded with its own special brand of vintage charm that is disappearing elsewhere. As one enchanted reader wrote us, "We're planning to recommend Statia only to especially nice people, in the hope it will stay especially nice."

Having known and enjoyed this hideaway ourselves for a good many years, we think it will.

USEFUL ADDRESSES

Golden Rock Artisan Foundation: Rosemary Lane, Upper Town (tel. 2352).

Henriquez Shop: Heyligerweg, Oranjestad.

Mazinga Gift Shop: Oranjestraat, Upper Town, Oranjestad (tel. 2245).

The Old Gin House: Shore Road, Lower Town, Oranjestad (tel. 2319).

St. Eustatius Foundation Museum Gift Shop: Doncker-deGraaff House, Oranjestraat, Oranjestad.

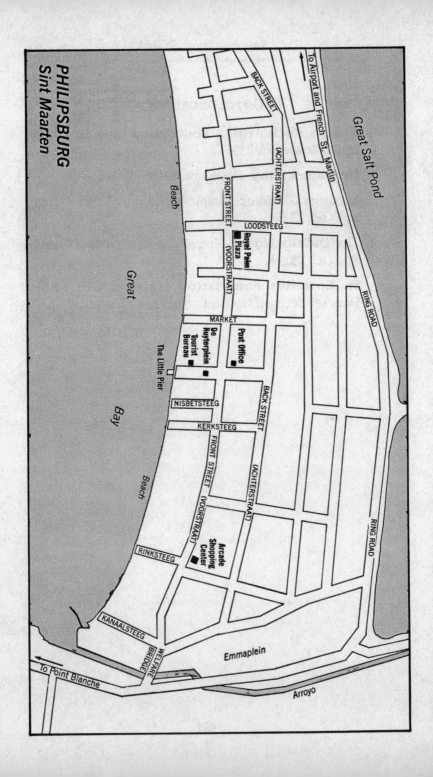

SINT MAARTEN / ST. MARTIN

SINT MAARTEN/ ST. MARTIN AT A GLANCE

GOVERNMENT TOURIST OFFICE: Sint Maarten (Dutch Side): Sint Maarten Tourist Office, De Ruyterplein, Philipsburg, Sint Maarten, N.A. (tel. 2337);

St. Martin (French Side): Syndicat d'Initiative, Mairie de Saint-Martin at Marigot, St. Martin, F.W.I. (tel. 87-50-04).

CURRENCY: Sint Maarten: The official unit of currency is the Netherlands Antilles florin or guilder (NAf). US$1 equals 1.77 NAf. So closely are the currencies entwined, even the soft drink machines are programmed to accept American money.

St. Martin: The French franc fluctuates, as it does in the mother country. Inquire about a possible 20% discount given on purchases made with traveler's checks and also with certain credit cards; the discount may not apply to all shops or to all merchandise on the French side.

OFFICIAL HOLIDAYS: Sint Maarten: New Year's Day, Good Friday, Easter Monday, Queen's Birthday (April 30), Labor Day (May 1), Ascension Day, Whit Monday, St. Maarten Day (November 11), Kingdom Day (December 15), Christmas Day, Boxing Day (December 26).

St. Martin: New Year's Day, Labor Day (May 1), Bastille Day (July 14), Armistice Day or St. Martin's Day (November 11), all Catholic Holy Days.

STORE HOURS: Sint Maarten: Monday through Saturday from 8 a.m. to 12 and 2 p.m. to 6 p.m. Many merchants

404

are open during the noon hour, and on Sundays and holidays, especially if there is a cruise ship in port.

St Martin: Monday through Saturday from 9 a.m.-ish to noon or 12:30 p.m. and from 2 or 2:30 to 6 p.m.—for the most part. The Port La Royale Complex opens and closes later.

LOCATIONS: For the addresses and telephone numbers of the shops, consult the alphabetical list at the end of this chapter.

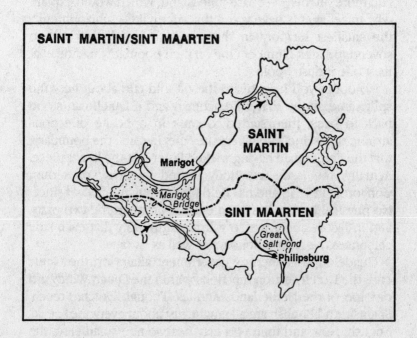

SAINT MARTIN/SINT MAARTEN

SAINT MARTIN

Marigot

Marigot Bridge

SINT MAARTEN

Great Salt Pond

Philipsburg

Thirty-six perfectly gorgeous beaches, a half a dozen casinos, and 150 restaurants. Tennis, golf, sailing, fishing, helicoptering, jet-skiing, nude bathing, parasailing, windsurfing, island hopping; amusing little hamlets to explore, sleek boats for cruising, late-model cars for hire, easy roads to drive. No big-city tension, a relaxed population all of whom speak English, a marvelously central geographic location—you'll find all this and more on this 37-square-mile island. Which would explain why travel agents have voted this sunny little schizophrenic, the smallest territory in the world to be shared by two sovereign states, Number One on their popularity parade in at least one industry poll.

No doubt you have heard the oft-told tale about how the split came about: that a Frenchman and a Dutchman stood back to back, then started to walk in opposite directions around the island, and where they met became the boundary; that the Frenchman having walked faster, got the larger piece. Actually, the issue was tidily settled by treaty on Mount Concordia in 1648 and has held force pretty much ever since. No physical border has been erected between the two parts, and in fact relations are so warm and friendly that each side celebrates the other's holidays as well as its own.

Guadeloupe chaperons government affairs on the Gallic end; the Dutch section functions within the Dutch Windward division of the Netherlands Antilles. Though Dutch, French, Spanish, and English are all taught, just about everyone speaks English. Now and then you may hear some Papiamento, the dialect of the Dutch islands, but, unfortunately, less and less is used as the communities become more Anglo-oriented.

If Sint Maarten/St. Martin is not the Super Bowl of Shopping in the Caribbean, with no less than 500 shops and boutiques to choose from, it certainly has to come close. On one score, it indisputably stands alone: *THIS IS THE ONLY, REPEAT ONLY, COMMUNITY IN THE CARIBBEAN WHICH IS TRULY, TOTALLY, 100% DUTY-FREE.*

Other resorts may claim this status but, in reality, each and every one levies some sort of surcharge on incoming merchandise, which of necessity must be passed on to the customer—EXCEPT Sint Maarten/St. Martin.

Philipsburg, capital "city" for the 10,000 or so Dutch residents, occupies a sliver of a sandspit between the Great Salt Pond and Great Bay Harbor (Groot Baai). It has just two thoroughfares: Voorstraat (Front Street), and Achterstraat (Back Street). Sometimes you will see these streets printed as solid words—Frontstreet and Backstreet; either way works. There's a touch of gingerbread here and there, some pretty pastel buildings, a fine beach—and a crowd on cruise ship days!

Marigot, the little town serving the somewhat smaller settlement on the French side, hugs the shoreline of Marigot Bay seven miles from Philipsburg. Both communities remain strongly West Indian in flavor, despite their soaring popularity as one of the busiest shopping destinations in the entire Caribbean.

Philipsburg has two advantages not always found elsewhere: it is compact, with most of the shops within walking distance; and dotted in between them are plenty of hotels and restaurants to which you can repair for the necessary pause to refresh and regroup.

Enjoy the breeze ruffling the palms bordering the bar at the **Pasanggrahan** (the word is Indonesian for "Guesthouse") on Front Street and over a cool drink debate whether to go back and get a half-a-dozen more of those dirt-cheap, embroidered-linen muffin baskets at The New Amsterdam Store. Have a seat and watch the passing parade from the **West Indian Tavern** at the "head" of Front Street. Pick up a bit to eat or a cold drink at any one of a number of locations all along your route. **Etna Gardens,** a few steps from the Main Square, dispenses cappuccino and croissants, tartufo or a fresh fruit drink (free flavor samples) on Front Street in Philipsburg as well as at its branch at Port La Royale in Marigot.

Let's face it, shopping is hard work, especially on a hot tropical day. And being able to take a break now and again is very helpful.

If you get a second wind after closing, note that many of the stores maintain boutiques in the major hotels, including a concentration of several in the Mullet Bay Shopping Arcade, and these stay open later.

Although this island has some of the top emporiums of the Caribbean, they are not always the most elegant in appearance. Some shop interiors are stunning; in others, ambience tends to be more one of comfortable clutter than glitzy design, more folksy than fancy. But make no mistake: as for the merchants themselves, you are dealing with professionals.

A couple of suggestions: just before you get ready to pay for an acquisition, ask the clerk if the price quoted you includes the traveler's check discount. Some merchants on the Dutch side deduct as much as 30% from the pricetag. On the French side you could save 20% by paying with traveler's checks.

Also, if you do not find what you are looking for in one establishment, ask the personnel there to direct you to where you might be able to get it. Retailers, on the Dutch side especially, have remarkably relaxed feelings about exclusivity. Although they do tend to divide the pie up in some way— artist Ruby Bute's hand-painted T-shirts, for example, turn up mainly at the Sea Breeze—an item you see in one shop may well also appear in several others.

Finally, a veteran member of the local tourist industry advises us to tell you not to turn your nose up at what appears to be a series of electrical shops. True, these marts do handle that kind of equipment, but you will find that many also peddle cameras, perfumes, and watches, often at most attractive prices. Our informant reports picking up a Seiko at half-price at The Wholesale House, on Front Street near the Caribbean Hotel. Obviously, no endorsement is intended nor given by this Guide. We merely pass on a tip from a knowledgeable source.

ARTS AND CRAFTS

Because of the island's small size and lack of natural resources, you will not find a bumper crop of made-on-Sint-Maarten crafts. There is, however, growing emphasis on spotlighting the output of the *region*. And because of the variety of items and the skill with which they are selected, you will enjoy surveying the collection of West Indian arts and crafts assembled here.

There is even a gallery in Philipsburg now featuring nothing but fine arts. Sue Parson's **Greenwich Gallery** at Marshall Mall showcases different painters, sculptors, and ceramists from the region working in oils, watercolors, acrylics, and a variety of other mediums; there's a broad range of prices, from budget-priced prints to $2,000 original canvases (Reproductions are available also). Among the more popular:

Harriet Sharkey's acrylics and watercolors
Oils by Donald Dahlke
The creations of Rose Cameron Smith from St. Kitts
Watercolors by Antoine Chapon
Nancy Usza's paintings
Pottery from Nevis, baked over flaming coconut husks
Lithographs by Alex Minguet, who works six months in France, the rest of the year in Sint Maarten
Ceramics by Marilyn Clark of Simpson Bay in Sint Maarten
The delicate pastels of Nusza

Among other intriguing entries are Ria Zonneveld's small (about 5 x 7 inches), framed collage/plaster sculptured busts of local faces.

You'll see these also at **Impressions**, 6 Promenade Arcade on Front Street, along with many other West Indian crafts—for example, the calabash purses that artisans in the Dominican Republic hand carve. We've seen these *Higueros*, as they are called, advertised in a U.S. catalog for $80. Get yours here for a fraction of that.

Have a look also at the hand-painted trays, cassette boxes, and chests by Moro of Haiti. Most spectacular, believe it or not, are the clothes hooks: impossible to describe the three-dimensional trickery involved, but suffice it to say that at $25 or so each, they march out of the store to hang on the wall as a decoration. Seldom, if ever, are they used for their ostensible purpose, because no one wants to cover them up with clothes. See also Moro's hand-carved and painted little tropical fish. If you need any help, ask either for Lane Derby, the proprietress, or her affable second-in-command, Francis Melfor.

Sint Maarten's most famous home-grown talent was born in Aruba, and began her career while she was still in school by winning, twice, UNESCO's first prize for her painting. Now that she is a member of the Sint Maarten community, Ruby Bute works full time as a bookkeeper for the government in the Education Department and moonlights by turning out an array of postcards, custom-made Christmas greetings, hand-painted fashions—along with the full assortment of oils and acrylics that have earned her wide recognition. The hibiscus is her trademark, and her favored subjects are still-lifes and vintage West Indian houses. Several shops, including Impressions, carry her cards.

Nancy Shepherd pretty much has a monopoly on the Ruby Bute hand-painted T-shirts at her **Sea Breeze** shop in the Promenade Arcade on Front Street (no phone); **Around the Bend,** at the head of Front Street, carries Ruby's big tops and painter's caps.

Another very popular artist, Gloria Lynn, is especially adept at capturing the persona of the island market women—one admirer compares here to work Gauguin's. In point of fact, the whole Lynn family is talented: son, Robert, produces serigraphs; husband, Martin, is a sculptor (you can visit him at his studio).

In the line of pottery, you'll see a good deal of the leaf-pattern designs—ashtrays, bric-a-brac—of Marguerite Schonenberger.

Among the shops emphasizing crafts, Janet Tucher's **Coconuts**, next door to The Yellow House near the Little Pier (tel. 2164), earned *Town and Country's* top nod as "Bloomingdale's Boutique of the Island." Stock flies out of here so fast that by the time we alert you to what's current, favored items will have already been scooped up—to be replaced, usually, with worthy substitutes.

More or less of a classic here is the needlepoint canvas featuring a Ruby Bute design—it comes with the yarns, the colors of which may or may not appeal to you. But the design itself is authentic Sint Maarten. You will also find needlepoint kits, some with island motifs, others of Dutch design, at **Thimbles and Things** on Back Street (tel. 2898).

Coconuts carries the works of Marilyn Clark and Marguerite Schonenberger (jars and vases), the lithographs of Minguet, as well as Antoine Chapon's watercolors and silkscreens—among others.

Jean McBeth pioneered in marketing regional crafts through her shop **Around the Bend** (see the entry above)—don't miss it. Handmade calypso dolls fashioned locally (note their little painted toenails); stuffed parrots; frogs, lizards, and merpersons (formerly known as mermaids), stuffed with snowy Sint Maarten sand to serve as paperweights or whatnots.

East Meets West, on Front Street across from L'Escargot, scours the surrounding islands for novel items, and comes up with quite a few. There are Taibisiri carpets, along with such oddities as Balat's sculptures fashioned out of hardened sap from trees, and an off-trail little curiosity known as a bitter cup. It's made of raw wood; about the diameter of a candlestick; the idea is to put water in it for several hours and when it tastes bitter, drink it—as a tonic, to clear up skin eruptions, whatever. At $2.50 each, there's not much to lose by trying.

The Caribbean Corner at the Holland House Hotel on Front Street comes on basically as a little souvenir shop, but it also carries watercolors and some of the works of Marguerite Schonenberger.

Scoffers may well dismiss the **Shipwreck Shop** chain as "Woolworth with Palms," and true, much of the inventory fails to ring our chimes also. Nevertheless, on whichever of the many islands with Shipwreck Shops we find ourselves, we usually stop in to see what's new. If, for example, Impressions is fresh out of the calabash purses, Shipwreck may have them—along with wooden plates, drugstore items, spices, beach towels, island books, and assorted baubles and beads. Find the main Shipwreck Shop on Front Street, the Pond side, next to the Callaloo Restaurant (tel. 2962).

In Marigot, **L'Artisanat/Galerie** exhibits crafts in a second-story situation on the main road leading out of town. The woodcarvings you may see in Marigot's native market likely come from Haiti or Jamaica.

In the village of Grande Case on the French side, American mystery writer Dee Forbes and her husband, Bill, preside over an interesting boutique known as **Pierre Lapin** (tel. 87-52-10). We still have the beguiling little wooden marionette caricature of the Ugly American tourist the Forbeses gave us years ago, a design she had made especially for her shop. Since then the stock has changed, expanded, and been perfected. As well as soft sculptures and rag dolls, the in-house art display exhibits the output of the previously mentioned Martin, Gloria, and Robert Lynn.

If you saw **Alexander Minguet's** work at the above-mentioned Greenwich Gallery and would like to know more, his studio is right on the main drag in Grande Case as well.

Another interesting Grand Case operation is the Etche-goyens' **l'Atelier**. This pottery studio opens to visitors every Wednesday afternoon and on Saturday too. Other handcrafts on sale include enamelware, leather, and woven articles.

Orléans' celebrity-in-residence is artist **Roland Richardson.** Visit him at home in this settlement inland on the eastern side of the island, back of the Baie de l'Embouchure and south of Orient beach. The studio is open from Monday through Friday from 9:30 a.m. to 1 p.m. You may want to acquire one of Mr. Richardson's island watercolors or prints.

CAMERAS

Only after first checking prices in the catalogs and discount houses in the States will you know how much of a bargain—if any, in some instances—you will strike here on photographic equipment.

Boolchand's, a.k.a. **Kohinoor,** a.k.a. **Taj Mahal,** all on Front Street in Philipsburg (tel. 2245 or 2445), handle Canon, Nikon, Olympus, Minolta, Pentax, and accessories.

Sonovision, Ramchand's and **Ashoka,** siblings also, at 57, 73, and 93 Front Street, respectively, handle cameras too. Sharp traders tell us they have been able to bargain with all these merchants.

CHINA, CRYSTAL, AND HOME FURNISHINGS

Nowhere else in the world will you find a larger concentration of international top-name brands in a smaller area. Royal Copenhagen, Georg Jensen, Royal Doulton, Swarovski, St. Louis, Lalique, Waterford, Lladró, Atlantis, Orreförs, Christofle—you will spot all of these represented at **Spritzer &**

Fuhrmann in the Mullet Bay Shopping Arcade on Grand Casino Way (tel. 4217) and also on the Rue de la République in Marigot and at Princess Juliana Airport. The main store of this long-established firm is in Curaçao. Spritzer & Fuhrmann also maintains a branch in New York City at 5 East 57 Street.

For his role in tourism and trade in the Dutch islands, Board Chairman Charles Fuhrmann, who co-founded Spritzer & Fuhrmann over sixty years ago, last year received from Queen Beatrix the highest civilian Dutch order, Knight in the Order of the Netherlands Lion. Ten years ago, the Netherlands Antilles government issued a special series of postal stamps to celebrate the company's golden anniversary, the first time any commercial enterprise was so honored.

For Aynsley, Rosenthal, and Thomas china; for Waterford, Baccarat, Lalique, and Rosenthal crystal; for Lladrò, Swarovski, and Goebel-Hummel figurines; for Christofle and Rosenthal hollow and flatware, shop at **Little Switzerland** at 42 and 69 Front Street in Philipsburg (tel. 2296) or in downtown Marigot on the Rue de la République (tel. 87-50-03).

Over thirty years ago, a pair of Swiss brothers emigrated to the West Indies and founded a luxury house of European imports. Soon Rudy Kelbert's South African–born, Swiss-educated wife, Helen, joined the team, adding her discerning taste to the mix. As the venture grew, the Kelberts lured a fourth member away from one of the most prestigious watchmakers in Geneva, a young Swiss by the name of Walter Fischer. Today Little Switzerland, now owned by an American corporation, operates shops on four islands—St. Martin, St. Thomas, St. Croix, and St. Barth.

Our regard for the organization grew when we paid $15 less for a Swiss watch at Little Switzerland than we had seen it priced in Lausanne three weeks before. An imposing seven-inch Baccarat cat, a facsimile of one discovered in an ancient Egyptian tomb, is shown in one of the U.S.'s fanciest stores at $192; Little Switzerland has it for $92. There are other savings—for example, Rosenthal Suomi white china, $65 the place setting in fine mainland shops, is priced here at about half, $30; a Baccarat jam pot tagged $65 up north costs $45 here. Check the catalog or price lists you have with you to see if the item you're considering acquiring represents a substantial saving.

The New Amsterdam Store at 54 Front St., Philipsburg (tel. 2787 and 2788), carries Murano glass, Capodimonte, Lladrò, and some Delft. Also represented at Mullet Bay and Maho Reef (tel. 4320).

Find Hummel figurines at **The Yellow House** at De Ruyterplein, Philipsburg (tel. 2332).

Worth scouting also is **Mille Fleurs** in the Promenade Arcade of Philipsburg (tel. 2473).

In Marigot, both **Vendôme** and **Printemps** have been selling quality china, crystal, and the like for longer than many a glitzier Johnny-come-lately. We've bought in both often, and have yet to be disappointed.

FASHIONS

One of the more memorable communiqués we received while toiling on the Letters To The Editor column of *Life* magazine read quite simply, "Dear Sir: Please send me all the information you have."

Summarizing the notable fashion offerings of Sint Maarten/ St. Martin offers about the same challenge as answering that *Life* correspondent to his satisfaction.

In no island in the Caribbean will you find represented more top-of-the-line manufacturers from the world over. When you remember that there are in fact over 500 shops on this island, and that, at the very least, half of them have some fashion orientation, the enormity of the choices awaiting you becomes apparent.

Where to begin!

Overview

Gucci has its own shop on Front Street.

Louis Vuitton items are at **Maurella Senesi** at 83 Front St. (tel. 3323).

Find Les must de Cartier at **Vanessa** in Galerie Périgourdine in Marigot and at **La Romana** on Front Street and Royal Palm Plaza, Philipsburg (tel. 2181). You will also spot Charles Jourdan shoes, Yves Saint Laurent accessories, Descamps linens, plus Daks, Liberty, Pringle, Valentino—the list is virtually endless.

Herewith, once over very lightly, are a few of the further choices that await you:

For strictly West Indian clothes, two American women are probably your best source: Jean McBeth at **Around the Bend** on Front Street in Philipsburg, directly across from Marshall's Mall, and Dee Forbes, who holds forth at **Pierre Lapin** in Grande Case on the French side (tel. 87-52-10). Neither is a dress designer in the professional sense, and neither maintains a huge stock. But the merchandise they have is usually fetching, and, more importantly, both are walking encyclopedias on what's where in Sint Maarten/St. Martin. And both are generous about sharing their knowledge with you.

Jean became acquainted with merchandising the Caribbean way when working in St. Thomas with Charlotte Paiewonsky—herself a one-time New York buyer before becoming a savvy Caribbean retailer. Since branching out on her own decades ago, Jean has earned her own enviable reputation. Her present lines include, among others, the hand-painted big tops and painters caps by Ruby Bute, and some interesting culottes and other articles of clothing utilizing a fabric that presents a photographic record of the making of Saba lace. New entries come in all the time.

Dee Forbes has been around the islands about as long as Jean McBeth, and the creative imagination reflected in the books she writes also translates into the way she operates her shop. Handwork—crochet, embroidery, batik—is a specialty, and you can have items made to order from West Indian fabrics created on Saba, St. Thomas, or St. Barth's. Dee Forbes also brings some garments in ready-made from elsewhere in the Caribbean.

For tropical fabrics by the yard, scout **Thimbles and Things** on Back Street, Philipsburg (tel. 2898), **Batik Caribe** in The Promenade at 42 Front St. (tel. 2185), and **Java Wraps**, Sint Maarten Shop, in Royal Palm Plaza, Philipsburg (tel. 3568). Batik also comes made up into resort wear.

Shipwreck Shop on Front Street (tel. 2962) also carries batik fabric made in the islands. In Port La Royale in Marigot, **Creations St. Martin** also sells fabric par le metre.

We first discovered **Continental**'s sometimes-overlooked charms over a decade ago, at 120 Front St. Within this rather fusty, mildly stuffy-looking-on-the-outside paradigm of the homey, provincial French mini-department store, we found enough luscious lengths of handsome cottons to make the most jaded home-stitcher flip out. Riotous South Pacific pareus, rich batik prints, exuberant African designs, imaginative tie-dyes—you could stagger out with bolt-loads.

From what the staff tells us, Monsieur le Patron first got into this business in the trading posts of Africa, and hence has special sources. Whatever the background, the results can be outstanding. From time to time we've come upon other buys here: one year it was puffy, cushy French Favo luggage priced, it seemed to us, way under U.S. costs. Another time we picked up good-quality, inexpensive Swiss handkerchiefs. There have even been some good-looking, bottom priced shirts for men on occasion.

Leather Goods

Of Gucci, enough said. Whether you side with Aldo, Maurizio, or Paolo, or one of the other Guccis in the well-publicized ongoing family feud, status continues to be the

Gucci trademark in loafers, handbags, and the rest of the output. The Sint Maarten **Gucci Boutique** is on the seaward side of lower Front Street, next to the Maurella Senesi Boutique.

MaximoFlorence, in the Promenade and at 102 Front St. (tel. 2608), features every kind of skin, from kid to iguana, meticulously crafted. Note the skillful use of snake, for instance, in pocketbook with matching shoes.

Desmo, next to Gemsland on upper Front Street in the St. Maarten Beach Club, offshoot of an established line represented in the U.S. as well as in Florence and Rome, also features top-of-the-line purses, so does **Penha & Sons** at 47 Front St. (tel. 2279), a fine old Dutch firm that features top-quality European sportswear, cosmetics, and perfumes.

One experienced Manhattan shopper reports acquiring a smashing lipstick-red suede suit for not much over a hundred dollars at **Sergio Moreta's** shop at 17 and 20 Front St., next to Around the Bend. Unfortunately, that was a year ago or more, and the cost is up. But you still might have a look.

La Romana, at Front Street in the Royal Palm Plaza Arcade (tel. 2181), possibly Sint Maarten's top fashion shop, has a wide selection of name-brand shoes: Maud Frizon, Andrea Pfister, Sergio Rossi, Rosetti, Cesare Paciotti, among them.

Boutique Smart in the Marina Royal Mall in Marigot handles avant-garde shoes and boots.

Swimsuits

On an island which has a different beautiful beach for every day in the month, it's no wonder there's such a wide assortment of bathing suits to choose from. The boutiques on the French side defy the laws of physics with the miniaturization of some of their bikinis—and the results are predictably bewitching. Shop the Port La Royale complex in Marigot especially. **Le Bastringue** (tel. 87-58-20), for example, handles the chic V de V swimwear for men and women in a variety of styles. **Bagatelle**, on Rue de la République, includes bikinis in its collection of creations from the Riviera.

On the Dutch side, look for the prestigious Gottex label in several locations, including **Lil' Shoppe**, next to the Pinocchio Restaurant on Front Street (tel. 2177). Try **Around the Bend,** also on Front Street, as well.

La Romana's upscale resort collection includes beachwear (see description above).

Venture upstairs to the mezzanine in **The New Amsterdam Store** at 54 Front St. (tels. 2787 and 2788) and you will find Gottex also, as well as Oberson from Israel, Aquasuit of Italy, and Hom swimming trunks.

Java Wraps at Royal Palm Plaza (tel. 3568) whips up swimwear from its own fabrics. **Penha & Sons** at 47 Front St. (tel. 2279) carries an extensive line of men's sportswear.

High Fashion

Because of the mind-boggling number of name brands available to you on this island, finding your favorites quickly can be a problem. Hopefully the following partial rundown on where to find what will make the task a little easier—and perhaps in the process you'll discover some new lines you like.

In Philipsburg:

E.G.R. Boutique, at 97 Front St. (tel. 2085), features French couture for large and tall sizes.

Elle, 79 Front St. (tel. 3486), and Port La Royale, Marigot, carries Italian-made Byblos linens, Kriss blouses, Giusi Slaviero skirts and sportswear.

La Romana, at Front Street in the Royal Palm Plaza Arcade (tel. 2181), features Giorgio Armani, Gianfranco Ferre, Gianni Versace, Fendi, Krizia, Bottega Veneta—at prices said to be up to 30% less than in the U.S. The Mullet Bay branch stays open at night until 11 p.m.

Leda of Venice, 96 Front St. (tel. 3441), specializes in Valentino, Carrano, and in Missoni sweaters. Good savings over Stateside prices also reported.

The New Amsterdam Store's mezzanine at Front Street (tel. 2787 or 2788) and satellite boutique at the Maho Reef and Beach Resort carries some well-known names: Adidas, Lacoste from Paris, Lanvin, Givenchy, Courrèges, Ferrari ready-to-wear.

On the French side:

Le Bastringue at Port La Royale in Marigot (tel. 87-58-20) is headquarters for Peppermint, Scooter, E.J. Jacobson, avant-garde Japanese designer Konsai Yamamoto, Verte Vallee, NW Dorotenns, Chipie, and Bo Bo Kaminsky.

Vertiges and **Boa**, also in Port La Royale, feature French fashions as well.

In the Marina Royal Shopping Arcade, Marigot, try **Dalila, Animale, St. Tropez, Aventura,** and **Raisonable.**

FOOD

Given Sint Maarten/St. Martin's growing stature as a center for Caribbean gastronomy, it's no wonder that the 150 restaurants operating on the island should have well-stocked supermarkets to supplement their own larders.

The Food Center, up the hill just outside Philipsburg (at 105 Bush Rd.) en route to Marigot (tel. 2315 or 2415), carries *Djahe*, the ginger-root-based seasoning essential to rijsttafel, delectable also to accent soups and salads. Saté, a clean, spicy, peanut-perfumed sauce in which to dip skewered beef bits for appetizer or main course, comes tinned. *Sajoeran kering*, that special mix of dried vegetables and herbs used in preparing *bahmi* (a sort of noodle), is on hand—along with a mélange of U.S., English, Danish, and of course, Holland cheeses, chocolates, and assorted sweets.

E.A.T. Royal, the little food store to the rear of Café Royal in Royal Palm Plaza on Front Street (tel. 3443), functions from 8 a.m. until 1 p.m. If you're in the market for a snack, they can provide smoked salmon, caviar, fresh croissants, and Dutch chocolates. In fact, they'll pack you a complete picnic basket if you like.

Emile's Place on De Ruyterplein (Little Pier) in Philipsburg (tel. 2145) is another worthy epicurean stop for Dutch cheeses and chocolates as well as spirits.

Shipwreck Shop on Front Street (tel. 2962) is the home of Lord & Hunter seasalt, cane sugar, and spices, which are marketed throughout the Caribbean.

On the main road to Grand Case, just inside the city limits of Marigot, stop in at **K-Dis** for a gallimaufry of Gallic gourmetry, fresh, tinned, or frozen, of such variety as to set the most fervent apositiac into transports of rapture. Terrine of venison, untold varieties of French cheeses, sauerkraut in champagne—on our last call the assortment was dazzling.

Tip: unless you're totally fluent in French, take along a dictionary; some personnel speak only the slighest *soupçon* of our language and deliver their own at such a rat-tat-tat machinegun pace you'll have trouble telling the escargots from the escarole. But for Cordon Bleu collectors, this epicerie is well worth a visit.

JEWELRY

Forty-six years ago Hans Stern, a penniless 16-year-old refugee from Nazi Germany, landed in Brazil because the U.S. rejected his application for admission. Since his first job was for a firm that exported mica and colored gems, Stern learned from the lapidaries how to cut stone, and started his own gem business at 23, with a bankroll of $200. At first only friends would come to him for rings and bracelets, but then one day a Latin American chief of state invested $22,000 in an aquamarine necklace, and the Stern luck turned.

By 1973, despite his expenditures of only 2% of sales on advertising and promotion, *The New York Times* was ranking H. Stern among the four top jewelers in the world—along with Boucherer of Switzerland and Harry Winston and Tiffany & Co. of New York. H. Stern is also the only concern that does its own mining of stones, plus cutting, manufacturing, designing, and marketing. The elimination of middlemen along the way is one method the firm cites for shaving costs.

H. Stern is especially well known for aquamarines (a favorite stone of his—Stern named his yacht *The Aquamarine*). We are most impressed with the caliber of design exhibited in even such inexpensive pieces as the garnet ring and amethyst locket we acquired early on. There's an **H. Stern** at 56 Front St., Philipsburg.

If you don't see what you have in mind at H. Stern, there certainly is no shortage of alternative places to shop. **La Romana** on Front Street in Philipsburg (tel. 2181) devotes one entire salon to its jewelry, which includes, by the way, the same Missani name you've seen featured at Bulgari. Beautiful pearl creations by Petochi can also be found.

From Via Mascagni, Milano, comes **Maurella Senesi,** housed in an elegant showroom at 83 Front St. (tel. 3323). The 18-karat-gold necklace in the leaf motif is especially striking, as is the Epoca watch. Interestingly enough, virtually all the Maurella Senesi designers are women.

Colombian Emeralds International, on Front Street a block south of De Ruyterplein (Little Pier), purveys what its name indicates—but not exclusively. You will also see diamond, ruby, and sapphire pieces here.

You may also find just what you are looking for in a number of other Philipsburg locations: **Mille Fleurs'** (The Promenade Arcade, Front Street—tel. 2473) high-fashion jewelry; and **Oro de Sol**'s (Front Street—tel. 2602) handsome French and Italian pieces. The latter also has an escale in Marigot (Rue de la République—tel. 87-57-02); **Carat**, next to Kischo on Front Street (tel. 2180); the **St. Trop Boutique** at 26 Front St. (tel. 2165).

The Jewel Box, at 65 Front St. (tel. 3538), has intriguing 18-karat-gold animal bracelets, enameled and set with rubies and diamonds. Worth a look too are the gold nuggets and freshwater pearls at **Gemsland,** 33 Front St., in the Holland House Hotel (tel. 2156).

Little Switzerland, at 42 and 69 Front St. (tel. 2296), and at Rue de la République in Marigot (tel. 87-50-03), has exquisite neckpieces, swirl bangle bracelets, and separate clasps of gold, black onyx, and diamonds that come with a special adapter so you can use them on any strand of pearls. Blue topaz and diamond pendants, frosted quartz beads accented with a peridot-and-diamond pendant—the assortment is extensive and impressive.

As for **Spritzer & Fuhrmann** (Grand Casino Way, Mullet Bay Shopping Arcade—tel. 4217), this firm broke precedent by being appointed jeweler to Her Majesty Queen Juliana at a time when only established corporations were eligible. In addition to this notable exception, Charles Fuhrmann was presented with the key to the House of Goldsmiths by the Federation of Jewelers in Valenza, Italy. Spritzer & Fuhrmann, in short, know their jewels.

How much money will you save? Many St. Maarten/St. Martin firms promise substantial, some even spectacular, savings. Whether or not you will feel you are making a rare buy depends on your expertise and upon the degree of your enthusiasm. Jewels belong to that category of blind items on which no direct, cut-and-dried price comparison can be made. But to paraphase the old Cunard slogan, "Finding out is half the fun." Even if you make no purchases whatsoever, you'll surely see some exquisite pieces in the process of scouting.

Those not of the Diamonds-Are-a-Girl's-Best-Friend persuasion will find plenty of costume jewelry to choose from. **Around the Bend,** Front Street, Philipsburg, carries handmade earrings—and charms in bone, silver, ceramic, and horn. **Shipwreck Shop** on Front Street (tel. 2962) has its own line of handcrafted items. See also **Bali Boutique's** (Little Pier—tel. 2520) shell jewelry.

LINENS

Anyone who has ever read a *Lifestyles of the Rich and Famous* type of a novel knows Porthault sheets. No self-respecting heiress would think of sleeping on anything else. Unfortunately, the cost of such luxury is not generally within everyone's reach. Shop the extensive linen assortment at **Oro de Sol** branch on the Rue de la République (tel. 87-57-02) in Marigot and you may find those exquisite designer Porthault sheets, tablecloths, and towels affordable. Some satisfied customers report them sold here at prices 50% under those quoted Stateside.

If you're more interested in a $25 drip-dry embroidered tablecloth or some budget-priced lace-trimmed placemats, these too may be readily available in any number of establishments.

The New Amsterdam Store at 54 Front St., Philipsburg (tel. 2787 and 2788), has been buying and selling plain and fancy tableware for over 55 years, during the course of which time its buyers have become uncommonly knowledgeable about where to find the best bargains.

Roy's at the Holland House Hotel on Front Street (tel. 2533) and the St. Maarten Beach Club, both in Philipsburg, spotlight linens of all kinds, from crib sheets to tablecloths of all sizes and shapes.

Albert's Store, away from the main concentration of shops (132 Front St.—tel. 2946), is a favorite target of the tourist guides, calling itself "The House of Fine Linens." Albert promises "the best prices in the Caribbean." To see if you agree, look in on Albert.

These are only some of the shops carrying linens, on both the French and the Dutch sides. If you find something you like in one of the electrical shops or in an Indian souk, and the price is right, more power to you. Do, however, double-check the fabric when making a purchase of any consequence.

We've been stung in shops on more than one island when we bought what appeared to be sturdy linens, only to have them turn unattractively limp when the sizing shipped out with the first washing.

PERFUMES AND COSMETICS

Again, watch your step. On American-made scents such as Giorgio—and there are more and more of these as U.S. perfumers become increasingly expert—oftentimes all you save is the tax. Imported perfumes, on the other hand, can represent a bargain.

We have found prices a bit lower on some brands in Marigot boutiques than in their Philipsburg counterparts, but the difference was not substantial, nor did it prevail across the board.

Because of the considerable volume and sophistication of stock available in Sint Maarten/St. Martin, this is an excellent place to sample some of the more recherché, less highly publicized commercial fragrances. The West Indian islands, for example, have their own indigenous patchouli and vetiver plants. In recent years, chemists in the Caribbean have been perfecting some first-rate scents. Jamaica's White Witch, Forget Me Not, and Khus-Khus are outstanding. So are the various perfumes of Grenada.

From the continent, **Maurella Senesi** at 83 Front St. (tel. 3323) has her own Eau de Toilette.

Lipstick at Port La Royale in Marigot carries the highly regarded Clarins cosmetics—along with Lancôme, Lancaster, Stendhal, and Yves Saint Laurent.

Jean Laporte Parfumeur at Port La Royale in Marigot features special blends of his own.

Conservative types who would rather stick with what they know and like than experiment will find a number of reliable purveyors competing for their patronage.

The Yellow House (La Casa Amarilla) on De Ruyterplein (Little Pier) to the left of the post office (tel. 2332) is a century-old member of the Dutch mercantile community both here and in Curaçao. It handles a wide range of offerings, including the ultra-chic Charles Blair, Van Cleef & Arpels, Dunhill, Galanos, Guerlain, Hermès, Givenchy, Dior, and Brigitte Bardot, to name just a few. Here also Stendhal cosmetics, as well as the hypoallergenic Roc.

Penha & Sons, in business for generations (47 Front St., Philipsburg—tel. 2279), feature Clinique, Orlane, Lancôme, Biotherm cosmetics, and a comprehensive collection of fragrances. **Little Switzerland** on 42 and 69 Front St., Philipsburg (tel. 2296) and Rue de la République in Marigot (tel. 87-50-03) also handles Balenciaga, Chanel, Worth, and other carriage-trade perfumes.

SPIRITS

Sint Maarten/St. Martin used to make a local rum that enjoyed a rather faithful following. The actual manufacturing has been moved elsewhere, but you will still find bottles of Potts Rum here and there. When you do, you might want to add one to your collection, since those left on the island have had time to age and mellow.

Exactly where the Saba Spice sold on Sint Maarten/St. Martin is made depends on which batch and whom you talk to. The original potion, an agreeable blend of spices with fennel overtones, is indisputably a Saban invention. Admiring, and resourceful, Sint Maartenites, demonstrating once again that imitation is the sincerest form of flattery, proceeded to copy the product—but did not, according to connoisseurs, duplicate it. On the other hand, the Sint Maarten product is considerably slicker in its presentation than that of Saba, which tends to be put up in discarded Dewars Scotch bottles or whatever other used container comes handy. Should you want to take an exploratory taste before investing in a whole fifth, there are miniatures available for very little outlay; the big bottle usually retails for under $5.

Sint Maarten/St. Martin's tolerant tax situation makes for great buys in conventional liquors. Johnnie Walker Red label, for example, priced $11.95 in Manhattan, can be had here for $4 or so. Wines don't always represent such a saving, though it depends on where you are accustomed to buying them. Compare $35 for Dom Perignon in Philipsburg with what you would pay Stateside and then decide whether or not it's worth hauling home.

As to where to shop for spirits, try the **Food Center,** the supermarket at the outskirts of Philipsburg at 105 Bush Rd. (tel. 2315 or 2415), where the supply is good and so are the prices.

Julio's Smoke 'n Booze Tasting House, on Back Street a block from the police station in Philipsburg, is an amusing place to browse: kegs serve as counters and display cases. You can also pick up Dutch cigars here.

Among other purveyors of liquors and wines are **Zig Zag Liquor Store** at 115 Front St. in Philipsburg (tel. 2343), next door to Le Bec Fins; **Emile's Place** on De Ruyterplein (Little Pier) in Philipsburg (tel. 2145); **Antillean Liquors N.V.** at Juliana Airport (tel. 4267); **Caribbean Liquors** at the Emmaplein in Philipsburg (tel. 2140 or 2141); **Anilina** on Front Street opposite the Holland House Hotel (tel. 2141); **Vendôme** on the waterfront on the French side in Marigot has a good assortment of liquor, in addition to some fine French wines and champagnes.

The **Caribe Cellar** branch on Rue de la République in Marigot is another source.

WATCHES

You pay your money and take your choice. And what

choices! You name it, you'll most certainly find the timepieces you've been longing for here in Sint Maarten/St. Martin. Here are some branches represented (in Philipsburg, unless otherwise noted):

Carat, Front Street (tel. 2180), and at Marigot: Les musts de Cartier, Piaget, Baume & Mercier

Caribbean Gems, Front Street: Seiko

Gandelman Jewelers, 50 Front St. (tel. 3396 or 3328): Baume & Mercier, Citizen, Raymond Weil, Heuer, Dior, Gucci

Gemsland Jewellers, 33 Front St. (tel. 2156): Favre Leuba, Seiko

La Romana, Front Street, Royal Palm Plaza Arcade, and Mullet Bay Shopping Arcade (tel. 2181): Hublot, Porsche Design, Mocassino, Les musts de Cartier

Little Europe Jewellers, 74 Front St. (tel. 3062): Piaget, Corum, Movado, Swatch, Seiko

Little Switzerland at 42 and 69 Front St., and Rue de la République, Marigot: Rolex, Audemars Piguet, Vacheron et Constantin, Borel, Concord, Girard-Pérregaux, Rado, Chopard

Maurella Senesi at 83 Front St. (tel. 3062): Epoka

Oro de Sol on Front Street (tel. 260), and Rue de la République, Marigot (tel. 87-57-02): Piaget, Cartier, Ebel, Concord, Corum

Roy's Jewelry & Solid Gold at the Holland House Hotel (tel. 2533) and the St. Maarten Beach Club: Movado, Seiko, Lassale, Raymond Weil, Citizen

Spritzer & Fuhrmann at Mullet Bay Shopping Arcade (tel. 4217), Juliana Airport; and Rue de la République, Marigot: Patek Phillippe, Piaget, Corum, Chopard, Omega, Tissot, Seiko

H. Stern Jewellers, 56 Front St.: Concord, Piaget,

Baume & Mercier, Corum, Oris, Movado, Raymond Weil, Heuer, Gucci

Before you make your purchase final from any of these shops—or from one of the number of other outlets offering timepieces for sale—a couple of cautionary notes.

First, if you are contemplating a substantial expenditure, you might want to invest in a phone call to your local jeweler at home to compare prices on the same item. The size of savings can vary considerably, and you would not want to use up your entire duty-free exemption unless it's for a real bargain.

Secondly, an authorized representative, namely one who has permission from the manufacturer to feature the logo of the watch in his advertising and his place of business, enjoys the endorsement of the maker by implication. That firm will stand by its product and repair it for you should it become necessary.

Case in point: We once bought on another island what we had no reason to believe was anything other than a bona fide Omega, in a shop which, while to all appearances reputable, did not display the distinctive Omega horseshoe logo. The watch never worked, was never successfully repaired. When we finally took it back to Switzerland with us we were informed that it was a "second," or otherwise flawed piece, rejected for sale by the Omega factory but that somehow found its way to market. Whether or not it came out of the Omega plant was open to question.

As a matter of fact, in any marketplace composed of 500 shops, the old *Caveat Emptor* applies. You will find most merchants are straight-arrow, on the up and up, with a long tradition to uphold. Some Sint Maarten firms go back 60 years and more. With this many veteran shopkeepers competing for your discretionary dollar, however, problems are not beyond the realm of possibility.

As in most communities, things are not always exactly what they seem on Sint Maarten either. To illustrate in another context, one longtime resident tells of his experience. It involved a prim ecclesiastical building known alternately as "The Japanese Fishing Club" because of its use for the diversion of the Japanese fishing fleet based in Sint Maarten, or as "The Church" in deference to a time when its premises were dedicated to less lubricious pursuits. The Fishing Club's feminine staff was government regulated, and the resident who met the Colombian señoritas every week at the medical clinic that provided him with vitamin shots, them with unspecified services, found the girls so demure it took him some time to realize that their house was neither a home nor a chapel.

Finally, given the vast array of tempting souks, suppose you had only one day to shop here?

In that unfortunate event, we would probably spend our time in these (check Useful Addresses section for exact locations):

La Romana and **Sergio's** for fashions on the Dutch side, **Le Bastringue** in Port La Royale, Marigot.

H. Stern Jewellers because their designs are so interesting and the price range usually includes something affordable.

Little Swizterland and **Oro de Sol** for one-stop luxury shopping, Dutch or French sides, including perfumes (if we did make it to the French side, we'd certainly include **Vendôme**).

In Philipsburg, **Coconuts** and **Impressions** for the fun of it, **The Yellow House** and/or **Penha & Sons** for hard-to-find perfumes. **The New Amsterdam Store** definitely—lazy shoppers sometimes bypass this crammed-to-the-scuppers emporium because there is indeed so much stuff here it takes a while to sort it out.

One indication of the worthiness of what's in The New Amsterdam Store from our standpoint is the number of previous acquisitions we continue to enjoy: a string of knotted cultured pearls acquired a decade ago for $10, an amusing Italian pocketbook well worth its $7.50 pricetag, perfume flagons gilded with filigree bands studded with big gloppy "jewels"—at 85¢ apiece. We bought them by the gross for stocking stuffers. You never know what you'll discover.

Around the Bend in Philipsburg and **Pierre Lapin** in Grand Case are musts, if only to find out what's going on, view Jean and Dee's last Caribbean-made finds, and generally feel the pulse of the island. If humanly possible, we'd fit in a stop at one or more of the food stores.

At the end of that one day, having barely tickled the top, we would depart gnashing our teeth in rage and frustration that time did not permit proper exploration of one of the top agoras in the Caribbean.

USEFUL ADDRESSES

Albert's Store: 132 Front St., Philipsburg (tel. 2946).

Anilina: Front Street, opposite the Holland House Hotel, Philipsburg (tel. 2141).

Animale: Marina Royal Shopping Arcade, Marigot.

Antillean Liquors N.V.: Juliana Airport (tel. 4267).

Around the Bend: Front Street, Philipsburg.

Ashoka: 93 Front Street, Philipsburg.

Aventura: Marina Royal Shopping Arcade, Marigot.

Bagatelle: Rue de la République, Marigot.

Bali Boutique: De Ruyterplein (Little Pier), Philipsburg (tel. 2520).

Batik Caribe: Promenade Arcade, Front Street, Philipsburg (tel. 2185).

Boa: Port La Royale, Marigot.

Boolchand's: 42 Front St., Philipsburg (tel. 2245 or 2445).

Boutique Smart: Marina Royal Shopping Mall, Marigot.

Carat: Front Street, Philipsburg (tel. 2180); Marigot.

The Caribbean Corner: Holland House Hotel, 33 Front Street, Philipsburg.

Caribbean Gems: Front Street, Philipsburg.

Caribbean Liquors: Emmaplein, Philipsburg (tel. 2140 or 2141).

Caribe Cellar: Front Street, De Ruyterplein (Little Pier), Philipsburg; Rue de la République, Marigot.

Coconuts: near De Ruyterplein (Little Pier), next door to The Yellow House, Philipsburg (tel. 2164).

Colombian Emeralds International: Front Street, Philipsburg.

Continental: 120 Front St., Philipsburg.

Creations St. Martin: Port La Royale, Marigot.

Dalila: Marina Royal Shopping Arcade, Marigot.

Desmo: St. Maarten Beach Club, Front Street, Philipsburg; also at Port La Royale, Marigot.

East Meets West: Front Street, Philipsburg.

E.A.T. Royal: Front Street at Royal Palm Plaza, Philipsburg (tel. 3443).

E.G.R. Boutique: 97 Front St., Philipsburg (tel. 2085).

Elle: 79 Front St., Philipsburg (tel. 3486); also at Port La Royale, Marigot.

Emile's Place: De Ruyterplein (Little Pier), Philipsburg (tel. 2145).

Etna Gardens: Front Street near Main Square, Philipsburg (tel. 3424); also at Port La Royale, Marigot.

Food Center: 105 Bush Rd., outside Philipsburg (tel. 2315 or 2415).

Gandelman Jewelers: 50 Front St., Philipsburg (tel. 3396 or 3328).

Gemsland Jewellers: Holland House Hotel, 33 Front St., Philipsburg (tel. 2156).

Greenwich Gallery: Marshall Mall, Front Street, Philipsburg.

Gucci Boutique: Front Street, Philipsburg.

H. Stern Jewellers: 56 Front St., Philipsburg.

Impressions: 6 Promenade Arcade, Front Street, Philipsburg.

Java Wraps: Royal Palm Plaza, Philipsburg (tel. 3568).

Jean Laporte Parfumeur: Port La Royale, Marigot.

The Jewel Box: 65 Front St., Philipsburg (tel. 3538).

Julio's Smoke 'n Booze Tasting House: Back Street, Philipsburg.

K-Dis: On the main road to Grand Case, outside Marigot.

Kohinoor: Front Street, Philipsburg (tel. 2245 or 2445).

L'Artisanat Galerie: Main road, Marigot.

L'Atelier: Grand Case, St. Martin.

La Romana: Front Street in the Royal Palm Plaza Arcade and Mullet Bay Shopping Arcade, Philipsburg (tel. 2181).

Le Bastringue: Port La Royale, Marigot (tel. 87-58-20).

Leda of Venice: 96 Front St., Philipsburg (tel. 3441).

Lil' Shoppe: Front Street, next to Pinocchio Restaurant, Philipsburg (tel. 2177).

Lipstick: Port La Royale, Marigot.

Little Europe Jewellers: 74 Front St., Philipsburg (tel. 3062).

Little Switzerland: 42 and 69 Front St., Philipsburg (tel. 2296); Rue de la République, Marigot (tel. 87-50-03); for full-color catalog call 800-524-2010.

Maurella Senesi: 83 Front St., Royal Palm Plaza, Philipsburg (tel. 3323).

MaximoFlorence: 102 Front St., Promenade Arcade, Philipsburg (tel. 2608).

Mille Fleurs: Front Street, Promenade Arcade, Philipsburg (tel. 2473).

Minguet, Alexander, studio: Grand Case, St. Martin.

The New Amsterdam Store: 54 Front St., Philipsburg (tel. 2787 and 2788); branches also at Grand Casino Way, Mullet Bay; Maho Reef (tel. 4320).

Oro de Sol: Front Street, Philipsburg (tel. 2602); Rue de la République, Marigot (tel. 87-57-02).

Pasanggrahan: Front Street, Philipsburg (tel. 3588).

Penha & Sons: 47 Front St., Philipsburg (tel. 2279).

Pierre Lapin: La Case, Grand Case (tel. 87-52-10).

Printemps: Marigot.

Raisonable: Marina Royal Shopping Arcade, Marigot.

Ramchand's: 73 Front St., Philipsburg.

Roland Richardson: Orléans, St. Martin.

Roy's Jewelry & Solid Gold: Holland House Hotel, Front Street, Philipsburg (tel. 2533); branch also at St. Maarten Beach Club, Philipsburg.

Sasha's: 57 Front St. (Pinocchio's Arcade), Philipsburg.

Sea Breeze: Front Street, Promenade Arcade, Philipsburg.

Sergio Moreta: 17 and 20 Front St., also Marshall's Mall, Philipsburg.

Shipwreck Shop: Front Street, Philipsburg (tel. 2962).

Sonovision: 57 Front Street, Philipsburg.

Spritzer & Fuhrmann: Grand Casino Way, Mullet Bay Shopping Arcade, Philipsburg (tel. 4217); branches also at Princess Juliana Airport and Rue de la République, Marigot.

St. Trop Boutique: 26 Front St., Philipsburg (tel. 2165).

St. Tropez: Marina Royal Shopping Arcade, Marigot.

Taj Mahal: Front Street, Philipsburg (tel. 2245 or 2445).

Thimbles and Things: Back Street, Philipsburg (tel. 2898).

Vanessa: Galerie Périgourdine, Marigot; branch also at Le Pirate.

Vendôme: Waterfront, Marigot.

Vertiges: Port La Royale, Marigot.

West Indian Tavern: "head" of Front Street, Philipsburg (tel. 2965).

The Wholesale House: 109 Front St., Philipsburg.

The Yellow House (La Casa Amarilla): De Ruyterplein (Little Pier), Philipsburg (tel. 2332).

Zig Zag Liquor Store: 115 Front St., Philipsburg (tel. 2343).

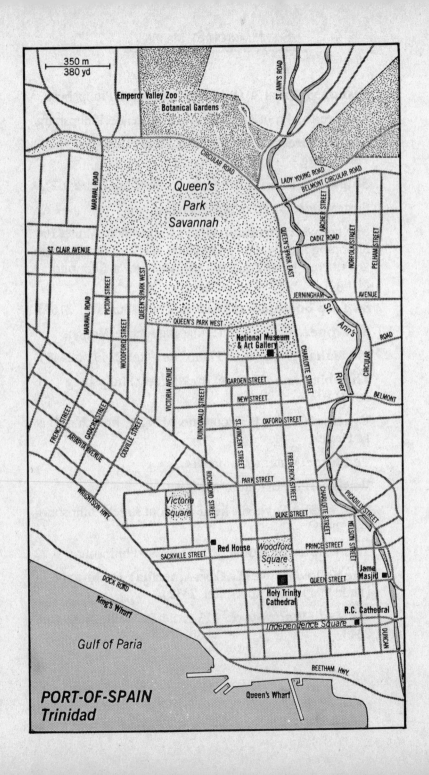

PORT-OF-SPAIN
Trinidad

TRINIDAD AND TOBAGO

TRINIDAD AND TOBAGO AT A GLANCE

GOVERNMENT TOURIST OFFICE: Trinidad and Tobago Tourist Board, 122-124 Frederick Street, Port-of-Spain, Trinidad (tel. 623-1932, 623-1933, 623-7405).

CURRENCY: Trinidad and Tobago dollars ($TT) are pegged to the U.S. dollar at an exchange rate of US$1 to $2.40TT. Hold on to your exchange receipts to reconvert your TT's to U.S. bills when you leave. You can change money at banks, or at your hotel. Traveler's checks get a slightly higher rate than bills. Here the symbols "$" and "¢" mean TT, not US$.

OFFICIAL HOLIDAYS: New Year's Day, Good Friday, Easter Monday, Whit Monday, Corpus Christi (June 10), Discovery Day (first Monday in August), Independence Day (August 31), Republic Day (September 24), Divali (Hindu Festival of Lights—November), Eidul-Fitr (Islamic Festival marking the end of Ramadan—December), Christmas Day, Boxing Day (December 26).

Note: The actual holiday dates can shift from year to year. Carnival Monday and Tuesday, the two days prior to Ash Wednesday, which marks the beginning of Lent, are not official holidays, but employers free nonessential workers and make other arrangements to relieve their staffs.

STORE HOURS: Most stores are open from 8 a.m. to 4 p.m., Monday through Friday. Saturday is half day, food and liquor stores excepted. However, these close Thursday afternoon.

LOCATIONS: For the addresses and telephone numbers of the shops, consult the alphabetical list at the end of this chapter.

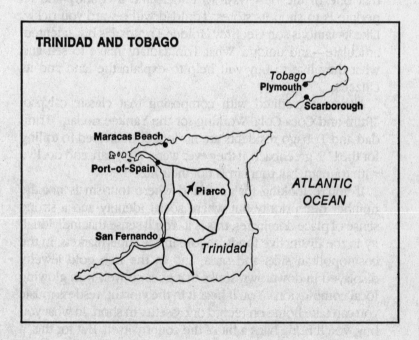

TRINIDAD AND TOBAGO

Tobago
Plymouth
Scarborough

Maracas Beach

Port-of-Spain

Piarco

ATLANTIC OCEAN

San Fernando

Trinidad

I f you like to shop in medinas tailored specifically to American visitors, you can skip the two-island nation of Trinidad. You'll find no abundance of glitzy boutiques here, few slick salons. Instead merchandise is generally chosen to serve the needs of the local population and of Venezuelan visitors, rather than to snag mass invasions of lumpen folk in flowered shirts.

On the other hand, if you are one of those who believes that one of the best ways to understand a country and its people is to shop its stores, Trinidad will reward you richly. Like its famous son Geoffrey Holder, Trinidad is big, talented, articulate—and unique. What Trinidadians make to sell and what they like to buy will help to explain the land and its citizens.

Although credited with composing that classic calypso, "Rum and Coca-Cola, Working for the Yankee dollar," Trinidad and Tobago residents are no longer dedicated to toiling for the U.S. greenback, if they ever were. They can, and do, live with tourism, but tourism is not their life.

If you're looking for an island where tourism is not the number one priority but where social identity and a strong sense of place dominates, this is it. You'll sense that individuality in the distinctive foods on sale in the supermarkets, in the cosmopolitan silks and saris, and in the rich gold jewelry displayed in downtown souks that goes so well with glowing local complexions. You'll hear it in the vibrant, restless music you can take home on record or cassette. In short, in what you buy, you'll bring back a bit of the country itself. But for this, a little background is indicated.

Trinidad is far from just another resort island. This ambitious country hums with an urgency and vibrates with a vitality that are at odds with her position as the southernmost of the generally somnolent, languorous West Indies. Barely fifteen miles from the South American coast, Trinidad's million-plus inhabitants, half of whom are under twenty-five, represent ethnic groups from almost every corner of the world.

Trinidad features birds that speak French, a lake you can walk on, and oysters growing on trees. Throughout the day an ubiquitous multicolored bird chirps the question, *"Qu'est-ce qu'il dit?"*—"What does he say?" Creole argot corrupts this to "kiskadee," which becomes the bird's local name.

The economy of the country does not depend on tourism and/or agriculture, as it must on so many Caribbean islands. Indeed, tourism represents less than 5% of the economy's Gross National Product. With the possible exceptions of Puerto Rico and Jamaica, Trinidad ranks as the most industrialized island of the West Indies and certainly the richest in natural resources: oil, bauxite, natural gas, bitumens from Pitch Lake, which Sir Walter Raleigh discovered in 1595.

For generations, this Delaware-size outpost was relegated to playing the role of a docile British Crown Colony, following instructions from Whitehall, toiling for the benefit of Britannia, accepting whatever crumbs dropped her way from the head table. This situation cast a pall over the naturally dynamic, gregarious, creative people.

When independence finally came to the two-island nation in 1962, this polyglot community had the rare good fortune to be guided by a leader of world stature. A gifted scholar and statesman, Doctor Eric E.I. Williams wrote his Ph.D. thesis at Oxford entitled "Capitalism and Slavery," which became a classic interpretation of industrialization financed by the slave trade and the emancipation made necessary by its success.

Eric Williams, compared by some academicians to Nehru, gave living proof that a native-born West Indian was indeed capable of great achievements in the world's highest centers of learning. Because of the foundation Dr. Williams laid before his death in 1981, Trinidad and its sister island of Tobago made the transition to independence with few headlines of strife and bloodletting. It was his sensitivity to the importance of his nation's heritage that contributed much to the degree of cultural integrity this country maintains today—an integrity that is the envy of many an island swallowed up by big-time tourism.

Port-of-Spain and its environs constitute the main shopping center. This bustling port, hub of administration, shipping, commerce, and culture, is about the size of Winston-Salem, North Carolina, or Cambridge, Massachusetts.

Some 120,000 wondrously disparate people live together in a fascinating hodgepodge of Victorian, Napoleon II Empire, Moorish, Renaissance, Gothic, and modern, high-rise architecture. One mansion lavishly copies a German Rhenish castle. Bustling, earthy, and totally cosmopolitan, Port-of-Spain is a pulsating blend of big metropolitan center, tropical shanties, and folksy country-seat.

Heartland of this community is Queen's Park, a 200-acre green belt surrounded by the city on three sides. Commonly called "The Savannah," this was once an old sugar estate (the family burial plot lies in the middle), and the deed of gift specified that no permanent building should ever be erected to mar the open field. Football, cricket, hockey, horseracing, and the glittering annual Carnival take place in the Savannah, but, to honor the deed, every structure was put together in "temporary" fashion; in the unlikely event that the letter of the law ever has to be enforced, even the grandstand could be taken apart piece by piece.

As you would expect in an area of this size, you have several shopping options.

Downtown Port-of-Spain—Frederick Street and Independence Square especially—is the traditional, longtime retail center.

The various malls offer fruitful foraging: **Gulf City**, near the metropolis of San Fernando and hailed by locals as the largest mall in the Caribbean; **Long Circular Mall**, in St. James;

West Mall, in West Moorings, Cocorite; **Val Park** and **Kirpalani's Roundabout**, en route to Piarco International Airport. Do not dismiss the malls out of hand as Yankee corruptions. Their merchandise retains its Trinidad flavor, and their convenience and creature comforts very definitely have their points.

If you are short on time, two easy ways to sample the wares of Trinidad are to patronize the shopping arcade at the Hilton Hotel (located near the Queen's Park Savannah in Port-of-Spain, and at the airport). You will find a wide range of items at both locations.

The Hilton arcade includes branches of two of the best freeport shops on the island—**Stecher's** (tel. 624-3322) and **Y. de Lima's** (tel. 624-3432). Shop them both for jewelry, watches, china, crystal, perfumes, and other imported luxury items. In the Hilton complex too, at **Kacal's Artist in Wood** (tel. 624-3356) you will find superior examples of what can be done with Trinidad's truly wonderful woods; the store also features local artwork. While less heavily stocked, airport shops also offer good selections.

ARTS AND CRAFTS

The trickle of foresighted buyers of Trinidadian art could well become a tidal wave. At least one art dealer from Haiti has been reported to be ferreting out canvases to take back to his own country. One delighted Texan built a room around one of Leo Glasgow's jumbo-sized canvases. Another collector picked up a series of impressionistic watercolors executed with—of all things—windshield wipers.

Clara de Lima's **Art Creators & Supplies, Ltd.**, 402 Aldegonda Park, 7 St. Ann's Road, Port-of-Spain (tel. 624-4369), is the insiders' choice for where to find the best in a bumper crop of fine paintings and sculptures. Although there are reproductions, small and large, and other inexpensive items, prices can run into the thousands—and are willingly paid by discerning art buffs. If you admired some of Geoffrey Holder's works when they were on exhibit in the States and would like to acquire one, you will find him represented here as well as works of Geoffrey's brother, Bosco.

Kacal's Artist in Wood in the Hilton arcade on Lady Young Road (tel. 624-3356), sells paintings as well.

Galleries we've been told about but can't vouch for from firsthand experience include **The Art Gallery**, Room D, Salavatori Building, Port-of-Spain (tel. 624-7904), and **Moart Gallery**, Kirpalani Roundabout Plaza, near Piarco International Airport (tel. 638-5887).

Artists whose works you might want to look for include Willi Chen, Nina Squires, Ken Critchlow, and Carlisle Harris.

You may also be advised to look for James Boodhoo, a good painter who exhibits locally.

Were we contemplating any serious investment in art, we would make every effort first to enlist the counsel of Carlisle Chang, a Trinidad-born, European-trained muralist-painter of extraordinary talent. For Port-of-Spain's Town Hall, he composed a 41-foot sand-cast (concrete poured on a bed of wet sand) mural dramatically portraying key elements of Trinidad's national character: the open door of hospitality, the sun of energy, and the Tree of Freedom, symbolizing the country's five main religious faiths. For the Hilton Hotel opening, Chang did an exciting three-dimensional *Carnival Parade*, in sensuous contrasts of metals, featuring lithe, liquid figures in Trinidadian "jump-up" costumes. When Carlisle Chang has the time, and the inclination, to create—which is not every day—knowing collectors snap up his works as fast as they come off the easel. Mr. Chang has designed some of the most exquisite of Trinidad's Carnival costumes, and is a moving force in the local art society. He eschews telephone service, but you should be able to reach him through his cousin, Gary Chang, at 627-6965. You might also drop Carlisle a line at 40 Murray St., Woodbrook, Port-of-Spain, Trinidad.

Insofar as crafts are concerned, they reflect the country's ethnic mix. The majority of Trinidad's population descends from the African Ashanti, Hausa, Ibo, Yoruba, Mandingo, and Rada tribes, very lightly flavored with Amerindians. This base has been seasoned and spiced with several hundred thousand East Indians, plus uncounted infusions of Chinese, French, Portuguese, British, Spanish, Lebanese, Syrians, and North Americans.

The problem for the visitor is to find them! Joyce Wong Sang, the gifted sister-in-law of the late Dr. Eric Williams, who coordinates the Prime Minister's "Best Village" program, has as one of her top priorities, to centralize and showcase the various crafts from the hamlets and towns throughout Trinidad and Tobago. The Best Village program stimulates competition in dance, cuisine, sports, and crafts—stuffed toys, dried flowers, creative shell jewelry, handmade dolls in Carnival costumes, woodcarvings, *shac-shac* musical instruments, crochet, embroidery, and *repoussé*. Other mediums appear in various exhibits and competitions, the largest of which—a ten-county event—takes place in October. Otherwise, look for crafts at the **Trinidad and Tobago Cooperative** at the Hilton Hotel in Port-of-Spain (tel. 624-3111). Another possible source is the **Trinidad & Tobago Blind Welfare Association Shop** at 118 Duke St., also in Port-of-Spain (tel. 625-4659). The baskets here, we were told, are fashioned according to an old Arawak design. Certainly they are the most durable we have ever owned. One still in active use in our household dates back to 1968.

Fuller's Ltd. at 22 Henry St., Port-of-Spain (tel. 623-5081), and **Jo-Di's Handicraft Shoppe** in the Galleria Shopping Plaza of St. James (tel. 622-8461) are on our list for next time.

CAMERAS

Nikon, Canon, Yashica—you'll find most of the big-name cameras, along with binoculars, at the **Y. de Lima** stores.

There are no less than sixteen Y. de Limas situated throughout the Caribbean, including those conveniently located in downtown Port-of-Spain, in the Hilton arcade, and at the Piarco International Airport (see Useful Addresses for details). As always, check your hometown prices before making a purchase. How much of a difference in your favor you will find depends on where in the U.S. you usually shop, and to a certain extent, for what. You may find accessories here especially lower in cost.

CHINA, CRYSTAL, AND HOME FURNISHINGS

Royal Doulton, Wedgwood, St. Louis, Waterford, Baccarat, Lalique—you'll note all these and more, handsomely presented, in any one of the several **Stecher's** shops in Trinidad and nearby islands (check the Useful Addresses section for details). For the best assortment at the best prices, for straight-arrow reliability, and for discerning guidance, Stecher's has been our preferred target of choice, for over two decades.

John Stecher's career as a Caribbean carriage-trade retailer began in Trinidad, where he lives, and although the Stecher empire has now expanded to encompass ten shops on three islands, and includes an operation at the Piarco International Airport, the spacious, air-conditioned main showroom at 27 Frederick St. in Port-of-Spain remains the lodestone. The leadership provided by this dynamic transplanted European, as chairman of the Chamber of Commerce's committee on Tourism and Industry and as a member of the Trinidad & Tobago Tourist Board, has made outstanding contributions to island development and at the same time, heightened his own insight into the land and his people.

Customers who have made their purchases at Stecher's include Lena Horne, Robert Mitchum, and, in years gone by, Nelson Rockefeller, Marlene Dietrich, Mahalia Jackson, as well as best-selling authors, senior senators, and legions of other knowledgeable shoppers.

To give you an idea of prices, note these comparisons:

Item	U.S. Price	Stecher's Price
Belleek Shamrock Tree Stump Vase	$32.50	$15.50
Wedgwood Cobalt Florentine 5-Piece Place Setting	195.00	118.00
Royal Doulton Character Mugs (large)	75.00	45.00
Swarovski Lotus Flower Candleholder	200.00	115.00
Waterford "Alana" Water Goblet	48.00	30.25

For made-in-Trinidad items, **Kacal's Artist in Wood** at the Hilton Hotel on Lady Young Road (tel. 624-3356) has handsome articles fashioned of purple heart, mahogany, lignum vitae, and other beautiful tropical woods. Some trays, tea carts, and the like combine the rainbow colors of the various woods with striking effect. You can acquire pieces at Kacal's from $15 up.

McLeod's Antiques at the corner of La Seiva and Saddle Road in Port-of-Spain (tel. 629-2224) is worth more than a cursory look. Find a branch also in the Hilton Hotel arcade.

Lakhan's Bazaar, at 32 West Main Road at Bombay Street, St. James (tel. 622-4688), in the heart of the Hindu section, offers a staggering array of casbah-style merchandise, some of which may remind you of stock you've seen in cities in the States: collapsible tables, brass servers in all shapes and sizes, ivory figurines, Indian rugs, carved chests. Viewed en masse, the effect is a little overpowering. On the other hand, if you need an exotic accent for an otherwise conventional room, perhaps you will find it here.

FASHIONS

At one time Trinidad was probably best known sartorially

for the superb British-style men's tailoring available on very short notice. The late Fitz Blackman, "The Bespoke Tailor," who doubled in brass as the mayor of Port-of-Spain, had clients in boardrooms, executive suites, and chancelleries the world over.

Unfortunately, this tradition is rather on the wane. Sydney Shim, "tailor to the stars" and at one time recommended to tourists, is out of business. Moreover, most of the tailors who are currently working are simply not geared to quick delivery. Some possibilities:

Manshak handles avant-garde haberdashery from its shop at 33 Charlotte St. (tel. 623-7061).

There's a **Tokiki Manshop** in the Hilton arcade (tel. 624-3111) that you might investigate.

You could investigate Christopher Lynch's service at **Habib's**, either at 48 Independence Square, Port-of-Spain (tel. 623-4485), or at Long Circular Mall, St. James (tel. 622-8895).

For haute couture with a Trinidadian accent, **Meiling** is your best bet. Headquarters are at 4 Cartos Street, Port-of-Spain, with a boutique also on Gray Street. When it comes to cost, Meiling has the customary three categories—low, medium, and high—but be forewarned: high is indeed high.

Shape, at 13 Fitzgerald Lane, Port-of-Spain (tel. 625-2119), offers quality merchandise, at quality prices.

Begum's Boutique, in the Hilton arcade, Port-of-Spain, is one of the livelier enclaves you're likely to find: ceremonial Kashmir headdresses, embroidered kaftans, come and go; even on one occasion there was even a trick dress with three sleeves. For men, we've seen fabulous satin and embroidered robes and smoking jackets, great sandals, buttons of intricate filigree, marriage turbans—the rapidly changing stock is uninhibited and flamboyant enough to suit the most adventurous of shoppers.

At the Hilton also, you might drop in on **Boutique Cybele** (tel. 624-4669) to see what's available there.

For young, trendy sportswear for either sex, it's **City Blues**, 15 Henry St., in downtown Port-of-Spain (tel. 623-4482).

If you're a home stitcher, keep an eye out for fabrics wherever you go, especially English imports, African prints, and Indian saris. Because there is a large local clientele for this kind of yard goods, the supply is eclectic and includes some you're not likely to find in your nearest sewing center.

Lakhan's Bazaar at 32 West Main Road, St. James (tel. 622-4688), has a representative selection of saris, along with beaded bags and assorted bazaar-style accessories.

FOOD

Wild game, stuffed crab back, pickled pork—these and all sorts of other exotica are to be found on Trinidad tables. The raw ingredients of delectable eating—hearts of palm, fresh spices, limes, homegrown vegetables and fruit—abound. And seasonings are as cosmopolitan as the people themselves.

Try *tulooms*—delicious little molasses cakes spiked with coconut, fresh ginger, orange peel, and nuts. Or cassava pone pudding, or pasteles. Many of the local delicacies are a little spicy for conventional palates, but the flavors are unusual, provocative, and distinctly Trinidadian.

One very readable monograph concerning Trinidad gastronomy is **Geoffrey Holder's Caribbean Cookbook** (New York, Viking Press). Holder not only writes most entertainingly about the local lore of eating in his native land, but also shares some of his special recipes, such as coq au rhum, king turtle stew, and shrimp cutlets. For better or for worse (we rather wish he had not) Holder has converted the ingredients into those readily available in the U.S. Still, the Trinidadian point of view is strongly evident, and the author's recollections of island cuisine are insightful.

There are over two dozen food manufacturers and distributors in Trinidad, so you will find no shortage of West Indian,

East Indian, Chinese, and local specialties for you to take home, tinned or dry-packaged, on sale on supermarket shelves.

Matouks, headquartered in the Glamour Girl Complex on Churchill Roosevelt Highway, San Juan (tel. 638-3391), makes a papaya-based hot sauce that is a staple in our larder. Trinidadian friends say it's too bland—but the heat is more than enough to ignite our timid tastebuds.

Rising Sun (93 St. Vincent St., Tunapuna, in case you want to write ahead—tel. 663-2546), produce ground geera, saffron, spices, and coffee.

As for the many varieties of Trinidad curry, ranging from superb to sublime, we lean toward the one produced by **Turban Brand Products**, at 186 Eastern Main Rd., on the fringe of Port-of-Spain.

All these condiments make great gifts. The hot sauce costs under $3 for 24 ounces. As for the curry powder, those who have shelled out small ransoms for a thimbleful at home will relish walking away here with a pound for less than $2.

To acquire your take-home supply of Trinidadian gourmetry, visit most any sizeable supermarket. **The Peoples Supermarket** at 10 Independence Square in Port-of-Spain is convenient to general shopping.

Others include the **Choo Quan Supermarket** at 24 Queen St., Port-of-Spain (tel. 623-5416); **Payless**, 75 St. Vincent St., Tunapuna (tel. 624-6895); and **Honey Comb Supermarket** at 7-11 Prince St., Port-of-Spain (tel. 623-6418). **Hilo Supermarkets**, with a number of branches in Port-of-Spain, is another possibility. There is no single stand-out, one so much better than the other markets that you need go out of your way to find it.

When you plan your overall schedule, ask your innkeeper, salesclerk, cashier, or maitre d'hotel to direct you to the store nearest you. Do tell them, however, that you want a proper, full-scale grocery. Too often they believe you merely want to pick up a pack of cigarettes or some such and send you to the closest mini hole-in-the-wall.

If you're into excursions, the honey harvested at and sold at **Mount St. Benedict's Abbey** on St. John's Road in Tunapuna (tel. 662-2105 and 662-4084) offers a savory pretext for an afternoon's outing. The lofty hilltop Benedictine monastery dominating the Piarco plain and Diego Martin Valley takes you back to the Middle Ages. It has large landholdings, as did European monasteries, a village nestled in the foothills that lives off the abbey, and a Vocational School and Woodworking Center.

Feverish production buzzes on multiple fronts. There is a boys' school, a Carmelite novitiate, and a seminary for training young recruits. The enterprising monks not only raise enough produce to feed themselves, their charges, and the paying visitors to their Pax Guest House, but they have enough left over to sell on the retail market. The abbey apiary exports tons of Pax honey; the wax is thriftily converted into candles. Indeed, the only major undertaking the brothers do not seem to be involved in is the blending of Benedictine liqueur. "And how," twinkled the holy one we asked about this, "do you know we don't? For strictly on-premises, private, medicinal consumption perhaps?"

To capitalize on the carloads of travelers who drive up to enjoy the lovely flowers, sweeping vistas, and generally soothing tranquillity of Mount St. Benedict, the brethren have installed a giftshop and last time we were there, even served tea to visitors for a small fee. Telephone them at 662-2105 to find out if they are still doing so and if reservations are required.

If you do go, and like Mount St. Benedict so much you'd like to linger longer, that too can be arranged. Check into the small Guest House the Order operates on the premises (tel. 662-4084).

JEWELRY

Everything **Y. de Lima** manufactures in its workrooms at 23A Frederick St. in Port-of-Spain (tel. 623-1364) is gold or silver and made in Trinidad. European and South American artists have contributed their expertise, originally creating some of the molds and supervising and execution.

Conch shells, ibises, hummingbirds, nutmeg branches—any island symbol is likely to be fashioned into jewelry. A charming orchid pin may balance a single cultured pearl on its stamen. Or there are steel-drum earrings and coco pods. The gold comes in 10, 14, and 18 karat, and some pieces wear a deep-orange finish which, we are told, can be buffed off while you wait. Apparently visitors from the other islands, who constitute a large percentage of Trinidad's tourists, find the finish becoming to their darker skins. On them it looks good—not so for some of us palefaces.

West Indian bangles, in silver or in gold, are a popular item. In some Caribbean areas, lovers young and old, married and unmarried, traditionally presented these to their wives or sweethearts on important occasions. On the theory that they can be redeemed for cash, they may serve as a sort of savings plan. Y de Lima makes island charms, friendship amulets, and up to thirty-three different styles of rings for men.

Y. de Lima also engraves and gold plates on order, and this opens up all sorts of gleaming possibilities. Pick up a standard chrome lighter, metal compact, car key or whatever, give it to Y. de Lima to be engraved and gold plated, you'll have an imposing gift, less costly than it looks. *Warning:* Have the engraving done *BEFORE* the plating, otherwise the etch mars the finish.

The de Lima mercantile empire dates back to 1885 and extends to a number of other islands. In Trinidad, there are shops in the Hilton arcade, at the Piarco International Airport, Long Circular Mall, and Gulf City and a variety of other locations, with prices beginning at $20. If you don't see something you like in any of these, ask about having a design made to order. Note the cultured pearls at de Lima also.

Of the several other houses featuring jewelry in stock or made to order, one of **Lousaing's** numerous escales—including Long Circular Mall, Port-of-Spain (tel. 623-6095) and Gulf City Shopping Complex, near San Fernando (tel. 657-9685)—might interest you. Or, try **Maraj**, 22 Frederick Street (tel. 623-8504) or 65 Prince Street (tel. 623-8284), both in Port-of-Spain.

Stecher's (see Useful Addresses list) is your best bet by far when it comes to elegant imported pieces of special interest: the stunning, very modern, textured-gold Lapponia line, and Mikimoto pearls in particular.

For assorted Indian baubles and beads, scout **Lakhan's Bazaar**, 32 West Main Road, St. James (tel. 622-4688). Remember, though, that ivory can pose a problem with customs.

PERFUMES AND COSMETICS

Trinidad does not as yet manufacture its own fragrances, but you can save substantially on Guerlain, Patou, all big-name French brands by buying duty-free at **Stecher's** at the Piarco International Airport. The same applies to Orlane and other European cosmetics.

SPIRITS

Trinidad's most celebrated libation, which consists of thirty separate ingredients, is a valuable (to some essential) accompaniment to many spiritous drinks. The formula, torn into four parts so that access to any one is useless, is hidden in bank vaults. Mixing takes place in a secret room. The elixir is Angostura bitters, and it was concocted by Dr. J. G. B. Siegert, a survivor of the Battle of Waterloo. He devised it as a stomachic for Simón Bolívar's soldiers. Grateful patients passed the word, as did visiting ships, and soon the Siegert potion was seasoning firewaters all over the world.

According to one account, the magic formula was only recently put to paper. Before that, each generation of the family was supposed to whisper it to the next. No outsider ever shared the secret.

When a Canadian stockholder offered a huge sum for the recipe and threatened to have the plant moved to Bermuda, the Trinidad government stepped in, bought most of the stock, and resold it to the Siegerts on condition they never take it out of the country. A bottle will cost you about $3.

To inquire about visiting the plant, telephone the public relations office at 623-1842. Worth a trip in itself: a collection of 3,000 butterfly specimens (Trinidad counts 622 varieties).

Old Oak is the most popular, locally made rum. You pay at least $10 a bottle for it in supermarkets. Mokatia, Trinidad's coffee liqueur, is about $15 U.S. By buying your liquor at the airport, you could save as much as 50%. Stag and Carib beers, a considerably smaller investment, are also delicious.

WATCHES

Patek Phillipe, Girard-Pérregaux, Seiko, Eterna, Piaget, Universal Genève, Borel—**Stecher's** (see Useful Addresses list for branches) has all these at duty-free prices. The Cartier "Le must" tank watch, selling for $675 plus tax in the U.S., costs $565 at Stecher's. On the Panther model you save $250. **Y. de Lima** also carries timepieces.

SPECIAL CATEGORY

As Memphis is to the blues, Port-of-Spain, and, in the larger context, Trinidad, is to West Indies music. Unquestionably and singlehandedly in fact, Trinidad created the means of expressing today's Caribbean culture that is used in most of today's performing arts. Steel bands, calypso, limbo; these all originated right here.

STEEL BANDS

You have not, no matter what you may think, really heard an authentic, proper steel band until you've heard one from Trinidad. And if you can bring back just one item from this Land of the Hummingbird, let it be the best of the steel-band recordings. Christmas is not complete at our house until the carols come wafting out of the stereo as played by a Trinidad steel band.

Listen to tapes or recordings of Mozart, Handel, and Bach as played on the "pans." It's music like nothing you have ever heard before. You may well become so fascinated you feel compelled to acquire a "pan" of your own. If so, call **Barbara Crichow** of the Catelli All Star Band at 625-6411 and enlist her advice on where to get the Real Thing. Also, be prepared to pay a good price for one—like $600.

In order to appreciate the magic of this, the first new musical instrument to have been invented in this century, consider how it evolved. Today's steel-band story goes back to V-E Day. Trinidad's Carnival had been suspended for six years, and to celebrate the peace, the government proclaimed a 24-hour resumption of Carnival. Jubilant celebrants rummaged in trunks for old costumes, but there were no conventional musical instruments to be had. So they grabbed garbage cans, cookie tins, bits and pieces of wreckage from old automobiles, any object that could be converted to make sound. They burst forth with a cacophony of thumping, jumping, and earsplitting din such as not even Trinidad had ever heard before. As irate housewives retrieved their kettles and cans, the melodists turned to the nearest substitute: empty oil drums. And then, to paraphrase Harold Arlen's *Birth of the*

Blues, "They nursed it, rehearsed it," and brought into the world a revolutionary, brand-new musical art form. The "pan" as the oil drum is called, has the advantage of being easy to come by. But the dedicated "pantuners" who transform it follow a ritual as meticulous as that of Stradivarius'.

First they pound in the top to make the sounding surface. Then, depending on what section of the orchestra this pan will play in, the drum is cut down.

As in a regular symphony, the steel band consists of four components: *ping-pongs*, or tenors, six-to-eight-inch deep drums that carry the melody; *guitars*, about twice as high, with two-thirds as many notes as the ping-pongs; *cellos* and *basses*, both full-size drums. The cello section involves several instruments at a time, while the bass players also beat on a number simultaneously.

Having cut the drum to size, the pantuner next scores the notes in to the top, grooving the lines from the middle to the rim in a pattern resembling the petals of a peony. He then heats the pan over a wood fire and lets it cool. If the sound is a little flat, he tunes it by hammering the underside with a sledge to stretch the metal. To lower a sharp tone, he bangs on the top of the pan head to flatten the pitch. A good pan takes at least a week of full-time work to produce. Each band has its own tuner. Panbeaters protect their precious drums from any outsider interference as they would the crown jewels.

Since the main band sounds are mostly melodic, a percussion section is also an inherent part of the orchestra. Car irons and hollowed out calabash gourds filled with seeds, beat out the rhythm. *Shac-shacs*, circles of home-cut steel, are used as cymbals. Ordinary goatskin kettles supply the timpani.

To Trinidad small-fry, becoming a steel-band man is about as impressive as passing the bar. No formal university exists for this music. The youngsters by and large teach themselves, and at Carnival time they audition to be allowed to play temporarily with one of the regular bands. If they make good, chances are they could be on their way. To quote one professional ping-ponger, "you can tell a good panbeater the minute he approaches his instrument."

Watch a live band perform and feel your pulses quicken. Most of the musicians cannot read a note; a leader verbally dictates to each of the thirty to one hundred players his part of the score. The individual musician not only memorizes his part flawlessly but understands, and applies, the most subtle gradations in phrasing.

When the first steel band sailed into New York, stevedores were reportedly all set to deepsix their drums, assuming they were trash. Customs officials agreed. Not until the panbeaters gave a concert on the dock were they able to prove that these were indeed bona-fide musical instruments. (Given the off-key mediocrity of the many imitations plaguing the Caribbean nowadays, there are times when purists long for confiscating officials to jettison some offending pans.)

Financially, a bandman's career is fairly good. Commercial enterprises sponsor the band, subsidize the instruments, costumes, and other expenses, including a band manager, and pay the players a subsistence allowance. In professional engagements, such as hotel bookings or mainland tours, the performers may divide the fee among themselves.

Most playing and rehearsing takes place at night, so the members can work at regular nine-to-five jobs and still belong to the band. Some groups do pursue their music full time. These are used for promotional purposes abroad and tend to be off the island quite a bit. But the best mostly stay home. In our experience, the most obscure of the Trinidad combines ranks head and shoulders above the best-known in other islands.

If there is one absolute *must* in Trinidad, hearing a proper steel band is it. *Do Not Miss* one of the outstanding attractions in the West Indies—and do not fail to bring home at least one recording. Catelli All Stars are the band of the moment; there are other excellent ones, and good quality recordings. You'll find them anywhere cassettes or disks are sold. Try **Rhyner's Record Shop**, at 54 Prince St. in Port-of-Spain (tel. 623-5673), or **Kaisoca Records** in Level One of Long Circular Mall in St. James (tel. 622-8570).

CALYPSO

The foot-tapping, finger-snapping sound of calypso is Trinidad's very own siren song. It spread first to other West Indian islands and eventually traveled to Broadway and chic international supper clubs. One of the most famous singers to adopt the calypso style, Harry Belafonte, is actually a native-born New Yorker.

Essentially, the calypso functions as a sort of singing scandal sheet—a *National Enquirer* set to music. The trick is to improvise, fast, and in rhyme, on any topical subject. A true calypsonian writes his own lyrics and works under such grandiose stage names as The Mighty Spoiler, or Attila the Hun.

Don't be surprised if you have trouble understanding the words; basically non-West Indians are not supposed to—and often it's better that way. Caribbean historians tell us that field hands dreamed up calypsos as one way of communicating when they were forbidden to talk while they worked, but did have permission to sing. To prevent their masters from eavesdropping on their melodic conversations, according to scholars they invented the baffling "broken talk" some still use today.

Although residents have been communicating by calypso for two centuries, not until this century did this music begin to come out of the shanty towns and spread to the general public. Gradually the folk music took hold much as it did in Memphis and New Orleans.

To become a true calypsonian, the neophyte should first pass muster with the Old Guard brigade, veterans with a decade's service in the art. At the Carnival King contest, aspiring balladiers pit their wits against the rivals in an all-out extemporaneous verbal war. Whoever gets the last word wins.

From January through to Carnival, the contestants compete in open-to-the-public calypso "tents" every night, and share in the gate receipts. The audience hisses, boos, and cheers. Subject matter tends to current events, with ditties ranging from bawdy to blue.

Fundamentally, though, the fascination of calypso lies in the powerful pull of the rhythm and the verbal dexterity of the performer. One respected practitioner of the art said it thus:

> *Calypso is a thing, I am telling you,*
> *When you are singing you must learn to be impromptu,*
> *Never mind your English but mind your rhymes,*
> *When you get the gist of it just say it in time,*
> *For veteran calypsonians are known to be*
> *Men who can sing on anything instantaneously.*

When selecting your calypso record(s), you might ask to hear the entries of the most recent Carnival winner, and, also, consult as to just how earthy are the lyrics. In many cases they are no gamier than current rock. On the other hand, it's nice to know what the singers are indeed saying before you make your purchase.

Tobago, the sister island, a 20-minute flight from Trinidad, is the complete opposite of its senior sibling. Claimed to be the unnamed island on which Defoe shipwrecked his Robinson Crusoe, it offers serenity-seeking travelers heavenly surcease from the comparative commercialism of the north. On the southern plain, endless coconut palms march in military precision from the beaches on the east coast to those on the west. In the higher northern district, 1,500-foot eminences tumble to the sand-bordered turquoise sea where water is so clear, sharp eyes can read the date on a dime at 30 feet.

Tobago has achieved world fame for its coral reefs, including fabulous and fantastic Buccoo Reef. To travelers who make it a point of honor to skip all so-called tourist attractions, we'd say, if you miss Buccoo you'll regret it the rest of your life. You may explore more extensive coralliferous formations elsewhere, and some may be wilder and more untamed, but none will be more accessible, and none have such a teeming agglomeration of drenchingly beautiful rainbow-hued fish. Once you've seen these multicolored marvels, you'll know what inspires the splendid chromatics in the paintings on sale in the art galleries of the region. Tobago's other major attraction consists of a bird-of-paradise sanctuary on Little Tobago.

Although shopping is not spectacular, you will not have to quit cold turkey.

The Handcraft Center on Bacolet Street in Scarborough, Tobago's principal settlement (tel. 623-2527), features straw and other local output.

Footprint Art Craft Shop, in Scarborough's Mount Irvine Bay Hotel (tel. 639-8523), is another possibility, as is **Khoury's** on Burnett Street (tel. 639-2273).

For your needs in crystal, china, fine jewelry, watches, perfume—most luxury goods—**Stecher's** maintains a beachhead at the Radisson Crown Reef Hotel, as well as in downtown Scarborough. If you don't see what you're looking for, Stecher's can whisk it over from Trinidad headquarters in a matter of hours.

Browse through the little emporiums in the Scarborough city center. Mount Irvine Bay and Crown Reef Hotels also house clusters of shops, and there's a **Best Valu Supermart** at the corner of Glen Road and Darrell Spring Road in Scarborough.

Trinidad and Tobago have yet to swing into full gear as a high-volume center for mainland tourists. And therein may lie much of their charm. Do not, however, expect to stroll through sleek salon after salon backed by warehouses bulging with sophisticated specialties of an affluent society. For this kind of variety, go to Sint Maarten, the Virgin Islands, or any of the more developed resorts to which group travelers throng, bringing higher volume sales. In some way, you have to work at shopping in Trinidad and Tobago. To many, the elusiveness of the quarry adds zest to the chase.

USEFUL ADDRESSES

Art Creators & Supplies, Ltd.: 402 Aldegonda Park, 7 St. Ann's Road, Port-of-Spain (tel. 624-4369).

The Art Gallery: Room D, Salavatori Building, Port-of-Spain (tel. 624-7904).

Begum's Boutique: Trinidad Hilton Hotel, Lady Young Road, Port-of-Spain.

Best Valu Supermart: Glen Road and Darrell Spring Road, Scarborough.

Boutique Cybele: Trinidad Hilton Hotel, Lady Young Road, Port-of-Spain (tel. 624-4669).

Chang, Carlisle: 40 Murray St., Woodbrook, Port-of-Spain (tel. c/o Gary Chang 627-6965).

Choo Quan Supermarket: 24 Queen St., Port-of-Spain (tel. 623-5416).

City Blues: 15 Henry St., Port-of-Spain (tel. 623-4482).

Footprint Art Craft Shop: Mt. Irvine Bay Hotel, Scarborough (tel. 639-8523).

Fuller's Ltd.: 22 Henry St., Port-of-Spain (tel. 623-5081).

Habib's: 48 Independence Square, Port-of-Spain (tel. 623-4485), Long Circular Mall, St. James (tel. 622-8895).

The Handcraft Center: Bacolet Street, Scarborough (tel. 623-2527).

Hilo Supermarkets: Numerous branches in Port-of-Spain.

Honey Comb Supermarket: 7-11 Prince St., Port-of-Spain (tel. 623-6418).

Jo-Di's Handicraft Shoppe: Galleria Shopping Plaza, St. James (tel. 622-8461).

Kacal's: 43-45 Frederick St., Port-of-Spain (tel. 623-2508).

Kacal's Artist in Wood: Trinidad Hilton Hotel, Lady Young Road, Port-of-Spain (tel. 624-3356).

Kaisoca Records: Long Circular Mall, St. James (tel. 622-8570).

Khoury's: Burnett Street, Scarborough (tel. 639-2273).

Lakhan's Bazaar: 32 West Main Road, St. James (tel. 622-4688).

Lousaing's: Long Circular Mall, St. James (tel. 623-6095); Gulf City Shopping Complex, near San Fernando (tel. 657-9685).

Manshak: 33 Charlotte St., Port-of-Spain (tel. 623-7061).

Maraj: 22 Frederick St., Port-of-Spain (tel. 623-8504); 65 Prince St., Port-of-Spain (tel. 623-8284).

Matouks: Glamour Girl Complex, Churchill Roosevelt Highway, San Juan (tel. 638-3391).

McLeod's Antiques: Le Seiva and Saddle Road, Port-of-Spain (tel. 629-2224); branch also at Trinidad Hilton Hotel.

Meiling: 4 Cartos St., Port-of-Spain; boutique on Gray Street.

Moart Gallery: Kirpalani Roundabout Plaza, en route to Piarco International Airport (tel. 638-5887).

Mount St. Benedict's Abbey: St. John's Road, Tunapuna (tel. 662-2105; 662-4084).

Payless: 75 St. Vincent St., Tunapuna (tel. 624-6895).

The Peoples Supermarket: 10 Independence Square, Port-of-Spain.

Rhyner's Record Shop: 54 Prince St., Port-of-Spain (tel. 623-5673).

Rising Sun: 93 St. Vincent St., Tunapuna (tel. 663-2546).

Shape: 13 Fitzgerald Lane, Port-of-Spain (tel. 625-2119).

Stecher's: 27 Frederick Lane, Port-of-Spain (tel. 623-5912); branches at Trinidad Hilton Hotel, Lady Young Road, Port-of-Spain (tel. 624-3322); West Mall, West Moorings (tel. 632-0502); Long Circular Mall, St. James (tel. 622-0017); Gulf City Shopping Complex, near San Fernando; Piarco International Airport. Branches also in Tobago at Radisson Crown Reef Hotel, Scarborough; downtown Scarborough.

Tokiki Manshop: Trinidad Hilton Hotel, Lady Young Road, Port-of-Spain (tel. 624-3111).

Trinidad & Tobago Blind Welfare Association Shop: 118 Duke St., Port-of-Spain (tel. 625-4659).

Trinidad and Tobago Cooperative: Trinidad Hilton Hotel, Lady Young Road, Port-of-Spain (tel. 624-3111).

Turban Brand Products: 186 Eastern Main Rd., St. James.

Y. de Lima: 23A Frederick St., Port-of-Spain (tel. 623-1364); branches also at Trinidad Hilton Hotel, Lady Young Road, Port-of-Spain (tel. 624-3432); Piarco International Airport; Long Circular Mall, St. James; and Gulf City Shopping Complex, near San Fernando.

U.S.
VIRGIN
ISLANDS

U.S. VIRGIN ISLANDS
AT A GLANCE

GOVERNMENT TOURIST OFFICE: U.S. Virgin Islands Division of Tourism, Charlotte Amalie, St. Thomas (tel. 775-8784); Christiansted, St. Croix (tel. 773-0495), or Custom House Building, Frederiksted, St. Croix (tel. 772-0357); Cruz Bay, St. John (tel. 776-6450).

CURRENCY: This is American territory, the U.S. dollar is the legal tender.

OFFICIAL HOLIDAYS: New Year's Day, Three Kings' Day (January 6), Martin Luther King's Birthday (January 15), Franklin Roosevelt's Birthday (January 30), Lincoln's Birthday (February 12), Washington's Birthday (February 22), Transfer Day (March 31), Holy Thursday, Good Friday, Easter Sunday and Monday, Children's Carnival Parade (usually falls in late April), Grand Carnival Parade (day after Children's Parade), Memorial Day (May 30), Organic Act Day—commemorating the passage of the Organic Act granting civil government and universal suffrage to the people of the U.S.V.I. (third Monday in June), Emancipation Day—commemorating freeing of the slaves in 1848 (July 3), Independence Day (July 4), Hurricane Supplication Day (July 25), Labor Day (first Monday in September), Columbus Day (second Monday in October), Thanksgiving Day—for hurricanes spared (third Monday in October), Liberty Day (November 1),

Veterans Day (November 11), Thanksgiving (last Thursday in November), Christmas Day (on St. Croix, Yuletide festivities begin in mid-December and run through January 6), Boxing Day (December 26).

STORE HOURS: Most shops are open from 9 a.m. until 5 p.m. daily except Sunday—theoretically. Some stores' business hours begin at 8:30 a.m., some stay open later, and some function on Sunday and holiday mornings when a cruise ship is in port. When it comes to the hotel emporiums, all bets are off: doors often do not close before 10 p.m. nor on Sunday. The custom of closing Thursday afternoons is mostly a thing of the past. Nor do all merchants shutter for holidays as religiously as they used to. Nevertheless, the holidays listed above are legal and therefore you should verify whether those of interest to you will be open.

LOCATIONS: For the addresses and telephone numbers of the shops, consult the alphabetical list at the end of this chapter.

When after three abortive tries the United States finally bought the Virgin Islands in 1917 for 45 tons of gold, or $25 million—the most ever paid for a piece of American real estate and considered scandalously high at the time—one of the conditions of the sale was that the islanders never be worse off under the Americans than they had been at the time of purchase. Which is why St. Thomas, St. John, and St. Croix are all free ports insofar as mainland tariffs are concerned. This has resulted in very special advantages for returning vacationers:

You can take back with you, or send home, twice as many duty-free imports from here as from elsewhere—$800 worth every 30 days. If you go over the $800 allowance, you will pay a flat 5% on the next $1,000, which is only half the going rate for foreign flag islands.

Only from the U.S. Virgin Islands, American Samoa, and Guam can packages follow by mail and be included in your exemption.

You can send as many duty-free gifts as you want, costing up to $100 each, to friends and relatives—provided you don't mail more than one per day or address any to yourself.

A family can pool their allowance (except for liquor which requires the buyer to be over 21). Thus, a couple traveling with their three children would start off with a $4,000 duty-free allowance.

You are permitted to import duty-free five fifths of liquor from St. Thomas (five times the allowance everywhere else) regardless of where it was made. Pick up a fifth of local rum or liqueur (Southern Comfort qualifies, believe it or not, because it is processed here), and *your quota goes to six fifths.*

THE VIRGIN ISLANDS

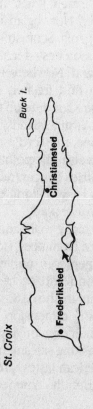

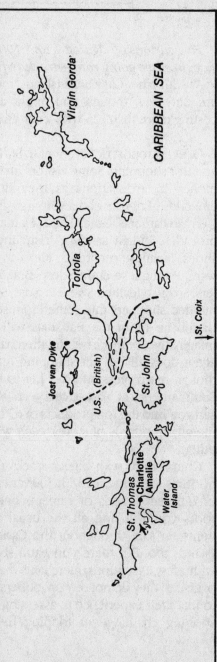

Five cartons of cigarettes and 100 hundred cigars—again, five times the going rate—are duty-free.

As with other Caribbean islands, most locally made products are duty-free, though you might accompany any of these costing more than $25 with a certificate of origin.

Of every tourist dollar spent in St. Thomas, an estimated 50¢ goes for shopping. Some visitors invest twice as much of their money in acquisitions as they do in hotels. Colombian emeralds, English china, Finnish fabrics, French brandies, German cameras, Greek shirts, Haitian mahogany, Hong Kong brocades, Indian sandals, Irish linens, Israeli knits, Italian shoes, Japanese recorders, Mexican silver, Norwegian ovenware, Portuguese embroidery, Brazilian gems, Scottish sweaters, Spanish leather, Swedish glass, Swiss watches—for single-minded shoppers this is the Promised Land. Nowhere in the Caribbean or in the Bahamas will you find fresher, more imaginative, or more tasteful merchandise. One veteran travel agent does all her gift shopping in the Virgin Islands, even though her profession takes her to Europe, the Far East, and South America at least once a year. Where else, she points out, can you find the top products of 67 countries concentrated in literally hundreds of stores, each within easy walking of the others.

China shops with bigger stocks than many mainland emporiums; perfumeries with 300 varieties of fragrances; dozens of different brands of cameras and timepieces under one roof—you will find all the usual in-bond and/or freeport items on sale throughout the Caribbean in the U.S. Virgin Islands too. But there's an extra shopping dimension here: with a few exceptions, merchants make their own buying trips overseas; they do not rely on jobbers or visiting salesmen. Add to that their experience in assessing American tastes, plus the sporting challenge of topping their friendly competitors.

These canny scouts search out finds distinctly their own—items you might well miss yourself on a trip to the country of origin.

Virginia Cavanagh, for example of Cavanagh's, Inc., more than once personally forded the rivers of Thailand, walking along rickety boards to find the best weavers to produce colors and patterns made up for her alone and available nowhere else. When Charlotte Paiewonsky comes across an unusual design in leather goods in Florence or Milan, she has the wallets, coin purses, etc., fashioned exclusively for her company's shops.

Obviously it is impossible to review within these few pages all the tempting, and reliable, emporiums competing for the discretionary dollar. All we can do is hit the high spots; and if your favorite mart is excluded, this certainly does not mean it is not recommended by this guide, only outspaced.

The bonanza these special provisions offer is not new: It began 265 years ago, when the King of Denmark decided since St. Thomas had no other major resources to attract commerce by declaring Charlotte Amalie (named after a Danish queen) a free port. Gradually the name of the town and that of the island became interchangeable, with St. Thomas more commonly used than Charlotte Amalie, the capital city.

Ever since then the island, by whichever name, St. Thomas, or Charlotte Amalie, has been known as "the emporium of the West Indies." As far back as 1701, priest-writer Père Labat described St. Thomas as "a market of great consequence, with large and handsome houses, tiled pavements, money plentiful, and visitors affluent."

St. Croix looks back on a tradition more agricultural than commercial. However, with the advent of post–World War II tourism, its shopping horizons have broadened considerably.

St. John, the littlest Virgin, while still something less than a thriving metropolis, offers imaginative browsing.

Inasmuch as each of these siblings is as different one from the other as three peas ever germinated in the same pericarp, their buying opportunities need to be considered separately. We begin with the most highly developed.

ST. THOMAS

Once the third-largest city in the Danish empire (only Copenhagen and Flensborg were more important), Charlotte Amalie became a top trading post for three reasons in addition to its freeport status: (1) a deep, commodious harbor fashioned from a former crater, protected from weather and hard to attack; (2) continued Danish neutrality, opening the port to shipping of all nations during the various West Indian skirmishes and battles; (3) a climate of corruption.

Privateers, soldiers of fortune, adventurers of all kinds could head for this harbor confident of a sympathetic reception and a not-too-close scrutiny of their affairs. Captain Kidd frequented St. Thomas. One of the early governors was himself a pirate. Indeed, some historians credit the pirates with the fact that so many of today's commercial buildings date back a century or more.

According to one theory suggested to us by a leading local historian, the late J. Antonio Jarvis (whose statue you see in the heart of town, facing the post office), this is the way it happened: Shortly after the island became accepted as the entrepot of choice for storing goods and merchandise, an $11-million fire decimated the city, followed shortly by still another disastrous blaze.

472

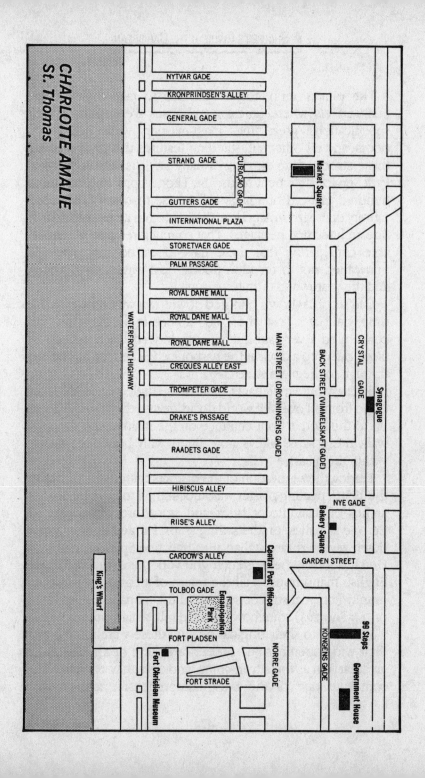

CHARLOTTE AMALIE
St. Thomas

NYTVAR GADE

KRONPRINDSEN'S ALLEY

GENERAL GADE

STRAND GADE

CURAÇAO GADE

GUTTERS GADE

INTERNATIONAL PLAZA

STORETVAER GADE

PALM PASSAGE

ROYAL DANE MALL

ROYAL DANE MALL

ROYAL DANE MALL

CREQUES ALLEY EAST

TROMPETER GADE

DRAKE'S PASSAGE

RAADETS GADE

HIBISCUS ALLEY

RIISE'S ALLEY

CARDOW'S ALLEY

TOLBOD GADE

FORT PLADSEN

FORT STRADE

WATERFRONT HIGHWAY

MAIN STREET (DRONNINGENS GADE)

BACK STREET (VIMMELSKAFT GADE)

Market Square

CRYSTAL GADE

Synagogue

NYE GADE

Bakery Square

GARDEN STREET

Central Post Office

NORRE GADE

KONGENS GADE

99 Steps

Government House

King's Wharf

Emancipation Park

Fort Christian Museum

The pirates reportedly threatened to take their storage business elsewhere unless warehouses were built to their specifications: great, thick mass-masonry walls, heavy iron doors, and all other still-standing features that have enabled these structures to survive virtually any disaster. A National Park Service statement reads: "St. Thomas probably has more hundred-year-old buildings still in use than any other community of its size in America. The island has an extraordinarily fine architectural heritage." That so much remains is remarkable considering that there have been no less than 130 hurricanes, not to mention floods, tidal waves, earthquakes, and the year-round termite season.

Old records show a hundred downtown warehouses at one time, built at a cost of $50,000 apiece in an era when this constituted a very substantial sum indeed. Each warehouse faced out onto a dock at the harbor's edge and ran all the way through to the main street

Today, where merchants, pirates, and traders once unloaded cargo from all over the world dockside and then ran the goods up to the store's front entrance on the main street, shoppers walk these same alleys now lined with boutiques tucked within the massive walls.

During the renovation of the district that took place during the 1950s, peeling plaster was knocked off to uncover soaring arches of magnificent brick and stone brought over from Europe as ballast on the sailing ships. Painted floors scraped down revealed rare Italian tiles and fine Spanish marble. A Dutch doorway here, French grillwork there, touches of the English manorhouse—all the traces of a cosmopolitan community (one census counted 140 different nationalities living on St. Thomas) somehow blended into a harmonious whole.

Restored to their original beauty, these warehouses, with their wide openings and breezeways, have become as much an attraction as the silver, china, and silks they contain. They constitute one of the most comprehensive and unusual shopping centers in this hemisphere, if not the world, featuring merchandise from 67 countries on four continents.

Tip: If the downtown congestion gets to you—and on a day when three cruise ships unload throngs of bargain-hunters all at once in these narrow streets it can—bear in mind that there are alternatives. Frenchman's Reef, Bluebeard's Castle, and Mountain Top all have a pretty representative cross-section of boutiques. The Havensight Mall, overlooking the cruise docks, already includes some of St. Thomas's old and reliable retail names and is growing constantly. Because of its proximity to the cruise ship berths, you may also find Havensight pretty hectic at times. But at least you have choices—town, Havensight, the hotels.

REST STOP

Project St. Thomas, an undertaking sponsored by the local business community, maintains a hospitality lounge on the ground floor of the Grand Hotel facing Emancipation Park, in the heart of downtown Charlotte Amalie. Here you can park your parcels, ask the friendly volunteers as many questions as you like, use the rest rooms, and generally enjoy a welcome pause that refreshes. Open 9 a.m. to 5 p.m., Monday through Saturday.

ARTS AND CRAFTS

One of the countless legends about the truly legendary Paiewonsky dynasty concerns the parent of current merchandising maven, Charlotte Paiewonsky. It seems her father, known to all of us as Mr. Kaufmann, decided to buy his daughter a Gauguin. But when he learned the price of a Gauguin original, he was horrified. "At that rate, I'll paint her one myself," he is reported to have said and, entirely self-taught, with no previous experience whatosever, he proceeded to suit action to words.

Once he took brush in hand, at an age only slightly younger than that of Grandma Moses when she began painting, Mr. Kaufmann became a widely appreciated talent and was featured in several one-man shows. Charlotte's interest in the subject continued beyond her father's death. She converted the old Danish kitchen upstairs over her **A. H. Riise Gift Shops** (37 Main St.—tel. 774-2303) into a gallery, and now exhibits and sells one of St. Thomas's more extensive art collections at two locations within the shop. Gallery I, on the ground floor, spotlights Caribbean scenes. On the second floor, Gallery II purveys pricier paintings, pottery, and some African sculptures.

Jim Tillett, whose work you may have read about in *The New York Times* and *Vogue*, when he ran his atelier in Mexico, is now a St. Thomas artist-in-residence. His studio is in the rolling hills at Estate Tutu, east of Charlotte Amalie. Jim's own landscapes and maps on canvas, hand done, 2 x 2½ feet in size, sell from under $20 and up. Available here also are the oeuvres of others: Eric Winter, one of St. Thomas's durable and popular artists, is perhaps best known for his oils; Arona Petersen's primitives and Eljay's marine compositions are worth investigating too.

The Tillett complex also includes a boutique featuring fabrics handscreened in the artist's own atelier on sale from $10 the yard or fashioned into shirts, skirts, caftans, and pants. You can observe silkscreeners as well as potters and stained-glass workers creating on the premises. If you need transportation, call ahead and ask about the free shuttle.

Three times a year, Jim and Rhoda Tillett put on an arts and crafts fair with as many as 60 exhibitors. There are fashion shows with local high school students modeling Tillett fashions, live music, and an appearance by the Mocko Jumbie, the stiltman who presides over St. Thomas's annual Carnival.

Usually the fairs are held the last weekend in March, the second weekend in August, and over the Thanksgiving holiday. For exact dates, query the Tilletts by writing them at Tutu Village, P.O. Box 7549, St. Thomas, VI 00801, or phoning them at 809/775-1405.

Generations, situated downstairs in the Frenchman's Reef resort (tel. 776-8500, ext. 877), bills itself as the only "pure" art gallery in St. Thomas. You will find for sale a wide variety of works by Diane Kreiner, Judith King, and other island residents and ex-residents, along with Europeans and mainland Americans. Also featured are some attractive, inexpensive four-color reproductions: of Bluebeard's Castle, Hotel 1829, and the Fort, each 11 x 14 inches, $9.95 for the set of three. The smaller cards, at $6.95 for eight, will also frame nicely.

L'Escargot Restaurant, in the Royal Dane Mall, Charlotte Amalie (tel. 774-8880), as well as **Alexander's Café** in Frenchtown (tel. 774-4340), also showcase local artists.

Joanna White has a studio in Bakery Square, off Back Street, Charlotte Amalie.

Half a dozen other emporiums offer pictures of varying quality, many of them imported from Haiti.

We hear interesting reports about the inventory at **Circe** in Palm Passage, Charlotte Amalie: Dan masks, Baga figures from Guinea, pre-Columbian sculptures—an enthusiastic editor from *Essence* waxed lyrical in discussing her finds here. We didn't make it to Circe on our most recent trip; hopefully we will next time. We have known the founder, Patti Birch, for many years as a professional in the business of dealing in art.

Insofar as crafts are concerned, bear in mind certain harsh economic realities: this is U.S. territory, subject to the laws of minimum wage; also, good-paying government jobs are plentiful. Thus the incentive to braid straw, string seeds, or otherwise engage in activities that may or may not pay off are far less compelling than in less fortunate islands down the chain. Still, you can find a considerable array of ethnic, regional,

West Indian/Caribbean offerings on sale, even though the majority may not be fabricated in the Virgin Islands.

The Straw Factory, 24 Garden St. in Charlotte Amalie (tel. 774-4849), specializes in, obviously, articles made from straw—pocketbooks, rugs, hats, etc. You'll find woodenware here as well.

Shipwreck Shop, in Palm Passage, Charlotte Amalie, one more link in the chain of establishments represented in many other islands, sells books, fabrics, souvenirs—most anything locally made that they can obtain in sufficient quantity to market.

The Sheltered Workshop, part of the government's Vocational Rehabilitation Program, has a store in town (on Crystal Gade behind the Reformed Church) and one at Frenchman's Reef, offering stuffed dolls and toys.

Caribbean Marketplace at Havensight Mall might be worth your while for a variety of reasons (see under "Food" as well).

If you're into feathered hair nets, toe rings, wind chimes and the like, look in on **Octopus Garden** in Trompeter Gade, Charlotte Amalie (tel. 774-7010).

There is a **Crafts Cooperative** also, on Back Street, across from the Christian Science Society.

CAMERAS

You can find Nikon L-35 F3HP at $489 on-island versus a "U.S. recommended dealer tag of $874.80," not counting the tax; or you may track down a Canon T-70 for $209 versus $400 or so up north; Minolta, Olympus, and Pentax for half-price—these are just some of the tempting bargains cited by the local wish book, *Here's How.*

However, as we have pointed out before—and cannot emphasize enough—buying photographic equipment in the Caribbean is tricky business. If you have done your pre-trip investigations, and know what constitutes rock-bottom prices at home, you may find yourself a real buy. But if you have not, and are planning anything resembling a substantial investment, we would suggest you pick up a copy of *The New York Times* at your nearest newsstand, check out the photographic ads therein, and, if in doubt, give one of the discounters a call and compare.

Where to look? **Boolchand's** is one name you may recognize from other islands or earlier trips; the firm has been around for a good while. Look for this establishment at 31 Main St. and in Havensight Mall (tel. 774-0794).

Of the other half a dozen possibilities, you might want to try **Royal Caribbean**, at 33 Main St. (tel. 776-4110).

China, Crystal, and Home Furnishings

These constitute some of St. Thomas's best bargains. A Rosenthal place setting, for example, the same pattern as that favored by Elizabeth Taylor, will retail for half its U.S. price tag. Baccarat goblets can be had for about a third the U.S. catalog quote. Two Lalique plates can be acquired in St. Thomas for approximately what you would pay for one back home. Experienced travelers report finding Irish coffee glasses priced higher at the Shannon Airport than in the islands.

Some years ago a journalist took one Baccarat jam pot as a test case and in her report tracked it down through the various Caribbean emporiums and luxury shops on the mainland. She wrote of finding the jam pot retailing for about $40 in Dallas in St. Thomas for under $10!

All in all, St. Thomas offers the upscale buyer as complete and enticing a selection of china, crystal, and fine home furnishings as are gathered in similar space anywhere in the world. As a shopper, there is simply no way you can cover all the bases. We recommend that whatever route you take, you should include visits to both **A. H. Riise Gift Shops** at 37 Main Street and Riise's Alley (tel. 774-2303) and the **Little Switzerland** emporiums at 5 Main St. (tel. 776-2010) and at Havensight Mall. The broad range of merchandise in these covers such a broad spectrum of price and selection that they might well be called the ultimate department stores for visitors.

First the oldest. A Danish pharmacist named A. H. Riise founded the empire bearing his name. But it took a pair of second-generation East European immigrants to raise the A. H. Riise complex to its present standard of excellence.

The original Paiewonsky patriarch emigrated from the Old Country with little more than the pack on his back, bound for South America. By the time the ship called at St. Thomas, he suffered so from seasickness that he disembarked for good, vowing never again to leave terra firma. Or so the story goes.

One of his two sons, Ralph Paiewonsky, served as governor of the U.S. Virgin Islands from 1961 to 1968, and it was at that time that big-time tourism came into its own. Ralph was also most influential in the creation of the College of the Virgin Islands.

His brother, Isidor, is a noted historian, newspaper columnist, and author of a highly respected monograph on the history of the Jewish colony in the area to which Herman Wouk wrote the preface. His most recent book is a collection of poems dedicated to a son lost in a skydiving accident when he was only eighteen. Isidor's wife, Charlotte, learned her trade as a New York buyer and perfected it through thirty years of traveling throughout Europe and the Far East in search of special treasures for her stores provided they'd sell at a minimum of 25% under U.S. prices.

Isidor Paiewonsky pioneered the transformation of Charlotte Amalie from a series of ramshackle warehouses into the elegant shopping district it has become. The Paiewonsky A. H. Riise Gift Shops on Main Street (A. H. Riise Gift Shops Alley—

or just Riise's Alley) and at Havensight Mall carry everything from Arpège to zircons, with plenty of Omega and Patek Philippe watches, Baccarat crystal, Royal Copenhagen china, Georg Jensen and Christofle silver in between. You also will find here Mikimoto pearls, Liberty silks, Pringle sweaters, Lladrò figurines, the superchic LALAoUNIS gold jewelery from Greece—among other lines. Riise's is among the shops which maintain a toll-free phone number, 1-800/524-2037, in case you have second thoughts when you get home.

Little Switzerland's St. Thomas beachhead was established early also, by a pair of brothers—almost forty years ago, in fact, beginning as a small watch and gift shop. As their empire grew, the Kelberts persuaded expert technicians and professionals from such prestigious firms as Girard-Pérregaux to leave Switzerland and move to St. Thomas. Helen Kelbert, Rudy's wife, served as president of the island Gift Shop Association.

Today the Little Switzerland complex is owned by the mainland Town & Country corporation. The operation sprawls over several islands, its stores purveying a dazzling variety of stock. In St. Thomas you will find some of it displayed in historic warehouses also. The branch store by the boat landing on the waterfront, with its arched and covered sidewalk, dates back to 1783.

Another branch is located at 5 Main St. in a former theater. Across the street is their **Rosenthal Studio**, devoted exclusively to merchandise from that one manufacturer, with prices often a third or more under Stateside. Sample china bargains they cite include Rosenthal Suomi at $29.50 for the five pieces versus $65 U.S.; an Iris goblet priced $23.40 as opposed to the $46 pricetag up north.

The lines here include Waterford—stemware, vases, chandeliers, fine jewelry—Baccarat, Lalique, Orrefors crystal; Hummel figurines; Wedgwood, Royal Doulton, Aynsley, Minton, and Royal Worcester china. Borel, Girard-Pérregaux, Audemars-

Piguet, Rolex, and Vacheron & Constantin are among the carried watches.

Walter Fischer, the dedicated dynamo who supervises this empire in St. Thomas, imports specialists from his native Switzerland and other European countries to inspect and repair watches, buy crystal and china of top quality, and generally run a tight ship. One expert learned his trade at the prestigious Bucherer company in Lausanne. Another trained at the Rosenthal headquarters in Hamburg. All in all, more than a dozen executives and technicians bring to the Caribbean the expertise they acquired in their native lands.

Many other stores also carry their own name brands, in a variety of categories. Generally, however, if you are looking for specific items, here are a few of the locations where you might find them.

A. H. Riise Gift Shops (37 Main St. at Riise's Alley—tel. 774-2303):

>*China*—Royal Copenhagen, Royal Crown Derby, Royal Doulton, Herend
>
>*Crystal*—Baccarat, Daum, Lalique, Waterford, Orreförs
>
>*Figurines*—Lladrò, Swarovski
>
>*Hollow and Flatware*—Christofle, Georg Jensen

The English Shop (Main Street at Market Square—tel. 774-5309):

>*China*—Coalport, Hammersley, Haviland, Limoges, Royal Worcester, Royal Albert, Spode, Wedgwood, Bing & Grøndahl, Minton, Villeroy & Bach
>
>*Crystal*—Val St. Lambert, Royal Brierly, Gobel, Bayel
>
>*Figurines*—Capodimonte, Bing & Grøndahl, Nao by Lladrò, Royal Doulton, Belleek, Coalport

Little Switzerland (5 Main St. and on Tolbod Gade opposite Emancipation Park—tel. 776-2010):

>*China*—Aynsley, Hutschenreuther, Minton, Rosenthal, Royal Doulton, Royal Worcester, Thomas, Villeroy & Boch, Wedgwood

Crystal—Atlantis, Baccarat, Lalique, Orreförs, Riedel, Rosenthal, Thomas, Waterford
Figurines—Goebel-Hummel, Lladrò
Hollow and Flatware—Christofle, Daniel Hechter, Georg Jensen, Rosenthal, Sabattini
Scandinavian Center (Main Street—tel. 776-0656):
China (Christmas plates especially)—Royal Copenhagen, Bing & Grøndahl, Arabia
Hollow and Flatware—David Anderson, Georg Jensen, Michelson
Crystal figurines—Littalia glassware

All of the above manufacturers maintain branches at Havensight Mall, dock side, Charlotte Amalie.

If you're an antique buff, drop in on **Carson Company Antiques** in the Royal Dane Mall. Could be you come up with the find of the century, or it could be a dry run. That's one of the fascinations of this hobby—you never know.

In **Cloth Horse**, on Bakery Square (tel. 774-4761), amidst the wall hangings, carpets, and assorted West Indies home furnishings, note the Haitian wild cotton, as well as the Marimekko, Oulivada, and French provincial fabrics. On these, savings of up to 40% have been recounted.

FASHIONS

The May 8, 1893, edition of the *St. Thomas Tidende* front-paged the arrival aboard two steamers of "Broadcloths, shirtings, white lawns, fine batistes, as well as eight or nine prints—new and pretty designs." From these, as local family albums indicate, Virgin Islanders fashioned stylish gowns with boned collars, skirts of tucked, trimmed, and embroidered fabrics, complemented by ostrich-trimmed bonnets, jeweled hair combs, and solid-gold collar buttons. For the men, there were made-to-order shirts and meticulously tailored white suits, changed twice a day.

Talented tailors and seamstresses no longer abound in these islands, but elegant ready-to-wear does. Ships and planes still bring bumper crops of new fashions from the four corners of the world. The sheer volume, variety, and value assembled for your consideration is bound to bewilder as well as bedazzle.

One singleminded shophound, with only hours in which to scan the vast stacks of St. Thomas, compared her frustration to that of the dedicated art buff being told to "do" the Louvre in a day.

No way.

No way, either, to lay out for you the endless options you have. Once again, as it too often becomes necessary to repeat, herewith a quick look at some of the happier hunting grounds you might want to explore.

A. H. Riise Gift Shops, 37 Main St. at Riise's Alley (tel. 774-2303), features Liberty of London fabrics, neckties, and accessories. Find also Braemar, Barrie, Lyle & Scott sweaters, as well as Scottish wool kilts and stoles.

Boutique Riviera and branches on Main Street, Charlotte Amalie, and Havensight Mall, as well as Frenchman's Reef. *The New York Times* and *Travel & Leisure* both singled out this store, as have regiments of shoppers in the twenty-five years the firm has been in St. Thomas. S. T. DuPont Paris, Daniel Hechter, Christian Dior, Pierre Cardin, Pringle—these are just a few of the brands you will find here. We thought, the Hermès scarves a little pricey at not much under $100 apiece; on the other hand, we've not seen the latest mainland quotations. Attractive and not seen on every street corner are the accessories shown with Riviera's Burberry raincoats, hats, wallets, pocketbooks, and mufflers, all in the familiar Burberry plaid.

Carib Shop, Riise's Alley, has for three decades provided visitors and locals alike with comfortable sandals imported from Europe, handbags, clothes, and general fashion merchandise. Among those who made purchases here is Clare Boothe Luce.

Catherine Marlet Boutique, at Post Office Alley (Cardow's Alley) between Main Street and the waterfront (tel. 776-3600), offers upscale French elegance for both sexes. You may have visited one of the other Catherine Marlet Boutiques in Marbella or Paris.

Cavanagh's, West Indian Company Docks, Havensight Mall (tel. 776-0737). The name "Cavanagh's" has been synonymous with St. Thomas shopping for legions of regulars since before the advent of big-time tourism. The familiar downtown location is no longer; look instead for its featured "fashions, gifts, and famous labels from over 50 countries" in Havensight Mall.

Coquina Court at Havensight Mall, another fashion pioneer, also formerly of Main Street, continues to emphasize relaxed styling in hand embroidery and batik.

Courrèges Boutique, on the waterfront end of Palm Passage, is a more recent arrival, but the name is sufficiently world-famous to be self-explanatory. Pace-setting designs for men as well as women created in Paris are for sale here, as is footwear.

Cosmopolitan, Inc., on the waterfront end of Drake's Passage, an offshoot of an established Curaçao company, represents a number of reassuringly stable name brands: Lanvin, Givenchy, Christian Dior, Amalfi, Bally shoes, Oberson and Gottex swimwear, plus entries from Sergio, Testoni, and Timberland.

Dilly D'Alley (one shop on Trompeter Gade, the other on Storetvaer Gade) specializes in sportswear, lace-trimmed separates, and a selection for small fry.

Gucci Boutique, located on the waterfront between Riise's Alley and Cardow's Alley, needs, as the saying goes, no introduction. Although you know the name in association with shoes, bags, wallets, etc., you may not have seen their newer sports clothes for men and women.

Guy Laroche, in Palm Passage, features designer clothes and shoes.

Hidey Hole Boutique, located on the second floor, Pisarro Building, Main Street, offers locally made resortwear.

J. Hook, the preppie U.S. pacesetter, maintains a beachhead here on the waterfront in Charlotte Amalie.

Java Wraps, in Palm Passage on the waterfront (tel. 774-3700), belongs to a ubiquitous chain of emporiums operating throughout the West Indies. The shop features sarongs, batiks, and a variety of Indonesian accessories.

At **La Caravelle**, with branches on Main Street, Charlotte Amalie, and at Frenchman's Reef resort, you'll find a bit of everything: Haitian hand-crocheted feminine frippery, some good-looking shell jewelry from the Philippines, the Fred Bernard Collection, and Kangaroo shirts. We thought the liquor here priced a little on the high side. You might disagree.

Lady of Paradise, at Secret Harbour Beach resort, Nazareth Bay, features Yves Saint Laurent, Bill Blass, Rose Marie Reid, Oscar de la Renta—also some more readily affordable alternatives.

The Leather Shop, 1 Main St. (tel. 776-3995) and at Havensight Mall, carries Fendi and Bottega Veneta Italian pocketbooks, as well as other imports for men and women.

Lion in the Sun, with shops in Riise's Alley and Palm Passage, trailblazed the importation of haute couture prêt-à-porter to the islands—and continues to bring in Yves Saint Laurent, Rive Gauche, Sonia Rykiel, Jean Paul Gaultier, Genny, and trendy Maud Frizon footwear, plus Kenzo and Yohji Yamamoto for both sexes, and New Man items for masculine shoppers.

Louis Vuitton, at 24 Main St., Palm Passage (tel. 774-3644), has a name that also speaks for itself: bags, luggage, watches, etc. Some satisfied customers say they've saved 25% to 30% over Stateside costs.

Michele Val, in the Royal Dane Mall, is another chic satellite—there's a Michele Val in Southampton (New York) too. The mood here tends to airy, delicate cottons and bright prints, some romantic wedding gown styles, and, by contrast, arresting sequinned tops reportedly selling for less than half what you would pay in Manhattan.

Sea Wench, with shops in the Royal Dane Mall and the Havensight Mall, specializes in Gallic lingerie, accessories, and *costumes de bain*.

Shanghai Silk and Handicrafts, in the Royal Dane Mall, purveys raw silks and brocades, by the yard at $8 or so, or made up into garments for men and women. Hand-crocheted sweaters can cost as little as $12.95, embroidered blouses under $10.

Takara, at Havensight Mall, offers more feminine French fashions, as well as Gossi shirts for both sexes (and Austrian crystal jewelry).

Zora of St. Thomas, on East Main Street (Norre Gade) beyond the Grand Hotel a block past the Lutheran Church, has been custom-making sandals, belts, and bags of leather and canvas for island residents for over a generation. She also does shoe repair.

FOOD

While very little is home-grown on St. Thomas, adventurous epicures will find fertile foraging.

The **Caribbean Marketplace**, Havensight Mall, presents an evocative turn-of-the-century ambience, purveys herbs and spices and "bush teas" with which to make magically curative potions. The Marketplace also puts together on the premises local liqueurs and fragrances. You will find some artwork and assorted island miscellany on display as well.

Down Island Traders, with branches in A. H. Riise Liquor Store and Bakery Square, Charlotte Amalie, and Frenchman's Reef resort (tel. 774-3419), handles preserves, spices, teas, coffees—also all tropical delicacies, and cookbooks.

The Wine Cellar, Creques Alley, has fresh coffee, Fortnum & Mason of London products, also represents Fauchon of Paris.

The large, conveniently located supermarkets are also worth strolling through. **Lucy's** (across Market Square between Gutters Gade and Strand Gade on Curaçao Street), founded by an old island family, was the first proper supermarket in St. Thomas.

Pueblo, in Sugar Estate, not far from the Havensight Mall, is a Puerto Rican import.

Both are strictly locally oriented, you will notice interesting reflections of ethnic tastes: the guava, orange, and mango canned nectars and "cheeses" (see the earlier section on "Food"), Sofrito seasonings, Spanish spices. Look also for Danish hams, Spanish olive oils, English marmalades and the like, not in a gourmet section, but stacked alongside the Armour, Crisco, Betty Crocker, and other U.S. brands. Take a look also at the wines and liquors—and at the prices. We often buy ours either in the supermarkets or at Woolworth's.

JEWELRY

Nowhere will you find a larger concentration of top-of-the-line jewelry in a more compact area than here in St. Thomas. Gold, platinum, diamonds, emeralds, rubies, opals, name brands or custom-designs, world-famous labels or the one-of-a-kind work of local artists—however arcane your preferences might be, St. Thomas can usually cater to them.

Inevitably, when dealing merchandise of high value, there can be pitfalls; certain articles may turn out to be not quite so precious as you might have been led to believe. The accuracy of those tales you might hear of $500 bracelets selling for twice that in St. Thomas, of so-called stones turning out to be glass backed with colored paper, is obviously not the purview of this guide to evaluate. The better part of wisdom does suggest, however, that you exercise every conceivable precaution in making any investment of substance. Two rules prudent shoppers might well live by:

(1) Beware of merchants offering discounts, either announced or pseudo spontaneous, "just for you, honey." Nine times out of ten the original price was hiked to accommodate the reduction. And (2) take a careful, very careful, look around the store to see what name brands are represented: Rolex, Braemar, Lalique . . . If you recognize the ones you see, chances are you're in good shape. No prestigious outfit is going to risk its reputation by allowing a fly-by-night to handle its product.

Of the many houses vying for your patronage, these are some you might consider when shopping for jewelry.

A. H. Riise Gift Shops, at 37 Main St. at Riise's Alley (tel. 774-2303), handles estate and antique pieces, Mikimoto cultured pearls, and, in the less expensive category, an exclusive on Majorca and Christian Dior jewelry.

Within the complex you will also find:

The FOREVER AMBER assortment of Caribbean and Baltic amber, supplemented with coral and crystal pieces as well.

The Larimar stone is said to be found only in the Dominican Republic, and at that only during the past eleven years. Negotiations are currently underway to have its present Geological Institute of America classification of "somewhat precious" upgraded to "precious," increasing the value proportionately. You can acquire a Larimar here for from $5 up. European-made settings come in 12- to 18-karat gold. Some designs also combine the Larimar stone with wild boar tusk.

Both the amber and Bonita Larimar lines are sold at additional locations in St. Thomas.

The **Fire Opal** features an array of gem-quality opals (accents of rubies, emeralds, sapphires, and diamonds as well) priced from under $10 up to $3,000.

Most exciting are the fabulous creations of master Greek goldsmith ilias LALAoUNIS. Aristotle Onassis brought this fourth-generation craftsman to world attention when he presented Jacqueline Kennedy with a Minoan-style 22-karat gold necklace as a wedding gift. Since then *Town & Country* has twice featured ilias LALAoUNIS, as has the *Paris Herald Tribune* and assorted upscale periodicals.

LALAoUNIS clients include Candice Bergen, Barbara Walters, Madame Valerie Giscard d'Estaing. There are now LALAoUNIS shops in New York, Paris, Zurich, Geneva, Vienna, as well as seven in Athens. We had heard of outlets in various Caribbean islands, too. However, when we queried Mr. Georgouses of the New York company headquarters, he informed us that St. Thomas is the only location in the Caribbean selling genuine LALAoUNIS creations. Be prepared for hefty pricetags—up to thousands of dollars. But what you will get in return is unquestionably top drawer.

At **Blue Carib Gems and Rocks**, located in Bakery Square (tel. 774-8525), on-site jewelers cut and set gem stones in silver or gold, design to order, repair your own damaged pieces. Or you can buy unset, coral, amber, agates, and the Dominican light blue turquoise Larimar stone.

Travel & Leisure likes **Boutique Riviera** on Main Street; you may also. If you have been coveting those plain smart Cartier bangles, the gold bands, or any other such accessories, you will find them here as well as at the **Cartier** Main Street establishment. We've also seen some outstanding costume creations at Boutique Riviera through the years—as, for example, at one time, dazzling reproductions of the Austrian crown jewels.

Cardow Jewelers, 39 Main Street, Charlotte Amalie, and a branch at Frenchman's Reef (tel. 774-1140), advertises a money-back guarantee of 30% to 50% savings on U.S. prices; keeps, on hand, $20 million worth of stock; and has included in its clientele Vincent Price, the late Cary Grant, Victoria Principal, the late Tennessee Williams, and a host of other high-profile travelers. We asked William Dowling, the enterprising Long Island M.I.T. graduate who started this empire from scratch, how it grew to this size and why. He has a simple answer: high volume, low markup.

Actually, our notes on the explanations are not so simple, studded, in fact, with such terms as grossitas, triple keystone, and other arcane jargon. What did come through loud and clear was an apparently built-in differential of 10.8% duty, plus 5% and up sales tax. On top of that is the fact that Cardow buys gold a kilo at a time (almost $15,000 at the moment), whereas smaller dealers pay a great deal more for their less sizable purchases because they must go through a middleman. This firm buys its own kilo and then parcels it out at a profit.

Whatever the facts are concerning the inner workings and economics of the Dowling empire, the result is a massive display of diamonds, emeralds, sapphires—and especially—gold. Whether it's a diamond necklace for $150,000 or a fluted gold nugget man's ring for $149, you'll find all price ranges here—along with chains, bangles, and earrings by the carload, and a lady's goldleaf ring at $39.50. A fetching little gold pendant set with an emerald and two small diamonds costs only $62.50. A ring with seven sapphires and two small diamonds, grape design, is $99.50. If you like old coins, two rings are worth a look. The feminine version features Helios, god of the sun, on the outside, while on the reverse inside the bas-relief of a rose is a pun on Rhodes: 18-karat gold, encircled by 45 points of diamonds—$645. The men's version is in 14-karat; the gold, bark design. The coin represents Alexander the Great as Hercules. Chains in 14-karat gold can be had for as little as $11.95, the 7-inch "S" model, a saving, Cardow claims, of 77%.

If you buy something at Cardow and are not happy with it when you get home, Bill tells us you'll get a prompt and cheerful refund, provided the item is in mint condition. If not, he'll still give you your money back, minus the cost of the repair.

Colombian Emeralds International maintains two shops on St. Thomas—Main Street and the Royal Dane Mall, Charlotte Amalie. You've seen this logo elsewhere in the Caribbean and in the Bahamas. In addition to its emeralds from Colombia, the firm offers gold chains, sapphires, and rubies.

G. Jesner's Jewelry Store, 13 Main St., represents the combined know-how of two generations of jewelers, father and son. They plied their trade in the big leagues up North before escaping to the tropics. Jesner's has a special room dedicated to economy-priced merchandise, which includes 14-karat nugget rings billed at 49% under U.S. price (men's rings $138.95 instead or $290; ladies' rings $89.50 instead of $175) and diamond stud earrings at $29.95—estimated at half the mainland price.

H. Stern, on 12 Main St. (tel. 774-1939), has branches also at Frenchman's Reef resort at Havensight Mall, and at Bluebeard's Castle Hotel. If you haven't visited Hans Stern in his Rio headquarters—or in Bogotá, Buenos Aires, Caracas, Cartagena, Lima, Santiago, or any of his other locales, Paris, Lisbon, Madeira, Frankfurt, Tel Aviv, Jerusalem, New York, you most certainly have read about him in *Time, Business Week, The New York Times*, or *Reader's Digest*, which calls him "The King of Colored Gems."

The company mines and cuts its own stones, designs and fabricates its own jewelry, handles its own marketing—in short controls the operation from beginning to end. You can pay a fortune for a gorgeous aquamarine, but you can also pick up a variety of inexpensive items set in 14-karat gold. We were particularly taken on our last trip by the garnet collection—as, for example, a fetching pair of earrings, with twelve garnets each, delicate and understatedly expensive looking, for only $62. There were gold charms for as little as $17.

Irmela, of **Irmela 's Jewel Studio**, in the Grand Hotel on Main Street (tel. 774-5875), first earned our high regard when she confected for our family's perfection-oriented matriarch a one-of-a-kind gold-and-topaz chain that became her pride and joy. Irmela continues to do business on the same personalized basis, and if you're not in the market for a custom-made piece, at least take a look at her assortment of freshwater pearls: Maobe, Biwa, Keshi—an imposing display.

The current owner of **Little Switzerland**, at 5 Main St. and on Tolbod Gade (tel. 776-2010), the Town & Country Company of Chelsea, Massachussetts, has always specialized in fine jewelry, maintaining and staffing its own factories overseas. If time permits (allow at least six weeks in advance), by all means telephone the toll-free number (1-800/524-2010) and ask for the Little Switzerland catalog. The full-color illustrations are mouth-watering. There's a smashing necklace at $12,650; a traffic-stopper ring consisting of 20 sizable diamonds is listed at $8,500. If these rather exceed your budget, take a look at the handsome Lady Di sapphire collection—earrings, ring, and pendant of sapphire framed in diamonds and set in 14-karat gold: the ring is $250, the pendant $275, and the earrings a hard-to-believe $450. These really look impressive.

Peach Bloom, 20-A Commandant Gade, two blocks north of Main Street (tel 776-2788), features vintage collections, from the early 1800s up to pre-World War II, selected by a pair of experts in antique jewelry (Lee Monaco and Cynthia Kline): memoriam pieces, tortoise shell inlaid with gold and silver, children's adornments, Victorian cuff bracelets in three-color gold. By buying lots, in Europe or America, instead of by the piece, the owners get a better price.

At the **Scandinavian Center** branches on Main Street and at Havensight Mall (tel. 776-0656), you will find smart silver pieces by Georg Jensen, David Anderson, and one of our favorites, the supermodern, Finnish Lapponia line. Also available here is FOREVER AMBER.

Sweet Passion Antique Jewelry, in the Royal Dane Mall (tel. 774-2990), carries early Victorian and Georgian bar pins and bangles, along with assorted little period-piece gifts for the antique lover on your list. You will also see jewelry of a later design—art nouveau and 1920s deco.

LINENS

Embroidered hand towels and hot-roll servers for $1 each; a 72 x 90-inch ecru tablecloth with eight napkins for $15.95—and these are just for-instances. Competition is keen on table linens in St. Thomas and the assortment is wide. Detecting the difference between the substantially solid texture of true quality fabric and the temporary, synthetically applied body which will disappear at the first washing requires some experience and an eagle eye. We've had it both ways: a lavishly hand embroidered bridge cloth and napkins hastily scooped up for $5 the set is still with us ten years later, sturdy, well worn, and growing handsomer all the time. On the other hand, our lovely but unthinkably costly embroidered pillowcases wilted at the first laundering.

The best-known, longest-established general-purpose shops in St. Thomas don't all carry much of this merchandise. Most selection is in the specialty houses.

The firm that operates **Boolchand's Linen Center**, 9B Main St. (tel. 776-8550), does carry other items at its other branches, but it has been handling imported linens ever since its inception in Curaçao a generation ago. A 17-piece luncheon set can be had for less than $10, placemats begin at $3.50 each;

$3.50 also for a pair of pillowcases. Embroidered hand-kerchiefs cost less than 50 cents apiece.

China Embroidery, 6C Vimmelskaft Gade (Back Street), 17 Main St., and in A. H. Riise Liquor Store, trades as the name indicates, direct with the Orient, bringing in linen, cotton, and drip-dry in various colors. Cloths range from $15.50 up for a 72-inch version with eight napkins.

You might find some linens at **The English Shop** on Main Street at Market Square (tel. 774-5309) or at the branch at the Havensight Mall (tel. 776-3776).

Hathi's II, 31 Radets Gade, and branch at Frenchman's Reef, has a perky bridge set, white embroidered with red strawberries and green stems, for $8 including the napkins. Napery in various sizes, shapes, and shades—along with some absurdly inexpensive little gifts. We bought a dozen $1 guest towels and roll servers on our last foray.

The **Linen House** has two locations, one at Royal Dane Mall (tel. 774-8117), and another at Palm Passage (tel. 774-8405). Four placemats, matching napkins, and the runner cost $8 here; a jumbo-sized, 72 x 144-inch cloth with a dozen napkins sells for $29.95.

Billed as "The Original Linen Shop in St. Thomas," **Mr. Tablecloth** in Palm Passage, Charlotte Amalie, is pleased to have been featured in *Sky*, the Delta Airlines magazine, as offering prices and quality on a par with that found in either Hong Kong or the People's Republic of China. In addition to the conventional table linen, the inventory includes fabric by the yard, embroidered dresser scarves—3,000 varieties, from $1 tip-towels to an $8,000 banquet set.

Royal Caribbean at 33 Main St. (tel. 776-4110) also handles linens.

PERFUMES AND COSMETICS

Forty years ago, an uppercrust retired West Point colonel

got involved in marketing the Virgin Islands' special brand of
bay rum—and in the process started one of the first such
operations in the Caribbean. To this day St. Johns Bay Rum,
with its distinctive packaging copied from the old-time fish-
traps made of stripped straw, can be found in luxury emporiums throughout the hemisphere. Eight ounces of the all-
purpose lotion costs $12.50 in St. Thomas, 35% less than the
Stateside price, and the firm has added scented cologne and
toilet water to the line. If you'd like to tour the factory, call the
West Indies Bay Company at 774-2166 to make arrangements.

St. Thomas had other innovators in the fragrance line,
including the Virgin Islands Perfume Corporation, and the
Fragrance & Cosmetic Factory, which you are also free to
visit (on the waterfront at the foot of the Royal Dane Mall).
New scent this year: La Te Da, at $35 the half-ounce. They also
manufacture Black Coral, Frangi Pani, and Jasmine, along with
assorted aloe products. Other island fragrances include Buccaneer—2 ounces of cologne $6.75—and various florals.

Insofar as imported perfumes and cosmetics are concerned,
the St. Thomas supply is overpowering: one shop alone
carries over 300 fragrances. Quite frankly, storage is so
efficiently climate-controlled and turnover so brisk here that
we don't think it makes a great deal of difference whether you
make your purchases at **Tropicana Perfume Shoppes** (two
stores on Main Street—tel. 774-0010), one of the better known
specialty houses in the hemisphere, or at Woolworth's, which
also stocks a representative assortment of name brands.

If you care to do some advance scouting before you leave
home, **A. H. Riise Gift Shops** offers you the convenience of
its toll-free number (1-800/524-2037), through which, incidentally, you can also place an order. Add $5 to the price of
your order for insured airmail.

How much do you save? It depends a great deal on the
brand. We've done a little better in the French West Indies on

occasion on some, on others—those with U.S. corporate connections in particular—the difference may not be perceptibly less. To give you an idea, herewith some sample comparisons as of presstime.

Yves Saint Laurent's Opium: $132 the ounce here, $172 including tax in New York.

Joy, $140 for one ounce in St. Thomas, $189 in Manhattan.

Van Cleef's First, $105 the ounce in the islands, as opposed to $162 up north.

Dioressence, $90 locally versus $162 on the mainland.

The fancy Patou Parfum 1000 retails in St. Thomas at $175 the ounce in contrast to $270 back home; Giorgio is $40 cheaper. You can save $12.52 or more a bottle on Paco Rabanne for men, $30 on a jar of La Prairie Wrinkle Cream, $17.40 on Lancôme's Forte Vital.

SPIRITS

Whether or not, as the story goes, George Washington's men really did drink Virgin Islands rum, the product has been, and remains, centrally important to the economy of this Territory. As of today, *97% of all rum imported into the United States comes from either Puerto Rico or the Virgin Islands*— the latter under the labels of Brugal, Cruzan, Carioca, and Old Mr. Boston.

Through the years, St. Thomians have developed their own variations on their *vin du pays* in addition to the combinations involving coconut, banana, and other tropical fruits and flavorings found elsewhere in the Caribbean.

On our first Christmas in St. Thomas one of our neighbors invited us to his house for a glass of guavaberry liqueur—a holiday custom we came to know as traditional to the island as eggnog is to the States. The St. Thomians make this distinctive elixir by soaking in rum from one year to the next a small fruit the size and color of a Concord grape. (Other than the similarity in nomenclature, the guavaberry bears no resemblance whatsoever to the several-times larger, light-yellow guava.) Traditionally, the liqueur matures in old wine bottles, discarded mayonnaise jars, or whatever comes to hand. For Christmas and New Year, it is transferred to the fanciest decanter in the house and is served to all comers. A glass of guavaberry supposedly guarantees good luck throughout the year.

Nowadays you can buy guavaberry liqueur, even watch it being prepared, at the **Caribbean Marketplace** in Havensight Mall—one of several flavors confected on site. Conducted tours go on throughout the day.

If you're not a rum drinker, you might want to pick up one or more bottles of whatever variety is your pleasure, to take home duty-free. Thanks to canny politicking, and Congress's sense that U.S. possessions deserve something of a break, Virgin Island visitors receive a special bonus: whereas one bottle is the maximum tax-exempt take-home allowance on spiritous liquors from foreign-flag areas into the U.S., you can bring in, duty-free, five bottles (fifths) from the American islands—plus a sixth one if it is processed in the islands. (This exemption also applies to Southern Comfort, incidentally, because it is bottled here.)

A. H. Riise Liquor Store, claiming an inventory of 100,000 bottles, advertises itself as "the largest liquor store in the West Indies." Besides its historic Main Street building, the company maintains outlets at the Grand Hotel, Havensight Mall, Mountain Top, Coral World, and the A. H. Riise Gift Shops.

Several other St. Thomas emporiums purvey alcoholic beverages. There's a liquor store at the airport, and at Havensight. If you're in the neighborhood, take a look in the supermarkets, **Al Cohen's** discount house at Havensight and Woolworth's.

How much of a bargain do St. Thomas prices represent as contrasted to what you pay at home depends very much on your state and local taxes and how keen the competition is in your area. To help you make that comparison, herewith some sample prices garnered at presstime:

Brand	Price per Fifth
Cruzan Rum	$2.95
Chivas Regal 12-year-old Scotch	11.50
Beefeater Gin	5.95
Jameson Irish Whiskey	6.95
Hennessy V.S.O.P. Fine Champagne Brandy	17.95
Kahlúa	7.75

WATCHES

When you consider the fact that local merchants cite such bargains as the Rolex Oyster Perpetual Air-King watch ticketed $740 U.S. as opposed to $525 in St. Thomas; the Rolex 16013 at $1,895 in St. Thomas as compared to $2,675 on the mainland; a $255 Oris for less than half that in St. Thomas—these and other impressive price differentials, especially on top-of-the-line timepieces—explain why watches constitute one of the most popular buys in the islands.

Fine Swiss watches engender a special loyalty in their owners, with many handed down from generation to generation. For this reason, it would seem useful to point out where you might find some of your favorite makes (see Useful Addresses List for details):

Audemars Piguet: **Little Switzerland**

Baume & Mercier: **H. Stern, Little Switzerland**

Borel: **Little Switzerland**

Cartier: **Boutique Riviera, Les must de Cartier**

Casio: **Boolchand's, Royal Caribbean**

Chopard: **Little Switzerland**

Citizen: **Boolchand's, Colombian Grand Jewelers, Emeralds International, Sparky's**

Concord: **A. H. Riise Gift Shops, H. Stern, Little Switzerland**

Consul: **Little Switzerland**

Corum: **H. Stern, Royal Caribbean**

Ebel: **A. H. Riise Gift Shops, Little Switzerland**

Ernest Borel: **Little Switzerland**

Girard-Pérregaux: **Little Switzerland**

Gucci: **Gucci**

Heuer: **Little Switzerland**

Longine's: **Brumney's Gem Shop**

Movado: **A. H. Riise Gift Shop, Cardow, H. Stern, Royal Caribbean**

Omega: **Arts & Jewels, Bolero, I,II, and III**

Orbit: **A. H. Riise Gift Shops, The English Shop, Sparky's**

Oris: **H. Stern**

Patek Phillipe: **A. H. Riise Gift Shops**

Piaget: **Bolero, I, Cardow, H. Stern**

Porsche: **Boutique Riviera**

Pulsar: **Accuracy, Inc., A. H. Riise Gift Shops, Artistic Boutique, Bolero I,II, and III, Cardow, The English Shop, Glamour Jewelers, Royal Caribbean, Sparky's, Solid Gold**

Rado: **Little Switzerland**

Raymond Weil: **G. Jesner's Jewelry Stores, Grand Jewelers**

Rolex: **Little Switzerland**

Seiko: **Accuracy, Inc., A. H. Riise Gift Shops, Artland, Arts & Jewels, Boolchand's, Cardow, The English Shop, Glamour Jewelers, H. Stern, Rikki's, Royal Caribbean, Solid Gold, Sparky's, Superior Trident Jewelers Shoppe**

Swatch: **A. H. Riise Gift Shops, Cardow, Royal Caribbean, H. Stern, Colombian Emeralds International**

Swiss Swatch: **A. H. Riise Gift Shops, Cardow, H. Stern, Royal Caribbean**

Tissot: **Colombian Emeralds**

Universal Genève: **Little Switzerland**

Vacheron et Constantin: **Little Switzerland**

St. Croix

Neither of St. Croix's two towns, Christiansted or Frederiksted, offer cruise ships the docking facilities and protected anchorages available in Charlotte Amalie. As a result, tourist volume on St. Thomas runs greatly above that of its larger, but quieter, sibling. Some major St. Thomas houses do maintain branches there, however, and resourceful St. Croix merchants have built up some bounteous browsing grounds of their own.

ARTS AND CRAFTS

The island's most celebrated resident artist has long been regarded as one of the most talented photographers in the world. **Fritz Henle's** pictures have been exhibited in fine galleries everywhere; they also appear as illustrations in quality books. If you have difficulty finding his work on the island, you might give him a call at 773-1067. Mr. Henle has designed a special photographer's tour of his island, by the way, beginning in Frederiksted and hitting what he considers the high spots: Columbus's landing place, the baobab trees unique to the island, Protestant Cay, and the tip of St. Croix (the easternmost point in the United States). For paintings and other art, look in on **The Gallery,** at Company and Queen Cross Streets, Christiansted, and **Libby Glasser** in King's Alley.

Trudi Gilliam offers one-of-a-kind copper and brass sculptures at 1 Strand St., Comanche Walk, Christiansted (closed Mondays).

Many Hands, in the Pan Am Pavilion, also in Christiansted (tel. 773-1990), specializes in Virgin Island art and in crafts: shellwork, basketry, canvases—and a year-round Christmas tree. If you don't see what you're looking for, ask for Anne Castruccio or Syd Corvinus.

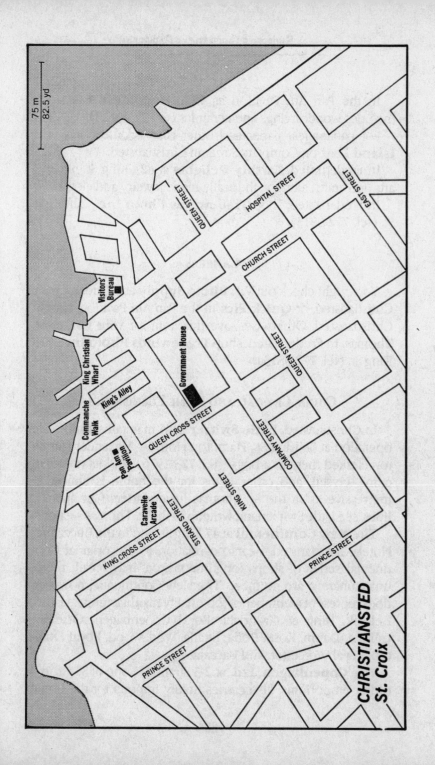

CHRISTIANSTED
St. Croix

75 m
82.5 yd

Hospital Street
Church Street
Queen Street
Queen Street
Company Street
King Street
East Street
Strand Street
Prince Street
Prince Street
King Cross Street
Queen Cross Street

Visitors' Bureau
King Christian Wharf
Commanche Walk
King's Alley
Pan Am Pavilion
Caravelle Arcade
Government House

In the Pan Am Pavilion as well, **Happiness Is**'s stock includes woodcarvings and ceramics (tel. 773-3123).

For banana-leaf paper and other island confections, visit **Island Leaf** on Company Street in Christiansted.

In Frederiksted, **Earthly Delights** at 429 King St. purveys arts and crafts, along with locally made jewelry and clothes.

In Frederiksted, shop **Tradewinds Photo Inc.,** 228 King St. (tel. 772-0813).

CAMERAS

You might check out **V.I. Photo Supply** at 3 Queen Cross, Christiansted, or **Quick Pics** in the Pan Am Pavilion, also in Christiansted. Otherwise, save this item for your visit to St. Thomas. In Frederiksted, shop **Tradewinds Photo Inc.**, 228 King St. (tel. 772-0813).

CHINA, CRYSTAL, AND HOME FURNISHINGS

In Christiansted, **Little Switzerland** maintains a full-scale operation at 56 King St., Hamilton House—Alexander Hamilton clerked there as a boy—(tel. 773-1976), and its variety of china, crystal, and other items for the home is almost as impressive as in the St. Thomas headquarters (for specific lines, see Little Switzerland writeup in the St. Thomas section).

The New Continental at 47 King St. and in the Buccaneer Hotel, Christiansted, bears no relation to the original Continental series of shops longtime visitors may recall; these, unfortunately, are no more. The New Continental, however, does represent a number of top-quality manufacturers: Lladrò, Belleek, Bing & Grøndahl, Royal Copenhagen, Orreförs, Lalique, Daum, Kosta Boda, littala, Wedgwood, Royal Doulton, Royal Worcester, and Baccarat.

The Copenhagen, Ltd. at 2-3 Strand St., one of St. Croix's oldest emporiums, also carries luxury imports for the home such as Dutch pewter and Scandinavian Christmas plates, as well as Arabia china.

Heritage House, 55 King St., often has excellent buys in crystal and pottery—the stock varies—tucked in amidst paintings, jewelry, and whatever the buyers consider new and different.

Find Limoges at **Violette's Boutique** in the Caravelle Arcade.

Fabulous Things Boutique, also in the Caravelle Arcade, features highball glasses depicting the local sugarbird, in five colors, gold-trimmed, at under $7 apiece.

House numbers, name plates, vases, lamps, wall plaques, and some ceramic jewelry are created by Conrad Knowles in his **Conrad's Ceramic Studio** at Estate Concordia, near the Gentle Winds Condominiums. A transplanted Antiguan, Conrad has had excellent training: at the Paul Soldner Workshop in Delaware, the School of Handicrafts and Industrial Arts in Copenhagen, and the Philadelphia School of Fine Arts. When we were last there inventory was low—whether because an enthusiastic buyer had cleaned out the shelves, or, more likely, because Conrad is doing much of his work to order, we don't know. In any event, if you're out that way, you might drop in (tel. 778-0122).

For individually crafted plates, cutting boards—woodenware of any kind—you should include in your touring itinerary a visit to **St. Croix LEAP** (St. Croix Life and Environmental Arts Project). Located off Mahogany Road (Route 76) on the western end of the island, 2 miles north of Frederiksted, this nonprofit carpentry and cabinetmaking shop was founded twelve years ago by Fletcher Pence, a master woodworker and environmentalist who himself fabricated many of the imposing pieces you'll spot in the better homes and hotels of St. Croix.

LEAP fells no mahogany trees, but does use wood from trees cut for other purposes. Additional tropical woods you will recognize by their color: the rich brown of Thibet, known in the Caribbean as woman's-tongue because of the constant clacking of the pods in the wind; Saman, a lighter café au lait; and the russet glow of mahoganies aged for two or more years. LEAP is hospitably open to visitors, but to verify time, telephone in advance (772-0421). For inquiries, write to Box 245, Frederiksted.

Other targets in the west include the restored **Whim Great House and Gift Shop,** on the grounds of an 18th-century West Indian plantation on Centerline Road, about 2 miles east of Frederiksted. The Gift Shop features island comestibles, assorted gifts, and will, we are told, custom-make for you one of the famous planter's chairs.

In Frederiksted, look for imported china and crystal, at the **Royal Frederik Shop,** 6 Strand St., or perhaps **Lucan's** on the waterfront.

FASHIONS

Violette's Boutique on 38 Strand St., at the corner of Queen Cross Street in Christiansted, offers a mini-department store array of merchandise. Fashion items include European imports for men and women, leather handbags, and lingerie by Dior, Iris, Lily of France.

For Pringle and Alan Paine sweaters, Bally and Bandolino shoes, and Dior and Givenchy accessories, browse **The New Continental** at 47 King St.

Nini of Scandinavia, at 16AB Church St., across from the post office (tel. 773-2269), serves up a swinging smörgåsbord of bounty from the Land of the Midnight Sun—including Finland's Marimekko fabrics at 20% or so under U.S. prices, made up or by the yard.

Spanish Main in the Pan Am Pavilion (tel. 773-0711), features tropical materials, including those designed by Jim

Tillett in St. Thomas, off the bolt or made up into fashions for men, women, and children.

Also in Christiansted, **Finesse,** at 53B Company St., runs the gamut of top-of-the-line apparel from tip to toe, priced accordingly.

Lady Martel, at the Buccaneer Hotel, 4 miles from Christiansted (tel. 773-2100), is another pace-setter.

Gold Coast, at 3AB Queen Cross St. in town, specializes in active sportswear.

Java Wraps, the ubiquitous purveyor of sarongs and sportswear seen in so many Caribbean islands, is represented here as well, at 2B Queen Cross St. and in the Pan Am Pavilion (tel. 773-7529).

Those of you who have shopped **Cavanagh's, Inc.,** religiously through the years will find a Cavanagh's Butik at 52 King St.

Designer lingerie? Try **K'Amil,** 1 Company St.

For shoes, bags, and assorted leathergoods, shop **Cruzan Carib** in the Pan Am Pavilion; **Leather Loft,** in King's Alley (tel. 773-2931); **JT's Sandals** (they make to order) at 53 Company St., **Nancee's Leather Awl,** Company Street, off Church Street.

Lisa's Sandal Shop, also on Strand Street, will handcraft to your specifications.

In Frederiksted, look into the **Royal Frederik Shop** at 6 Strand St. for cashmeres and dressy handbags, and **Raines' of St. Croix,** 310 Strand St., for both men's and women's clothes.

FOOD

If there's a super-terrific gourmet shop on St. Croix, we've missed it. The **Grand Union, Pueblo,** and other supermarkets are worth visiting for the off-trail canned and packaged West Indian comestibles, as well as the Danish hams, Dutch cheeses, English marmalades, and other imports the Virgin

Islands exemption from U.S. Customs duties makes as economical as Kraft or Hormel.

JEWELRY

St. Croix is extremely well served in this department. Of the leading St. Thomas emporiums represented in Christiansted, **Little Switzerland's** (56 King St.—tel. 773-1976) collection is as wide-ranging in price as it is in tasteful design.

Colombian Emeralds, at the corner of Queen Cross and Strand Streets, offers the full range of rubies, sapphires, diamonds, and Colombian emeralds showcased in its other shops in the Caribbean.

George Jesner, the professional jeweler who migrated from Manhattan to St. Thomas several decades ago, holds forth at the Pan Am Pavilion in a boutique called, simply, **The Jewelry Store**.

From farther afield—Sun Valley, Idaho, to be exact—comes another St. Croix outpost, **Gem Exposé**, at 2-3 Strand St.: it features gold chains, rings of topaz or diamond, and assorted earrings.

St. Croix also has its own homegrown specialists. **Pegasus,** at 58 Company St. (tel. 773-6926), offers a wide assortment of handcrafted designs featuring island motifs.

Pegasus and **Ay Ay Gold,** at King's Wharf, both purvey handmade pieces as well as finished designs in gold, silver, coral, and pearls. If you have a special creation in mind, ask to speak to Laura at Pegasus.

Violette's Boutique, 38 Strand St., carries both gold and costume jewelry.

Find jade in bangles or pins at **The Compass Rose** (tel. 773-0444), along with Oriental pearls.

Find some handcrafted pieces at **Many Hands,** Pan Am Pavilion (tel. 773-1990).

Black coral and some interesting jewelry made from old Danish pottery is available at **Happiness Is,** also in the Pan Am Pavilion (tel. 773-3123).

One of our favorite Danish silver bracelets came from **Nini of Scandinavia,** 16 AB Church St. (tel. 773-2269).

If you like Nordic styling, try **The Copenhagen, Ltd.** 2-3 Strand St., as well.

Look for antique estate jewelry at **The Gold Shop** in King's Alley and at **Ritsu's** in the Caravelle Arcade, amidst Burma jade, Kobe pearls, and designer pieces from Singapore.

The **Jewelry Factory,** also in the Caravelle Arcade, comes on strong, with full-page ads offering free earrings, coconut jewelry, mother-of-pearl hair barrettes, along with shells and leaves dipped in gold.

In Frederiksted, the **Tradewinds Shop** at 320 King St. (tel. 772-0939) and **Lucan's** on the waterfront are probably your likeliest prospects.

LINENS

Choices here are not nearly as varied as in St. Thomas. However, you may well find attractive buys at **The Compass Rose,** 5 Company St. (tel. 773-0444), or **The New Continental,** at 47 King St.

PERFUME AND COSMETICS

As might be expected of a French owner, the **Violette's Boutique** in the Caravelle Arcade carries the largest selection of perfume on the island, and cosmetics as well.

However, in the event that your favorite brand happens to be sold out, you'll find no shortage of alternative sources in Christiansted.

St. Croix Perfume Center, in the King's Alley Arcade, opposite Government House, handles both American and

French fragrances, also Estée Lauder and Giorgio, and exclusive on Clinique.

The **New Continental** at 47 King St. carries perfumes and cosmetics by Nina Ricci, Guerlain, Gucci, Givenchy—most of the big names.

In Frederiksted, **Lucan's** on the waterfront or the **Tradewinds Shop** at 320 King St. are probably your best bets.

Cruzan for Men, widely featured in the U.S. in such disparate forums as *Town & Country* and J.C. Penney's, we were unable to find anywhere. Not even in the phone book.

SPIRITS

St. Croix offers its visitors the same unique advantage as St. Thomas: you can take home five fifths of alcoholic beverages instead of the one allowed elsewhere, plus a sixth, provided it is island-produced. As a result, there is no shortage of liquor stores (including the supermarkets, where wines are attractively priced and well stocked, as are stronger libations).

Grog 'N Spirits, at King's Wharf in Christiansted, stays open on Sunday in case you leave this item as last on your list.

Pan Am Liquors, in the Pan Am Pavilion (tel. 773-5641), supplements standard brands with arcane West Indian elixirs and European exotica.

Carib Cellars at 53 King St. (tel. 773-1260) in addition to stocking standard brands, will introduce you to samples of unusual to off-the-wall liqueurs combining local rum with tropical fruits—bananas, pineapple, and coconut—as well as flowers, hibiscus and roses.

In Frederiksted, stock up at the **Tradewinds Shop,** 320 King St. (tel. 772-0939), and while you're on the west end of the island, you might take the free tour of the **Cruzan Rum Distillery.** It's given Monday through Friday at 8:30 and 11:15 a.m., 1 and 4:15 p.m. Telephone 772-0799 for information and reservations.

WATCHES

Little Switzerland in Christiansted (tel. 773-1976), handles Rolex (island quipsters call it the Texas Timex), along with all the brands listed previously in the St. Thomas section.

Several shops carry Seiko, among them **The Compass Rose** at 5 Company St. (tel. 773-0444), **The New Continental** at 47 King St., and the **Violette's Boutique** in the Caravelle Arcade, all in Christiansted.

In Frederiksted, try the **Tradewinds Shop** at 320 King St. (tel. 772-0939).

Omega timepieces are on sale at **Colombian Emeralds** at the corner of Queen Cross and Strand Streets, Christiansted. **The Copenhagen, Ltd.,** 2-3 Strand St., Christiansted, also handles watches.

A SPECIAL SERVICE

St. Croix shows a unique, laudable concern for its guests as well as residents by providing a **Hot Line** number for their convenience. In case of any difficulty or personal problem— "a fear, worry, confusion, or dilemma"—visitors are invited to phone 773-1780 any day from 9 a.m. until midnight. Compassionate islanders are on call, waiting to be of help. Other islands might consider following this example.

St. John

Less than 3,000 people inhabit St. John's 20 square miles. Bermuda, roughly the same size, supports 50,000 residents. Over half of St. John is set aside and preserved as the Virgin Islands National Park, excluded from development. Thus it is not surprising to find little commercial activity there. Most of what there is clusters around the little port of entry, the village of Cruz Bay. What shopping there is tends to be distinctive and interesting, though not necessarily indigenous.

Those really handsome wooden dinner plates included in the display of crafts at **The Art Project** in Cruz Bay, for example, come from Haiti. The internationally popular Jean-Yves Froment fabrics are made in St. Barthélémy. The batiks at **Batik Caribe** are imported. The beach and sportswear in **Porto Cruz Boutique** are manufactured in Brazil and Spain, the sports shirts in Hawaii.

There is, however, a bank of extraordinary on-island talent as well. Some of the designers' output is outstanding, and much of it is on sale at a baker's dozen of boutiques known as **Mongoose Junction,** a short walk from either the public or National Park dock.

ARTS AND CRAFTS

The Art Project, mentioned above, located next door to Cruz Bay Moped Rental, exhibits paintings and watercolors by local artists, along with its collection of West Indian basketware and tapestries. **Zebra Gallery** also shows paintings and cartoons, as well as ready-to-wear.

Wickerwood and Shells, in Mongoose Junction, offers straw baskets, hats, and off-trail accessories.

You might also look in on **Virgin Canvas,** next door to Fred's Patio Bar.

CHINA, CRYSTAL, AND HOME FURNISHINGS

Insofar as treasures for the home are concerned, the **Donald Schnell Studio,** also in Mongoose Junction (tel. 776-6420), is not to be missed. Water fountains, coral pottery, wind chimes, lamps, glassware, house signs—the output of this Michigan-born craftsman is distinctive and worth a second look. The studio will ship anything back home for you, no matter where you live.

In Mongoose Junction also shop **Ardec** and **Wire Works** for home decorating.

Virgin Canvas, mentioned above, does some upholstery.

For antique brass lanterns, charts suitable for framing, and other nautical heirlooms, visit the **Posh Bosun Box,** next door to the Lime Inn.

FASHIONS

Lots of entries appear in this category, some local, some imported.

Batik Caribe carries fashions fabricated by Cloud Burst in addition to the wraps and sarongs. (Find it next to the Bird's Nest Restaurant and opposite the Chase Manhattan Bank.)

The **Canvas Factory** in Mongoose Junction (tel. 776-9196) makes everything of canvas, including tote bags and fashions. If the jib on your ketch rips, see the experts here about having it repaired.

C & M Boutique, in The Lemon Tree shopping center smack in the middle of Cruz Bay, caters to all members of the family, large and small.

The Clothing Studio in Mongoose Junction (tel. 776-3585) will hand-paint and make to order whatever shirt, skirt, or coverup you have in mind.

Coconuts, next door to St. John Investments in Cruz Bay, serves both men and women with its line of cotton clothes, including imports from down-island as well as the States. Look especially at the hand-knit sweaters from Holland.

Dock Shop, at the foot of the public dock in Cruz Bay; **Sailor's Delight,** next to Cruz Bay Watersports; **Stitches,** on the other side of Sailor's Delight; and **Stitches II,** adjoining Cruz Bay Park, all specialize in sportswear.

Fabric Mill in Mongoose Junction (tel. 776-6194) purveys yardgoods of tropical origin and motif. Also find interesting accessories and soft sculptures.

At **Islandia,** look for the smart Finnish Marimekkos, off the bolt or made up. The shop is just this side of Mongoose Junction.

The **Porto Cruz** Boutique imports fashion miscellany from Europe, South America, and the Pacific, for men as well as women. You will find Tahitian pareos and casual clothes from Cyprus as well.

The boutique at **Caneel Bay Plantation Boutique** (tel. 776-6111) is not so different in stock or tariffs from hotel shops most anywhere in the world in our view: it's chic and top-priced.

FOOD

If a visit to a local supermarket is an essential part of your visit to any new area, as it is with us, check out **Lillian Smith's Grocery,** next to the police station in Cruz Bay.

JEWELRY

R and I Patton Goldsmithing, Mongoose Junction (tel. 776-6548), create their own jewelry in 14-karat gold and sterling silver, motifs taken from the islands.

Coconuts Tropical Clothing Company in Cruz Bay also carries jewelry. And for imports, try **Sparky's,** behind the Tourist Information Office in Cruz Bay. (If you saw something in the St. Croix or St. Thomas Sparky's main stores that is not here, perhaps they can send for it for you.)

Find coral pieces at **Stitches II** and Spanish jewelry at **Porto Cruz Boutique,** both in Cruz Bay.

The aforementioned Sparky's is probably your best bet in St. John for liquor, perfumes, and watches.

As we indicated earlier, St. John is not the place for single-minded shoppers, or indeed any kinetic, action-oriented vacationer, for that matter. Although today's St. John is not as somnolent as in the days when St. Thomians used to refer to it as the "place old people go to visit their parents," the island is still very slow-paced indeed. And distinctly not for everyone.

A few years ago a totally unathletic, urban-oriented, New York couple whose idea of a perfect vacation is a week in Paris, and who would have loved St. Thomas, were mistakenly booked by their travel agent for two weeks on St. John. After only three days of complete peace and quiet, their nerves frazzled, they went to the desk to check out—only to be told they could not leave yet, because their reservation was for two weeks.

To which the frustrated wife responded, "But hasn't it BEEN two weeks already?"

So be forewarned. Cruz Bay has some marvelously imaginative places to browse. But if shopping is your number one pastime, don't book a holiday on St. John without making plans for at least a day's excursion into the souks of St. Thomas.

USEFUL ADDRESSES

St. Thomas

Accuracy, Inc.: Main Street at International Plaza, Charlotte Amalie.

A. H. Riise Gift Shops: 37 Main St. at Riise's Alley, Charlotte Amalie (tel. 774-2303; tel. toll-free U.S. 1-800/524-2037).

A. H. Riise Liquor Store: Coral World, Mountain Top, Havensight Mall, plus Main Street, Riise's Alley, and Grand Hotel, Charlotte Amalie.

Al Cohen's: Havensight, 18A Estate Thomas (tel. 774-3690).

Alexander's Café: Frenchtown (tel. 774-4340).

Artistic Boutique: Main Street.

Artland: 27 Main St., and 32 Radets Gade.

Arts & Jewels: Main Street.

Blue Carib Gems and Rocks: Bakery Square, Charlotte Amalie (tel. 774-8525).

Bolero I, II, and III: 21 and 38 Main St., Drake's Passage.

Boolchand's: 31 Main St., (tel. 774-0794); Havensight Mall.

Boolchand's Linen Center: 9B Main St., (tel. 776-8550).

Boutique Riviera: Main Street, Charlotte Amalie; Frenchman's Reef; Havensight Mall.

Brumney's Gem Shop: 25 Main St.

Cardow Jewelers: 39 Main St., Charlotte Amalie, and Frenchman's Reef (tel. 774-1140).

Carib Shop: corner of Riise's Alley.

Caribbean Marketplace: Havensight Mall.

Carson Company Antiques: Royal Dane Mall.

Cartier Boutique: Main Street.

Catherine Marlet Boutique: Post Office Alley between Main Street and waterfront, (tel. 776-3600).

Cavanagh's: Havensight Mall (tel. 776-0737).

China Embroidery: 6C Vimmelskaft Gade (Back Street), 17 Main St., and A. H. Riise Liquor Store (see above entry).

Circe: Palm Passage.

Cloth Horse: Bakery Square, Charlotte Amalie (tel. 774-4761).

Colombian Emeralds International: Main Street and Royal Dane Mall, (tel. 774-4401).

Coquina Court: Havensight Mall.

Cosmopolitan, Inc.: Drake's Passage.

Courrèges Boutique: Palm Passage.

Crafts Cooperative: Back Street.

Dilly D'Alley: Trompeter Gade and Storetvaer Gade, Charlotte Amalie.

Down Island Traders: A. H. Riise Liquor Store and Bakery Square, Charlotte Amalie, and Frenchman's Reef (tel. 774-3419).

The English Shop: Main Street at Market Square, (tel. 774-5309); Havensight Mall (tel. 776-3776).

Fragrance & Cosmetic Factory: Royal Dane Mall.

Generations: Frenchman's Reef (tel. 776-8500, ext. 877).

G. Jesner's Jewelry Store: 13 Main St., Charlotte Amalie.

Glamour Jewelers: 17 Main St.

Gucci Boutique: Waterfront, between Cardow's and Riise's Alleys.

Guy Laroche: Palm Passage.

Hathi's II: 31 Radets Gade, Charlotte Amalie, and Frenchman's Reef.

Hidey Hole Boutique: second floor, Pisarro Building, Main Street.

H. Stern: 12 Main St., Charlotte Amalie (tel. 774-1939); branches also at Bluebeard's Castle Hotel, Havensight Mall, and Frenchman's Reef.

Irmela's Jewel Studio: Grand Hotel, Main Street (tel. 774-5875).

Java Wraps: Palm Passage (tel. 774-3700).

J. Hook: on the waterfront, Charlotte Amalie.

Jim Tillet's Boutique and Art Gallery: Tillett Gardens, Tutu, St. Thomas (tel. 775-1405).

Joanna White: Bakery Square, Charlotte Amalie.

La Caravelle: Main Street, and Frenchman's Reef.

Lady of Paradise: Secret Harbour Beach resort, Nazareth Bay.

The Leather Shop: 1 Main Street and Havenside Mall (tel. 776-3995).

L'Escargot In-Town: Royal Dane Mall (tel. 774-8880).

Les must de Cartier: Main Street at Palm Passage (tel. 774-1590).

Linen House: 7A Royal Dane Mall (tel. 774-8117), and Palm Passage (tel. 774-8405).

Lion in the Sun: Riise's Alley and Palm Passage.

Little Switzerland: 5 Main St., opposite Emancipation Park, and Havensight Mall (tel. 776-2010).

Louis Vuitton: 24 Main St., Palm Passage (tel. 774-3644).

Lucy's: between Gutters Gade and Strand Gade on Curaçao Street, Charlotte Amalie.

Michele Val: Royal Dane Mall.

Mr. Tablecloth: Palm Passage.

Octopus Garden: Trompeter Gade (tel. 774-7010).

Peach Bloom: 20-A Commandant Gade, Charlotte Amalie (tel. 776-2788).

Pueblo: Sugar Estate.

Rikki's: Main Street.

Rosenthal Studio: Main Street.

Royal Caribbean: 33 Main St. (tel. 776-4110).

Royal Dane Mall: Charlotte Amalie.

Scandinavian Center: Main Street, Havensight Mall (tel. 776-0656).

Sea Wench: Royal Dane Mall and Havensight Mall.

Shanghai Silk and Handicrafts: Royal Dane Mall.

The Sheltered Workshop: Crystal Gade, Charlotte Amalie; Frenchman's Reef.

Shipwreck Shop: Palm Passage.

Solid Gold: 35 Main St.

Sparky's: Main Street, Airport Gift Shop; Bluebeard's Castle Hotel.

The Straw Factory: 24 Garden St., Charlotte Amalie (tel. 774-4849).

Superior Trident Jewelers Shoppe: Main Street at Royal Dane Mall.

Sweet Passion Antique Jewelry: Royal Dane Mall (tel. 774-2990).

Takara: Havensight Mall.

Tropicana Perfume Shoppes: Main Street (tel. 774-0010).

The Wine Cellar: Creques Alley.

Zora of St. Thomas: East Main Street (Norre Gade).

St. Croix

Ay Ay Gold: King's Wharf, Christiansted.

Carib Cellars: 53 King St., Christiansted (tel. 773-1260).

Cavanagh's, Inc.: 52 King St., Christiansted.

Colombian Emeralds: corner of Queen Cross and Strand Streets, Christiansted.

The Compass Rose: 5 Company St., Christiansted (tel. 773-0444).

Conrad's Ceramic Studio: Estate Concordia, near Gentle Winds Condominiums (tel. 778-0122).

The Copenhagen, Ltd.: 2-3 Strand St., Christiansted.

Cruzan Carib: Pan Am Pavilion, Christiansted.

Earthly Delights: 429 King St., Frederiksted.

Fabulous Things Boutique: Caravelle Arcade, Christiansted.

Finesse: 53B Company St., Christiansted.

Fritz Henle: tel. 773-1067

The Gallery: Company Street at Queen Cross Street, Christiansted.

Gem Exposé: 2-3 Strand St., Christiansted.

Gold Coast: 3AB Queen Cross St., Christiansted.

The Gold Shop: King's Alley, Christiansted.

Grog 'N Spirits: King's Wharf, Christiansted.

Happiness Is: Pan Am Pavilion, Christiansted (tel. 773-3123).

Heritage House: 55 King St., Christiansted.

Hot Line: tel. 773-1780.

Island Leaf: Company Street, Christiansted.

Java Wraps: 2B Queen Cross St.; Pan Am Pavilion, Christiansted (tel. 773-7529).

The Jewelry Factory: Caravelle Arcade, Strand and Queen Cross Streets, Christiansted.

The Jewelry Store: Pan Am Pavilion, Christiansted.

JT's Sandals: 53 Company St., Christiansted.

K'Amil: 1 Company St., Christiansted.

Lady Martel: Buccaneer Hotel, 4 miles from Christiansted (tel. 773-2100).

Leather Loft: King's Alley, Christiansted (tel. 773-2931).

Libby Glasser: King's Alley, Christiansted.

Lisa's Sandal Shop: Strand Street, Christiansted.

Little Switzerland: 56 King St., Christiansted (tel. 773-1976).

Lucan's: Waterfront, Frederiksted.

Many Hands: Pan Am Pavilion, Christiansted (tel. 773-1990).

Nancee's Leather Awl: Company Street, Christiansted.

The New Continental: 47 King St., Christiansted; branch also at the Buccaneer Hotel, Christiansted.

Nini of Scandinavia: 16AB Church St., Christiansted (tel. 773-2269).

Pan Am Liquors: 12 Pan Am Pavilion, Christiansted (tel. 773-5641).

Pegasus: 58 Company St., Christiansted (tel. 773-6926).

Quick Pics: Pan Am Pavilion, Christiansted.

Raines' of St. Croix: 310 Strand St., Frederiksted.

Ritsu's: Caravelle Arcade, Christiansted.

Royal Frederik Shop: 6 Strand St., Frederiksted.

Spanish Main: Pan Am Pavilion, Christiansted (tel. 773-0711).

St. Croix LEAP: Mahogany Road, Route 76, 2 miles north of Frederiksted (tel. 772-0421).

St. Croix Perfume Center: King's Alley Arcade, 55 King St., Christiansted.

Tradewinds Shop: 320 King St., Frederiksted (tel. 772-0939).

Trudi Gilliam: 1 Strand St., Comanche Walk, Christiansted.

Violette's Boutique: Caravelle Arcade, Christiansted.

V.I. Photo Supply: 3 Queen Cross St., Christiansted.

Whim Great House and Gift Shop: Centerline Road, 2 miles east of Frederiksted.

St. John

Ardec: Mongoose Junction.

The Art Project: Cruz Bay.

Batik Caribe: opposite the Chase Manhattan Bank, Cruz Bay.

C & M Boutique: The Lemon Tree shopping center, Cruz Bay.

Canvas Factory: Mongoose Junction (tel. 776-9196).

The Clothing Studio: Mongoose Junction (tel. 776-3585).

Coconuts: next door to St. John Investments, Cruz Bay.

Dock Shop: near public dock, Cruz Bay.

Donald Schnell Studio: Mongoose Junction (tel. 776-6420).

Fabric Mill: Mongoose Junction (tel. 776-6194).

Islandia: near Mongoose Junction.

Lillian Smith's Grocery: next to police station, Cruz Bay.

Mongoose Junction: near the docks, Cruz Bay.

Porto Cruz Boutique: Cruz Bay.

Posh Bosun Box: Mongoose Junction.

R and I Patton Goldsmithing: near Mongoose Junction (tel. 776-6548).

Sailor's Delight: next to Cruz Bay Watersports, Cruz Bay.

Sparky's: behind Tourist Information Office, Cruz Bay.

Stitches: next to Sailor's Delight, Cruz Bay. **Stitches II** adjoining Cruz Bay Park.

Virgin Canvas: next door to Fred's Patio Bar, near Mongoose Junction.

Wickerwood and Shells: Mongoose Junction.

Wire Works: Mongoose Junction.

Zebra Gallery: Cruz Bay.

The $25-A-Day Travel Club— How to Save Money on All Your Travels

In this book you've been looking at how to get your money's worth in the Caribbean, but there is a "device" for saving money and determining value on **all** your trips. It's the popular, international $25-A-Day Travel Club, now in its 25th successful year of operation. The Club was formed at the urging of numerous readers of the $$$-A-Day and Dollarwise Guides, who felt that such an organization could provide continuing travel information and a sense of community to value-minded travelers in all parts of the world. And so it does!

In keeping with the budget concept, the annual membership fee is low and is immediately exceeded by the value of your benefits. Upon receipt of $18 (U.S. residents), or $20 U.S. by check drawn on a U.S. bank or via international postal money order in U.S. funds (Canadian, Mexican, and other foreign residents) to cover one year's membership, we will send all new members the following items.

(1) **Any two of the following books**

Please designate in your letter which two you wish to receive:

Frommer's $-A-Day Guides
Europe on $25 a Day
Australia on $25 a Day
Eastern Europe on $25 a Day
England on $35 a Day
Greece including Istanbul and Turkey's Aegean Coast on $25 a Day
Hawaii on $45 a Day
India on $15 and $25 a Day
Ireland on $30 a Day
Israel on $30 a Day
Mexico on $20 a Day (plus Belize and Guatemala)
New York on $45 a Day
New Zealand on $35 a Day
Scandinavia on $50 a Day
Scotland and Wales on $35 a Day
South America on $30 a Day
Spain and Morocco (plus the Canary Is.) on $40 a Day

Turkey on $25 a Day
Washington, D.C., on $40 a Day

Frommer's Dollarwise Guides
Dollarwise Guide to Austria and Hungary
Dollarwise Guide to Belgium, Holland & Luxembourg
Dollarwise Guide to Bermuda and the Bahamas
Dollarwise Guide to Canada
Dollarwise Guide to the Caribbean
Dollarwise Guide to Egypt
Dollarwise Guide to England and Scotland
Dollarwise Guide to France
Dollarwise Guide to Germany
Dollarwise Guide to Italy
Dollarwise Guide to Japan and Hong Kong
Dollarwise Guide to Portugal, Madeira, and the Azores
Dollarwise Guide to South Pacific
Dollarwise Guide to Switzerland and Liechtenstein
Dollarwise Guide to Alaska
Dollarwise Guide to California and Las Vegas
Dollarwise Guide to Florida
Dollarwise Guide to New England
Dollarwise Guide to New York State
Dollarwise Guide to the Northwest
Dollarwise Guide to Skiing USA-East
Dollarwise Guide to Skiing USA-West
Dollarwise Guide to the Southeast and New Orleans
Dollarwise Guide to the Southwest
Dollarwise Guide to Texas

(Dollarwise Guides discuss accommodations and facilities in all price ranges, with emphasis on the medium-priced.)

Frommer's Touring Guides
Egypt
Florence
London
Paris
Venice

(These new, color illustrated guides include walking tours, cultural and historic sites, and other vital travel information).

A Shopper's Guide to Best Buys in England, Scotland, and Wales
(Describes in detail hundreds of places to shop—department stores, factory outlets, street markets, and craft centers—for great quality British bargains.)

A Shopper's Guide to the Caribbean
Two experienced Caribbean hands guide you through this shopper's paradise, offering witty insights and helpful tips on the ware and emporia of more than 25 islands.

Bed & Breakfast—North America
(This guide contains a directory of over 150 organizations that offer bed & breakfast referrals and reservations throughout North America. The scenic attractions and major schools and universities near the homes of each are also listed.)

Dollarwise Guide to Cruises
(This complete guide covers all the basics of cruising—ports of call, costs, fly-cruise package bargains, cabin selection booking, embarkation and debarkation and describes in detail over 60 or so ships cruising the waters of Alaska, the Caribbean, Mexico, Hawaii, Panama, Canada, and the United States.)

Dollarwise Guide to Skiing Europe
(Describes top ski resorts in Austria, France, Italy, and Switzerland. Illustrated with maps of each resort area plus full-color trail maps.)

The Fast 'n' Easy Phrase Book
(French, German, Spanish, and Italian—all in one convenient, easy-to-use phrase guide.)

How to Beat the High Cost of Travel
(This practical guide details how to save money on absolutely all travel items—accommodations, transportation, dining, sightseeing, shopping, taxes, and more. Includes special budget information for seniors, students, singles, and families.)

Marilyn Wood's Wonderful Weekends
(This very selective guide covers the best mini-vacation destinations within a 175-mile radius of New York City. It describes special country inns and other accommodations, restaurants, picnic spots, sights, and activities—all the information needed for a two- or three-day stay.)

Motorist's Phrase Book
(A practical phrase book in French, German, and Spanish designed specifically for the English-speaking motorist touring abroad.)

Swap and Go—Home Exchanging Made Easy
(Two veteran home exchangers explain in detail all the money-saving benefits of a home exchange, and then describe precisely how to do it. Also includes information on home rentals and many tips on low-cost travel.)

The Candy Apple: New York for Kids
A spirited guide to the wonders of the Big Apple by a savvy New York

grandmother with a kid's eye view to fun. Indispensable for visitors and residents alike.

Travel Diary and Record Book
(A 96-page diary for personal travel notes plus a section for such vital data as passport and traveler's check numbers, itinerary, postcard list, special people and places to visit, and a reference section with temperature and conversion charts, and world maps with distance zones.)

Where to Stay USA
(By the Council on International Educational Exchange, this extraordinary guide is the first to list accommodations in all 50 states that cost anywhere from $3 to $30 per night.)

(2) A one-year subscription to *The Wonderful World of Budget Travel*

This quarterly eight-page tabloid newspaper keeps you up to date on fast-breaking developments in low-cost travel in all parts of the world bringing you the latest money-saving information—the kind of information you'd have to pay $25 a year to obtain elsewhere. This consumer-conscious publication also features columns of special interest to readers: **Hospitality Exchange** (members all over the world who are willing to provide hospitality to other members as they pass through their home cities); **Share-a-Trip** (offers and requests from members for travel companions who can share costs and help avoid the burdensome single supplement); and **Readers Ask...Readers Reply** (travel questions from members to which other members reply with authentic firsthand information).

(3) A copy of *Arthur Frommer's Guide to New York*

This is a pocket-size guide to hotels, restaurants, nightspots, and sightseeing attractions in all price ranges throughout the New York area.

(4) Your personal membership card

Membership entitles you to purchase through the Club all Arthur Frommer publications for a third to a half off their regular retail prices during the term of your membership.

So why not join this hardy band of international budgeteers and participate in its exchange of travel information and hospitality? Simply send your name and address, together with your annual membership fee of $18 (U.S. residents) or $20 U.S. (Canadian, Mexican, and other foreign residents), by check drawn on a U.S. bank or via international postal money order in U.S. funds to: $25-A-Day Travel Club, Inc., Frommer Books, Gulf + Western Building, One Gulf + Western Plaza, New York, NY 10023. And please remember to specify which **two** of the books in section (1) above you wish to receive in your initial package of members' benefits. Or, if you prefer, use the last page of this book, simply checking off the two books you select and enclosing $18 or $20 in U.S. currency.

Once you are a member, there is no obligation to buy additional books. No books will be mailed to you without your specific order.

INDEX

ESTABLISHMENTS

GENERAL

INDEX

Linens, 22, 36–9, 76, 99, 131, 146, 150–1, 169, 225, 255–6, 285, 323, 335, 336, 337, 350, 365, 376, 380, 424–5, 495, 509. *See also* Bath linens; Bed linens; Kitchen linens; Table linens
Lingerie, 166, 279, 336, 487, 506, 507
Liqueurs, 43–4, 78, 119, 171, 212, 226, 259–60, 338, 351, 454, 489, 497–8, 510. *See also* Spirits
Liquors, 44, 78, 103, 195–6, 228, 400, 427, 454, 486, 488, 498. *See also* Spirits
Lithographs, 409, 411

Macramé, 64, 93, 185
Madras, 281
Mahogany, 505, 506; carvings, 18, 205, 275; home furnishings, 89, 297; tableware, 206, 221, 389. *See also* Wood
Mailing purchases, 6, 11, 468
Mail order, 38, 217, 220–1, 481, 493, 496
Mango, 29, 320
Maps, 205; antique, 204, 278; reproductions of, 358
Marmalades. *see* Jellies, jams, preserves, and marmalades
Martinique, 269–92
Masks, 311, 477
Meat, import restrictions on, 283; turtle, 147–8. *See also* Food
Medicines, 208, 245–6, 247, 487
Menswear, 61, 73, 74, 96, 115, 145, 146, 165–6, 207, 279, 281, 319, 363, 364, 377, 378, 419, 448, 449, 484, 486, 487, 506, 507, 513
Merchants, reliability of, 36. *See also* Imitation(s)
Metal sculpture, 16, 218, 502
Money, brought into or out of U.S., reporting, 13–14
Money changing, 10–11, 182, 228, 438
Montserrat, 293–301
Murals, 16, 444
Music, 454–9; calypso, 458–9, recorded, 290, 455, 458, 459; steel bands, 455–8
Musical instruments, 312; *cuatro,* 311, 312, 315; in steel bands, 455, 456, 457

Nautical items, heirlooms, 513, model boats, 388
Nectars. *See* Drinks, non-alcoholic
Needlepoint supplies, 411
Nevis, 355–69

Opals, 488, 490
Ornaments, Christmas tree, 296, 314; liquor bottle, 296

Paintings, 17, 49, 57, 71, 90–1, 112, 128, 142, 163–4, 186–7, 204, 217–18, 221, 232–3, 234, 276, 295, 307, 308, 310, 337, 345–6, 358, 374, 409, 410–11, 412, 413, 443–4, 475–6, 477, 502, 505, 412. *See also* Arts and crafts
Palm, fronds, 320; hearts of, 320; import restrictions on, 320
Papaya, 320
Paper, banana-leaf, 504
Papier-mâché items, 314, 315
Pareos, 50, 206, 389, 514
Peanut butter, 224
Pearls, 32, 35, 150, 169, 251, 390–1, 423, 453, 481, 489, 493, 508, 509; testing for imitation, 35
Pens and pencils, 285
Perfumes, 39–42, 64, 77, 99–100, 119, 131, 140, 151, 169–70, 195, 210–11, 225, 256–7, 285–6, 324, 336, 350, 366, 380, 400, 408, 425–6, 443, 453, 469, 495–7, 509–10, 515; imported, 41–2, 64, 77, 99, 131, 151, 170, 256–7, 285–8, 366, 380, 418, 425, 426, 453, 481, 496–7, 509–10; import restrictions on, 13; local; 41, 64, 119, 170–1, 210–11, 225, 257, 366, 380, 425, 487, 496
Pewter, imported, 505; reproductions, 22, 238–9
Photographs, 204
Photography, 502
Pimiento, 247
Pineapple, 320; black, 63
Plastic surgery, 133
Platinum, 488
Pocketbooks, 50, 166, 178, 191, 223, 236, 275, 279, 297, 377, 410, 412, 449, 478, 486, 507.
Postcards, 400, 410; handpainted, 388; recipe, 248
Potpourri, 211
Pottery, 71, 92, 93, 178, 275, 296, 311, 347, 361, 374, 409, 411, 413, 476, 505; jewelry, 509; reproductions, 22; tableware, 22. *See also* Arts and crafts
Preserves. *See* Jellies, jams, preserves, and marmalades
Price comparisons, 8, 9–10, 12, 19–20
Prints, 205, 308, 312, 358, 409, 413
Puerto Rico, 303–32

Quartz jewelry, 423
Qué Pasa?, 305

Records, 290; calypso, 459; steel band, 455, 458

545

PURCHASES IN THE CARIBBEAN

DATE OF PURCHASE	STORE & PRODUCT	GIFT FOR	COST	DATE & PLACE MAILED	AIR OR SURFACE

PURCHASES IN THE CARIBBEAN

DATE OF PURCHASE	STORE & PRODUCT	GIFT FOR	COST	DATE & PLACE MAILED	AIR OR SURFACE

PURCHASES IN THE CARIBBEAN

DATE OF PURCHASE	STORE & PRODUCT	GIFT FOR	COST	DATE & PLACE MAILED	AIR OR SURFACE

PURCHASES IN THE CARIBBEAN

DATE OF PURCHASE	STORE & PRODUCT	GIFT FOR	COST	DATE & PLACE MAILED	AIR OR SURFACE

PURCHASES IN THE CARIBBEAN

DATE OF PURCHASE	STORE & PRODUCT	GIFT FOR	COST	DATE & PLACE MAILED	AIR OR SURFACE

PURCHASES IN THE CARIBBEAN

DATE OF PURCHASE	STORE & PRODUCT	GIFT FOR	COST	DATE & PLACE MAILED	AIR OR SURFACE

Date_____

FROMMER BOOKS
PRENTICE HALL PRESS
ONE GULF + WESTERN PLAZA
NEW YORK, NY 10023

Friends:

Please send me the books checked below:

FROMMER'S $-A-DAY GUIDES™

(In-depth guides to sightseeing and low-cost tourist accommodations and facilities.)

☐ Europe on $25 a Day $12.95
☐ Australia on $25 a Day $10.95
☐ Eastern Europe on $25 a Day $10.95
☐ England on $35 a Day $10.95
☐ Greece on $25 a Day $10.95
☐ Hawaii on $50 a Day $10.95
☐ India on $15 & $25 a Day $9.95
☐ Ireland on $30 a Day $10.95
☐ Israel on $30 & $35 a Day $10.95
☐ Mexico on $20 a Day $10.95

☐ New Zealand on $25 a Day $10.95
☐ New York on $45 a Day.............. $9.95
☐ Scandinavia on $50 a Day........... $10.95
☐ Scotland and Wales on $35 a Day..... $10.95
☐ South America on $30 a Day $10.95
☐ Spain and Morocco (plus the Canary Is.) on $40 a Day $10.95
☐ Turkey on $25 a Day $10.95
☐ Washington, D.C., on $40 a Day $10.95

FROMMER'S DOLLARWISE GUIDES™

(Guides to sightseeing and tourist accommodations and facilities from budget to deluxe, with emphasis on the medium-priced.)

☐ Alaska $12.95
☐ Austria & Hungary $11.95
☐ Belgium, Holland, Luxembourg $11.95
☐ Egypt............................ $11.95
☐ England & Scotland $11.95
☐ France.......................... $11.95
☐ Germany $11.95
☐ Italy............................ $11.95
☐ Japan & Hong Kong $12.95
☐ Portugal (incl. Madeira & the Azores) . $11.95
☐ South Pacific..................... $12.95
☐ Switzerland & Liechtenstein $11.95
☐ Bermuda & The Bahamas........... $10.95
☐ Canada $12.95
☐ Caribbean $12.95

☐ Cruises (incl. Alaska, Carib, Mex, Hawaii, Panama, Canada, & US) $12.95
☐ California & Las Vegas $11.95
☐ Florida.......................... $10.95
☐ Mid-Atlantic States $12.95
☐ New England..................... $11.95
☐ New York State $11.95
☐ Northwest....................... $11.95
☐ Skiing in Europe $12.95
☐ Skiing USA—East $10.95
☐ Skiing USA—West $10.95
☐ Southeast & New Orleans........... $11.95
☐ Southwest....................... $11.95
☐ Texas........................... $11.95

TURN PAGE FOR ADDITIONAL BOOKS AND ORDER FORM.